Autodesk Fusion 360
A Step-By-Step Tutorial Guide for Beginners

Provider of High Quality Learning Material at Affordable Price
www.sdcadacademy.com

Autodesk Fusion 360: A Step-By-Step Tutorial Guide for Beginners

Published by
SDCAD Academy
www.sdcadacademy.com

Copyright © 2020 SDCAD Academy

NOTICE TO THE READER

The publisher and the author make no representations or warranties with respect to the accuracy or completeness of the contents of this work/text and specifically disclaim all warranties, including without limitation warranties of fitness for a particular purpose. The publisher does not guarantee any of the products described in the text nor has performed any independent analysis in connection with any of the product information contained in the text. No warranty may be created or extended by sales or promotional materials. This work is sold with the understanding that the publisher is not engaged in rendering legal, accounting, or other professional services. Neither the publisher nor the author shall be liable for damages arising herefrom. Further, readers should be aware that Internet websites listed or referenced in this work may have changed or may have been removed in the time between the writing and the publishing of this work.

Examination Copies

Textbooks received as examination copies in any form such as paperback or eBook are for review only and shall not be made available for the use of the student. These files shall not be transferred to any other party. Resale of examination copies is prohibited.

Electronic Files

The electronic file/eBook in any form of this textbook is licensed to the original user only and shall not be transferred to any other party.

Disclaimer

The author has made sincere efforts to ensure the accuracy of the material described herein, however the author makes no warranty, expressed or implied, with respect to the quality, accuracy, or freedom from error of this document or the products it describes.

www.sdcadacademy.com

Dedication

To my mum and dad,
who have always supported me unconditionally in my endeavors.

To my wife and my sisters,
whose motivation, support, and inspiration made this textbook possible.

To teachers,
who share their invaluable wisdom with young and
curious minds of our future generations.

To students,
who are dedicated to learning new technologies and
striving to make the world a better place to live in.

Thanks

To the employees of SDCAD Academy
for their dedication in editing the contents of this textbook.

Contents at a Glance

Table of Contents

Preface

Autodesk Fusion 360 is a product of Autodesk Inc., one of the biggest providers of technology for engineering, architecture, construction, manufacturing, media, and entertainment industries. It offers robust software tools for design, engineering, and entertainment industries that let you design, visualize, simulate, and publish your ideas before they are built or created. Moreover, Autodesk continues to develop a comprehensive portfolio of state-of-the-art CAD/CAM/CAE software for the global market.

Autodesk Fusion 360 delivers a rich set of integrated tools that are powerful and intuitive to use. It is the first cloud-based 3D CAD/CAM/CAE software that combines the entire product development cycle into a single cloud-based platform. It allows you to design feature-based, parametric mechanical designs by using simple but highly effective 3D modeling tools. Fusion 360 provides a wide range of tools that allow you to create real-world components and assemblies. These components and assemblies can be converted into 2D engineering drawings for production, used for validating designs by simulating their real world conditions, and assessing the environmental impact of your products. It also enables you to create photorealistic renderings, animations, and toolpaths for CNC machines, in addition to creating rapid prototypes of your design by using the 3D printing workflow.

Autodesk Fusion 360: A Step-By-Step Tutorial Guide for Beginners textbook is intended to help students, designers, engineers, and professionals who are interested in learning Autodesk Fusion 360 step-by-step for creating real world 3D mechanical designs. It is a great starting point for new users of Autodesk Fusion 360 and for those moving from other CAD software. This textbook contains tutorials that provide users with step-by-step instructions for creating parametric 3D solid components, assemblies, animations, and 2D drawings with ease. Every tutorial in this textbook is created based on real-world projects. This textbook consists of 11 chapters, a total of 408 pages covering major workspaces of Autodesk Fusion 360 such as DESIGN, ANIMATION, and DRAWING. **This textbook has been developed using software version: 2.0.8950.**

Every chapter ends with exercises that allow users to experience for themselves the user friendly and powerful capacities of Autodesk Fusion 360, followed by chapter summary and questions which help users to assess their knowledge.

Who Should Read This Textbook

This textbook is written to benefit a wide range of Autodesk Fusion 360 users, varying from beginners to advanced users. The step-by-step tutorials in each chapter of this textbook allow easy comprehension of different design techniques, concepts, tools, and design principles.

What Is Covered in This Textbook

Autodesk Fusion 360: A Step-By-Step Guide for Beginners textbook is designed to equip you with everything you need to know to start using Autodesk Fusion 360 with straightforward, step-by-step tutorials. This textbook covers the following topics:

Chapter 1: Introducing Autodesk Fusion 360, discusses system requirements for installing Autodesk Fusion 360 and how to invoke a new design file. It explains user interface of Autodesk Fusion 360 and its various workspaces. It also discusses about managing data by using the **Data Panel**, saving a design file, exporting design to other CAD formats, opening an existing design file, working in the offline mode, recovering unsaved design data, sharing design, invoking a Marking Menu, and exporting your design for 3D printing.

Chapter 2: Creating and Editing Sketches, discusses how to invoke the Sketching environment for creating a sketch by selecting a sketching plane. It explains how to specify the unit system as well as the grids and snaps settings. This chapter also introduces methods for drawing lines, rectangles, circles, arcs, polygons, ellipses, conic curves, slots, and splines by using the respective sketching tools. Besides, it discusses about editing a spline, adding text into a sketch, editing and modifying sketches by performing various editing operations such as trim, extend, mirror, and offset. Moreover, this chapter discusses about applying constraints, applying dimensions, and different states of a sketch.

Chapter 3: Creating Extrude and Revolve Features, discusses how to create extrude and revolve base features.

Chapter 4: Creating Multi-Feature Models, discusses how to navigate a 3D model in the graphics area by using various navigation tools, shortcut keys, and ViewCube. It explains step-by-step creating multi-feature models by using various modeling tools. This chapter also discusses about creating a rib feature, a chamfer, a circular pattern, and a mirror feature, in addition to the extrude and revolve features by using their respective tools. Besides, this chapter explains how to assign a material and calculate the mass properties of a model.

Chapter 5: Creating Sweep and Loft Features, discusses how to create sweep and loft features by using the **Sweep** and **Loft** tools, respectively.

Chapter 6: Creating Holes, Threads, and Shell Features, discusses how to create holes, threads, and shell features. It also explains about creating rectangular pattern and fillet.

Chapter 7: Creating 3D Sketches and Helical Coils, discusses how to create 3D sketches in the Sketching environment by using the sketching tools. It explains about creating helical and spiral coils of different cross-sections. This chapter also discusses about creating a solid or a hollow pipe and combining multiple solid bodies into a single body by performing boolean operations such as join, cut, or intersect.

Chapter 8: Creating Assemblies - I, discusses how to create assemblies by using the bottom-up assembly approach. It explains the application of rigid, revolute, slider, cylindrical, pin-slot, planar, and ball joints to assemble components of an assembly and defines relative motion with respect to each other. This chapter also discusses how to insert components in a design file, ground the first component, apply various types of joints, define joint limits, animate a joint, animate a model, and define relative motion between two joints.

Chapter 9: Creating Assemblies - II, discusses how to create assemblies by using the Top-down assembly approach. It explains various methods of creating all components of an assembly within a design file. This chapter also discusses about applying as-built joints between the components of the assembly by using the **As-built Joint** tool.

Chapter 10: Creating Animation and Exploded Views, discusses how to create an animation of an assembly in the **ANIMATION** Workspace. To animate an assembly, you need to capture various views and actions on the **Timeline** of a storyboard, the method for which is described in this chapter. It explains various methods for creating exploded views of the assembly (manually or automatically), turning on or off the visibility of the components, and creating callouts. This chapter also discusses about customizing and deleting views and actions on the **Timeline**, creating new storyboards, turning on or off the recording of the views, and publishing animation as .avi file format.

Chapter 11: Creating 2D Drawings, discusses how to create 2D drawings of components and assemblies. It explains the concept and definition of the angle of projections, and how to edit the annotations and sheet settings. This chapter also discusses about creating exploded views of an assembly, applying and editing dimensions, creating the Bill of Material (BOM)/Parts list, adding balloons, and exporting the Parts list (BOM) as a CSV file. Besides, it discusses how to export or output the current drawing as a PDF, DWG, or DXF file.

Icons/Terms used in this Textbook
The following icons and terms are used in this textbook:

Note
 Notes highlight information requiring special attention.

Tip
 Tips provide additional advice, which increases the efficiency of the users.

Drop-down Menu
A drop-down menu is a menu in which a set of tools is grouped together, see Figure 1.

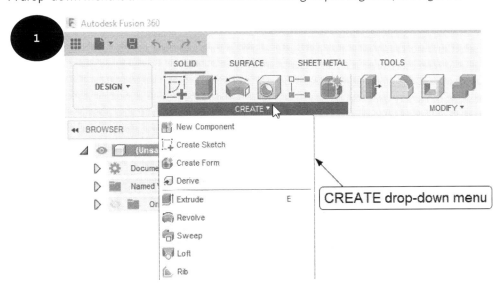

Drop-down List

A drop-down list is a list in which a set of options is grouped together, see Figure 2.

Field

A Field allows you to enter a new value, or modify an existing/default value, as per your requirement, see Figure 2.

Button

A Button appears as a 3D icon and is used for confirming or discarding an action, see Figure 2.

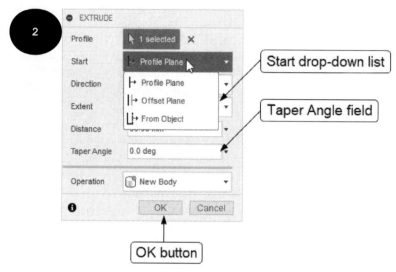

Rollout

A rollout is an area in which buttons, drop-down lists, fields, selection options, check boxes, and so on are available to specify various parameters, see Figure 3. A rollout can either be in the expanded or collapsed form. You can expand or collapse a rollout by clicking on the arrow available on the left side of its title bar.

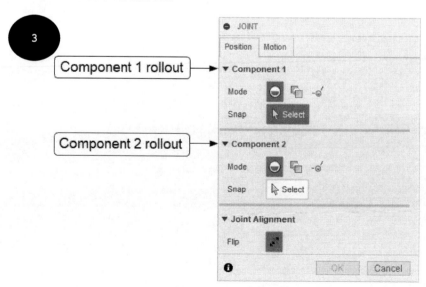

Check box

A check box allows you to turn on or off the uses of a particular option, see Figure 4.

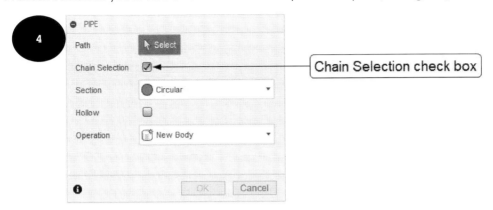

How to Download Online Resources

The author has provided all the models used in the Tutorials and Exercises of this textbook. To download these files:

1. Visit www.sdcadacademy.com
2. Click on **Textbooks > Autodesk Fusion 360 > Autodesk Fusion 360: A Step-By-Step Tutorial Guide for Beginners**.
3. On the bottom of the textbook page, click on **DOWNLOAD TUTORIALS** and **DOWNLOAD EXERCISES** for downloading the tutorial and exercise files, respectively.

If you face any problems in downloading the files or need any technical assistance, please contact the publisher at *info@sdcadacademy.com*.

We would like to express our sincere gratitude to you for purchasing the **Autodesk Fusion 360: A Step-By-Step Tutorial Guide For Beginners** textbook. We hope that the information and concepts introduced in this textbook help you to accomplish your professional goals.

Introducing Autodesk Fusion 360

In this chapter, you will learn the following:

- Installing Autodesk Fusion 360
- Getting Started with Autodesk Fusion 360
- Working with User Interface
- Invoking a New Design File
- Working with Workspaces
- Managing Data by Using the Data Panel
- Saving a Design File
- Exporting a Design to Other CAD Formats
- Opening an Existing Design File
- Working in the Offline Mode
- Recovering Unsaved Data
- Sharing a Design
- Invoking a Marking Menu
- 3D Printing

Welcome to the world of Computer-aided design (CAD) with Autodesk Fusion 360. It is a product of Autodesk Inc., one of the biggest technology providers for engineering, architecture, construction, manufacturing, media, and entertainment industries. It offers robust software tools for 3D design, engineering, and entertainment industries that let you design, visualize, simulate, and publish your ideas before they are built or created. Autodesk continues to develop a comprehensive portfolio of state-of-the-art CAD/CAM/CAE software for global markets.

Autodesk Fusion 360 delivers a rich set of integrated tools that are powerful and intuitive to use. It is the first cloud-based 3D CAD/CAM/CAE software that combines the entire product development cycle into a single cloud-based platform. It allows you to design feature-based, parametric, mechanical designs by using simple but highly effective 3D modeling tools. Autodesk Fusion 360 provides a wide range of tools that allow you to create real-world components and assemblies. These components and assemblies can be converted into engineering 2D drawings for production, for validating designs by simulating their real world conditions, and assessing the environmental impact of your products. It also enables you to create photo-realistic renderings, animations, and toolpaths for CNC machines. Additionally, it allows to create rapid prototypes of your design by using the 3D printing workflow.

Autodesk Fusion 360 enables multiple design teams to work together on a single project for collaborative product development. You can save your designs on a cloud which is secure and provides unlimited storage and access. It allows you to share your designs with your partners, subcontractors, and colleagues in smart new ways and tracks each version of your design, which improves knowledge transfer and effectively shortens the design cycle. Autodesk Fusion 360 is compatible with Windows and iOS operating systems.

Installing Autodesk Fusion 360

If you do not have Autodesk Fusion 360 installed in your system, you first need to get it installed. However, before you start installing Autodesk Fusion 360, you need to evaluate the system requirements and make sure that you have a system capable of running it adequately. Below are the system requirements for installing Autodesk Fusion 360:

- **Operating Systems:** Microsoft® Windows® 8.1 (64-bit only), or Windows 10 (64-bit only)
- **CPU Type:** 64-bit processor (32-bit not supported)
- **RAM:** 4 GB RAM (6 GB or more recommended)
- **Disk Space:** 3 GB minimum (10 GB or more recommended)
- **Graphics Card:** Supported for DirectX 11 or greater, Dedicated GPU with 1 GB or more of VRAM, or Integrated graphics with 6 GB or more of RAM

For more information about the system requirements for Autodesk Fusion 360, visit Autodesk website at *https://knowledge.autodesk.com/support/fusion-360/troubleshooting/caas/sfdcarticles/ sfdcarticles/System-requirements-for-Autodesk-Fusion-360.html*

Once the system is ready, install Autodesk Fusion 360 by using the downloaded Autodesk Fusion 360 software setup file. You can download the setup file by logging in to your Autodesk account.

Getting Started with Autodesk Fusion 360

Once the Autodesk Fusion 360 is installed on your system, double-clicking on the **Autodesk Fusion 360** icon on the desktop of your system. The system prepares for starting Fusion 360 by loading all required files. Once all the required files are loaded, the startup user interface of Autodesk Fusion 360 appears, see Figure 1.1.

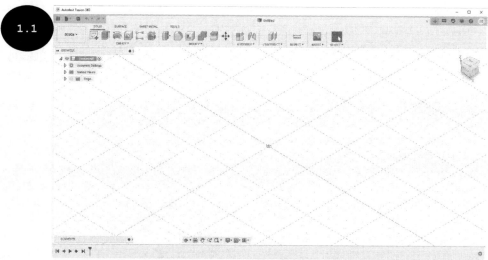

1.1

If you are starting Autodesk Fusion 360 for the first time after installing the software, the QUICK SETUP dialog box appears with the startup user interface, see Figure 1.2. You can also access this dialog box by invoking the **Help** menu in the top right corner of the screen and then clicking on the **Quick Setup** tool, see Figure 1.3. In this dialog box, you can specify default units for the new file. You can also customize the navigation and view settings for Autodesk Fusion 360 by using this dialog box. If you are familiar with any other CAD software such as SOLIDWORKS or Inventor, you can customize the settings in accordance with that software by using the options in this dialog box. You will learn about navigation settings in later chapters.

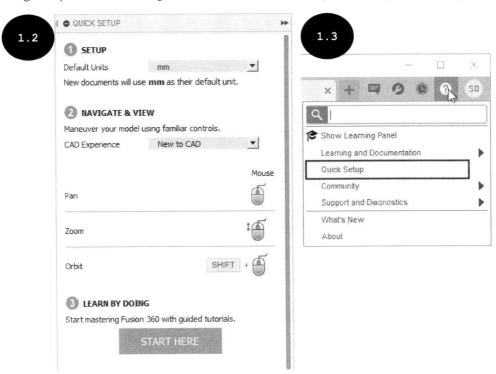

*If you are not already logged in to your Autodesk account then on starting Autodesk Fusion 360, the **Sign in** window appears, see Figure 1.4. In this window, enter your E-mail ID and then click on the **NEXT** button. The **Welcome** window appears. In this window, enter the password and then click on the **SIGN IN** button. The startup user interface of Autodesk Fusion 360 appears.*

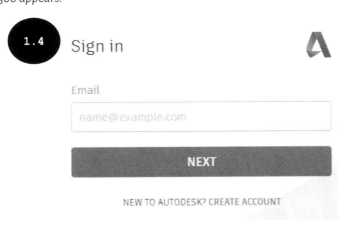

Working with User Interface

It is evident from the startup user interface of Autodesk Fusion 360 that it is intuitive and user friendly. Various components of the startup user interface are shown in Figure 1.5 and are discussed next.

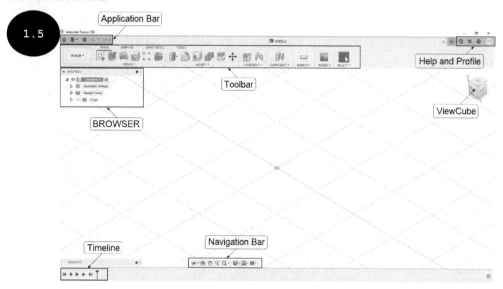

Toolbar

Toolbar provides access to various Autodesk Fusion tools for accomplishing different tasks depending upon the activated workspace, see Figure 1.6. You can activate a workspace by using the **Workspace** drop-down menu of the **Toolbar**, see Figure 1.7. By default, the **DESIGN** workspace is activated in the **Workspace** drop-down menu. As a result, the tools for creating and editing solid 3D models (components and assemblies), surface models, and sheet metal models are available in the **SOLID**, **SURFACE**, and **SHEET METAL** tabs of the **Toolbar**, respectively, see Figure 1.7. You will learn more about different workspaces available in Autodesk Fusion 360 later in this chapter.

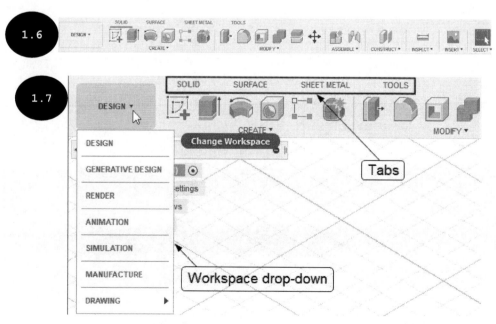

Application Bar

Application Bar consists of frequently used tools to access design files, manage data, create a new design file, export data, save design file, undo/redo operations, and so on, see Figure 1.8. You will learn about these tools later in this chapter.

BROWSER

BROWSER appears on the left side of the graphics area and keeps a record of all objects in the design which includes sketches, bodies, components, and construction geometries, see Figure 1.9. You can use BROWSER to control the visibility of each object of the design. For example, to toggle the visibility of an object in the graphics area, click on the **Show/Hide** icon of the object, see Figure 1.9. In BROWSER, a set of similar objects are grouped together under different nodes.

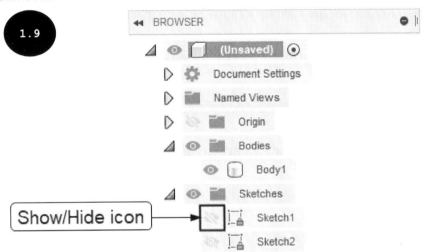

Help and Profile Menus

Help and Profile menus appear on the upper right corner of the interface. The **Help** menu allows you to access help documents, community forum, what's new in Fusion 360 information, and so on, see Figure 1.10. The **Profile** menu allows you to control your profile, account settings, and design preferences settings, see Figure 1.11.

ViewCube

ViewCube is available at the upper right corner of the graphics area and is used for navigating the design, see Figure 1.12. You can orbit or switch between the standard and isometric views of a model by using the ViewCube. You will learn to navigate a design by using the ViewCube in later chapters.

Timeline

Timeline appears in the lower left corner of the interface and keeps a record of all features or operations performed on the design, see Figure 1.13. Note that the features appear in the **Timeline** in the order they are created. The Rollback Bar appears on the right side of the last feature in the **Timeline**. You can drag the Rollback Bar to the left or right in the **Timeline** to step forward or backward through the regeneration order of the features. Note that the features present after the Rollback Bar get suppressed and do not appear in the graphics area.

Navigation Bar

Navigation Bar available at the lower middle part of the graphics area, see Figure 1.14. **Navigation Bar** contains navigation tools such as **Zoom**, **Pan**, and **Orbit** to navigate the design, as well as tools to control the display settings such as appearance of the interface and the visual style of the design. You will learn about navigating and display settings in later chapters.

Invoking a New Design File

Every time you start Autodesk Fusion 360, a new design file with the default name "**Untitled**" is invoked, automatically, see Figure 1.15. Various components such as **Application Bar**, **Toolbar**, **BROWSER**, and **Timeline** of the startup user interface of the new design file are discussed earlier.

In addition to the default design file, you can invoke a new design file by using the **New Design** tool of the **File** drop-down menu in the **Application Bar**, see Figure 1.16. To do so, a new design file with the default name "**Untitled (1)**" is invoked and it becomes active by default. You can also click on the +sign, next to the name of the existing design file to start a new design file, see Figure 1.17. Alternatively, press the CTRL + N key.

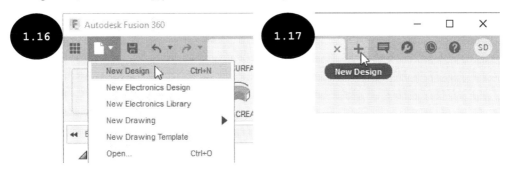

As discussed earlier, the tools available in the **Toolbar** depend upon the active workspace. By default, the **DESIGN** workspace is active. As a result, the tools related to design 3D models, surface models, and sheet metal models are available in various tabs of the **Toolbar**. The different workspaces available in Autodesk Fusion 360 are discussed next.

Working with Workspaces

Workspaces are defined as task-oriented environments in which different tools and commands are organized according to particular design objectives. In Autodesk Fusion 360, different workspaces namely, **DESIGN, GENERATIVE DESIGN, RENDER, ANIMATION, SIMULATION, MANUFACTURE,** and **DRAWING** are available. You can switch between these workspaces by using the **Workspace** drop-down menu of the **Toolbar**, see Figure 1.18. Different workspaces are discussed next.

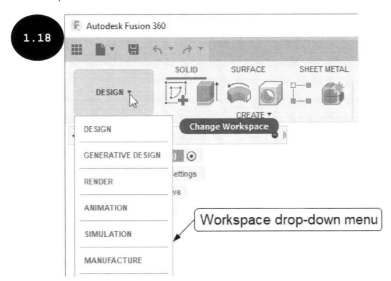

DESIGN Workspace

The **DESIGN** workspace consists of different sets of tools that are used for creating 3D solid models, surface models, sheet metal models, as well as free form 3D solid or free form surface models in the respective tabs of the **Toolbar**. Different tabs of the **Toolbar** in the **DESIGN** workspace are discussed next.

SOLID

The SOLID tab consists of different sets of tools that are used for creating 3D solid models, which includes designing of 3D solid components and assemblies. Figure 1.19 shows a component and Figure 1.20 shows an assembly.

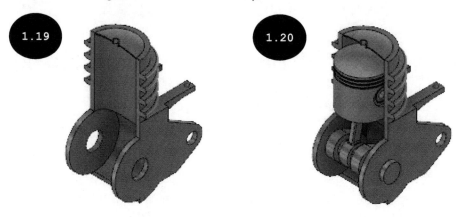

SURFACE

The SURFACE tab consists of different sets of tools that are used for creating surface models, see Figure 1.21. Surface models are of zero thickness and generally used for creating models of complex shapes, see Figure 1.22.

SHEET METAL

The SHEET METAL tab consists of different sets of tools that are used for creating sheet metal components, see Figures 1.23 and 1.24.

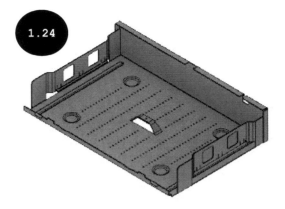

FORM

The **FORM** contextual tab is provided with different sets of tools that are used for creating or editing free form 3D solid or free form surface models by manipulating (pushing and pulling) faces, edges, and vertices of the design to achieve the desired shapes, see Figure 1.25. Note that the **FORM** contextual tab is the sub-environment of the **DESIGN** Workspace and can be invoked by clicking on the **Create Form** tool in the **CREATE** panel of the **SOLID** tab, see Figure 1.26. To return to **SOLID** tab, you need to click on the **FINISH FORM** tool in the Toolbar.

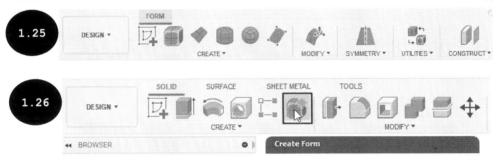

SKETCH

The **SKETCH** contextual tab is provided with different sets of tools that are used for creating sketches for the solid, surface, and sheet metal models, see Figure 1.27. Note that the **SKETCH** contextual tab is invoked by clicking on the **Create Sketch** tool in the **CREATE** panel of the **DESIGN** workspace, see Figure 1.28.

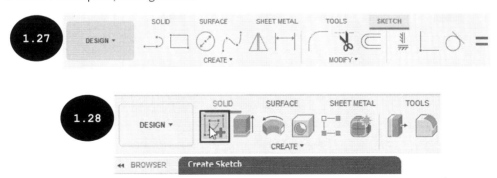

TOOLS

The **TOOLS** tab is provided with different sets of tools that are used for creating 3D prints of the design, determining area and volume of models, detecting interference between components, and so on, see Figure 1.29.

GENERATIVE DESIGN Workspace

GENERATIVE DESIGN workspace consist of different sets of tools that are used for defining a design problem through goals and constraints and generate a set of designs that meet the requirements, see Figure 1.30.

RENDER Workspace

The RENDER workspace consists of different sets of tools that are used for rendering photo-realistic images, see Figure 1.31.

ANIMATION Workspace

The ANIMATION workspace consists of different sets of tools that are used for creating exploded views of an assembly as well as animation of a design to represent how the components of an assembly are assembled, operated, or repaired, see Figure 1.32.

SIMULATION Workspace

The SIMULATION workspace allows you to perform various types of finite element analysis on a design for simulating its performance under applied loads and conditions, see Figure 1.33. It helps engineers to bring product performance knowledge into the early stages of the design cycle.

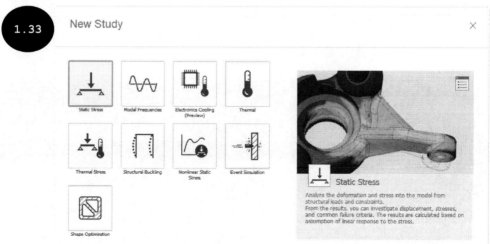

MANUFACTURE Workspace

The **MANUFACTURE** workspace consists of different sets of tools that are used for creating toolpaths for CNC machines, see Figure 1.34.

1.34

DRAWING Workspace

The **DRAWING** workspace consists of different sets of tools that are used for creating 2D drawings of a design (component or assembly), see Figures 1.35 and 1.36.

1.35

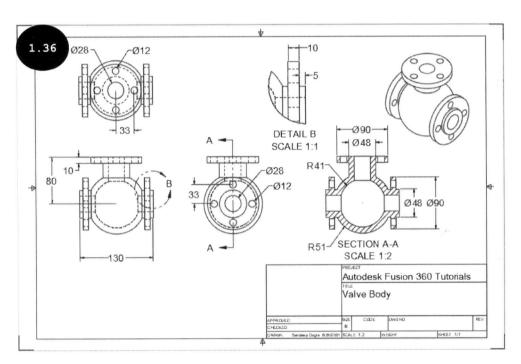

1.36

Managing Data by Using the Data Panel

Autodesk Fusion 360 is a cloud-based 3D CAD/CAM/CAE software that allows you to store all your designs, safe and secure in the cloud by using the **Data Panel**. It is a smart new way to manage the data in cloud. To access the **Data Panel**, click on the **Show Data Panel** tool in the **Application Bar**, see Figure 1.37. The **Data Panel** appears on the left, see Figure 1.38. The homepage of the **Data Panel** is divided into three areas: PROJECTS, LIBRARIES, and SAMPLES. The PROJECTS area allows you to create a new project folder and sub-folders to save the files, upload files, collaborate with other users, and access recently used data. The LIBRARIES area allows you to store projects that contain assets used by Fusion 360 including templates, libraries, and other configuration files. The SAMPLES area provides access to sample projects and training exercises. The methods for creating a new project folder and sub-folders, uploading files, and collaborating with other users are discussed next.

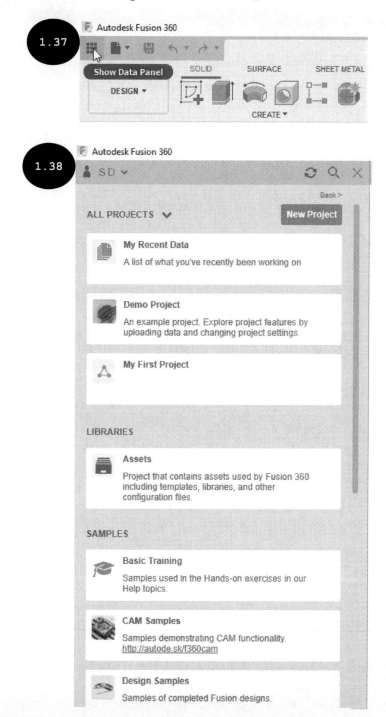

Creating a New Project Folder and Sub-Folders

In Autodesk Fusion 360, the first and foremost step is to organize the **Data Panel** by creating the project folder and sub-folders to save files. To do so, invoke the **Data Panel** and then click on the **New Project** button, see Figure 1.39. A new project folder is created in the **PROJECTS** area of the **Data Panel** and its default name "**New Project**" appears in an edit field, see Figure 1.39. Write the name of the project in this edit field and then press ENTER. The new project folder is created in the **PROJECTS** area of the **Data Panel** with the specified name.

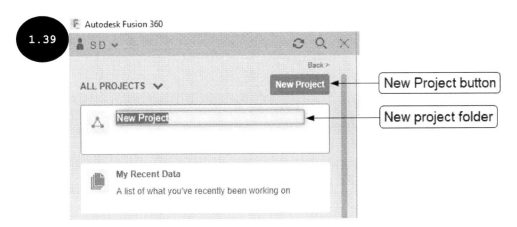

After creating the project folder, you can access it to save files. You can also create sub-folders in the project folder to organize sets of similar project files. To do so, double-click on the name of the project folder in the **PROJECTS** area of the **Data Panel**. The selected project folder is opened in the **Data Panel** and its name appears at the top, see Figure 1.40. Next, click on the **New Folder** button. A new sub-folder is created and its default name "**New Folder**" appears in an edit field, see Figure 1.41. Write the name of the sub-folder in this edit field and then press FNTER. A sub-folder with the specified name is created inside the selected project folder. Similarly, you can create multiple sub-folders in a project folder.

*If you are not connected to the Internet or loose the Internet connection, you cannot create project folders and sub-folders in the **Data Panel**. However, you can still continue to work on your designs in the offline mode. You will learn more about offline mode later in this chapter.*

Uploading Existing Files in a Project

In Autodesk Fusion 360, you can upload one or more existing files in an active project. To do so, click on the **Upload** button available at the top of an active project folder or sub-folder in **Data Panel**. The **Upload** dialog box appears, see Figure 1.42.

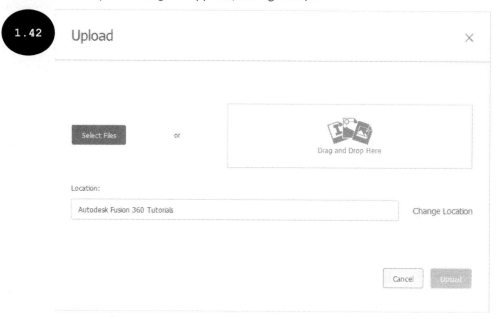

In the **Upload** dialog box, the **Location** field displays the location for uploading files in the **Data Panel**. You can change the location by using the **Change Location** option available on the right of the **Location** field. After specifying the location for uploading the files, click on the **Select Files** button. The **Open** dialog box appears. By using the **Open** dialog box, you can select the following types of files to be uploaded:

- Alias Files (*.wire)
- AutoCAD DWG Files(*.dwg)
- Autodesk Eagle Files(*.sch, *.brd, *.lbr)
- Autodesk Fusion 360 Archive Files(*.f3d, *.f3z, *.fsch, *.fbrd, *.flbr)
- Autodesk Inventor Files (*.iam, *.ipt)
- Catia V5 Files (*.CATProduct, *.CATPart)
- DXF Files (*.dxf)
- FBX Files (*.fbx)
- IGES Files (*.iges, *.ige, *.igs)
- NX Files (*.prt)
- OBJ Files (*.obj)
- Parasolid Binary Files (*.x_b)
- Parasolid Text Files (*.x_t)
- Pro/ENGINEER and Creo Parametric Files (*.asm, *.prt)
- Pro/ENGINEER Granite Files (*.g)
- Pro/ENGINEER Neutral Files (*.neu)
- Rhino Files (*.3dm)
- SAT/SMT Files (*.sab, *.sat, *.smb, *.smt)
- SolidWorks Files (*.prt, *.asm, *.sldprt, *.sldasm)
- SolidEdge Files(*.par, *.asm, *.psm)
- STEP Files (*.ste, *.step, *.stp)
- STL Files (*.stl)

- SketchUp Files (*.sku)
- 123D Files(*.123dx)

 *You can also drag and drop the files to be uploaded in the **Upload** dialog box.*

Select one or more files in the **Open** dialog box and then click on the **Open** button. The selected file(s) gets listed in the **Upload** dialog box. Next, click on the **Upload** button. The **Job Status** dialog box appears which displays the current status of uploading the files on the specified location in the **Data Panel**. Once the uploading is completed and the status appears as **Complete** in the dialog box, click on the **Close** button. The thumbnails of the uploaded files appear in the specified location of the **Data Panel**. Now, you can open the uploaded file in Fusion 360. To do so, double-click on the thumbnail of the file in the **Data Panel**. The selected file gets opened in Fusion 360. Now, you can edit the file, as required.

Collaborating with Other Users

Autodesk Fusion 360 enables multiple design teams to work together on a single project for collaborative product development. To collaborate with other users or to share the design with your partners, subcontractors, and colleagues, click on the **People** tab in the **Data Panel**, see Figure 1.43. The **People** tab gets activated and displays the list of people working on the project. Also, the **Invite** field appears in the **Data Panel**, see Figure 1.44.

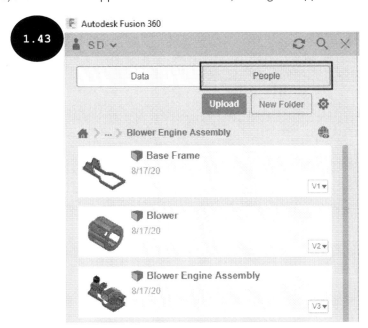

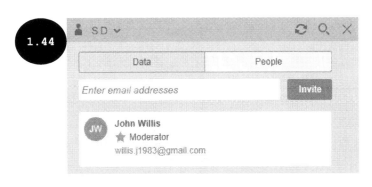

Now, you can enter an E-mail ID in the **Invite** field of the **Data Panel** and then click on the **Invite** button to allow specified people to access your design.

You can also create or switch teams using the **Team Switcher** in the top left corner of the **Data Panel**, see Figure 1.45. Click the drop-down arrow besides your name in the **Data Panel**. The **Team Switcher** drop-down menu displays a list of teams you are a member of. To create or join a team, click on the **Create or join team** tool, see Figure 1.46. The **Create or Join Team** window appears. In this window, follow the instructions for creating or joining a team. A team is a collaborative environment where you can store design data and either work on your own or with collaborators.

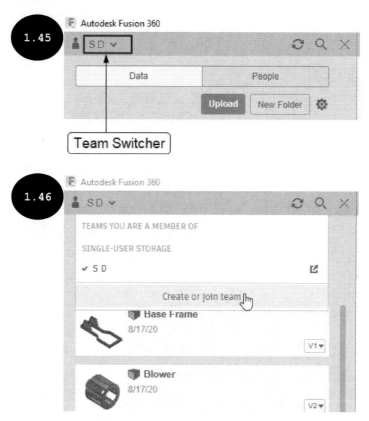

Filtering Project Display in the Data Panel

You can choose to display a set of projects by using the **Project Filter** drop-down list on the upper left area of the **Data Panel**, see Figure 1.47. You can choose to show all projects, pinned projects, owned projects, or shared projects by choosing the respective option in this drop-down list. You can also filter the display of projects by typing in the **Filter** field available at the bottom of the **Data Panel**.

Opening Data Panel in Web Browser

In Autodesk Fusion 360, you can also view and manage a project on a web browser. To do so, open the project folder by double clicking on its name in the **Data Panel** and then click on the **Open on the Web** tool available at the top right of the **Data Panel**, see Figure 1.48. The selected project opens in the default web browser and you can perform various operations such as uploading a file, deleting a file, creating folders, and so on in the project.

Saving a Design File

To save a design file created in any of the workspaces of Autodesk Fusion 360, click on the **Save** tool in the **Application Bar**, see Figure 1.49. The **Save** dialog box appears. In this dialog box, enter the name of the design file in the **Name** field. The **Location** field of the dialog box displays the current location for saving the file. To specify a new location for saving the file, click on the down arrow next to the **Location** field of the dialog box. The **Save** dialog box gets expanded, see Figure 1.50.

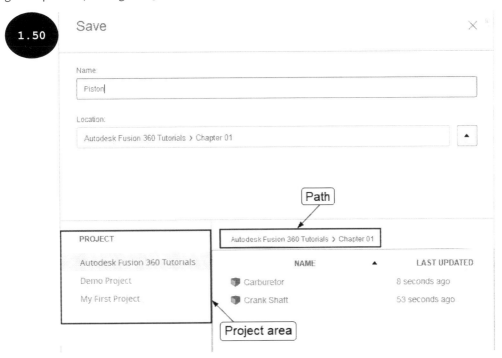

In the expanded **Save** dialog box, you can specify the location to save the file. The **Project** area of the dialog box displays the list of projects. You can select the required project folder to save the file in this area. On selecting the project folder, its sub-folders appear on the right panel of the dialog box. You can double-click on the sub-folder to access it for saving the file. Note that the **Path** area of the dialog box displays the current path/location for saving the file. You can also click on the project folder or sub-folder in the **Path** area of the dialog box to change the location. Besides, you can also create a new project and sub-folders by using the **New Project** and **New Folder** buttons in the **Save** dialog box, respectively.

After specifying the name and location, click on the **Save** button in the dialog box. The design file is saved at the specified location.

In Autodesk Fusion 360, every time you save a file by using the **Save** tool, a new version of the file is saved because Autodesk Fusion 360 keeps a track of each version of your design. By default, when you open a design file, the latest version of the file will be opened in Fusion 360. However, you can also open an older version of the design file as well. You will learn about opening design files later in this chapter.

You can also save an already saved design file with a different name. To do so, invoke the **File** drop-down menu in the **Application Bar** and then click on the **Save as** tool, see Figure 1.51. The **Save As** dialog box appears. In this dialog box, specify a new name for the design file and the location for saving it. Next, click on the **Save** button. The design file gets saved with the specified name without affecting the original design file.

Exporting a Design to Other CAD Formats

In Autodesk Fusion 360, you can export the Fusion 360 design files to other CAD formats, neutral file formats, or the native Fusion file format. To do so, invoke the **File** drop-down menu in the **Application Bar** and then click on the **Export** tool. The **Export** dialog box appears, see Figure 1.52.

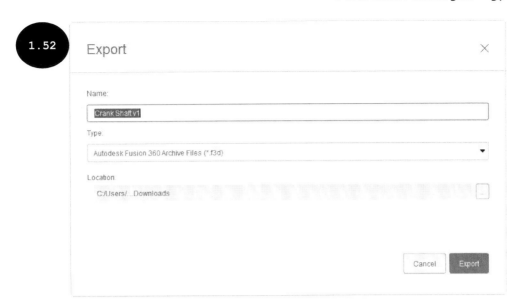

1.52

In the **Type** drop-down list of the **Export** dialog box, select the required file format [Autodesk Fusion 360 Archive Files (*.f3d), **Autodesk Inventor 2019 Files (*.ipt), DWG Files (*.dwg), DXF Files (*.dxf), FBX Files (*.fbx), IGES Files (*.igs *.iges), OBJ Files (*.obj), SAT Files (*.sat), SketchUp Files (*.skp), SMT Files (*.smt), STEP Files (*.stp *.step), or STL Files (*.stl)**] in which you want to export the file. To specify the location for saving the file in a local drive of your computer, click on the **Browse** button. The **Save As** dialog box appears. In this dialog box, specify a location to save the file and then click on the **Save** button. The file is saved in the specified file format.

Opening an Existing Design File

In Autodesk Fusion 360, you can open an existing design file of a project from the **Data Panel** or the **Open** dialog box. You can also open an existing **Fusion** (*.f3d), IGES (*.iges; *.igs), SAT (*.sat), SMT (*.smt), STEP (*.step; *.stp), etc. file that is saved in your local computer. The various methods for opening an existing file are discussed next.

Opening an Existing File from the Data Panel

To open an existing design file of a project from the **Data Panel,** click on the **Show Data Panel** tool ▦ in the **Application Bar**. The **Data Panel** gets invoked. Next, browse to the location of the file to be opened and then double-click on it. The selected file gets opened in Fusion 360. Alternatively, right-click on the file to be opened and then click on the **Open** option in the shortcut menu that appears, see Figure 1.53.

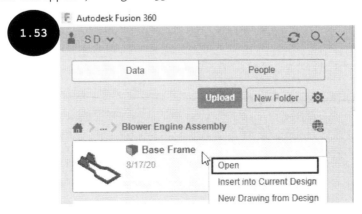

1.53

By default, when you open a design file, its latest version will get opened in Fusion 360. However, you can also open an older version of the file. To do so, click on the Version icon ⬛ available on the lower right corner of the design thumbnail in the **Data Panel**, see Figure 1.54. All the versions of the respective design file appear in the **Data Panel**, see Figure 1.55. Note that in this figure, the **V5** icon indicates that a total of 5 versions are available for the selected design file.

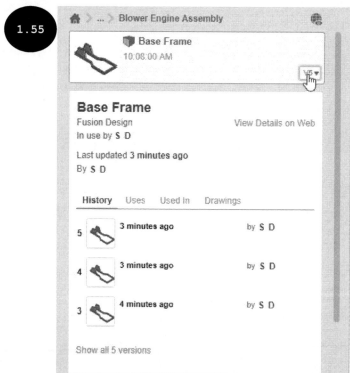

Hover the cursor over the desired version of the file to be opened. The **Promote** and **Open** buttons appear in front of it. The **Promote** button 👕 is used for promoting the older version of the file to the latest version. The **Open** button 📂 is used for opening the older version of the file. Click on the **Open** button. The selected version of the file gets opened in Fusion 360. If all versions of the selected files do not appear in the **Data Panel**, then click on the **Show all versions** option in the **Data Panel**.

Opening an Existing File by using the Open tool

To open an existing design file of a project by using the **Open** tool, invoke the **File** drop-down menu in the **Application Bar** and then click on the **Open** tool, see Figure 1.56. The **Open** dialog box appears, see Figure 1.57. In this dialog box, click on the name of the project that appears on the left panel of the dialog box. All the sub-folders or files of the selected project appear on the right panel of the dialog box. Select the required design file to be opened from the right panel of the dialog box. Note that if the design file to be opened is saved in a sub-folder of the selected project, then you need to double-click on the sub-folder to display its files. After selecting the design file, click on the **Open** button in the dialog box. The selected file gets opened.

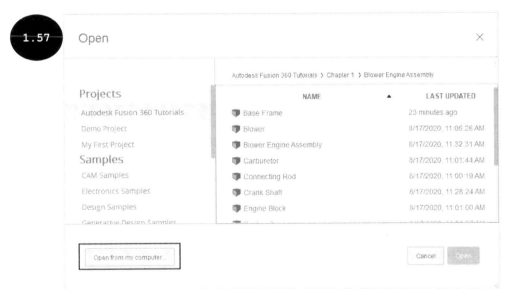

Opening an Existing File from the Local Computer

As discussed earlier, you can open an existing **Fusion** (*.f3d), IGES (*.iges; *.igs), SAT (*.sat), SMT (*.smt), STEP (*.step; *.stp), etc. file that is saved in your local computer. To do so, invoke the **Open** dialog box, as discussed earlier and then click on the **Open from my computer** button, refer to Figure 1.57. Another **Open** dialog box appears. In this dialog box, browse to the location where the file to be opened is saved. You can open **Alias** files, **AutoCAD DWG** files, **Autodesk Fusion 360** files, **Autodesk Inventor** files, **Catia V5** files, **NX** files, **IGES** files, **STEP** files, and so on. After selecting the required file, click on the **Open** button in the dialog box. The **Job Status** window appears with the current status of the file in the **Status** column. When the status of the file appears as **Complete** in the **Status** column of the dialog box, click on the **Open** option in the **Action** column of the dialog box. The selected file gets opened in Fusion 360.

After opening an existing file, you can edit it by adding new features. However, before you add the new features, it is recommended to turn on the process of capturing design history in the **Timeline** for the newly added features. To do so, right-click on the name of the file (top browser node) in the **BROWSER** and then click on the **Capture Design History** tool in the shortcut menu that appears, see Figure 1.58. Similarly, if you do not want to capture design history for a design, click on the **Do not capture Design History** tool in the shortcut menu that appears.

Working in the Offline Mode

Autodesk Fusion 360 automatically goes to offline mode when you are not connected to the Internet, lose the Internet connection, an unexpected outage is detected, or service is under maintenance. However, Autodesk Fusion 360 allows you to continue work on your designs in the offline mode. You can also switch between the online and offline modes, manually. To do so, click on the **Job Status** icon in the upper right corner of the screen, see Figure 1.59. The **Job Status** flyout appears, see Figure 1.60. In this flyout, click on the **Working Online** icon. The offline mode gets activated and the **Working Offline** icon ⬤ appears in the flyout.

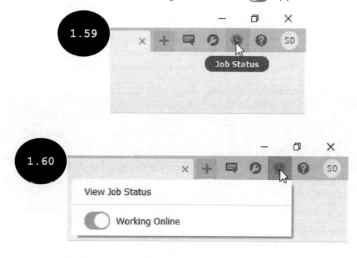

As discussed, Autodesk Fusion 360 allows you to work in the offline mode. However, certain file operations such as uploading files, creating project folders, and sub-folders cannot be performed. Note that the designs saved in the offline mode will be automatically synced and uploaded to the **Data Panel** when you are back to the online mode. However, when you save a design in the offline mode, only the last saved version of the design is captured.

Recovering Unsaved Data

Autodesk Fusion 360 allows you to recover the data in case an unexpected error occurs and Autodesk Fusion 360 closes automatically. To do so, invoke the **File** drop-down menu in the **Application Bar** and then click on the **Recovered Documents** tool. The **File Recovery** window appears. In this window, click on the unsaved file to be recovered and then click on the **Open** tool in the menu that appears. The file is recovered and opened in Fusion 360. Note that the **Recovered Documents** tool is only active if unsaved data is available for recovery. To delete a recovered file from the list, select the **Delete** tool in the menu that appears on clicking the name of the recovered file.

Sharing a Design

In Autodesk Fusion 360, you can share your design with anyone using a link. You can also share your design to Autodesk gallery and GrabCAD (*www.grabcad.com*). In addition, you can create a video of your design by recording your screen and share it with anyone. The methods for sharing your design are discussed next.

Sharing Design Using a Link

To share your design with anyone using a link, invoke the **File** drop-down menu in the **Application Bar** and then move the cursor over the **Share** tool. A cascading menu appears, see Figure 1.61. Next, click on the **Public Link** tool. The **Share Public Link** window appears. In this window, select the **Share the latest version with anyone using this public link** check box, see Figure 1.62. A unique link is generated and appears in the window. Next, click on the **Copy** button to copy the link and then you can share this link with anyone through e-mail or any other mode to allow access to your design.

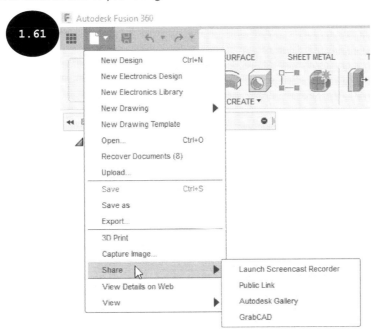

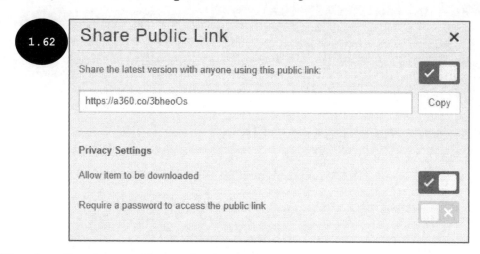

Sharing Design to Autodesk Gallery

You can also share your design to Autodesk Gallery so that all the registered members of Autodesk Gallery can access your design. To do so, click on **File** > **Share** > **Autodesk Gallery** in the **Application Bar**. The **SHARE TO AUTODESK GALLERY** dialog box appears. In this dialog box, click on the **NEW PROJECT** button and then enter project title, description, and so on. Next, accept the terms and conditions, and then click on the **Publish** button to share the design/project in Autodesk Gallery.

Sharing Design to GrabCAD

To publish or share your design to GrabCAD (*www.grabcad.com*), click on **File** > **Share** > **GrabCAD** in the **Application Bar**. The **PUBLISH TO GRABCAD** dialog box appears, see Figure 1.63. By using this window, log in to your GrabCAD account to publish your design, publicly for all registered members of GrabCAD.

Sharing Design by Recording Screen

In Autodesk Fusion 360, you can also record your screen by using the Screencast Recorder and create a video of your design for sharing it with anyone. To do so, click on **File > Share > Launch Screencast Recorder** in the **Application Bar**. The Autodesk webpage gets opened for downloading the Screencast Recorder application. Download and install the Screencast Recorder application. After installing the Screencast Recorder, launch it by double-clicking on the **Screencast Recorder** icon on your desktop. The **Screencast** window appears, see Figure 1.64. Next, click on the **Record** button in this window to start recording your screen. After capturing all the operations of your design process or workflow, stop the recording by clicking on the **Stop** button in the **Screencast** window. The **Screencast Recording Preview** window appears. In this window, click on the **Save and Upload** button. The **Screencast Details** dialog box appears, see Figure 1.65. In this dialog box, specify the required details such as title name and description of the video. Next, select the required option in the **Share with** drop-down list and then click on the **Upload** button. The video gets uploaded and shared depending upon the option selected in the **Share with** drop-down list of the dialog box.

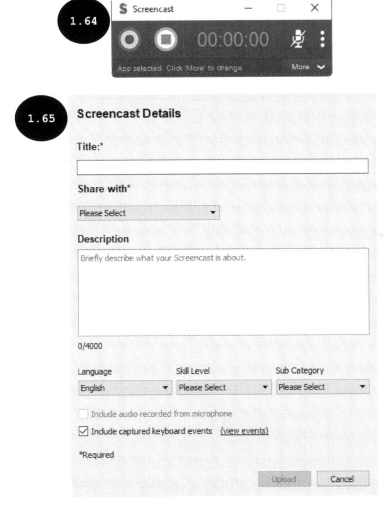

Invoking a Marking Menu

The Marking Menu gets invoked when you right-click in the graphics area. It provides quick access to the most frequently used tools in the Wheel, see Figure 1.66. It also includes an Overflow menu that provides quick access to navigation tools and workspace selection menu, see Figure 1.66. Note that the availability of the tools in the Marking Menu depends on the active workspace.

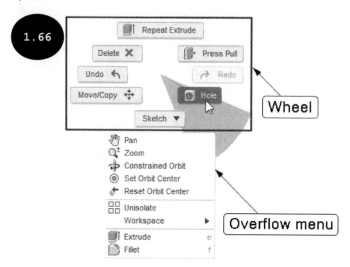

3D Printing

After creating a design in Autodesk Fusion 360, you can create a prototype of your design by using the additive manufacturing or 3D printing. Additive manufacturing is a technique where a 3D printer builds the model in 3 dimensions by joining material layer by layer as per the design. Generally, different grades of plastic material are used for building the 3D prototype of your design. However, you can also use metal material for building the prototype. Note that for creating a 3D prototype of your design by using 3D printing, you need to export your design in a .STL file as an input to a 3D printer, since the .STL file is the most popular file format for 3D printing. The method for exporting your design in .STL file format for 3D printing is discussed next.

Exporting a Design in .STL File Format for 3D Printing

1. Invoke the **MAKE** drop-down menu in the **TOOLS** tab of the **DESIGN** workspace and then click on the **3D Print** tool, see Figure 1.67. The **3D PRINT** dialog box appears, see Figure 1.68. Alternatively, you can also click on the **File > 3D Print** in the **Application Bar** or right-click on the name of the model (top browser node) in the **BROWSER** and then click on the **Save As STL** tool in the shortcut menu that appears.

By default, the **Selection** button is activated in the **3D PRINT** dialog box. As a result, you can select a component in the graphics area.

2. Select a component to be exported as .stl file for 3D printer.

3. Select the **Preview Mesh** check box in the dialog box. The mesh preview of the model appears in the graphics area as per the default refinement settings.

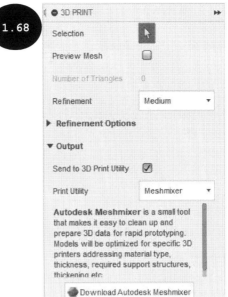

4. Select the required option in the **Refinement** drop-down list to define the refinement quality of the mesh. You can further define the refinement settings by expanding the **Refinement Options** rollout of the dialog box.

5. Ensure that the **Send to 3D Print Utility** check box is selected in the **Output** rollout of the dialog box for sending the .STL file directly to a 3D print utility application.

*Instead of sending the .STL file directly to a 3D print utility, you can also save the .STL file in your local computer. This .STL file can later be imported to any 3D print utility application for 3D printing. To do so, clear the **Send to 3D Print Utility** check box in the **Output** rollout of the dialog box and then click on the **OK** button. The **Save STL** dialog box appears. In this dialog box, browse to the required location and then click on the **Save** button.*

6. Select the required 3D print utility in the **Print Utility** drop-down list of the dialog box for defining the print settings and further preparing the design for printing by defining material properties and other related settings. Note that if the selected utility is not installed on your computer then you need to download and install it by using the link given at the bottom of the dialog box.

7. After selecting the required print utility, click on the **OK** button in the dialog box. The process for loading the selected utility gets started and once that is done, the selected utility gets invoked, see Figure 1.69. Note that Figure 1.69 shows the PreForm utility.

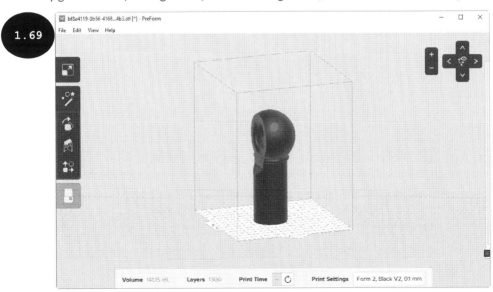

Once the design is opened in the selected 3D print utility application, you can define the settings for 3D printing such as orientation, placement of the model on printing tray, scale, repair model for any geometrical defects, add supports for overhanging parts, and so on. Also, you need to connect your computer with a 3D printer. After defining all the parameters for 3D printing, click on the **Start a print** tool in the toolbar to print the model.

Summary

This chapter discussed system requirements for installing Autodesk Fusion 360 and how to invoke a new design file. It explained user interface of Autodesk Fusion 360, various workspaces, and how to create a new design from file. It also discussed about managing data by using the **Data Panel**, saving a design file, exporting design to other CAD formats, opening an existing design file, working in the offline mode, recovering unsaved design data, sharing design, invoking a Marking Menu, and exporting your design for 3D printing.

Questions

Answer the following questions:

* In Autodesk Fusion 360, _____ are defined as task-oriented environments in which different tools and commands are organized according to particular design objectives.

* The _____ workspace is used for creating exploded views of an assembly as well as animation of a design.

* The _____ appears in the lower left corner of the interface and keeps a record of all features or operations performed on the design.

* The _____ tool is used for turning on the process of capturing design history in the **Timeline** for an imported design.

* To create a 3D prototype of a design by using 3D printing, you need to export your design in a _____ file as an input to a 3D printer.

* Autodesk Fusion 360 allows you to store all your designs in the cloud by using the _____.

* The _____ tool in the **Application Bar** is used for exporting designs in other CAD formats.

* In Autodesk Fusion 360, every time you save a file by using the **Save** tool, a new version of the file gets saved. (True/False)

* Autodesk Fusion 360 does not allow you to work in the offline mode. (True/False)

* The .IGES file is the most popular file format for 3D printing. (True/False)

* In Autodesk Fusion 360, you can publish your design to GrabCAD (*www.grabcad.com*). (True/False)

Creating and Editing Sketches

In this chapter, you will learn the following:

- Invoking the Sketching Environment
- Drawing a Line
- Drawing a Tangent Arc by Using the Line Tool
- Drawing a Rectangle
- Drawing a Circle
- Drawing an Arc
- Drawing a Polygon
- Drawing an Ellipse
- Drawing a Slot
- Drawing a Conic Curve
- Drawing a Spline
- Editing a Spline
- Adding Text into a Sketch
- Editing and Modifying Sketches
- Applying Constraints
- Applying Dimensions
- Working with Different States of a Sketch
- Creating a Sketch
- Creating and Editing a Sketch

Autodesk Fusion 360 is a feature-based, parametric, solid modeling mechanical design, and automation software. Before you start creating solid 3D components in Autodesk Fusion 360, you need to understand the software. To design a component using this software, you need to create all its features one by one, see Figures 2.1 and 2.2. Note that the features are divided in two main categories: sketch based features and placed features. A feature created by using a sketch is known as a sketch based feature, whereas a feature created on an existing feature without using a sketch is known as a placed feature. Of the two categories, the sketch based feature is the first feature of any real world component to be designed. Therefore, it is important to focus first on drawing a sketch.

Figure 2.1 shows a component consisting of an extrude feature, a cut feature, a chamfer, and a fillet. Of all these features, the extrude and cut features are created by using a sketch, refer to Figure 2.2. Therefore, these features are known as sketch based features. On the other hand, the fillet and the chamfer are known as placed features because no sketch is used for creating these features. Figure 2.2 depicts the process for creating this model.

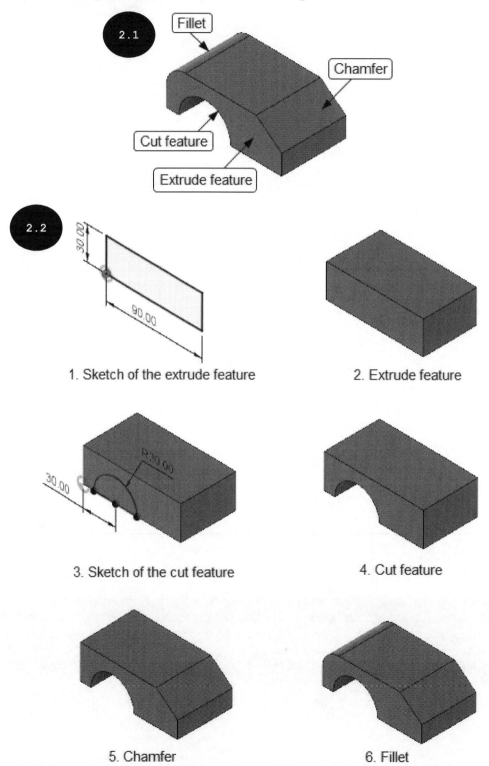

1. Sketch of the extrude feature

2. Extrude feature

3. Sketch of the cut feature

4. Cut feature

5. Chamfer

6. Fillet

As the first feature of any component is a sketch based feature, you first need to learn how to create sketches. Note that the first feature is also know as the base feature of a model. In Autodesk Fusion 360, you can create sketches by using the various sketching tools available in a design file.

Invoking the Sketching Environment

In Autodesk Fusion 360, you can create a sketch of a feature in the Sketching environment. To do so, launch Autodesk Fusion 360 and then click on the **Create Sketch** tool in the **Toolbar**, see Figure 2.3. Three default planes: Front, Top, and Right, which are mutually perpendicular to each other appear in the graphics area. Next, select any one of the three default planes as the sketching plane for creating the sketch. The Sketching environment gets invoked and the **SKETCH** contextual tab appears in the **Toolbar**. Now, you can start creating the sketch by using the sketching tools available in the **CREATE** panel and the **CREATE** drop-down menu of the **SKETCH** contextual tab, see Figures 2.4 and 2.5.

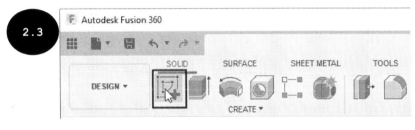

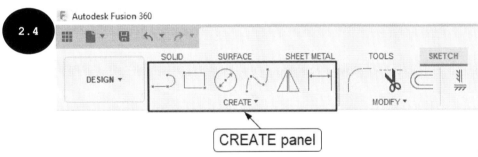

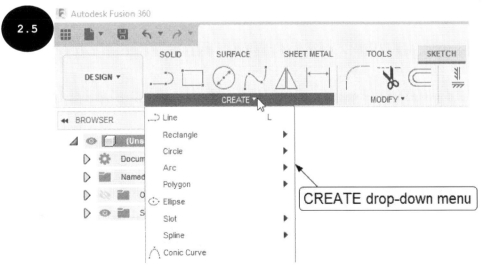

Drawing a Line

A line is defined as the shortest distance between two points. You can draw a line by using the **Line** tool. To do so, click on the **Line** tool in the **CREATE** panel of the **SKETCH** contextual tab, see Figure 2.6 or press the **L** key. Next, click to specify the start point and the endpoint of the line in the drawing area, see Figure 2.7. A line between the specified points is drawn. Also, a rubber band line appears with one of its ends fixed to the last specified point and the other end attached to the cursor. This indicates that a chain of continuous lines can be drawn by clicking the left mouse button in the drawing area. After drawing the line, press the ESC key to exit the **Line** tool or right-click in the drawing area and then click on the **OK** tool in the Marking Menu that appears.

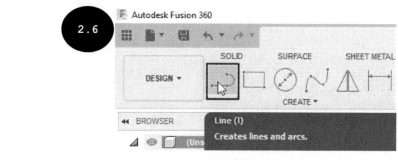

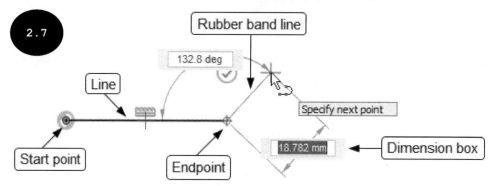

You can also enter the length of the line in the Dimension box that appears in the drawing area and then press ENTER for creating a line of specified length.

When you move the cursor horizontally or vertically after specifying the start point of the line, the symbol of horizontal or vertical constraint appears near the line. The symbol of constraint indicates that if you click the left mouse button to specify the endpoint of the line, the corresponding constraint will be applied. You will learn more about constraints later in this chapter.

Drawing a Tangent Arc by Using Line Tool

In Autodesk Fusion 360, you can also draw a tangent arc by using the **Line** tool. To do so, invoke the **Line** tool and then draw a line by specifying two points in the drawing area. Next, move the cursor over the last specified point of the line, see Figure 2.8 and then drag the cursor toward the other side of the line. The arc mode gets activated and a preview of a tangent arc appears in the drawing area, see Figure 2.9.

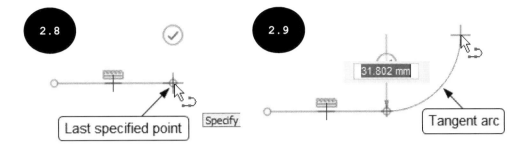

 *To draw a tangent arc by using the **Line** tool, at least one line or arc entity has to be available in the drawing area. Also, the tangency of the arc depends upon how you drag the cursor from the last specified point in the drawing area.*

Drawing a Rectangle

You can draw a rectangle by using the **2-Point Rectangle**, **3-Point Rectangle**, and **Center Rectangle** tools. You can access these tools in the **CREATE** drop-down menu of the **SKETCH** contextual tab in the **Toolbar**, see Figure 2.10. The tools for creating a rectangle are discussed next.

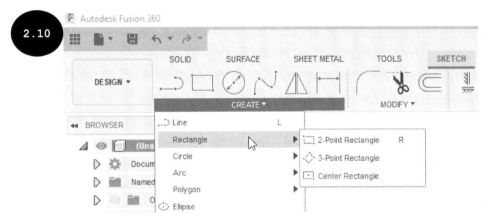

2-Point Rectangle Tool

The **2-Point Rectangle** tool is used for drawing a rectangle by specifying two points (diagonally opposite corners of the rectangle) in the drawing area, see Figure 2.11.

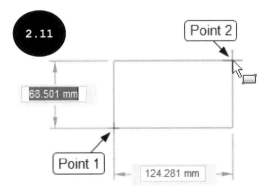

3-Point Rectangle Tool

The 3-Point Rectangle tool is used for drawing a rectangle by specifying 3 points in the drawing area, see Figure 2.12.

Center Rectangle Tool

The Center Rectangle tool is used for drawing a rectangle by specifying its center point and a corner point, see Figure 2.13.

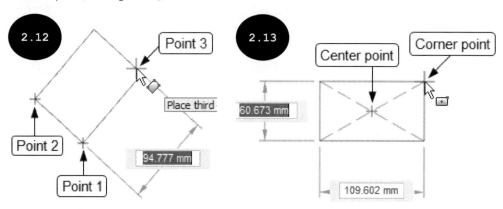

Drawing a Circle

You can draw a circle by using the Center Diameter Circle, 2-Point Circle, 3-Point Circle, 2-Tangent Circle, and 3-Tangent Circle tools. You can access these tools in the CREATE drop-down menu of the Toolbar, see Figure 2.14. The tools for drawing a circle are discussed next.

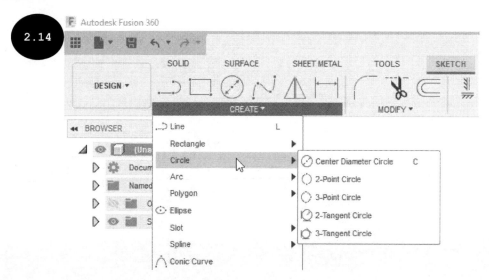

Center Diameter Circle Tool

The Center Diameter Circle tool is used for drawing a circle by specifying the center point and a point on the circumference of the circle, see Figure 2.15.

2-Point Circle Tool

The 2-Point Circle tool is used for drawing a circle by specifying two points on the circumference of the circle, see Figure 2.16.

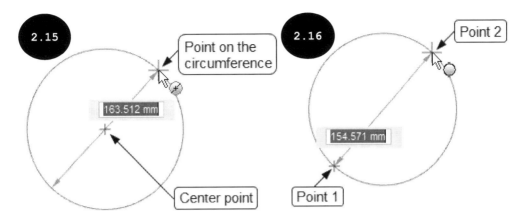

3-Point Circle Tool

The 3-Point Circle tool is used for drawing a circle by specifying three points on the circumference of the circle, see Figure 2.17.

2-Tangent Circle Tool

The 2-Tangent Circle tool is used for drawing a circle, tangent to two line entities, see Figure 2.18. To do so, you need to define two line entities and the radius of the circle.

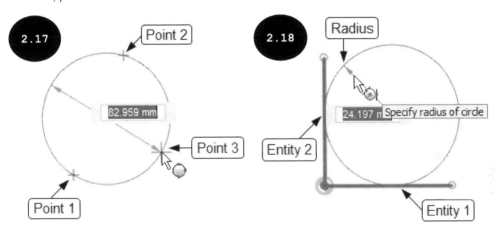

3-Tangent Circle Tool

The 3-Tangent Circle tool is used for drawing a circle that is tangent to three line entities, see Figure 2.19.

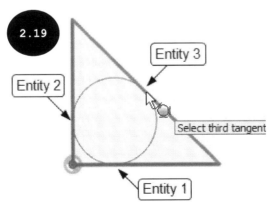

Drawing an Arc

You can draw an arc by using the 3-Point Arc, Center Point Arc, and Tangent Arc tools. You can access these tools in the CREATE drop-down menu of the SKETCH contextual tab, see Figure 2.20. The tools for drawing an arc are discussed next.

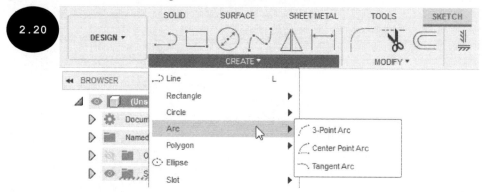

3-Point Arc Tool

The 3-Point Arc tool is used for drawing an arc by defining three points on its arc length, see Figure 2.21.

Center Point Arc Tool

The Center Point Arc tool is used for drawing an arc by defining its center point, start point, and endpoint, see Figure 2.22.

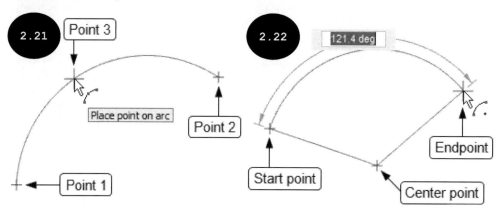

Tangent Arc Tool

The Tangent Arc tool is used for drawing an arc tangent to an existing entity by specifying its start point and the endpoint, see Figure 2.23. You can draw an arc tangent to a line, an arc, or a spline entity.

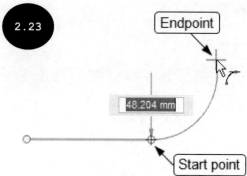

Drawing a Polygon

A polygon is a closed multi-sided geometry having equal sides as well as equal angles between all sides. Figure 2.24 shows a polygon having six sides. You can draw a polygon by using the **Circumscribed Polygon**, **Inscribed Polygon**, and **Edge Polygon** tools. You can access these tools in the **CREATE** drop-down menu of the **SKETCH** contextual tab, see Figure 2.25. The tools for drawing a polygon are discussed next.

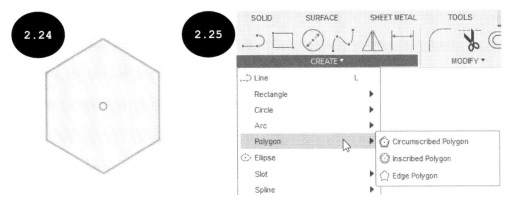

Circumscribed Polygon Tool

The **Circumscribed Polygon** tool is used for drawing a circumscribed polygon which is created outside an imaginary circle such that the midpoints of the polygon sides touch the imaginary circle, see Figure 2.26. You can draw a circumscribed polygon by specifying the center point, number of polygon sides, and the midpoint of a polygon side or the radius of the imaginary circle, refer to Figure 2.26.

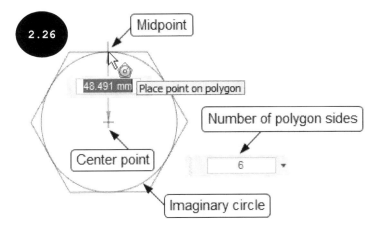

Inscribed Polygon Tool

The **Inscribed Polygon** tool is used for drawing an inscribed polygon which is created inside an imaginary circle such that its vertices touch the imaginary circle, see Figure 2.27. You can draw an inscribed polygon by specifying the center point, number of polygon sides, and a vertex of the polygon or the radius of the imaginary circle, refer to Figure 2.27.

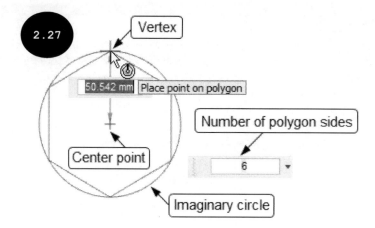

Edge Polygon Tool

The **Edge Polygon** tool is used for drawing a polygon by specifying the start point and the endpoint of an edge of the polygon as well as the number of polygon sides, see Figure 2.28. Note that after specifying the start point, endpoint, and number of polygon sides, you also need to specify the side of the polygon by clicking the left mouse button on either side of the polygon edge.

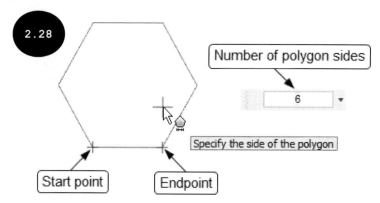

Drawing an Ellipse

An ellipse is drawn by defining a center point, first axis point (major axis), and a point on the ellipse, see Figure 2.29. You can draw an ellipse by using the **Ellipse** tool of the **CREATE** drop-down menu.

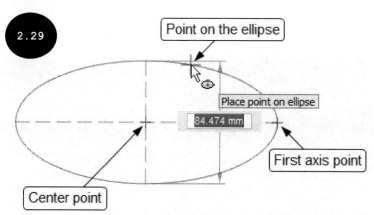

Drawing a Slot

You can draw straight and arc slots by using the slot tools: **Center to Center Slot**, **Overall Slot**, **Center Point Slot**, **Three Point Arc Slot**, and **Center Point Arc Slot**. You can access these tools in the **CREATE** drop-down menu of the **SKETCH** contextual tab, see Figure 2.30. The tools for drawing slots are discussed next.

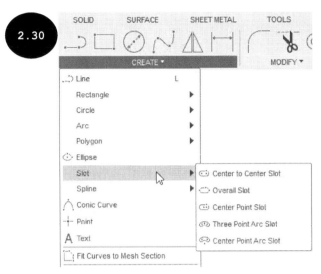

Center to Center Slot Tool

The **Center to Center Slot** tool is used for drawing a straight slot by defining the center points of both the slot arcs (Point 1 and Point 2) and a point (Point 3) to define the width of the slot, see Figure 2.31.

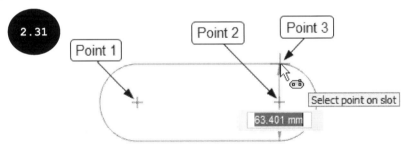

Overall Slot Tool

The **Overall Slot** tool is used for drawing a straight slot by defining the start and end of the overall slot length (Point 1 and Point 2) and a point (Point 3) to define the width of the slot, see Figure 2.32.

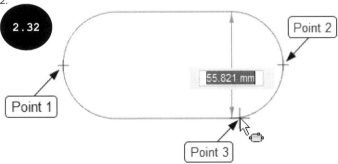

Center Point Slot Tool

The **Center Point Slot** tool is used for drawing a straight slot by defining the slot center point (Point 1), center point of a slot arc (Point 2), and a point (Point 3) to define the width of the slot, see Figure 2.33.

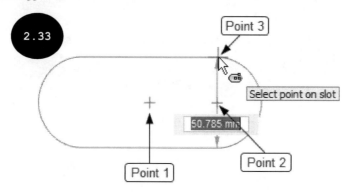

Three Point Arc Slot Tool

The **Three Point Arc Slot** tool is used for drawing an arc slot by defining three points on the slot center arc and a point to define the width of the slot, see Figure 2.34.

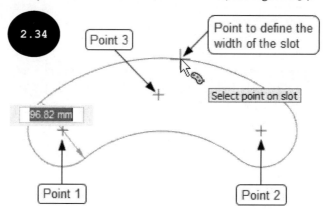

Center Point Arc Slot Tool

The **Center Point Arc Slot** tool is used for drawing an arc slot by defining the center point of the slot (Point 1), center point of the first slot arc (Point 2), center point of the second slot arc (Point 3), and a point to define the width of the slot (Point 4), see Figure 2.35.

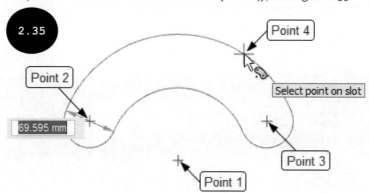

Drawing a Conic Curve

You can draw a conic curve by specifying its start point, endpoint, top vertex, and the Rho value by using the **Conic Curve** tool available in the **CREATE** drop-down menu of the **SKETCH** contextual tab, see Figure 2.36.

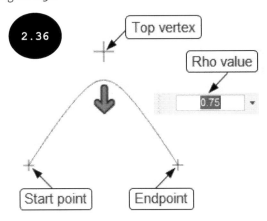

 The Rho value of the conic curve defines the type of curve. If the Rho value is less than 0.5 then the conic curve will be an ellipse. If the Rho value is equal to 0.5 then the conic curve will be a parabola. If the Rho value is greater than 0.5 then the conic curve will be a hyperbola.

Drawing a Spline

A Spline is defined as a curve having a high degree of smoothness and is used for creating free form features. You can draw a spline by specifying two or more than two points in the drawing area. You can draw a spline by using the **Fit Point Spline** and the **Control Point Spline** tools. You can access these tools in the **CREATE** drop-down menu of the **SKETCH** contextual tab, see Figure 2.37. The tools for creating a spline area discussed next.

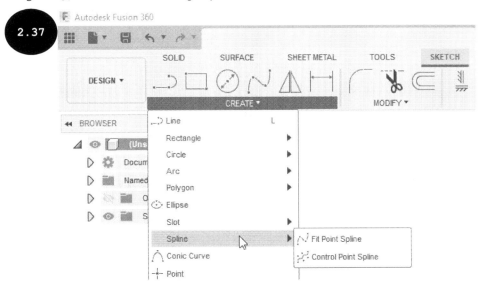

Fit Point Spline Tool

The **Fit Point Spline** tool is used for drawing a spline by defining two or more than two fit points in the drawing area, see Figure 2.38. Note that the spline is created such that it passes through the specified fit points. Figure 2.38 shows the preview of a spline with five fit points specified in the drawing area. After specifying all the fit points, click on the tick-mark that appears in the drawing area, see Figure 2.38. The spline is drawn and all its tangent handles appear in the drawing area, see Figure 2.39. Also, the **Fit Point Spline** tool is still active. To exit the **Fit Point Spline** tool, right-click in the drawing area and then click on the **OK** tool in the Marking Menu that appears. You can edit the spline by using its tangent handles, if needed. Next, click anywhere in the drawing area to exit the editing mode of the spline.

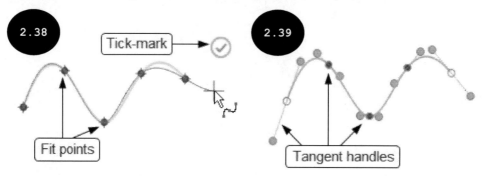

Control Point Spline Tool

The **Control Point Spline** tool is used for creating a spline by defining two or more than two control points in the drawing area. Note that the spline is created such that it passes near the control points specified in the drawing area, see Figure 2.40. In this figure, four control points have been specified in the drawing area to create a spline by using the **Control Point Spline** tool. After specifying all the control points, click on the tick-mark that appears in the drawing area. The spline is drawn and the **Control Point Spline** tool is still active. To exit the **Control Point Spline** tool, right-click in the drawing area and then click on the **OK** tool in the Marking Menu that appears.

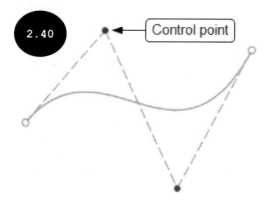

Editing a Spline

Editing a spline is important in order to achieve the complex shape and maintain a high degree of smoothness and curvature. You can edit a spline by dragging its fit points, tangent handles, or control points.

 *When you click on a fit point of a spline, its tangent handle appears in the drawing area. Also, the **Curvature display** and **Tangent display** buttons appear in the SKETCH PALETTE dialog box, see Figure 2.41. You can choose the **Curvature display** or **Tangent display** button to display the respective (curvature or tangent) handle in the drawing area.*

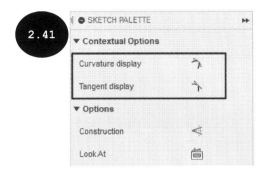

Adding Text into a Sketch

You can add text into an active sketch by using the **Text** tool of the **CREATE** drop-down menu. To do so, invoke the **CREATE** drop-down menu in the **SKETCH** contextual tab and then click on the **Text** tool. Next, click anywhere in the drawing area to specify the insertion point of the text. The **TEXT** dialog box appears, see Figure 2.42. Also, the Insertion and Rotation handles appear in the drawing area, see Figure 2.43.

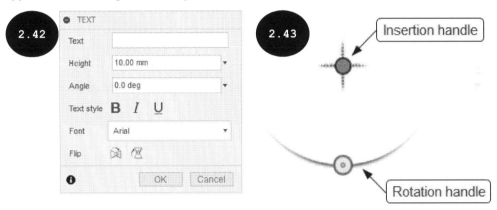

Enter the text in the **Text** field of the dialog box. A preview of the text appears in the drawing area. You can specify the height, angle, style, and font of the text in the respective fields of the dialog box. You can also flip the text, horizontally and vertically by using the **Horizontal Flip** and **Vertical Flip** buttons in the dialog box, respectively. You can drag the Insertion handle that appears in the drawing area to change the position of the text. You can also drag the Rotation handle that appears in the drawing area to rotate the text in the drawing area. After specifying all the parameters, click on the **OK** button in the dialog box. The text gets added in the drawing area.

Editing and Modifying Sketches

Editing and modifying a sketch is very important to give it a desired shape. In Autodesk Fusion 360, various editing operations such as trim, extend, mirror, and offset can be performed on a sketch. Some of the editing operations are discussed next.

Trimming Sketch Entities

You can trim the unwanted sketch entities to their nearest intersection by using the **Trim** tool. To do so, click on the **Trim** tool in the **MODIFY** panel of the **SKETCH** contextual tab, see Figure 2.44. You can also press the **T** key to activate the **Trim** tool. After activating the **Trim** tool, click on the sketch entity to be trimmed, see Figure 2.45. A portion of the entity gets trimmed up to its nearest intersection in the drawing area, see Figure 2.46.

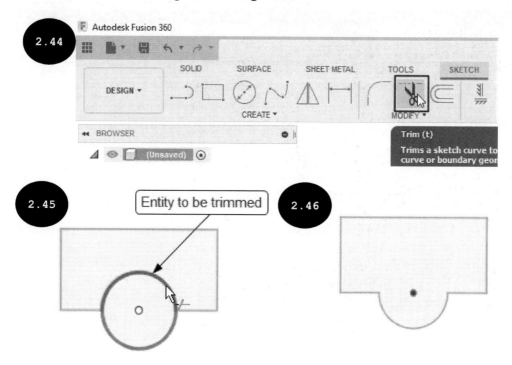

You can continue trimming sketch entities one by one up to their next intersection by clicking the left mouse button. After trimming undesired entities of the sketch, right-click in the drawing area and then click on the **OK** tool in the Marking Menu to exit the **Trim** tool or press the ESC key.

 *You can also trim sketch entities by dragging the cursor over the entities to be trimmed after activating the **Trim** tool.*

Extending Sketch Entities

You can extend sketch entities up to their nearest intersection by using the **Extend** tool. To do so, invoke the **MODIFY** drop-down list in the **SKETCH** contextual tab and then click on the **Extend** tool, see Figure 2.47. Next, move the cursor over the entity to be extended, see Figure 2.48 and then click on it when the preview of the extended line appears up to its next intersection, see Figure 2.49. The entity gets extended and the **Extend** tool remains activated. You can continue extending sketch entities up to their next intersection by clicking the left mouse button. After extending the entities, press the ESC key to exit the tool.

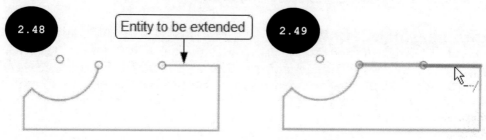

Mirroring Sketch Entities

You can mirror sketch entities about a mirroring line by using the **Mirror** tool. To do so, click on the **Mirror** tool in the **CREATE** panel of the **SKETCH** contextual tab, see Figure 2.50. The **MIRROR** dialog box appears, see Figure 2.51.

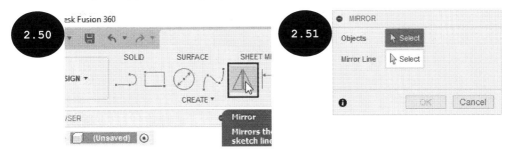

After invoking the **MIRROR** dialog box, select the entities to be mirrored in the drawing area individually, by clicking the left mouse button or by drawing a window around the entities to be mirrored, see Figure 2.52. After selecting the entities to be mirrored, click on the **Mirror Line** selection option in the dialog box and then select a mirroring line in the drawing area, see Figure 2.53. Next, click on the **OK** button in the dialog box. The selected entities get mirrored about the mirroring line, see Figure 2.54.

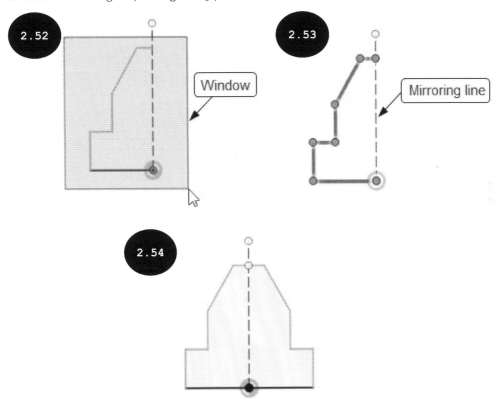

Offsetting Sketch Entities

You can offset the entities of a sketch or the edges of a feature at a specified offset distance by using the **Offset** tool. To do so, click on the **Offset** tool in the MODIFY panel of the SKETCH contextual tab, see Figure 2.55 or press the O key. The OFFSET dialog box appears, see Figure 2.56.

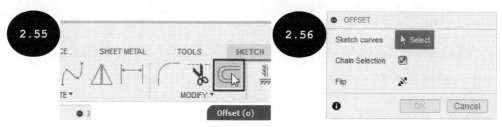

By default, the **Chain Selection** check box is selected in the dialog box. As a result, on selecting an entity of a sketch to offset, all the contiguous entities (closed or open loop) of the selected entity get automatically selected in the drawing area. To offset an individual selected entity, you need to clear this check box in the **OFFSET** dialog box.

After invoking the **OFFSET** dialog box, select an entity of the sketch to offset in the drawing area, see Figure 2.57. Next, enter the required offset distance value in the **Offset position** field that appears in the dialog box. You can also drag the spinner arrows that appear in the drawing area to set the offset distance. Next, click on the **OK** button in the dialog box or press ENTER. The offset entities get created, see Figure 2.58. In this figure, the offset entities are created by selecting the **Chain Selection** check box in the dialog box.

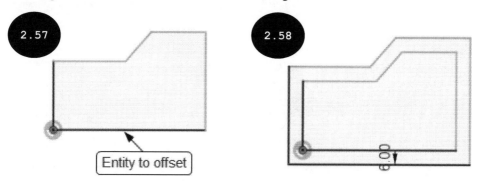

Entity to offset

To reverse the direction of offset entities, click on the **Flip** button in the **OFFSET** dialog box or drag the spinner arrows that appear in the drawing area on the other side of the selected entity. You can also enter a negative value in the **Offset position** field to reverse the offset direction.

Applying Constraints

Constraints are used for restricting some of the degrees of freedom of a sketch. You can apply constraints on a sketch entity, between sketch entities, and between sketch entities and planes, axes, edges, or vertices. Some of the constraints such as horizontal, vertical, and coincident are applied automatically while drawing sketch entities. You can apply constraints by using the constraints tools available in the **CONSTRAINTS** panel of the **SKETCH** contextual tab in the **Toolbar**, see Figure 2.59.

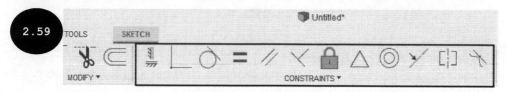

To apply a constraint, click on its tool in the **CONSTRAINTS** panel of the **SKETCH** contextual tab and then select the entities in the drawing area. For example, to apply a concentric constraint between a circle and an arc, click on the **Concentric** tool in the CONSTRAINTS panel. Next, click on the circle and then the arc in the drawing area one by one, see Figure 2.60. The concentric constraint gets applied and the selected entities become concentric to each other such that they share the same center point, see Figure 2.61. Some of the constraints are discussed next.

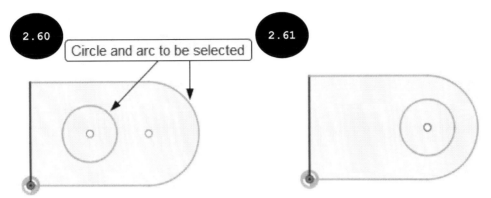

In Figures 2.60 and 2.61, the display of applied constraints is turned off. You can turn on or off the display of applied constraints in the drawing area by selecting or clearing the Show Constraints check box in the SKETCH PALETTE dialog box.

Horizontal Constraint

Horizontal constraint is used for changing the orientation of an entity to horizontal and then forcing it to remain so. This constraint can be applied to a line, a construction line, or between two points or vertices by using the **Horizontal/Vertical** tool of the CONSTRAINTS panel.

Vertical Constraint

Vertical constraint is used for changing the orientation of an entity to vertical and then forcing it to remain so. This constraint can be applied to a line, a construction line, or between two points or vertices by using the **Horizontal/Vertical** tool of the CONSTRAINTS panel.

Coincident Constraint

Coincident constraint is used for coinciding two points/vertices and then forcing them to remain coincident with each other. You can apply this constraint between two points or a point and a line/arc/circle/ellipse by using the **Coincident** tool of the CONSTRAINTS panel. Besides, you can also apply a coincident constraint between a sketch point and the origin.

Collinear Constraint

Collinear constraint is used for making two lines collinear to each other and then forcing them to remain collinear to each other. You can apply this constraint by using the **Collinear** tool of the CONSTRAINTS panel.

Perpendicular Constraint

Perpendicular constraint is used for making two line entities perpendicular to each other and then forcing them to remain perpendicular to each other. You can apply this constraint by using the **Perpendicular** tool of the CONSTRAINTS panel.

Parallel Constraint

Parallel constraint is used for making two lines parallel to each other and then forcing them to remain parallel to each other. You can apply this constraint by using the **Parallel** tool ⊘ of the CONSTRAINTS panel.

Tangent Constraint

Tangent constraint is used for making two sketch entities such as a circle and a line tangent to each other. You can also make two circles, two arcs, two ellipses, or a combination of these entities tangent to each other by using the **Tangent** tool ⊘ of the CONSTRAINTS panel. Besides, you can also make a sketch entity (line, circle, arc, or ellipse) tangent to a linear or a circular edge.

Concentric Constraint

Concentric constraint is used for making two arcs, two circles, two ellipses or a combination of these entities concentric to each other. In concentric constraint, the selected entities share the same center point. You can apply this constraint by using the **Concentric** tool ⊚ of the CONSTRAINTS panel.

Equal Constraint

Equal constraint is used for making two entities (arcs, circles, or lines) equal to each other. In equal constraint, the length of line entities and the radii of arc entities become equal. You can apply this constraint by using the **Equal** tool ═ of the CONSTRAINTS panel.

Midpoint Constraint

Midpoint constraint is used for making a point coincident to the midpoint of a line entity. You can apply a midpoint constraint between a sketch point and a line or a sketch point and a linear edge by using the **Midpoint** tool △ of the CONSTRAINTS panel.

Symmetry Constraint

Symmetry constraint is used for making two points, two lines, two arcs, two circles, or two ellipses symmetric about a line entity. You can apply this constraint by using the **Symmetry** tool ⊞ of the CONSTRAINTS panel.

Curvature Constraint

Curvature constraint is used for maintaining a smooth curvature continuity at the transition point of two sketch entities (two splines or a spline and a line). You can apply this constraint by using the **Curvature** tool ◥ of the CONSTRAINTS panel.

Fix Constraint

Fix constraint is used for fixing the current position and the size of a sketch entity. However, in case of a fixed line or arc entity, the endpoints are free to move without changing the position of the entity. You can apply this constraint by using the **Fix/Unfix** tool ⬜ of the CONSTRAINTS panel.

Applying Dimensions

Once a sketch has been drawn and the required geometric constraints have been applied, you need to apply the required dimensions to the sketch. As Autodesk Fusion 360 is a parametric software, the parameters of sketch entities such as length and angle are controlled or driven by dimension values. On modifying a dimension value, the respective sketch entity also gets modified accordingly. You can apply various types of dimensions such as horizontal dimension, vertical dimension, aligned dimension, angular dimension, diameter dimension, radius dimension, and linear diameter dimension by using the **Sketch Dimension** tool. You can access this tool in the **CREATE** panel of the **SKETCH** contextual tab, see Figure 2.62. Alternatively, press the **D** key.

 *The dimension applied by using the **Sketch Dimension** tool depends upon the type of entity selected. For example, if you select a circle, the diameter dimension is applied and if you select a line, the linear dimension is applied.*

Working with Different States of a Sketch

A sketch can be either Under-defined or Fully defined. Both these states of a sketch are discussed next.

Under-Defined Sketch

An under-defined sketch is a sketch, whose all degrees of freedom are not fixed. This means that the entities of the sketch can change their shape, size, and position on being dragged. Figure 2.63 shows a rectangular sketch in which the length of the rectangle is defined as 50 mm. However, the width and the position of the rectangle with respect to the origin are not defined. This means that the width and position of the rectangle can be changed by dragging the respective entities of the rectangle. Note that the entities of an under-defined sketch appear in light blue color in the drawing area.

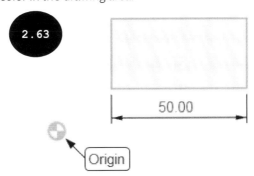

Fully Defined Sketch

A fully defined sketch is a sketch, whose all degrees of freedom are fixed. This means that the entities of the sketch cannot change their shape, size, and position on being dragged. Figure 2.64 shows a rectangular sketch in which the length, width, and position of the sketch are defined. Note that the entities of a fully defined sketch appear in black color. Also, a small lock icon appears on the sketch in the expanded **Sketches** folder in the **BROWSER**, see Figure 2.65.

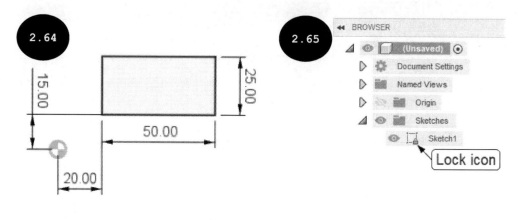

Tutorial 1: Creating a Sketch

Create the sketch shown in Figure 2.66 and make it fully defined by applying all the required dimensions and constraints. The model shown in this figure is for your reference only. You will learn about creating 3D models in later chapters. All dimensions are in mm.

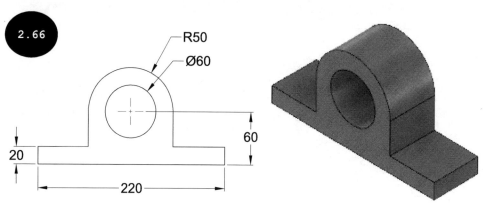

The following sequence summarizes the tutorial outline:

- Invoking Autodesk Fusion 360
- Starting a New Design File
- Organizing the Data Panel
- Specifying Units
- Invoking the Sketching Environment
- Specifying Grid and Snap Settings
- Creating a Sketch
- Applying Dimensions
- Applying Constraints
- Saving the Sketch

Invoking Autodesk Fusion 360

1. Start Fusion 360 by double-clicking on the **Autodesk Fusion 360** icon on your desktop. The startup user interface of Fusion 360 appears, see Figure 2.67.

Every time you start Autodesk Fusion 360, a new design file with default name "Untitled" is invoked, automatically, see Figure 2.67. You can start creating your design in this default design file. However, in this Tutorial, you will start a new design file for creating the sketch of this tutorial.

2.67 — New Design File (Untitled)

Starting a New Design File

1. Invoke the **File** drop-down menu in the **Application Bar** and then click on the **New Design** tool, see Figure 2.68. The new design file gets started with the default name and a new tab "**Untitled(1)**" is added next to the tab of the existing design file, see Figure 2.69. Alternatively, press the CTRL + N key or click on the + sign, next to the name of the existing design file to start a new design file.

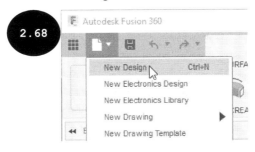

2.68

2.69 — DESIGN Workspace — New Design File "Untitled(1)"

The newly started design file is activated by default. You can switch between the design files by clicking on the respective tabs.

2. Make sure that the **DESIGN** workspace is selected in the **Workspace** drop-down menu of the **Toolbar** as the active workspace for the design file, refer to Figure 2.69.

*The tools available in the **Toolbar** of a design file depend upon the activated workspace. By default, the DESIGN workspace is activated. As a result, the tools used for designing 3D mechanical solid, surface, and sheet metal models are available in the respective tabs of the Toolbar.*

Organizing the Data Panel

In Autodesk Fusion 360, the first and foremost step is to organize the data panel by creating the project folder and sub-folders to save the design.

1.   Click on the **Show Data Panel** tool in the **Application Bar**, see Figure 2.70. The **Data Panel** appears, see Figure 2.71.

2.   Click on the **New Project** button at the top right corner of the **Data Panel**, refer to Figure 2.71. The new project is added in the **Data Panel** and its default name **New Project** appears in an edit field. You can edit or change the default name of the newly added project.

3.   Enter **Autodesk Fusion 360 Tutorials** in the edit field as the name of the newly added project and then click anywhere in the drawing area. The new project with the name **Autodesk Fusion 360 Tutorials** is created in the **Data Panel**, see Figure 2.72.

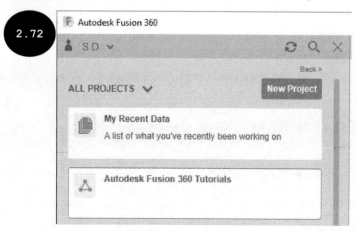

Now, you need to create sub-folders inside the **Autodesk Fusion 360 Tutorials** project.

4. Double-click on the **Autodesk Fusion 360 Tutorials** project in the **Data Panel**. The project is opened and appears in the **Data Panel**, see Figure 2.73.

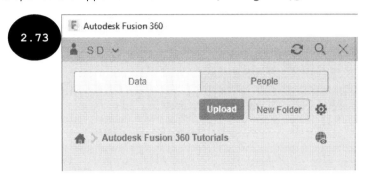

5. Click on the **New Folder** button in the **Autodesk Fusion 360 Tutorials** project of the **Data Panel** to create a folder inside it. The new folder is added inside the project and its default name **New Folder** appears in an edit field.

6. Enter **Chapter 02** in the edit field as the name of the folder and then click anywhere in the drawing area. The new folder with the name **Chapter 02** is created inside the **Autodesk Fusion 360 Tutorials** project in the **Data Panel**, see Figure 2.74.

7. Double-click on the **Chapter 02** folder in the **Data Panel** to open it for saving the design file.

In Data Panel, you can create multiple folders and sub-folders inside a project for saving files.

After organizing the **Data Panel**, you need to close it.

8. Click on the **Hide Data Panel** tool in the **Application Bar** to close the **Data Panel**, see Figure 2.75. Alternatively, click on the cross-mark [×] at its top right corner.

Specifying Units

Now, you need to specify millimeter as the unit for creating this tutorial.

1. In the **BROWSER**, expand the **Document Settings** node by clicking on the arrow in front of it, see Figure 2.76.

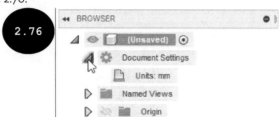

2. Move the cursor over the **Units** option in the expanded **Document Settings** node. The **Change Active Units** tool appears, see Figure 2.77.

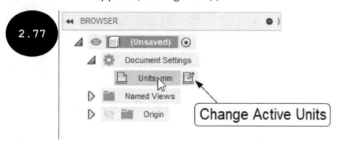

3. Click on the **Change Active Units** tool. The **CHANGE ACTIVE UNITS** dialog box appears on the right side of the graphics area, see Figure 2.78.

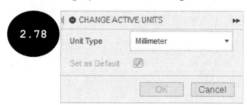

4. Make sure that the **Millimeter** unit is selected in the **Unit Type** drop-down list of this dialog box. Next, click on the **OK** button.

    Set as Default: You can define the unit selected in the **Unit Type** drop-down list of the dialog box as the default unit for all new documents by selecting the **Set as Default** check box in the **CHANGE ACTIVE UNITS** dialog box. If this check box is cleared then the selected unit gets defined only for the currently active document. Note that this check box is not enabled, if the selected unit is the default unit of Autodesk Fusion 360.

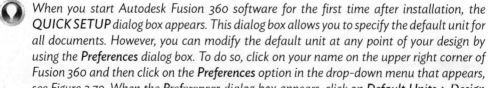   *When you start Autodesk Fusion 360 software for the first time after installation, the QUICK SETUP dialog box appears. This dialog box allows you to specify the default unit for all documents. However, you can modify the default unit at any point of your design by using the Preferences dialog box. To do so, click on your name on the upper right corner of Fusion 360 and then click on the Preferences option in the drop-down menu that appears, see Figure 2.79. When the Preferences dialog box appears, click on Default Units > Design on the left panel of the dialog box. Next, select the required unit in the Default units for new design drop-down list of the dialog box as the default unit for all new documents. After defining the default unit, click on the Apply button and then the OK button to accept the change and close the dialog box.*

2.79

Invoking the Sketching Environment

Now, you need to invoke the Sketching environment for creating the sketch.

1. Click on the **Create Sketch** tool in the **Toolbar**, see Figure 2.80. Three default planes: Front, Top, and Right, which are mutually perpendicular to each other appear in the graphics area, see Figure 2.81.

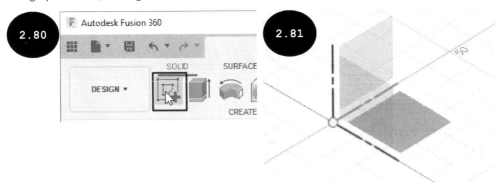

2.80

2.81

2. Move the cursor over the Front plane (XZ) and then click the left mouse button when it gets highlighted in the graphics area. The Front plane becomes the sketching plane for creating the sketch and it is oriented normal to the viewing direction. Also, the **SKETCH** contextual tab and the **SKETCH PALETTE** dialog box appear, see Figure 2.82.

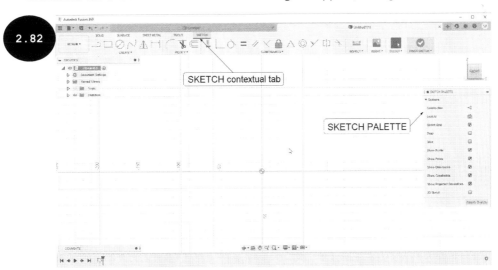

2.82

SKETCH contextual tab

SKETCH PALETTE

Specifying Grid and Snap Settings

Now, you need to specify the grid and snap settings for creating the sketch. Grids help you to specify points in the drawing area while creating sketch entities and act as reference lines.

1. Invoke the **Grid and Snaps** flyout in the **Navigation Bar**, see Figure 2.83.

2. Click on the **Grid Settings** tool in the **Grid and Snaps** flyout. The **GRID SETTINGS** dialog box appears, see Figure 2.84.

Adaptive: By default, the **Adaptive** radio button is selected in the **GRID SETTINGS** dialog box. As a result, the size of the grid adjusts automatically when you zoom in and out of the drawing display area.

Fixed: The **Fixed** radio button is used for specifying the grid size which remains the same and does not change nor does it adjust when you zoom in or out of the drawing display area.

Reference Numbers: The Reference Numbers check box is used for turning on or off the display of the grid's reference numbers in the drawing area.

3. Make sure that the **Adaptive** radio button is selected in the **GRID SETTINGS** dialog box.

4. Click on the **OK** button in the **GRID SETTINGS** dialog box.

5. Make sure that the **Sketch Grid** and **Snap** check boxes are selected in the **SKETCH PALETTE** dialog box to display the grids and to snap the movement of the cursor on the grid lines, see Figure 2.85.

Creating a Sketch

1. Click on the **Center Diameter Circle** tool of the **CREATE** panel in the **SKETCH** contextual tab, see Figure 2.86. The **Center Diameter Circle** tool gets activated. Alternatively, press the C key to activate the **Center Diameter Circle** tool.

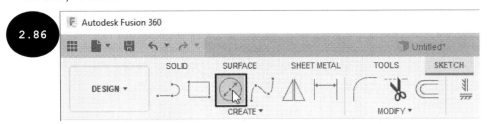

2.86

2. Click to specify the center point of the circle at the origin in the drawing area.

3. Move the cursor horizontally toward right and then click to specify a point when the diameter of the circle appears 60 mm in the Dimension box, see Figure 2.87. A circle of diameter 60 mm is drawn. Note that you may need to zoom in to or out of the drawing view to adjust the grid size so that the cursor snaps to the grid lines when the diameter of the circle measures 60 mm.

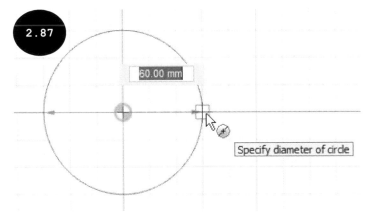

2.87

60.00 mm

Specify diameter of circle

4. Right-click in the drawing area and then click on the **OK** tool in the Marking Menu to exit the **Center Diameter Circle** tool. Alternatively, press the ESC key.

Now, you need to create an arc of the sketch.

5. Invoke the **CREATE** drop-down menu in the **SKETCH** contextual tab of the **Toolbar** and then click on **Arc > Center Point Arc**, see Figure 2.88. The **Center Point Arc** tool gets activated.

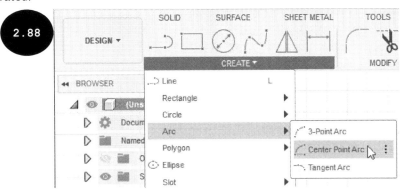

2.88

6. Click to specify the center point of the arc at the origin in the drawing area.

7. Move the cursor horizontally toward right and then click to specify the start point of the arc when the radius of the arc appears as 50 mm in the Dimension box, see Figure 2.89.

8. Move the cursor anti-clockwise in the drawing area and then click to specify the endpoint of the arc when the angle value appears as 180 degrees, see Figure 2.90. The arc is drawn. Next, press the ESC key to exit the tool.

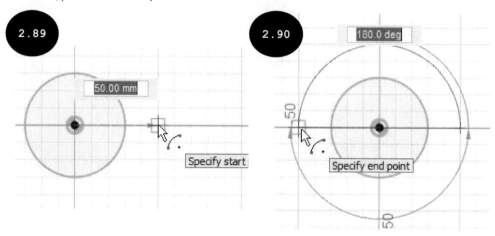

Now, you need to create the line entities of the sketch.

9. Click on the Line tool in the Toolbar, see Figure 2.91. The Line tool gets activated. Alternatively, press the L key to activate the Line tool.

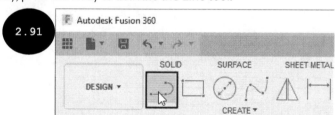

10. Click to specify the start point of the line at the endpoint of the previously drawn arc, see Figure 2.92.

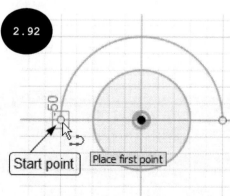

11. Move the cursor vertically downward and click when the length of the line appears 40 mm in the Dimension box, see Figure 2.93. A line of length 40 mm is drawn and the **Line** tool remains active.

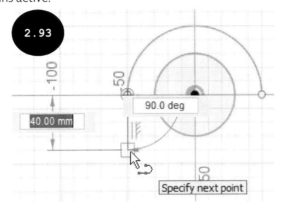

12. Move the cursor horizontally toward left and click when the length of the line appears 60 mm, see Figure 2.94.

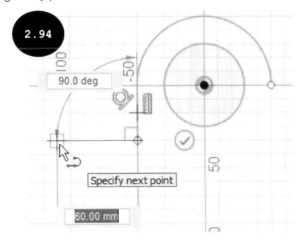

13. Move the cursor vertically downward and click when the length of the line appears 20 mm, see Figure 2.95. A line of length 20 mm is drawn and the **Line** tool remains active.

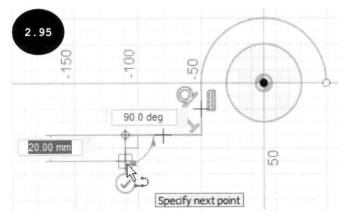

14. Similarly, continue drawing the remaining line entities of the sketch by specifying the points in the drawing area. Figure 2.96 shows the sketch after drawing all sketch entities.

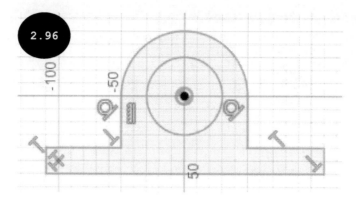

 *In Figure 2.96, the display of automatically applied constraints such as horizontal and vertical is turned on. To turn on or off the display of constraints in the drawing area, select or clear the **Show Constraints** check box in the **SKETCH PALETTE** dialog box, respectively.*

15. Right-click in the drawing area and then click on the **OK** tool in the Marking Menu to exit the **Line** tool.

Applying Dimensions

Once a sketch has been drawn, you need to make it fully defined by applying the required constraints and dimensions.

1. Click on the **Sketch Dimension** tool in the **CREATE** panel of the **SKETCH** contextual tab, see Figure 2.97 or press the **D** key. The **Sketch Dimension** tool gets activated.

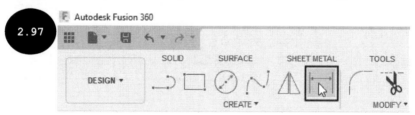

2. Click on the circle of the sketch. The diameter dimension of the selected circle gets attached to the cursor, see Figure 2.98.

3. Click outside the sketch to specify the placement point for the attached dimension. A Dimension box appears with the display of current dimension value, see Figure 2.99.

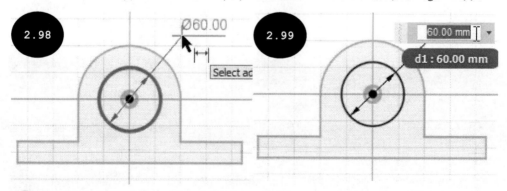

 *In Figures 2.98 and 2.99, the display of constraints is turned off. To do so, clear the **Show Constraints** check box in the **SKETCH PALETTE** dialog box.*

4. Ensure that the value 60 mm is entered in the Dimension box as the diameter of the circle and then press ENTER. The diameter dimension is applied to the circle and the **Sketch Dimension** tool remains active.

5. Click on the center point of the circle and the horizontal line at the bottom as the entities to apply the dimension between them, see Figure 2.100. A linear dimension between the selected entities appears attached to the cursor, see Figure 2.101.

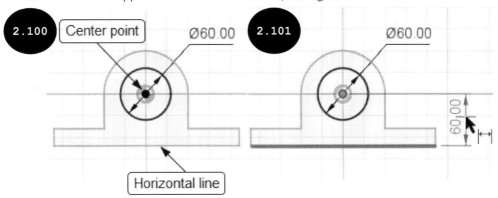

6. Click to specify the placement point for the attached linear dimension. A Dimension box appears with the display of current dimension value.

7. Ensure that the value 60 mm is entered in the Dimension box as the linear dimension between the selected entities of the sketch and then press ENTER. The dimension gets applied, see Figure 2.102. Also, the **Sketch Dimension** tool is remains active.

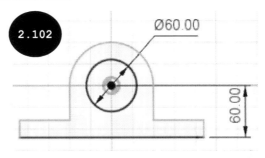

8. Similarly, apply the remaining dimensions of the sketch. Figure 2.103 shows the sketch after applying all the dimensions.

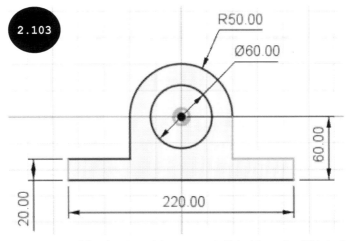

 In Figure 2.103, some of the sketch entities appear in light blue color. This indicates that even after applying dimensions, the sketch is not yet fully defined and you need to apply required constraints to make it fully defined.

Applying Constraints

Now, you need to apply the required constraints.

1. Click on the **Equal** tool in the **CONSTRAINTS** panel in the **SKETCH** contextual tab to apply equal constraints between the entities having equal length, see Figure 2.104.

2. Click on the vertical lines on the extreme left and extreme right of the sketch one by one as the entities for applying the equal constraint, see Figure 2.105. An equal constraint gets applied between the selected line entities. Also, the **Equal** tool remains active.

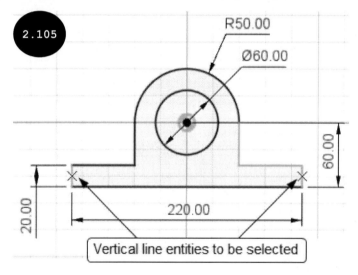

3. Click on the left and right horizontal lines one by one as the entities for applying equal constraint, see Figure 2.106. An equal constraint gets applied between the selected line entities. Also, the **Equal** tool remains active.

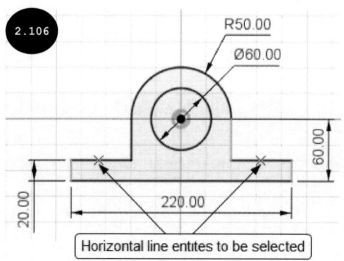

4. Similarly, click on the vertical lines (line 1 and line 2) at the top of the sketch one by one to apply the equal constraint, see Figure 2.107. All entities of the sketch turn black in color and the sketch becomes fully defined, see Figure 2.108.

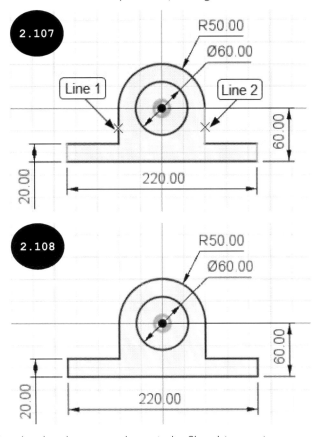

After creating the sketch, you need to exit the Sketching environment.

5. Click on the **FINISH SKETCH** tool in the **SKETCH** contextual tab to confirm the creation of sketch and to exit the Sketching environment, see Figure 2.109.

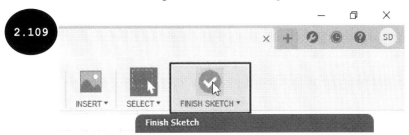

Saving the Sketch

1. Click on the **Save** tool in the **Application Bar** or press CTRL + S. The **Save** dialog box appears.

2. Enter **Tutorial 1** in the **Name** field of the dialog box as the name of the model.

3. Click on the down arrow next to the **Location** field in the dialog box. The expanded **Save** dialog box appears with the **PROJECT** area in its left panel, see Figure 2.110.

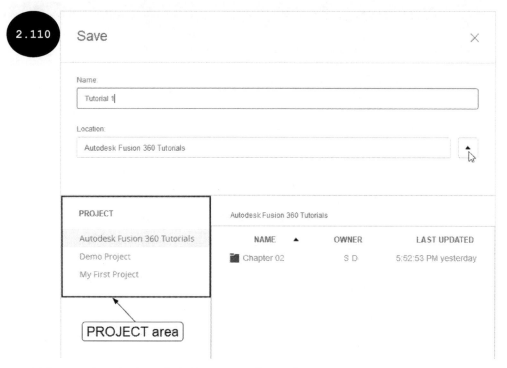

2.110

4. Make sure that the **Autodesk Fusion 360 Tutorials** project is selected in the **PROJECT** area. All the folders created in the selected project appear on the right panel of the dialog box.

5. Specify the location **Autodesk Fusion 360 Tutorials** > **Chapter 02** for saving the sketch. Note that you need to double-click on the folder/sub-folder of the project on the right panel of the dialog box to access the required location for saving the sketch.

6. Click on the **Save** button in the dialog box. The sketch gets saved with the name **Tutorial 1** at the specified location (*Autodesk Fusion 360 Tutorials > Chapter 02*) in the **Data Panel**.

Tutorial 2: Creating and Editing a Sketch

Create the sketch shown in Figure 2.111 and make it fully defined by applying all dimensions and constraints. The model shown in this figure is for your reference only. You will learn how to create 3D models in the later chapters. All dimensions are in mm.

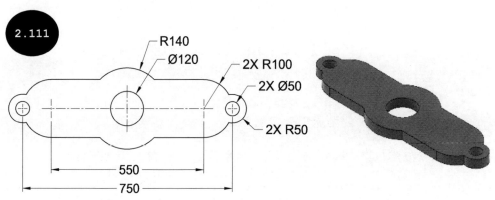

2.111

The following sequence summarizes the tutorial outline:

- Starting a New Design File and Specifying Units
- Specifying Grid Settings
- Creating a Sketch
- Trimming Sketch Entities
- Applying Constraints
- Applying Dimensions
- Saving the Sketch

Starting a New Design File and Specifying Units

1. Start Fusion 360 by double-clicking on the **Autodesk Fusion 360** icon on your desktop, if not started already. The startup user interface of Fusion 360 appears.

2. Invoke the **File** drop-down menu in the **Application Bar** and then click on the **New Design** tool, see Figure 2.112. The new design file is started with the default name and a new tab "**Untitled**" is added next to the tab of the existing design file. Alternatively, press the CTRL + N key or click on the + sign, next to the name of the existing design file to start a new design file.

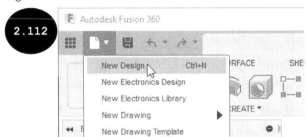

Now, you need to specify the units for the newly added design file.

3. In the **BROWSER**, expand the **Document Settings** node by clicking on the arrow in front of it, see Figure 2.113.

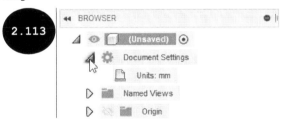

4. Move the cursor over the **Units** option in the expanded **Document Settings** node. The **Change Active Units** tool appears, see Figure 2.114.

5. Click on the **Change Active Units** tool. The **CHANGE ACTIVE UNITS** dialog box appears on the right side of the graphics area, see Figure 2.115.

6. Make sure that the **Millimeter** unit is selected in the **Unit Type** drop-down list of this dialog box. Next, click on the **OK** button.

 If millimeter is defined as the default unit for Autodesk Fusion 360 then you can skip the above steps from 3 to 6. The method for specifying a default unit is discussed in Tutorial 1 of this chapter.

Specifying Grid Settings

1. Invoke the **Grid and Snaps** flyout in the **Navigation Bar**, see Figure 2.116.

2. Click on the **Grid Settings** tool in the **Grid and Snaps** flyout. The **GRID SETTINGS** dialog box appears, see Figure 2.117.

The options in the GRID SETTINGS dialog box are discussed in Tutorial 1 of this chapter.

3. Ensure that the **Adaptive** radio button is selected in the **GRID SETTINGS** dialog box.

4. Click on the **OK** button in the **GRID SETTINGS** dialog box.

Creating a Sketch

1. Click on the **Create Sketch** tool in the **Toolbar**, see Figure 2.118. Three default planes: Front, Top, and Right, which are mutually perpendicular to each other, appear in the graphics area.

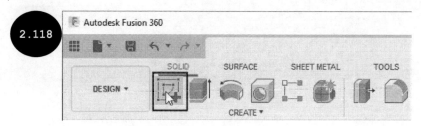

2. Move the cursor over the Top plane (XY) and then click the left mouse button when it gets highlighted in the graphics area. The Top plane becomes the sketching plane for creating the sketch and it is oriented normal to the viewing direction. Also, the SKETCH contextual tab and the SKETCH PALETTE dialog box appear.

3. Make sure that the Sketch Grid and Snap check boxes are selected in the SKETCH PALETTE dialog box to display the grids and to snap the movement of the cursor on the grid lines.

4. Click on the Center Diameter Circle tool of the CREATE panel in the SKETCH contextual tab, see Figure 2.119 or press the C key.

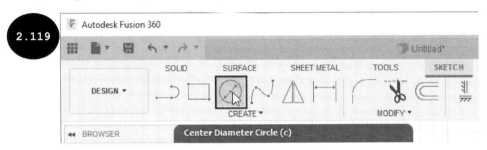

2.119

5. Click to specify the center point of the circle at the origin.

6. Move the cursor horizontally toward right and then click when the diameter of the circle appears as 120 mm in the Dimension box, see Figure 2.120. A circle of diameter 120 mm is drawn and the Center Diameter Circle tool is still active.

2.120

120.00 mm

7. Click to specify the center point of another circle at the origin.

8. Move the cursor horizontally toward right and click when the diameter of the circle appears as 280 mm. The circle is created and the Center Diameter Circle tool remains active.

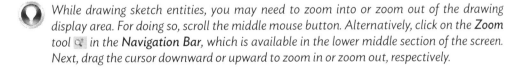 *While drawing sketch entities, you may need to zoom into or zoom out of the drawing display area. For doing so, scroll the middle mouse button. Alternatively, click on the Zoom tool ⌕ in the Navigation Bar, which is available in the lower middle section of the screen. Next, drag the cursor downward or upward to zoom in or zoom out, respectively.*

9. Right-click in the drawing area and then click on the OK tool in the Marking Menu that appears to exit the Center Diameter Circle tool.

10. Invoke the CREATE drop-down menu in the SKETCH contextual tab of the Toolbar and then click on Slot > Center Point Slot, see Figure 2.121. The Center Point Slot tool is activated.

11.   Click to specify the center point of the slot at the origin.

12.   Move the cursor horizontally toward right and click when the half length of the slot appears as 275 mm, see Figure 2.122. Next, move the cursor to a distance in the drawing area. A preview of the slot appears.

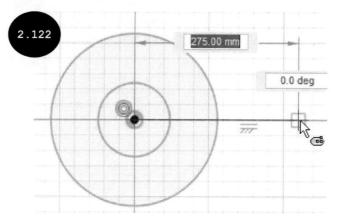

13.   Click on the left mouse button when the width of the slot appears as 200 mm, see Figure 2.123. The slot is created. Next, press the ESC key to exit the **Center Point Slot** tool.

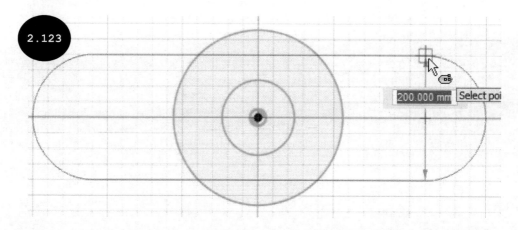

14. Click on the **Center Diameter Circle** tool in the **CREATE** panel of the **SKETCH** contextual tab or press the C key. The **Center Diameter Circle** tool gets activated.

15. Move the cursor toward the midpoint of the right slot arc, see Figure 2.124 and then click to specify the center point of the circle when the cursor snaps to it.

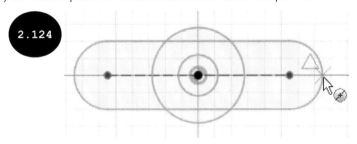

16. Move the cursor horizontally toward right and click when the diameter of the circle appears as 50 mm. A circle of diameter 50 mm is created and the **Center Diameter Circle** tool remains active.

17. Move the cursor to the center point of the previously created circle of diameter 50 mm and then click to specify the center point of another circle when the cursor snaps to it.

18. Move the cursor horizontally toward right and click when the diameter of the circle appears as 100 mm. Another circle of diameter 100 mm is created, see Figure 2.125.

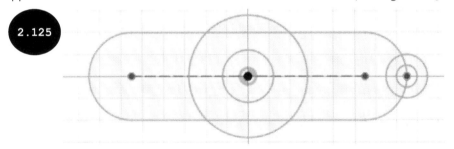

19. Similarly, create two circles of diameters 50 mm and 100 mm on the left slot arc, see Figure 2.126. Next, press the ESC key to exit the **Center Diameter Circle** tool.

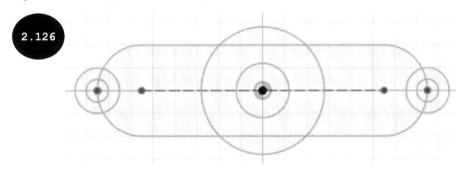

Now, you need to create a vertical construction line.

20. Click on the **Line** tool in the **Toolbar** or press the L key. The **Line** tool gets activated.

21. Click on the **Construction** button in the **SKETCH PALETTE** dialog box for activating the construction mode and creating construction entities, see Figure 2.127.

22. Create a vertical construction line of any length starting from the origin, see Figure 2.128. Next, press the ESC key to exit the **Line** tool. Note that in Figure 2.128, the display of grids is turned off for clarity of the image.

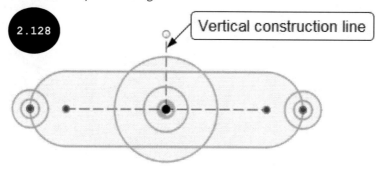

Trimming Sketch Entities

1. Click on the **Trim** tool in the **MODIFY** panel of the **SKETCH** contextual tab or press the T key. The **Trim** tool gets activated.

2. Move the cursor over the portion of the lower horizontal slot entity which lies inside the outer circle, see Figure 2.129. Next, click when it is highlighted. The selected portion of the entity gets trimmed, see Figure 2.130. Also, a warning message appears at the lower right section of the drawing area which informs you that the constraints or dimensions were removed during the trimming operation. Ignore this warning message.

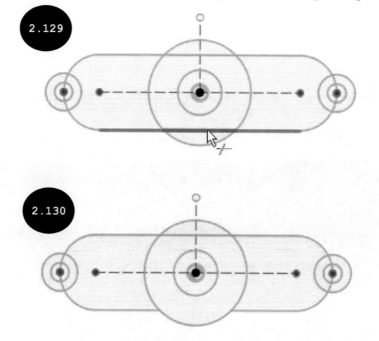

3. Similarly, click on the other unwanted entities of the sketch one by one to trim them. Figure 2.131 shows the sketch after trimming all the unwanted entities.

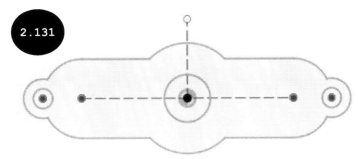

While trimming sketch entities, you may need to zoom in or out of the drawing display area. To do so, scroll the middle mouse button or click on the Zoom tool $\boxed{Q^{\pm}}$ *in the Navigation Bar and then drag the cursor downward or upward to zoom in or zoom out, respectively. Next, to exit the tool, press the ESC key.*

4. Once you have completed trimming operations, press the ESC key to exit the **Trim** tool.

Applying Constraints

1. Click on the **Equal** tool in the CONSTRAINTS panel in the SKETCH contextual tab of the **Toolbar** to apply equal constraints between the entities having equal dimensions.

2. Click on the circles having diameter 50 mm one by one, see Figure 2.132. An equal constraint is applied between the selected circles and the **Equal** tool remains active.

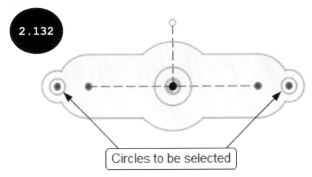

Now, you need to apply equal constraints between arcs having the same radius.

3. Click on the arcs of the sketch having radius 50 mm one by one to apply equal constraint between them, see Figure 2.133. Next, press the ESC key to exit the **Equal** tool.

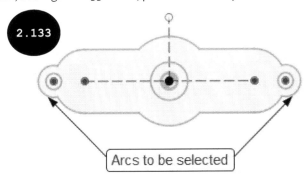

Now, you need to apply symmetric constraint to the sketch entities.

4.   Click on the **Symmetry** tool in the **CONSTRAINTS** panel in the **SKETCH** contextual tab of the **Toolbar** to apply symmetric constraint between the entities.

5.   Select the center points of the two circles of diameter 50 mm one by one and then select the vertical centerline, see Figure 2.134. A symmetric constraint is applied between the selected center points of the circles and the vertical centerline.

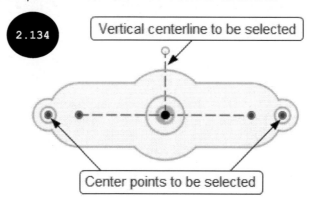

2.134

Vertical centerline to be selected

Center points to be selected

 In Figure 2.134, the display of constraints is turned off. You can turn on or off the display of the constraints in the drawing area by selecting or clearing the Show Constraints check box in the SKETCH PALETTE dialog box, respectively.

Applying Dimensions

Now, you need to apply required dimensions to make the sketch fully defined.

1.   Click on the **Sketch Dimension** tool in the **CREATE** panel of the **SKETCH** contextual tab or press the **D** key to activate the **Sketch Dimension** tool.

2.   Select a circle whose center point is at the origin. The diameter dimension of the selected circle gets attached to the cursor, see Figure 2.135.

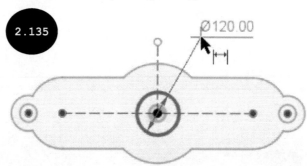

2.135

⌀120.00

3.   Move the cursor to a location where you want to place the dimension in the drawing area and then click to specify the placement point. A Dimension box appears, see Figure 2.136.

4.   Ensure that the value 120 mm is entered in the Dimension box as the diameter of the circle. Next, Press ENTER. The diameter dimension is applied to the circle. Also, the **Sketch Dimension** tool remains active.

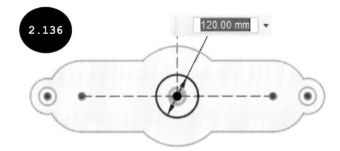

5. Click on the right circle of the sketch. The diameter dimension of the selected circle gets attached to the cursor, see Figure 2.137.

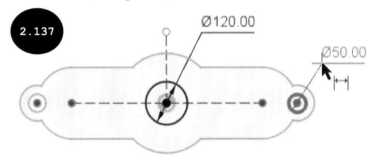

6. Click to specify the placement point in the drawing area. A Dimension box appears.

7. Ensure that the value 50 mm is entered in the Dimension box as the diameter of the circle. Next, press the ENTER key. The diameter dimension is applied to the circle.

8. Similarly, apply the remaining dimensions of the sketch. Figure 2.138 shows the sketch after applying all the required dimensions. Note that the sketch becomes fully defined and all its entities appear in black color.

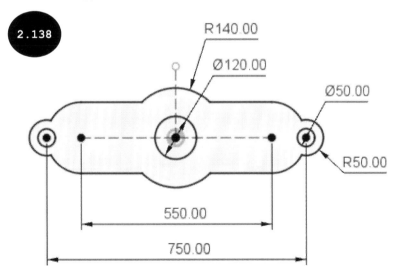

 *In Figure 2.138, the display of constraints is turned off. You can turn on or off the display of the constraints in the drawing area by selecting or clearing the **Show Constraints** check box in the **SKETCH PALETTE** dialog box, respectively.*

Saving the Sketch

1. Click on the **Save** tool in the **Application Bar**. The **Save** dialog box appears.

2. Enter **Tutorial 2** in the **Name** field of the dialog box.

3. Ensure that the location *Autodesk Fusion 360 Tutorials > Chapter 02* is specified in the **Location** field of the dialog box. To specify the location, you need to expand the **Save** dialog box by clicking on the down arrow next to the **Location** field of the dialog box.

 *You need to create these folders in the **Data Panel**, if not created earlier.*

4. Click on the **Save** button in the dialog box. The sketch is saved with the name **Tutorial 2** in the specified location (*Autodesk Fusion 360 Tutorials > Chapter 02*).

Exercise 1

Create a sketch of the model shown in Figure 2.139 and make it fully defined. The model shown in this figure is for your reference only. All dimensions are in mm.

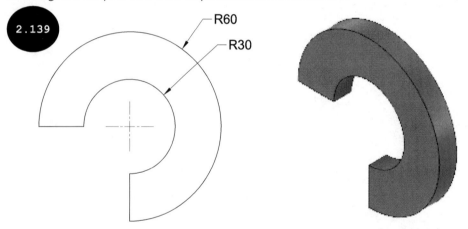

Exercise 2

Create a sketch of the model shown in Figure 2.140 and make it fully defined. The model shown in this figure is for your reference only. All dimensions are in mm.

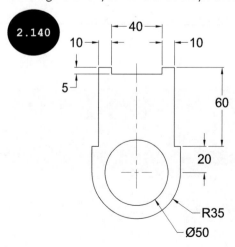
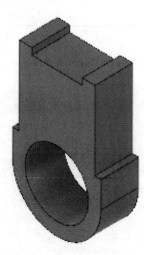

Exercise 3

Create a sketch of the model shown in Figure 2.141 and make it fully defined. The model shown in this figure is for your reference only. All dimensions are in mm.

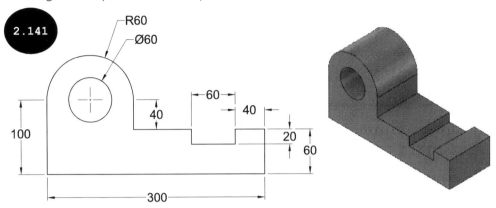

2.141

Exercise 4

Create a sketch of the model shown in Figure 2.142 and make it fully defined. The model shown in this figure is for your reference only. All dimensions are in mm.

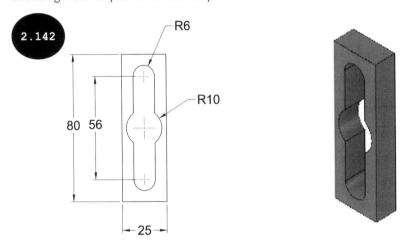

2.142

Exercise 5

Create a sketch of the model shown in Figure 2.143 and make it fully defined. The model shown in this figure is for your reference only. All dimensions are in mm.

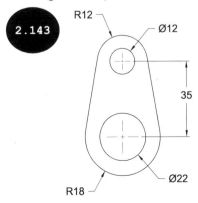

2.143

Summary

This chapter discussed how to invoke the Sketching environment for creating a sketch by selecting a sketching plane. It explained how to specify the unit system as well as the grids and snaps settings. Besides, this chapter introduced methods for drawing lines, rectangles, circles, arcs, polygons, ellipses, conic curves, slots, and splines by using the respective sketching tools. Editing a spline, adding text into a sketch, editing and modifying sketches by performing various editing operations such as trim, extend, mirror, and offset have also been discussed. Moreover, the chapter also discussed application of constraints, application of dimensions and different states of a sketch.

Questions

Answer the following questions:

- Features are divided into two main categories: _____ and _____.

- The _____ feature of any real world component is a sketch based feature.

- You can draw a rectangle by using the _____, _____, and _____ tools.

- The _____ tool is used for drawing a rectangle by specifying its center point and a corner point.

- The _____ tool is used for drawing an arc by defining three points on its arc length.

- The _____ tool is used for drawing an inscribed polygon which is created inside an imaginary circle.

- If the Rho value of a conic curve is less than 0.5 then the conic curve is an _____.

- You can trim the unwanted sketch entities to their nearest intersection by using the _____ tool.

- _____ constraint is used for making two sketch entities tangent to each other.

- You cannot draw a tangent arc by using the **Line** tool. (True/False)

- A fully defined sketch is a sketch, whose all degrees of freedom are fixed. (True/False)

CHAPTER

3

Creating Extrude and Revolve Features

In this chapter, you will learn the following:

- Introduction to an Extrude Feature
- Creating an Extrude Feature
- Introduction to a Revolve Feature
- Creating a Revolve Feature

Once a sketch has been created and fully defined, you can convert it into a 3D solid feature by using the feature modeling tools, see Figure 3.1.

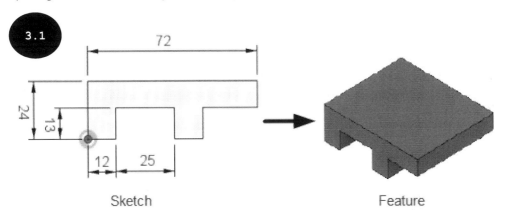

Sketch   Feature

All the feature modeling tools are available in the **CREATE** drop-down menu of the **SOLID** tab in the **Toolbar**, see Figure 3.2. To create a 3D solid model, you need to create all its feature one by one using the feature modeling tools, see Figure 3.3. The first created feature of a model is known as the base feature or the parent feature of the model.

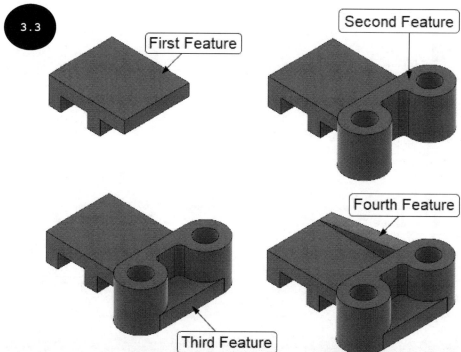

In Autodesk Fusion 360, you can create a base feature by using various feature modeling tools such as **Extrude, Revolve, Sweep**, and **Loft**. In this chapter, you will learn about creating a base feature by using the **Extrude** and **Revolve** tools. You will learn about the remaining tools in later chapters.

Introduction to an Extrude Feature

An extrude feature is created by adding or removing material, normal to the sketching plane. Note that the sketch of the extrude feature defines its geometry. The first or base extrude features are essentially created by adding material. Figure 3.4 shows different base extrude features that are created from the respective sketches. In Autodesk Fusion 360, you can create an extrude feature by using the **Extrude** tool of the **CREATE** panel in the **SOLID** tab of the **Toolbar**.

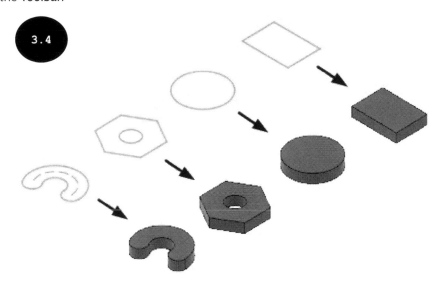

Tutorial 1: Creating an Extrude Feature

Create a sketch of the model shown in Figure 3.5 and then extrude it to a depth of 6 mm symmetrically about the sketching plane. All dimensions are in mm.

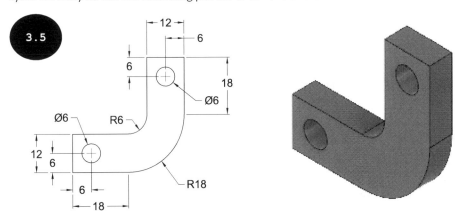

The following sequence summarizes the tutorial outline:

- Invoking Autodesk Fusion 360
- Starting a New Design File
- Specifying Units
- Creating a Sketch of the Extrude Feature
- Creating the Extrude Feature
- Saving the model

Invoking Autodesk Fusion 360

1. Start Fusion 360 by double-clicking on the **Autodesk Fusion 360** icon on your desktop. The startup user interface of Fusion 360 appears.

 Every time you start Autodesk Fusion 360, a new design file with the default name "Untitled" is invoked, automatically. You can start creating your design in this default design file. However, in this Tutorial, you will start a new design file for creating the model.

Starting a New Design File

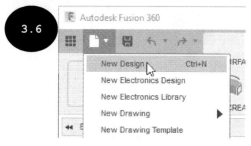

1. Invoke the **File** drop-down menu in the **Application Bar** and then click on the **New Design** tool, see Figure 3.6. The new design file is started with the default name and a new tab "**Untitled(1)**" is added next to the tab of the existing design file. Alternatively, press the CTRL + N key or click on the + sign, next to the name of the existing design file to start a new design file.

 The newly started design file is activated by default. You can switch between the design files by clicking on the respective tabs.

Specifying Units

Now, you need to specify millimeters as the unit for creating this tutorial.

1. In the **BROWSER**, expand the **Document Settings** node by clicking on the arrow in front of it, see Figure 3.7.

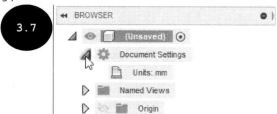

2. Move the cursor over the **Units** option in the expanded **Document Settings** node. The **Change Active Units** tool appears, see Figure 3.8.

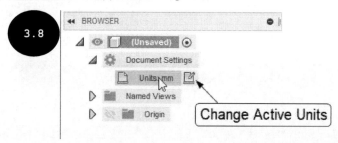

3. Click on the **Change Active Units** tool. The **CHANGE ACTIVE UNITS** dialog box appears on the right side of the graphics area, see Figure 3.9.

3.9

4. Ensure that the **Millimeter** unit is selected in the **Unit Type** drop-down list of this dialog box. Next, click on the **OK** button.

 If millimeter is defined as the default unit for Autodesk Fusion 360 then you can skip the above steps from 1 to 4. The method for specifying the default unit is discussed in Chapter 2.

Creating a Sketch of the Extrude Feature

1. Click on the **Create Sketch** tool in the **Toolbar**, see Figure 3.10. Three default planes: Front, Top, and Right, which are mutually perpendicular to each other appear in the graphics area.

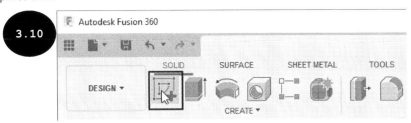

3.10

2. Move the cursor over the Front plane and then click the left mouse button when it gets highlighted in the graphics area. The Sketching environment gets invoked and the Front plane becomes the sketching plane for creating the sketch. Also, it is oriented normal to the viewing direction and the **SKETCH** contextual tab appears in the **Toolbar**.

   Now, you need to turn off the grids and snap modes. As Autodesk Fusion 360 is a parametric software, you can turn off the grids and snap modes and create a sketch by specifying points arbitrarily in the drawing area and then apply the required dimensions.

3. Clear the **Sketch Grid** and **Snap** check boxes in the **SKETCH PALETTE** dialog box to turn off the grids and snap modes, see Figure 3.11.

   Now, you can create the sketch.

4. Click on the **Line** tool in the **CREATE** panel of the **SKETCH** contextual tab, see Figure 3.12 or press the **L** key. The **Line** tool gets activated.

3.11

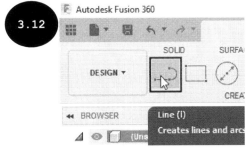

3.12

5.   Click to specify the start point of the line at the origin.

6.   Move the cursor horizontally toward the right and then click to specify the endpoint of the line when the length of the line appears close to 36 mm in the Dimension box, see Figure 3.13. A horizontal line of length close to 36 mm is created.

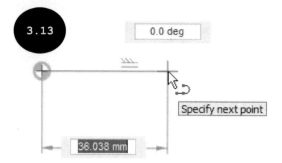

7.   Move the cursor vertically upward and then click to specify the endpoint of the line when the length of the line appears close to 36 mm. A vertical line of length close to 36 mm is created.

8.   Press the ESC key to exit the **Line** tool.

Now, you need to create a sketch fillet of radius 18 mm at the corner of the entities.

9.   Click on the **Fillet** tool in the **MODIFY** panel of the **SKETCH** contextual tab, see Figure 3.14. The **Fillet** tool gets activated.

10. Mover the cursor over the corner of the line entities created and then click when the preview of the fillet appears in the drawing area, see Figure 3.15. The **Fillet radius** field appears in the drawing area. Also, an arrow appears along with the fillet preview, see Figure 3.16.

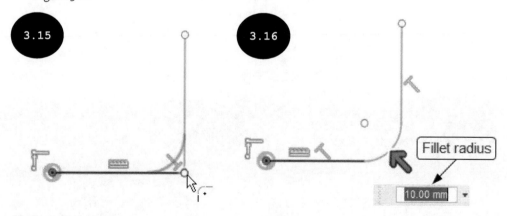

Instead of selecting a corner for creating a fillet, you can also select two intersecting or parallel sketch entities one by one.

11. Enter **18** mm as the radius of the fillet in the **Fillet radius** field and then press ENTER. A fillet of radius 18 mm is created, see Figure 3.17. Note that in Figure 3.17, the display of constraints is turned off by clearing the **Show Constraints** check box in the SKETCH PALETTE dialog box.

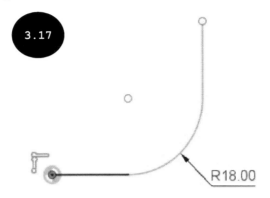

3.17

You can also drag the arrow that appears in the preview to adjust the fillet radius, dynamically.

Now, you need to offset the sketch entities to a distance of 12 mm.

12. Click on the **Offset** tool in the **SKETCH** contextual tab, see Figure 3.18 or press the O key. The **OFFSET** dialog box appears.

3.18

13. Ensure that the **Chain Selection** check box is selected in the **OFFSET** dialog box.

14. Select an entity of the sketch in the drawing area. All contiguous entities of the selected entity get selected and a preview of the offset entities appears in the drawing area, see Figure 3.19. Also, the **Offset position** field appears in the dialog box as well as in the drawing area.

15. Enter **12** in the **Offset position** field of the dialog box. The preview of the offset entities gets modified, see Figure 3.20.

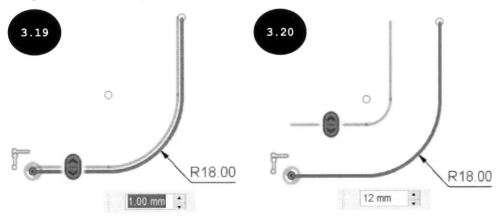

3.19

3.20

*Ensure that the direction of offset entities is on the upper side of the sketch as shown in Figure 3.20. To reverse the direction of offset entities, you can click on the **Flip** button in the dialog box or enter a negative offset value in the **Offset position** field.*

16. Click on the **OK** button in the dialog box. The offset entities are created.

Now, you need to close the sketch by creating lines on both sides of the sketch.

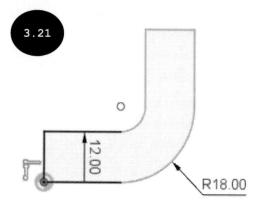

17. Invoke the **Line** tool and then create lines on both the open ends of the sketch one by one. Figure 3.21 shows the sketch after creating lines on both the open ends of the sketch.

Now, you need to create two circles of the sketch.

18. Press the C key to invoke the **Center Diameter Circle** tool and then create two circles of diameter close to 6 mm inside the closed profile of the sketch, see Figure 3.22. Next, press ESC key to exit the tool.

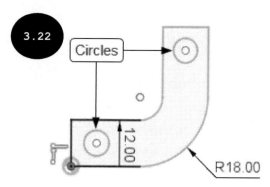

Now, you need to apply an equal constraint between the circles.

19. Click on the **Equal** tool in the **CONSTRAINTS** panel of the **SKETCH** contextual tab, see Figure 3.23.

20. Click both the circles of the sketch one by one. An equal constraint is applied between the selected circles and the **Equal** tool remains active. Next, press the ESC key.

Now, you need to apply dimensions to make the sketch fully defined.

21. Press the **D** key to invoke the **Smart Dimension** tool and then apply dimensions to the sketch, see Figure 3.24.

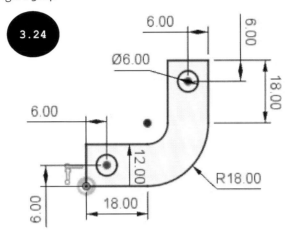

After creating the sketch, you need to exit from the Sketching environment.

22. Click on the **FINISH SKETCH** tool in the **SKETCH** contextual tab, see Figure 3.25, to confirm the creation of the sketch and exit the Sketching environment.

23. Click on the **Home** icon in the **ViewCube** to change the orientation of the sketch to isometric, see Figure 3.26, if not changed by default. The sketch appears similar to the one shown in Figure 3.27.

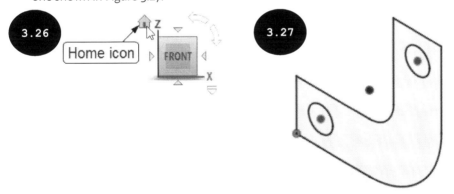

Creating the Extrude Feature

1. Click on the **Extrude** tool in the **SOLID** tab of the **Toolbar**, see Figure 3.28. The **EXTRUDE** dialog box appears, see Figure 3.29. You can also press the **E** key to activate the **Extrude** tool.

2. Click on the outer closed profile of the sketch to be extruded, see Figure 3.30. The profile gets selected. Also, an arrow, a manipulator handle, and a Dimension box appear in the graphics area, see Figure 3.31.

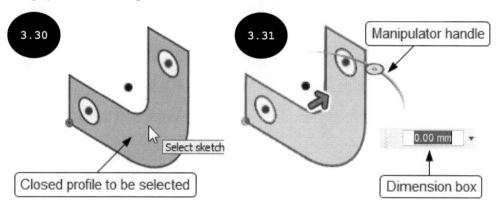

You can select multiple closed profiles of a sketch for creating an extrude feature by clicking the left mouse button. You can also remove an already selected profile. To do so, click again on the selected profile, or press and hold the CTRL or SHIFT key and then click on the profile to be removed from the selection set.

3. Enter **6** in the **Distance** field of the **EXTRUDE** dialog box as the extrusion distance, see Figure 3.32. The preview of an extrude features appears, see Figure 3.33.

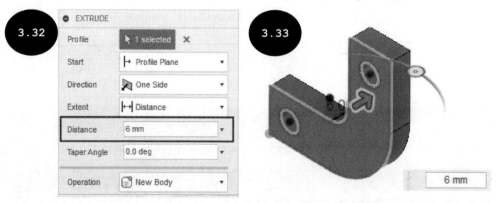

*You can also drag the arrow that appears in the graphics area to set the extrusion distance in the graphics area, dynamically. The manipulator handle that appears along with the preview in the graphics area is used for setting the taper angle of extrusion in the graphics area. You can also specify the taper angle value in the **Taper Angle** field of the dialog box.*

4. Select the **Symmetric** option in the **Direction** drop-down list of the dialog box for extruding the sketch profile symmetrically about the sketching plane. The **Half Length** and **Whole Length** buttons appear below the **Direction** drop-down list in the dialog box, see Figure 3.34.

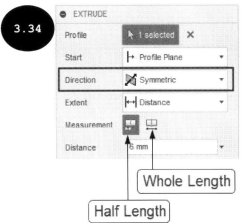

Direction: The options in the **Direction** drop-down list of the **EXTRUDE** dialog box are used for defining the direction of extrusion. The **One Side** option is used for defining the direction of extrusion on either side of the sketching plane. The **Two Sides** option is used for extruding the sketch profile on both sides of the sketching plane with different depths of extrusion. The **Symmetric** option is used for extruding the sketch profile symmetrically on both sides of the sketching plane. On selecting this option, the **Half Length** and **Whole Length** buttons appear. The **Half Length** button is activated by default. As a result, the distance value specified in the **Distance** field of the dialog box is measured as the half length of the extrusion. For example, if the specified distance value is 10 mm then the resultant feature will be created by adding material measuring 10 mm on each side (side 1 and side 2) of the sketching plane. On activating the **Whole Length** button, the distance value specified in the **Distance** field is measured as the total length of the extrusion. For example, if the specified distance value is 10 mm then the resultant feature will be created by adding material measuring 5 mm on each side of the sketching plane.

5. Select the **Whole Length** button in the **Measurement** area of the dialog box. The preview of the extrude feature gets modified such that 3 mm material is added on each side of the sketching plane maintaining a total length of the extrusion as 6 mm, see Figure 3.35.

6. Accept the remaining default specified options in the dialog box and then click on the **OK** button. The extrude feature gets created, see Figure 3.36.

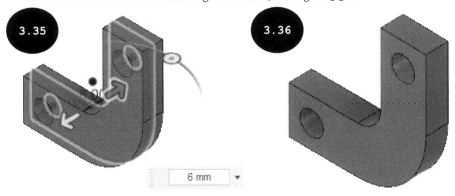

Saving the Model

1. Click on the **Save** tool in the **Application Bar** or press CTRL + S. The **Save** dialog box appears.

2. Enter **Tutorial 1** in the **Name** field of the dialog box as the name of the model.

3. Click on the down arrow next to the **Location** field in the dialog box. The expanded **Save** dialog box appears with the **PROJECT** area on its left.

4. Ensure that the **Autodesk Fusion 360 Tutorials** project is selected in the **PROJECT** area. All the folders created in the selected project appear on the right panel of the dialog box.

5. Create a folder with the name **Chapter 03** inside the **Autodesk Fusion 360 Tutorials** project by using the **New Folder** button of the expanded **Save** dialog box.

6. Double-click on the newly created **Chapter 03** folder to open it for saving the model at the location (*Autodesk Fusion 360 Tutorials > Chapter 03*).

7. Click on the **Save** button in the dialog box. The model gets saved with the name **Tutorial 1** at the specified location (*Autodesk Fusion 360 Tutorials > Chapter 03*) in the **Data Panel**.

Introduction to a Revolve Feature

A revolve feature is created by revolving a sketch around an axis of revolution. You can create a revolve feature by adding or removing material. The base revolve feature of a model is essentially created by adding material. The sketch of the revolve feature should be on either side of the axis of revolution. You can use a line, a construction line, an axis, or a linear edge as the axis of revolution. Figure 3.37 shows sketches and the resultant base revolve features created by revolving the sketches around the respective axes of revolution. In Autodesk Fusion 360, you can create a revolve feature by using the **Revolve** tool of the **CREATE** panel in the **SOLID** tab of the **Toolbar**.

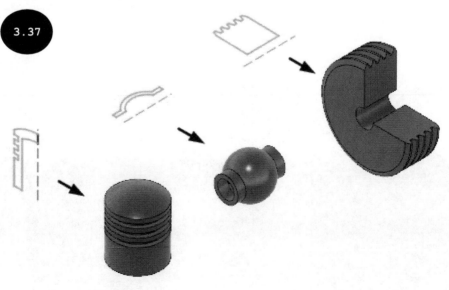

3.37

Tutorial 2: Creating a Revolve Feature

Draw a sketch of the revolve model shown in Figure 3.38 and then revolve it around the vertical centerline at an angle of 270 degrees. All dimensions are in mm.

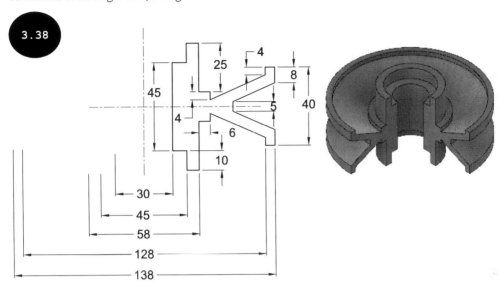

3.38

The following sequence summarizes the tutorial outline:

- Starting a New Design File and Specifying Units
- Creating a Sketch of the Revolve Feature
- Mirroring the Sketch Entities
- Applying Dimensions
- Creating a Revolve Feature
- Saving the Model

Starting a New Design File and Specifying Units

1. Invoke the **File** drop-down menu in the **Application Bar** and then click on the **New Design** tool, see Figure 3.39. The new design file is started with the default name and a new tab "**Untitled**" is added next to the tab of the existing design file. Alternatively, press the CTRL + N key or click on the + sign, next to the name of the existing design file to start a new design file.

   Now, you need to specify the units for the newly added design file.

2. In the **BROWSER**, expand the **Document Settings** node by clicking on the arrow in front of it, see Figure 3.40.

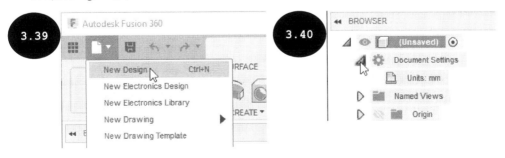

3.39

3.40

3. Move the cursor over the **Units** option in the expanded **Document Settings** node. The **Change Active Units** tool appears, see Figure 3.41.

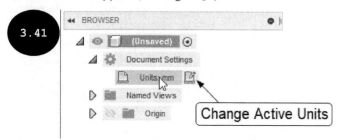

4. Click on the **Change Active Units** tool. The **CHANGE ACTIVE UNITS** dialog box appears on the right side of the graphics area, see Figure 3.42.

5. Ensure that the **Millimeter** unit is selected in the **Unit Type** drop-down list of this dialog box. Next, click on the **OK** button.

 If millimeter is defined as the default unit for Autodesk Fusion 360 then you can skip the above steps from 2 to 5.

Creating a Sketch of the Revolve Feature

Now, you need to create a sketch of the revolve feature. Note that the sketch of the revolve feature should be on either side of the axis of revolution. You can use a line, a construction line, or a linear edge as the axis of revolution.

1. Click on the **Create Sketch** tool in the **Toolbar**, see Figure 3.43. Three default planes: Front, Top, and Right appear in the graphics area.

2. Move the cursor over the Front plane and then click the left mouse button when it gets highlighted in the graphics area. The Sketching environment gets invoked and the Front plane becomes the sketching plane for creating the sketch. Also, it is oriented normal to the viewing direction and the **SKETCH** contextual tab appears in the **Toolbar**.

3. Clear the **Sketch Grid** and **Snap** check boxes in the **SKETCH PALETTE** dialog box to turn off the grids and snap modes, see Figure 3.44.

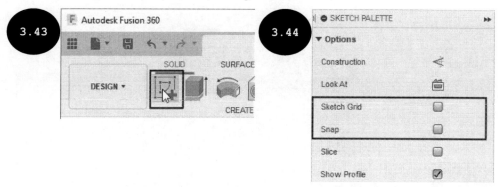

As Autodesk Fusion 360 is a parametric software, you can turn off the grids and snap modes and create a sketch by specifying points arbitrarily in the drawing area and then apply the required dimensions.

Now, you can create the sketch.

4. Click on the **Line** tool in the **Toolbar** or press the **L** key. The **Line** tool gets activated.

5. Click on the **Construction** button < in the **SKETCH PALETTE** dialog box for activating the construction mode and creating construction lines in the drawing area.

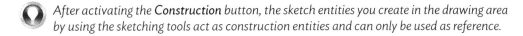 *After activating the Construction button, the sketch entities you create in the drawing area by using the sketching tools act as construction entities and can only be used as reference.*

6. Click to specify the start point of the construction line at the origin and then move the cursor vertically upward, see Figure 3.45.

7. Click to specify the endpoint in the drawing area for creating a vertical construction line of any length, see Figure 3.46. Next, click on the tick-mark that appears near the line segment in the drawing area to end the creation of continuous lines, see Figure 3.46. A vertical construction line gets created and the **Line** tool is still active.

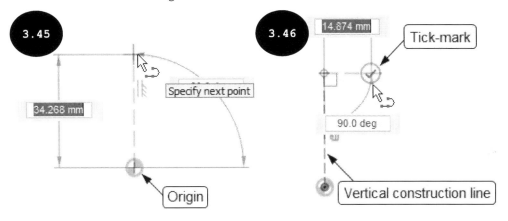

8. Similarly, create a horizontal construction line of any length starting from the origin, see Figure 3.47. After creating the construction lines, do not exit the **Line** tool.

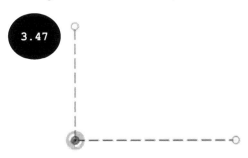

9. Deactivate the construction mode by clicking on the **Construction** button again in the **SKETCH PALETTE** dialog box.

10. Move the cursor over the horizontal construction line to a distance from the origin, see Figure 3.48 and then click to specify the start point of the line.

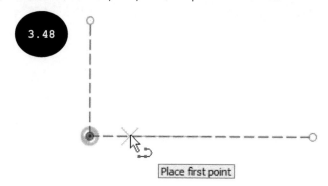

11. Move the cursor vertically upward and then click to specify the endpoint of the line when the length of the line appears close to 22.5 mm near the cursor, see Figure 3.49. A vertical line of length close to 22.5 mm is created.

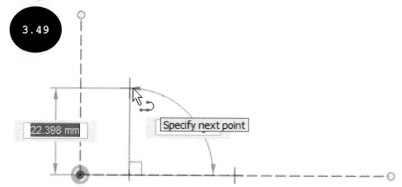

12. Move the cursor horizontally toward right and click to specify the endpoint of the second line when the length of the line appears close to 7.5 mm. A horizontal line of length close to 7.5 mm is created.

13. Move the cursor vertically upward and click to specify the endpoint of the line when the length of the line appears close to 10 mm. A vertical line of length close to 10 mm is created.

14. Move the cursor horizontally toward right and click when the length of the line appears close to 6.5 mm. A horizontal line of length close to 6.5 mm is created.

15. Move the cursor vertically downward and click when the length of the line appears close to 25 mm.

16. Move the cursor horizontally toward right and click when the length of the line appears close to 6 mm.

17. Move the cursor vertically downward and click when the length of the line appears close to 4 mm.

18. Move the cursor toward right at an angle, see Figure 3.50 and then click to specify the endpoint of the inclined line when the line appears similar to the one shown in Figure 3.50.

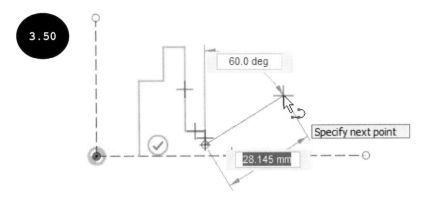

19. Move the cursor vertically upward and click when the length of the line appears close to 4 mm.

20. Move the cursor horizontally toward right and click when the length of the line appears close to 5 mm.

21. Move the cursor vertically downward and click when the length of the line appears close to 8 mm.

22. Move the cursor parallel to the inclined line toward left, see Figure 3.51 and then click the left mouse button just above the horizontal construction line, see Figure 3.51. Note that if the symbol of parallel constraint does not appear, then first move the cursor over the existing inclined line and then move it in a direction parallel to it.

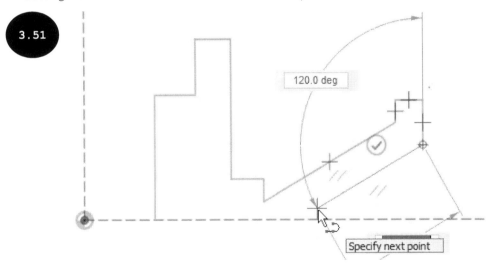

23. Move the cursor vertically downward and then click the left mouse button when the cursor snaps to the horizontal centerline. Next, press the ESC key to exit the **Line** tool. Figure 3.52 shows the sketch after creating its upper half.

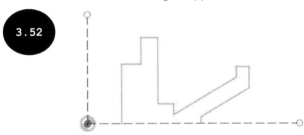

Mirroring Sketch Entities

After creating the upper half of the sketch, you need to mirror it to create the lower half of the sketch.

1. Click on the **Mirror** tool in the **CREATE** panel in the **SKETCH** contextual tab of the **Toolbar**, see Figure 3.53. The **MIRROR** dialog box appears, see Figure 3.54.

2. Select all the sketch entities except the vertical and horizontal construction lines as the entities to be mirrored. You can select the entities individually by clicking the left mouse button or by drawing a window around the entities to be selected, see Figure 3.55. You can draw a window by dragging the cursor.

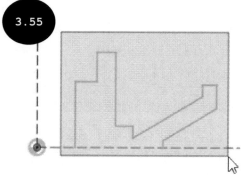

3. Click on the **Mirror Line** selection option in the **MIRROR** dialog box to activate it and then click on the horizontal construction line as the mirroring line in the drawing area. A preview of the lower half of the sketch appears.

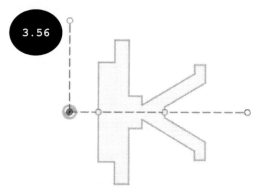

4. Click on the **OK** button in the **MIRROR** dialog box. The lower half of the sketch is created, see Figure 3.56.

Applying Dimensions

Now, you need to apply dimensions to make the sketch fully defined. Constraints such as horizontal, vertical, and parallel are already applied to the sketch entities while drawing them.

1. Press the **D** key. The **Sketch Dimension** tool gets activated. Alternatively, click on the **Sketch Dimension** tool in the **CREATE** panel of the **SKETCH** contextual tab for activating this tool.

2. Click to select both the end points of the vertical line on the extreme left of the sketch one by one, see Figure 3.57. The linear dimension appears attached to the cursor.

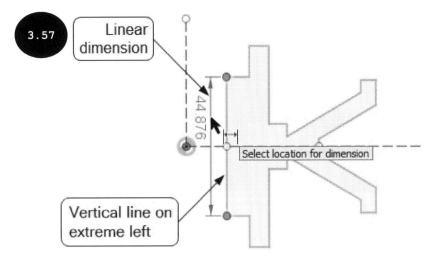

3. Move the cursor toward left to a distance and then click to specify the placement point. A Dimension box appears.

4. Enter **45** in the Dimension box and then press ENTER. The length of the line is modified and the dimension is applied, see Figure 3.58. Also, the tool remains active.

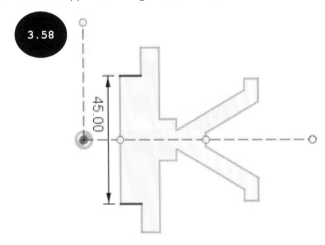

5. Click on the next vertical line, see Figure 3.59. The linear dimension is attached to the cursor. Next, click to specify the placement point. A Dimension box appears.

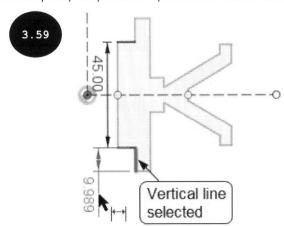

6. Enter **10** in the Dimension box and then press ENTER. The length of the line is modified to 10 mm and the linear dimension is applied. Also, the **Sketch Dimension** tool remains active.

7. Similarly, apply the remaining linear dimensions to the sketch entities, see Figure 3.60.

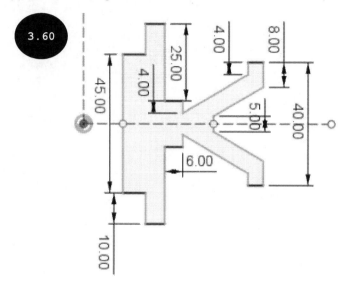

After applying the linear dimensions, you need to apply the linear diameter dimensions.

8. Ensure that the **Sketch Dimension** tool is activated, and then select the vertical construction line. The linear dimension of the vertical construction line is attached to the cursor. Next, select the vertical sketch line on the extreme left. The linear dimension between the vertical construction line and the vertical sketch line is attached to the cursor, see Figure 3.61.

9. Right-click in the drawing area and then click on the **Diameter Dimension** option in the Marking Menu that appears, see Figure 3.62.

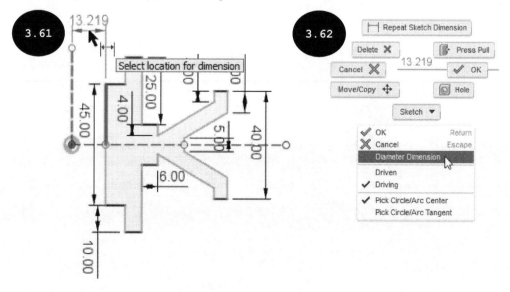

10. Move the cursor to the other side of the vertical construction line. The linear diameter dimension appears attached to the cursor. Next, click to specify the placement point in the drawing area. A Dimension box appears.

11. Enter **30** in the Dimension box and then press ENTER. The linear diameter dimension is applied, see Figure 3.63.

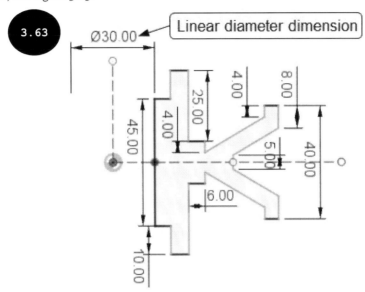

3.63

To apply the linear diameter dimensions, you need to first select the vertical construction line and then the sketch entity. This is because, the first selected entity will be used as the centerline for applying the diameter dimension.

12. Similarly, apply the remaining linear diameter dimensions to the sketch, see Figure 3.64. Next, press the ESC key. Figure 3.64 shows the fully defined sketch after applying all the dimensions.

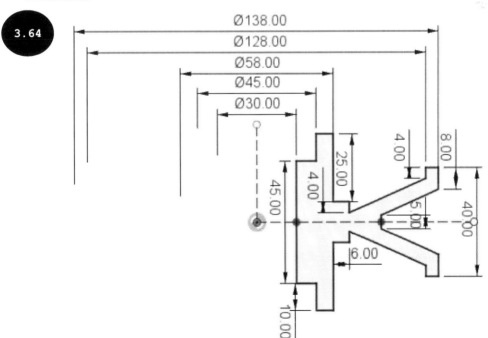

3.64

After creating the sketch, you need to exit from the Sketching environment.

13. Click on the **FINISH SKETCH** tool in the **SKETCH** contextual tab to confirm the creation of the sketch and exit the Sketching environment.

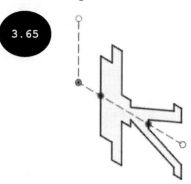

3.65

14. Click on the **Home** icon of the **ViewCube** to change the orientation of the sketch to isometric. The sketch appears similar to the one shown in Figure 3.65.

Creating a Revolve Feature

Now, you can convert the sketch into a revolve feature by revolving the sketch around the vertical construction line at an angle of 270 degrees.

1. Click on the **Revolve** tool in the **SOLID** tab of the **Toolbar**, see Figure 3.66. The **REVOLVE** dialog box appears, see Figure 3.67. Also, the closed profile of the sketch gets selected automatically and you are prompted to select an axis of revolution.

3.66   3.67

 In Autodesk Fusion 360, if a single valid profile is available in the graphics area, then it gets selected automatically on invoking the EXTRUDE or REVOLVE tool.

2. Ensure that the **Axis** selection option is activated in the **REVOLVE** dialog box for selecting an axis of revolution.

3. Click on the vertical construction line of the sketch as the axis of revolution, see Figure 3.68. The preview of a revolve feature appears in the graphics area with a default angle of revolution, see Figure 3.69.

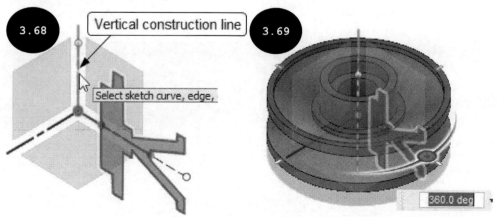

3.68   Vertical construction line   3.69

4. Ensure that the **Angle** option is selected in the **Type** drop-down list of the dialog box.

   Type: The options in the **Type** drop-down list of the **REVOLVE** dialog box are used for specifying the end condition for revolving the sketch profile around the axis. The **Angle** option is used for specifying the end condition of the revolution by specifying the angle value in the **Angle** field of the dialog box. The **Full** option is used for revolving a sketch profile 360 degrees around the axis of revolution.

5. Enter **-270** in the **Angle** field of the **REVOLVE** dialog box. The preview of the revolve feature gets modified in the graphics area, see Figure 3.70.

   A negative angle value is used to reverse the direction of revolution. You can also drag the manipulator handle that appears in the graphics area, to set the angle of revolution of the feature, dynamically.

6. Accept the remaining default specified options in the dialog box and then click on the **OK** button. The revolve feature is created, see Figure 3.71.

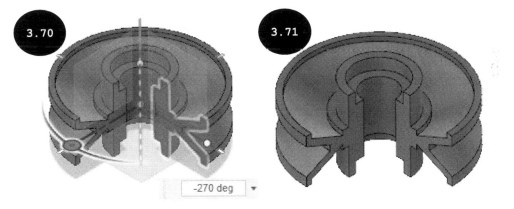

Saving the Model

Now, you need to save the model in the project folder of the **Data Panel**.

1. Click on the **Save** tool in the **Application Bar** or press CTRL + S. The **Save** dialog box appears.

2. Enter **Tutorial 2** in the **Name** field of the dialog box as the name of the model.

3. Ensure the location **Autodesk Fusion 360 Tutorials > Chapter 03** is specified in the **Location** field of the dialog box to save the file of this tutorial. To specify the location, you need to expand the **Save** dialog box by clicking on the down arrow next to the **Location** field of the dialog box, as discussed in Tutorial 1.

4. Click on the **Save** button in the dialog box. The model gets saved with the name **Tutorial 2** at the specified location (*Autodesk Fusion 360 Tutorials > Chapter 03*) in the **Data Panel**.

Exercise 1

Create a sketch of the model shown in Figure 3.72 and then extrude it to a depth of 35 mm, symmetrically about the sketching plane. All dimensions are in mm.

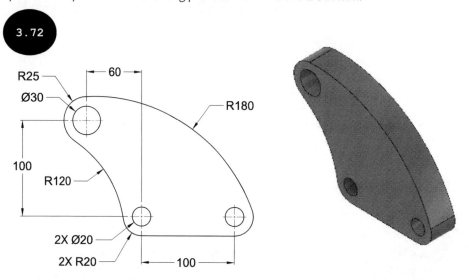

3.72

Exercise 2

Create a sketch of the model shown in Figure 3.73 and then extrude it to a depth of 6 mm. All dimensions are in mm.

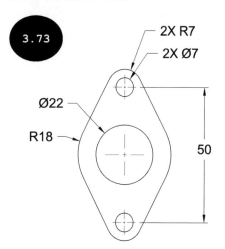

3.73

Exercise 3

Draw a sketch of the revolve model shown in Figure 3.74 and then revolve it around the vertical centerline at an angle of 270 degrees. All dimensions are in mm.

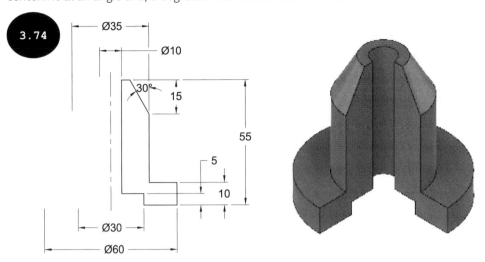

Exercise 4

Draw a sketch of the revolve model shown in Figure 3.75 and then revolve it around the vertical centerline at full angle of 360 degrees. All dimensions are in mm.

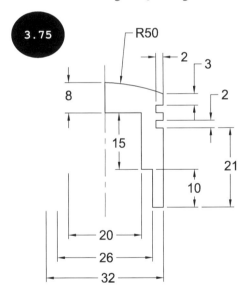

Summary

This chapter discussed how to create extrude and revolve base features by using the **Extrude** and **Revolve** tools. An extrude feature is created by adding or removing material normal to the sketching plane, whereas a revolve feature is created by revolving a sketch around an axis of revolution.

Questions

Answer the following questions:

- The _____ tool is used for creating an extrude feature by adding or removing material, normal to the sketching plane.

- On pressing the _____ key, the **EXTRUDE** dialog box appears in the graphics area.

- The first created feature of a model is known as the _____ feature of a model.

- The _____ field in the **EXTRUDE** dialog box is used for specifying the taper angle value of extrusion.

- On selecting the **Symmetric** option in the **Direction** drop-down list of the **EXTRUDE** dialog box, the _____ and _____ buttons appear in the dialog box.

- The _____ option in the **Direction** drop-down list of the **EXTRUDE** dialog box is used for extruding the sketch profile on both sides of the sketching plane with different depths of extrusion.

- The _____ tool is used for creating a revolve feature by revolving a sketch around an axis of revolution.

- The _____ option in the **Type** drop-down list of the **REVOLVE** dialog box is used for specifying the end condition of the revolution by specifying the angle value.

- The _____ option in the **Type** drop-down list of the **REVOLVE** dialog box is used for revolving a sketch profile 360 degrees around the axis of revolution.

- You cannot select multiple closed profiles of a sketch for creating an extrude feature. (True/False)

- The first feature of a model is essentially created by adding material. (True/False)

- The sketch of a revolve feature should be on either side of the axis of revolution. (True/False)

- The manipulator handle that appears along the preview in an extrude feature in the graphics area is used for setting the extrusion distance of the feature.   (True/False)

Creating Multi-Feature 3D Models

In this chapter, you will learn the following:

- Navigating a 3D Model in Graphics Area
- Creating Fixture Block
- Creating Toggle Lever
- Creating Valve Body

In this chapter, you will learn about creating multi-feature models by using various modeling tools. While creating multi-feature models, you will learn about creating a rib feature, a chamfer, a circular pattern, and a mirror feature, in addition to the extrude and revolve features by using their respective tools. You will also learn about assigning a material and calculating the mass properties of a model. However, before learning to create multi-feature models, it is important to understand about navigating a 3D model in the graphics area.

Navigating a 3D Model in Graphics Area

You can navigate a model by using the mouse buttons and the navigation tools. You can access the navigation tools in the **Navigation Bar** available at the lower middle section of the screen, see Figure 4.1. Alternatively, you can also navigate a model by using the ViewCube. However, before you start navigating a model, you need to understand the navigation settings. In Autodesk Fusion 360, you can control the shortcuts for panning, zooming, and orbiting a model similar to the Fusion, Alias, Inventor, Tinkercad, or SolidWorks CAD package. The method for controlling the navigation settings and different navigation tools are discussed next.

Controlling the Navigation Settings

In Autodesk Fusion 360, you can control the navigation settings by using the **Preferences** dialog box. To invoke the **Preferences** dialog box, click on your name in the upper right corner of Fusion 360. The **User Account** drop-down menu appears, see Figure 4.2. In this drop-down menu, click on the **Preferences** tool. The **Preferences** dialog box appears, see Figure 4.3.

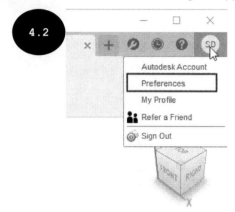

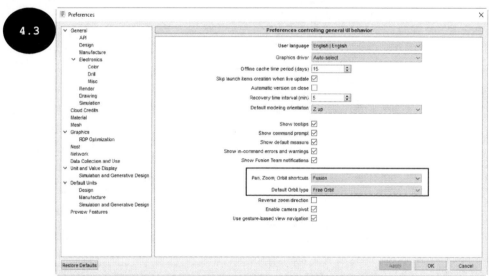

In the **Preferences** dialog box, make sure that the **General** option is selected in the left panel of the dialog box. The options to control the navigation settings appear on the right panel of the dialog box, refer to Figure 4.3. Next, in the **Pan, Zoom, Orbit shortcuts** drop-down list of the dialog box, select the required option (**Fusion, Alias, Inventor, Solidworks,** or **Tinkercad**), see Figure 4.4. Note that depending upon the option selected in the **Pan, Zoom, Orbit shortcuts** drop-down list, you can navigate the model by using the shortcuts used in the respective CAD package, see the Table given below:

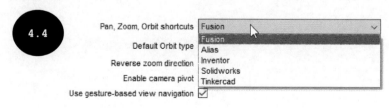

	Pan 🖐	Zoom 🔍	Orbit 🔄
Fusion	Hold Middle Mouse Button & Drag	Scroll Middle Mouse Button Up & Down	SHIFT +
Alias	SHIFT + ALT +	SHIFT + ALT +	SHIFT + ALT +
Inventor	F2 +	F3 +	F4 +
SolidWorks	CTRL +	SHIFT +	
Tinkercad	Hold Middle Mouse Button	Scroll Middle Mouse Button	

You can also set the default option to orbit the model: **Constrained Orbit** or **Free Orbit** by using the **Default Orbit type** drop-down list in the **Preferences** dialog box.

After specifying the navigation settings, as per the requirement, click on the **Apply** button and then on the **OK** button in the **Preferences** dialog box.

Now, you can navigate the model as per the navigation settings specified in the **Preferences** dialog box. The various navigation tools are discussed next.

 In this textbook, the default navigation settings are used for panning, zooming, and orbiting the model. The Fusion navigation settings are the default settings.

Pan 🖐

You can pan or move a model in the graphics area by using the **Pan** tool. To do so, click on the **Pan** tool in the **Navigation Bar**, see Figure 4.5. The **Pan** tool gets activated. Next, drag the cursor after pressing and holding the left mouse button.

Alternatively, you can also pan the model by dragging the cursor after pressing and holding the middle mouse button.

Zoom

You can zoom into or out of the graphics area, dynamically by using the **Zoom** tool. In other words, you can enlarge or reduce the view of a model, dynamically by using the **Zoom** tool. To do so, click on the **Zoom** tool in the **Navigation Bar**. The **Zoom** tool gets activated. Next, drag the cursor upward or downward in the graphics area by pressing and holding the left mouse button. On dragging the cursor upward, the view gets reduced, whereas on dragging the cursor downward, the view gets enlarged. You can also reverse the zoom direction. For doing so, invoke the **Preferences** dialog box, as discussed earlier and then select the **Reverse zoom direction** check box, see Figure 4.6. Note that in the process of zooming in or zooming out, the scale of the model remains the same. However, the viewing distance gets modified in order to enlarge or reduce the view of the model.

Alternatively, you can also zoom in or zoom out by scrolling the middle mouse button in the graphics area.

Zoom Window

The **Zoom Window** tool is used for zooming a particular portion or area of a model by defining a window. To do so, invoke the **Zoom** flyout in the **Navigation Bar** by clicking on the arrow next to an active zoom tool, see Figure 4.7. Next, click on the **Zoom Window** tool and then draw a window by dragging the cursor around the portion or area of the model to be zoomed. The area inside the window gets enlarged.

Fit

The **Fit** tool is used for fitting a model completely inside the graphics area. To do so, invoke the **Zoom** flyout in the **Navigation Bar** by clicking on the arrow next to an active zoom tool, see Figure 4.7 and then click on the **Fit** tool. The model fits completely inside the graphics area. You can also press the **F6** key to fit the model inside the graphics area.

Free Orbit

The **Free Orbit** tool is used for rotating the model freely inside the graphics area. To do so, invoke the **Orbit** flyout by clicking on the arrow next to an active orbit tool in the **Navigation Bar**, see Figure 4.8 and then click on the **Free Orbit** tool. A circular rim with lines at its four quadrants and a cross mark at its center appears in the graphics area, see Figure 4.9.

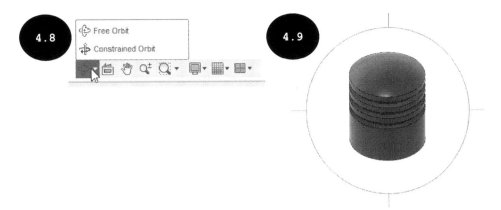

To rotate a model freely, drag the cursor after pressing and holding the left mouse button in the graphics area. Alternatively, drag the cursor after pressing and holding the SHIFT key and the middle mouse button.

To rotate a model about the vertical axis, move the cursor over the horizontal line at the right or left quadrant of the circular rim. The cursor icon changes to a horizontal elliptical arrow. Next, drag the cursor by pressing the left mouse button to rotate the model about the vertical axis. Similarly, you can rotate the model about the horizontal axis by dragging the cursor after positioning it over a vertical line at the top or bottom quadrant of the circular rim.

Constrained Orbit
The **Constrained Orbit** tool is used for rotating a model by constraining the view of the model along the XY plane of the Z axis. To do so, invoke the **Orbit** flyout in the **Navigation Bar**, refer to Figure 4.8 and then click on the **Constrained Orbit** tool. Next, drag the cursor after pressing and holding the left mouse button. You can also rotate the model around the vertical or horizontal axis by using the horizontal or vertical lines of the circular rim that appear in the graphics area, respectively as discussed earlier.

Look At
The **Look At** tool is used for displaying the selected face of a 3D model normal to the viewing direction. To do so, click on the **Look At** tool in the **Navigation Bar** and then click on a face. The selected face becomes normal to the viewing direction. If you are in the Sketching environment, then you can use this tool to make the current sketching plane normal to the viewing direction.

Navigating a 3D Model by Using the ViewCube
ViewCube is available at the upper right corner of the graphics area, see Figure 4.10. It is used for changing the view or orientation of a model.

By using the ViewCube, you can switch between standard and isometric views. By default, it is in the inactive state. When you move the cursor over the ViewCube, it becomes active and works as a navigation tool. You can navigate a model by using the ViewCube components, see Figure 4.11. The various ViewCube components are discussed next.

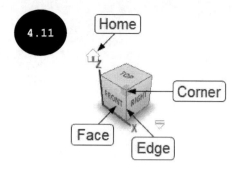

Home

The **Home** icon of the ViewCube is used for bringing the current view of the model to the default home or isometric view.

Corner

A corner of the ViewCube is used for getting an isometric view or to rotate the view freely in all directions. To get an isometric view, click on a corner of the ViewCube. To rotate the view freely in all directions, drag a corner of the ViewCube by pressing and holding the left mouse button.

Edge

An edge of the ViewCube is used for getting an edge-on view or to rotate the view freely in all directions. To get an edge-on view, click on an edge of the ViewCube. To rotate the view freely in all directions, drag an edge by pressing and holding the left mouse button.

Face

A face of the ViewCube is used for getting an orthogonal view such as a top, front, or right. For example, to get the top view of the model, click on the top face of the ViewCube.

You can also display additional options to control the view of a model or the ViewCube settings. To do so, click on the arrow available at the bottom of the ViewCube to display options for controlling the ViewCube settings, see Figure 4.12. Alternatively, right-click on the ViewCube to display these options. Some of the options are discussed next.

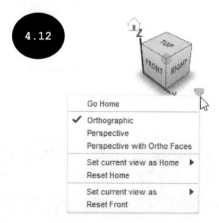

Go Home

The **Go Home** option is used for bringing the current view of the model to the default home view.

Orthographic

By default, the **Orthographic** option is selected. As a result, the model appears in the orthographic view in the graphics area.

Perspective

The **Perspective** option is used for displaying a model in the perspective view.

Perspective with Ortho Faces

The **Perspective with Ortho Faces** option is used for displaying a model in the perspective view with orthographic faces.

Set current view as Home

In Autodesk Fusion 360, you can set the current view of a model as the Home view with a fixed distance or fit to view. To do so, move the cursor over the **Set current view as Home** option. A cascading menu appears with the **Fixed Distance** and **Fit to View** options, see Figure 4.13. The **Fixed Distance** option is used for setting the current view of the model as the Home view with a fixed view distance as it is currently set for the model. The **Fit to View** option is used for setting the current view of the model as the Home view with the fit to view distance. This means that the view of the model adjusts automatically and fits in the graphics area.

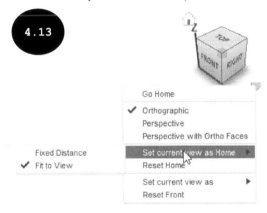

Reset Home

The **Reset Home** option is used for resetting the Home view of the model to the default settings.

Set current view as

You can set the current view of the model as the Front or Top view. To do so, move the cursor over the **Set current view as** option. A cascading menu appears with the **Front** and **Top** options. Click on the required option in this menu.

Reset Front

The **Reset Front** option is used for resetting the Front view of the model to the default settings.

Tutorial 1: Creating Fixture Block

Create the model shown in Figure 4.14. After creating the model, assign the Cast Iron material and calculate the mass properties of the model. All dimensions are in mm.

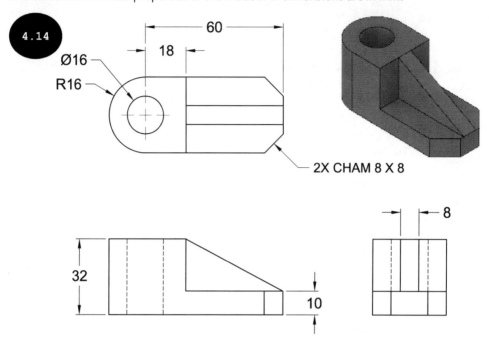

The following sequence summarizes the tutorial outline:

- Starting a New Design File
- Creating the Base Extrude Feature
- Creating the Second Extrude Feature
- Creating an Extrude Cut Feature
- Creating a Rib Feature
- Creating a Chamfer
- Assigning the Material
- Calculating Mass Properties
- Saving the model

Starting a New Design File

1. Start Fusion 360 by double-clicking on the **Autodesk Fusion 360** icon on your desktop. The startup user interface of Fusion 360 appears.

2. Invoke the **File** drop-down menu in the **Application Bar** and then click on the **New Design** tool, see Figure 4.15. The new design file is started with the default name and a new tab "**Untitled**" is added next to the tab of the existing design file.

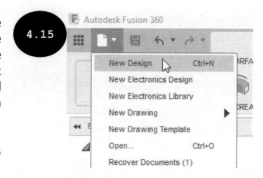

3. Ensure that millimeter (mm) unit is defined for the active design file.

Creating the Base Extrude Feature

1. Click on the **Create Sketch** tool in the **Toolbar**, see Figure 4.16. Three default planes: Front, Top, and Right, which are mutually perpendicular to each other appear in the graphics area.

2. Move the cursor over the Top plane (XY) and then click the left mouse button when it gets highlighted in the graphics area. The Sketching environment gets invoked and the Top plane becomes the sketching plane for creating the sketch. Also, it is oriented normal to the viewing direction and the **SKETCH** contextual tab appears in the **Toolbar**.

   Now, you can create the sketch.

3. Create the sketch of the base extrude feature and then apply the required constraints and dimensions to the sketch, see Figure 4.17.

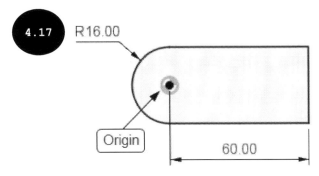

4. After creating the sketch, click on the **SOLID** tab in the **Toolbar** for displaying the solid modeling tools, see Figure 4.18.

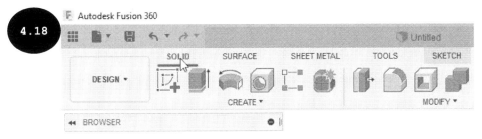

5. Click on the **Extrude** tool in the **CREATE** panel of the **SOLID** tab or press the E key. The **EXTRUDE** dialog box appears. Also, the closed profile of the sketch gets selected automatically for extrusion.

 If a single valid profile is available in the graphics area, then it gets selected automatically on invoking the EXTRUDE tool.

6. Change the orientation of the sketch to isometric by clicking on the Home icon of the ViewCube, if not changed by default.

7. Enter 10 in the **Distance** field of the **EXTRUDE** dialog box as the extrusion distance, see Figure 4.19. The preview of an extrude features appears in the graphics area, see Figure 4.20. Alternatively, you can also drag the arrow that appears in the graphics area to set the extrusion distance in the graphics area, dynamically.

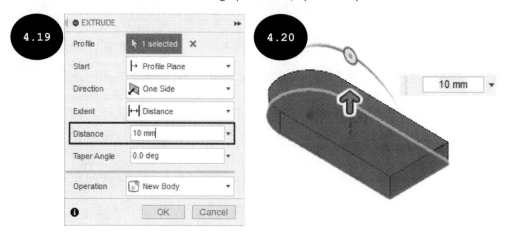

If you are creating the first or base feature of a model, then the **New Body** option is selected in the **Operation** drop-down list of the **EXTRUDE** dialog box, by default. As a result, the resultant base extrude feature is created by adding material and acts as a new body. You will learn about remaining options in the **Operation** drop-down list later in this chapter.

8. Accept the remaining default specified options in the dialog box and then click on the **OK** button. The extrude feature is created, see Figure 4.21.

Creating the Second Extrude Feature

1. Click on the **Create Sketch** tool in the **Toolbar**, see Figure 4.22. Three default planes: Front, Top, and Right which are mutually perpendicular to each other appear in the graphics area and you are prompted to select a sketching plane.

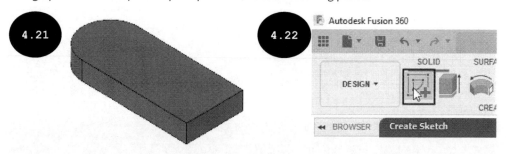

2. Click on the top planar face of the base feature, see Figure 4.23. The top planar face of the base feature becomes the sketching plane for creating the sketch and it is oriented normal to the viewing direction.

In addition to selecting a plane, you can also select a planar face of an existing feature as a sketching plane for creating the sketch.

3. Create the sketch of the second extrude feature, see Figure 4.24.

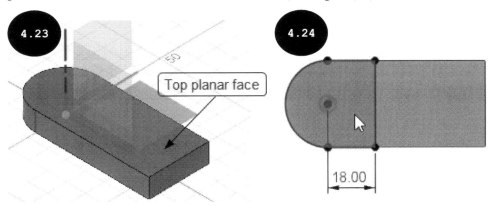

The entities of the sketch shown in Figure 4.24 have been created by taking reference from the edges of the existing feature of the model. Also, in Figure 4.24, the display of the automatically applied constraints is turned off by clearing the **Show Constraints** check box in the **SKETCH PALETTE** dialog box.

4. After creating the sketch, click on the **SOLID** tab in the **Toolbar** for displaying the solid modeling tools, see Figure 4.25.

5. Click on the **Extrude** tool in the **CREATE** panel of the **SOLID** tab or press the **E** key. The **EXTRUDE** dialog box appears.

6. Click to select the closed profile of the sketch to be extruded, see Figure 4.26. The profile gets selected.

7. Enter **22** in the **Distance** field of the **EXTRUDE** dialog box. A preview of the extrude feature appears in the graphics area, see Figure 4.27.

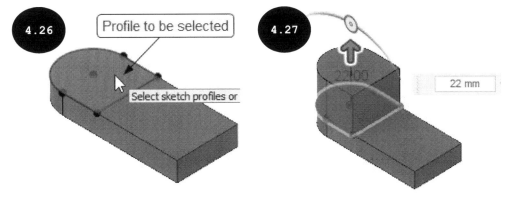

8. Ensure that the **Join** option is selected in the **Operation** drop-down list of the dialog box to join the feature with the base feature of the model, see Figure 4.28.

4.28

Operation: The Operation drop-down list is used for defining the type of operation to be performed for creating the extrude feature. The **Join** option is used for merging or joining the feature with the existing features of the model so that they act as a single body. The **Cut** option is used for creating a feature by removing material from the model. The **Intersect** option is used for creating a feature by only keeping the intersecting/common material between the existing feature and the feature being created. The **New Body** option is used for creating a separate new body in the graphics area. The **New Component** option is used for creating a new component in the currently active design file. On selecting this option, the design file acts as an assembly file. You will learn about assembly files in later chapters.

9. Click on the **OK** button in the dialog box. The second extrude feature is created in the graphics area, see Figure 4.29.

Creating an Extrude Cut Feature

Now, you need to create an extrude cut feature by removing the material from the model.

1. Click on the **Create Sketch** tool in the **Toolbar**. Three default planes appear in the graphics area and you are prompted to select a sketching plane.

2. Click on the top planar face of the second extrude feature, see Figure 4.30. The top planar face of the second feature becomes the sketching plane for creating the sketch and it is oriented normal to the viewing direction.

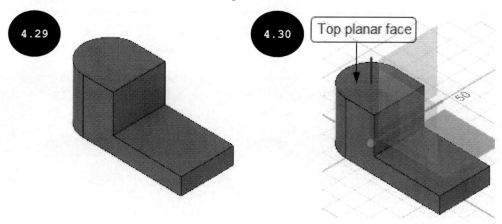

4.29

4.30

Top planar face

3. Create a circle of diameter 16 mm as the sketch of the extrude cut feature, see Figure 4.31.

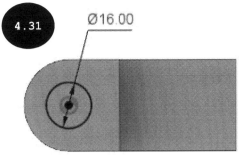

4. After creating the sketch, click on the **SOLID** tab in the **Toolbar** for displaying the solid modeling tools, see Figure 4.32.

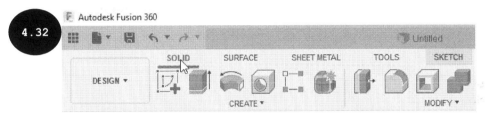

5. Click on the **Extrude** tool in the **CREATE** panel of the **SOLID** tab or press the E key. The **EXTRUDE** dialog box appears.

6. Change the orientation of the model to isometric by clicking on the Home icon of the ViewCube, if not changed by default.

7. Click on the closed profile of the sketch, see Figure 4.33. The profile gets selected.

8. Invoke the **Extent** drop-down list in the **EXTRUDE** dialog box and then select the **All** option, see Figure 4.34.

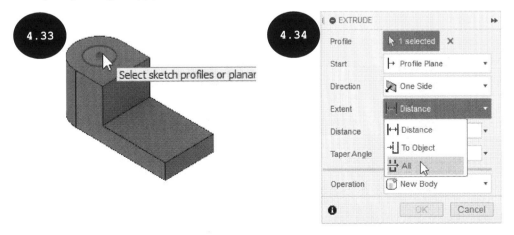

Extent: The options in the **Extent** drop-down list are used for defining the end condition or termination method of the extrusion. The **Distance** option is used for specifying the end condition or termination of the extrusion by defining the distance value in the **Distance** field of the dialog box. The **To Object** option is used for defining the end condition or termination of the extrusion by selecting a face, a plane, a vertex, or a body. The **All** option is used for defining the extrusion through all the faces of the model.

9. Click on the **Flip** button ⊠ in the **EXTRUDE** dialog box to reverse the direction of extrusion downward, see Figure 4.35.

10. Ensure that the **Cut** option is selected in the **Operation** drop-down list of the dialog box for creating an extrude cut feature by removing material from the model, see Figure 4.36.

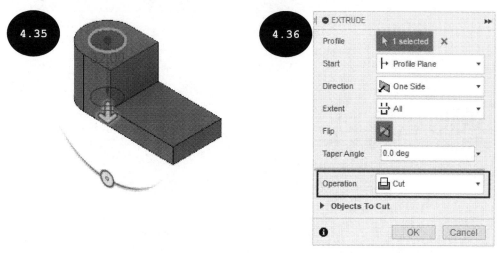

11. Click on the **OK** button in the dialog box. The extrude cut feature is created, see Figure 4.37.

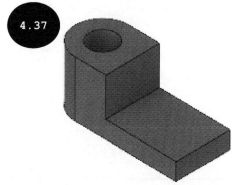

Creating a Rib Feature

A Rib feature acts as a supporting feature and is generally used for increasing the strength of a model. You can create a rib feature from a single line sketch or a curve by adding thickness in a specified direction.

1. Click on the **Create Sketch** tool in the **Toolbar** and then select the front plane as the sketching plane for creating the sketch of the rib feature.

2. Click on your name in the upper right corner of Autodesk Fusion 360 and then click on the **Preferences** tool in the **User Account** drop-down menu that appears, see Figure 4.38. The **Preferences** dialog box appears, see Figure 4.39.

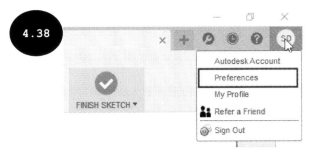

4.38

3. Click on the **Design** option in the right panel of the **Preferences** dialog box and then select the **Auto project edges on reference** check box on the right panel of the dialog box, see Figure 4.39.

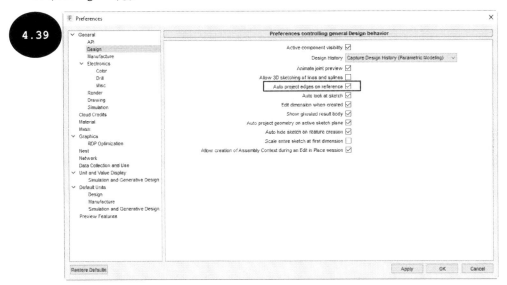

4.39

Auto project edges on reference: On selecting the **Auto project edges on reference** check box in the **Preferences** dialog box, the edges of the existing features of the model get projected automatically onto the sketching plane as reference for creating the sketch.

4. Click on the **Apply** button and then the **OK** button in the **Preferences** dialog box.

Now, you can create an open sketch of the rib feature by taking reference from the existing geometries of the model.

5. Create a single line as the sketch of the rib feature by using the **Line** tool, see Figure 4.40. The line shown in Figure 4.40 has been created by taking reference from the vertices of the existing features of the model.

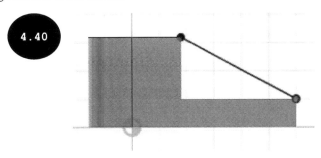

4.40

The projection of both the ends of the rib sketch should lie on the geometry of the model.

6. After creating the sketch, click on the **SOLID** tab in the **Toolbar** for displaying the solid modeling tools.

7. Invoke the **CREATE** drop-down menu in the **SOLID** tab and then click on the **Rib** tool, see Figure 4.41. The **RIB** dialog box appears.

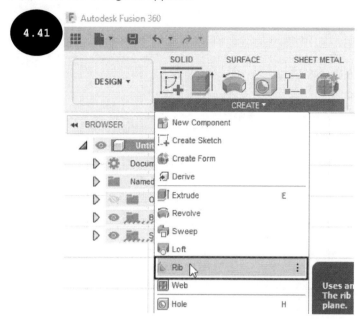

8. Change the orientation of the model to isometric by clicking on the **Home** icon of the ViewCube, if not changed by default.

9. Select the sketch of the rib feature. An arrow appears in the graphics area, see Figure 4.42. Also, the **Thickness** field appears in the graphics area as well as in the **RIB** dialog box.

10. Ensure that the **Symmetric** option is selected in the **Thickness Options** drop-down list of the **RIB** dialog box, see Figure 4.43.

Thickness Options: The **Symmetric** option of the **Thickness Options** drop-down list is used for adding thickness symmetrically on both sides of the rib sketch. The **One Direction** option is used for specifying thickness on either side of the rib sketch. To reverse the direction of thickness from one side of the sketch to the other side, you need to enter a negative thickness value in the **Thickness** field of the dialog box.

11. Ensure that the **To Next** option is selected in the **Depth Options** drop-down list of the dialog box, refer to Figure 4.43.

    Depth Options: The **To Next** option of the **Depth Options** drop-down list is used for terminating the rib feature up to its next intersection. The **Depth** option is used for terminating the rib feature up to a depth value specified in the **Depth** field that appears in the dialog box on selecting this option.

12. Enter 8 in the **Thickness** field of the **RIB** dialog box as the thickness of the rib feature. A preview of the rib feature appears in the graphics area.

13. Click on the **Flip Direction** button 👒 in the dialog box to reverse the direction of the rib feature. A preview of the rib feature appears similar to the one shown in the Figure 4.44.

14. Click on the **OK** button in the dialog box. The rib feature is created, see Figure 4.45.

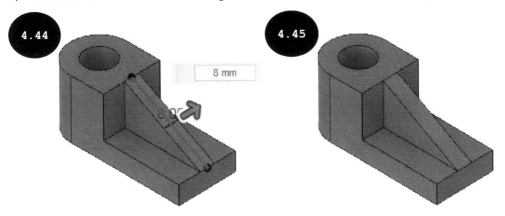

Creating a Chamfer

A chamfer is a bevel face that is non perpendicular to its adjacent faces. You can create a chamfer by using the **Chamfer** tool.

1. Invoke the **MODIFY** drop-down menu in the **SOLID** tab and then click on the **Chamfer** tool, see Figure 4.46. The **CHAMFER** dialog box appears, see Figure 4.47.

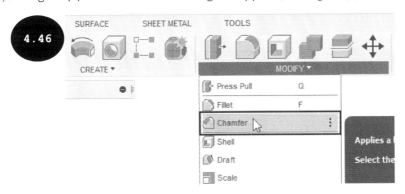

2. Ensure that the **Equal distance** option is selected in the **Chamfer Type** drop-down list of the **CHAMFER** dialog box, see Figure 4.47.

Chamfer Type: The **Equal distance** option of the **Chamfer Type** drop-down list is used for creating a chamfer with equal/symmetric distance on both sides of the chamfer edge. The **Two distances** option is used for creating a chamfer with different distance values on both sides of the chamfer edge. The **Distance and angle** option is used for creating a chamfer by specifying its distance and angle values.

3.   Click on the edges of the model to be chamfered one by one in the graphics area, see Figure 4.48. The **Distance** field appears in the graphics area as well as in the dialog box. Also, an arrow appears in the graphics area along the last selected edge.

4.   Enter **8** in the **Distance** field of the dialog box. A preview of the chamfer appears with 8 mm distance on both sides of the selected edges, see Figure 4.49. You can also drag the arrow that appears in the graphics area to specify the chamfer distance value.

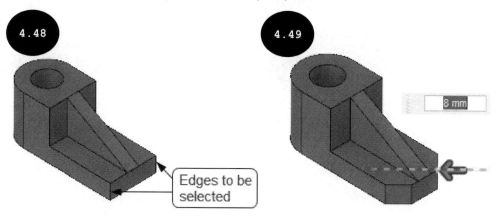

Edges to be selected

5.   Click on the **OK** button in the **CHAMFER** dialog box. The chamfer is created on both the selected edges of the model, see Figure 4.50. Figure 4.50 shows the final model of the Fixture Block after creating all its features one by one.

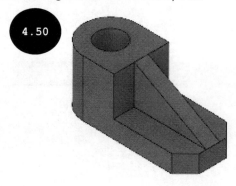

Assigning the Material

Now, you need to assign the Cast Iron material to the model.

1. Right-click on the *name of the design file* in the **BROWSER** and then click on the **Physical Material** tool in the shortcut menu that appears, see Figure 4.51. The **PHYSICAL MATERIAL** dialog box appears, see Figure 4.52. Alternatively, invoke the **MODIFY** drop-down menu in the **SOLID** tab of the **Toolbar** and then click on the **Physical Material** tool.

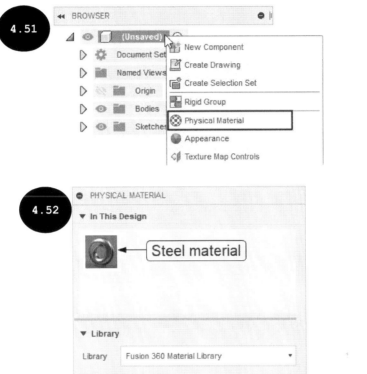

By default, the Steel material is added in the **In This Design** rollout of the **PHYSICAL MATERIAL** dialog box, see Figure 4.52. This means that the Steel material is applied to the currently active design file.

2. Ensure that the **Fusion 360 Material Library** is selected in the **Library** drop-down list of the dialog box. The different material categories such as Ceramic, Glass, Metal, Plastic, and Wood available in the material library appear in the dialog box.

3. Click on the **Metal** material category in the dialog box. The **Metal** material category gets expanded and all the materials available in this category appear.

4. Scroll down to the list of available materials in the **Metal** material category and then pause the cursor over the **Iron, Cast** material, see Figure 4.53.

5. Drag and drop the **Iron, Cast** material over the model in the graphics area by pressing and holding the left mouse button, see Figure 4.54. The **Iron, Cast** material is applied to the model. Next, close the **PHYSICAL MATERIAL** dialog box.

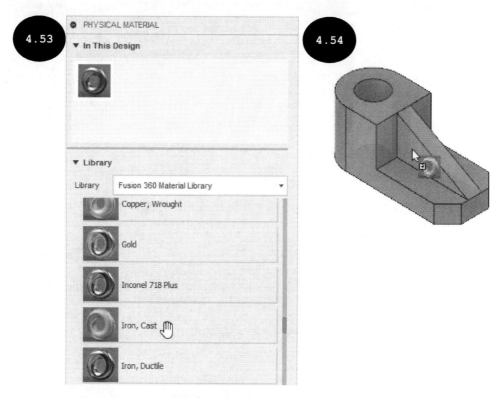

Calculating Mass Properties

Now, you need to calculate the mass properties of the model.

1. Right-click on the *name of the design file* in the **BROWSER** and then click on the **Properties** tool in the shortcut menu that appears, see Figure 4.55. The **PROPERTIES** dialog box appears in the graphics area, which displays the properties of the model including area, mass, volume, bounding box dimensions, center of mass, moment of inertia at center of mass, and moment of inertia at origin, see Figure 4.56.

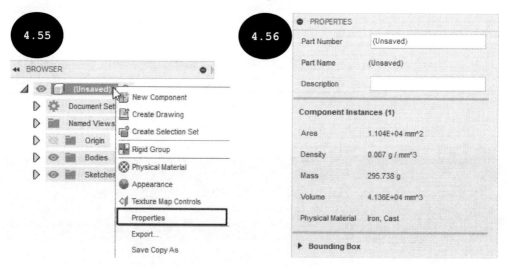

2. The mass of the model is **295.738 grams**.

3. After reviewing the mass properties, exit the **PROPERTIES** dialog box.

Saving the Model

1. Click on the **Save** tool in the **Application Bar** or press CTRL + S and then enter **Fixture Block** in the **Name** field of the **Save** dialog box that appears.

2. Click on the down arrow next to the **Location** field in the dialog box. The expanded **Save** dialog box appears with the **PROJECT** area on its left.

3. Make sure that the **Autodesk Fusion 360 Tutorials** project is selected in the **PROJECT** area. All the folders created in the project appear on the right panel of the dialog box.

4. Create a folder with the name **Chapter 04** inside the **Autodesk Fusion 360 Tutorials** project by using the **New Folder** button of the expanded **Save** dialog box.

5. Double-click on the newly created **Chapter 04** folder and then click on the **Save** button in the dialog box. The model gets saved with the name **Fixture Block** at the specified location (*Autodesk Fusion 360 Tutorials > Chapter 04*) in the **Data Panel**.

Tutorial 2: Creating Toggle Lever

Create the model shown in Figure 4.57. After creating the model, assign the Mild Steel material and calculate the mass properties of the model. All dimensions are in mm.

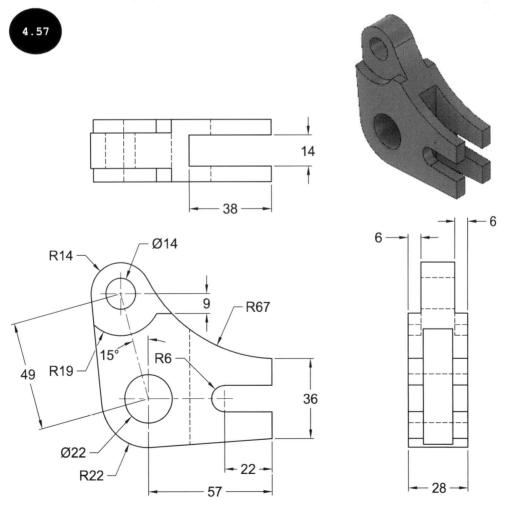

4.57

The following sequence summarizes the tutorial outline:

- Starting Fusion 360 and a New Design File
- Creating the Base Extrude Feature
- Creating the Extrude Cut Feature
- Mirroring a Feature
- Creating the Second Extrude Cut Feature
- Assigning the Material
- Calculating Mass Properties
- Saving the model

Starting Fusion 360 and a New Design File

1. Start Fusion 360 by double-clicking on the **Autodesk Fusion 360** icon on your desktop.

2. Invoke the **File** drop-down menu in the **Application Bar** and then click on the **New Design** tool, see Figure 4.58. The new design file is started with the default name and a new tab "**Untitled**" is added next to the tab of the existing design file.

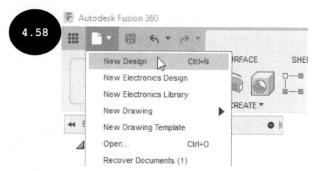

3. Ensure that millimeter (mm) unit is defined for the active design file.

Creating the Base Extrude Feature

1. Click on the **Create Sketch** tool in the **Toolbar**, see Figure 4.59. Three default planes: Front, Top, and Right, which are mutually perpendicular to each other appear in the graphics area.

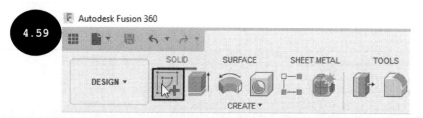

2. Move the cursor over the Front plane and then click the left mouse button when it gets highlighted in the graphics area. The Sketching environment gets invoked and the Front plane becomes the sketching plane for creating the sketch. Also, it is oriented normal to the viewing direction and the **SKETCH** contextual tab appears in the **Toolbar**.

   Now, you can create the sketch.

3. Create the sketch of the base extrude feature and then apply the required constraints and dimensions to the sketch, see Figure 4.60.

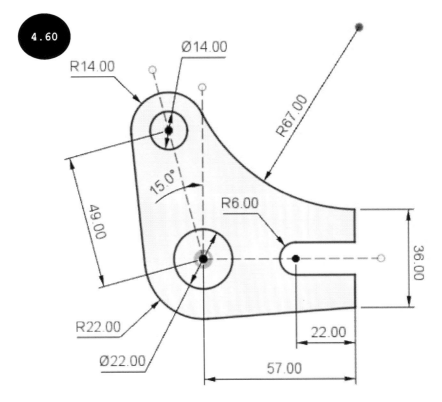

In Figure 4.60, the dimension measuring 49 mm is an aligned dimension applied between the center points of the two circles of the sketch. To apply an aligned dimension, activate the **Sketch Dimension** tool and then select the center points of the two circles one by one. Next, right-click in the drawing area and then click on the **Aligned** option in the Marking Menu that appears. An aligned dimension appears between the selected points. Next, click to specify the placement point for the aligned dimension and then enter the dimension value in the Dimension box that appears in the graphics area. Next, press ENTER.

Also, in Figure 4.60, the tangent constraint is applied between all sets of connecting sketch entities to make the sketch fully defined. Also, the display of constraints in the drawing area is turned off by clearing the **Show Constraints** check box in the **SKETCH PALETTE** dialog box.

4. After creating the sketch, click on the **SOLID** tab in the **Toolbar** for displaying the solid modeling tools, see Figure 4.61.

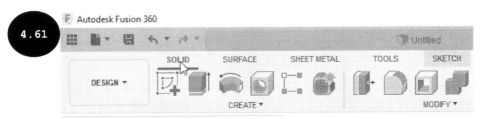

5. Click on the **Extrude** tool in the **CREATE** panel of the **SOLID** tab or press the **E** key. The **EXTRUDE** dialog box appears.

6. Change the orientation of the sketch to isometric by clicking on the Home icon of the ViewCube, if not changed by default.

7.   Click to select the closed profile of the sketch, see Figure 4.62. The profile gets selected.

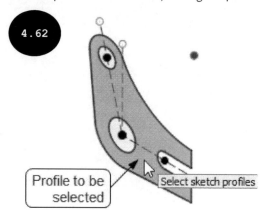

8.   Enter **28** in the **Distance** field of the **EXTRUDE** dialog box as the extrusion distance, see Figure 4.63. The preview of an extrude feature appears, see Figure 4.64.

9.   Select the **Symmetric** option in the **Direction** drop-down list of the dialog box for extruding the sketch profile symmetrically about the sketching plane. The **Half Length** and **Whole Length** buttons appear below the **Direction** drop-down list in the dialog box, see Figure 4.65.

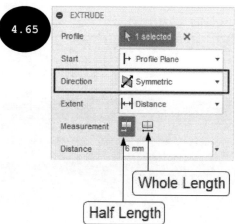

10. Select the **Whole Length** button in the **Measurement** area of the dialog box. The preview of the extrude feature gets modified such that 14 mm material is added on each side of the sketching plane maintaining the total length of the extrusion as 28 mm, see Figure 4.66.

 Adding material symmetrically keeps the sketching plane exactly at the middle of the feature, so that it can be used later as a mirroring plane for mirroring a feature about it.

11. Accept the remaining default specified options in the dialog box and then click on the **OK** button. The extrude feature is created, see Figure 4.67.

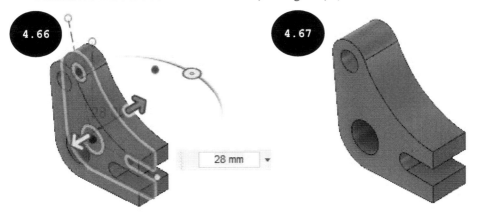

Creating the Extrude Cut Feature

1. Click on the **Create Sketch** tool in the **Toolbar**, see Figure 4.68 and then select the front planar face of the base feature as the sketching plane, see Figure 4.69. The front planar face of the base feature becomes the sketching plane for creating the sketch and it is oriented normal to the viewing direction.

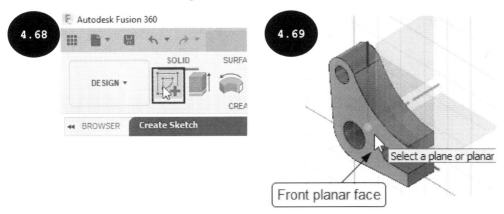

Now, you can create the sketch of the extrude cut feature. Note that to create the sketch of this extrude cut feature, you need to project the existing edges of the model as sketch entities on to the current sketching plane.

2. Invoke the **CREATE** drop-down menu in the **SKETCH** contextual tab of the **Toolbar** and then click on **Project / Include > Project**, see Figure 4.70. The **PROJECT** dialog box appears. Alternatively, press the **P** key to invoke the **PROJECT** dialog box.

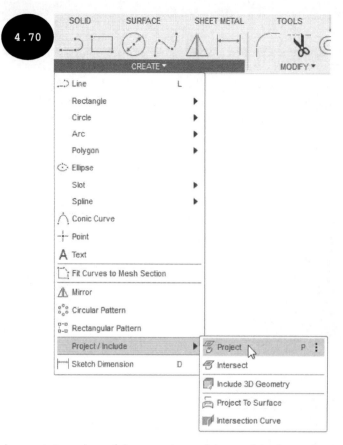

3. Select top three existing edges of the outer loop of the model to be projected one by one, see Figure 4.71. Next, click on the **OK** button in the **PROJECT** dialog box. The selected edges get projected onto the active sketching plane, see Figure 4.72.

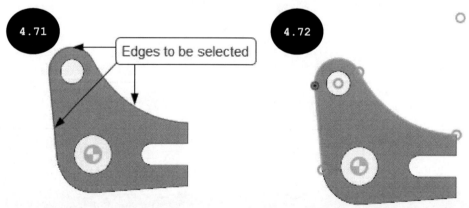

4. Create a circle and a line similar to the one shown in Figure 4.73 by using the **Center Diameter Circle** and **Line** tools. Note that the center point of the circle is at the center of the upper circular edge of the model.

5. Trim the unwanted entities of the sketch by using the **Trim** tool, see Figure 4.74.

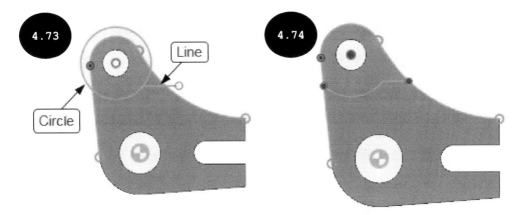

6. Apply dimensions to the sketch by using the **Sketch Dimension** tool, see Figure 4.75.

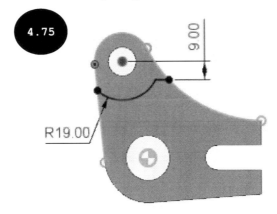

7. After creating the sketch, click on the **SOLID** tab in the **Toolbar** for displaying the solid modeling tools, see Figure 4.76.

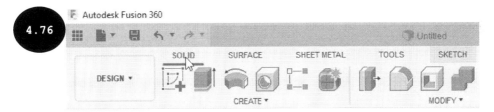

8. Click on the **Extrude** tool in the **CREATE** panel of the **SOLID** tab or press the **E** key. The **EXTRUDE** dialog box appears.

9. Change the orientation of the sketch to isometric by clicking on the **Home** icon of the ViewCube, if not changed by default.

10. Click on the closed profile of the sketch, see Figure 4.77. The profile gets selected.

11. Enter **-6** in the **Distance** field of the **EXTRUDE** dialog box. The preview of an extrude cut feature appears in the graphics area, see Figure 4.78.

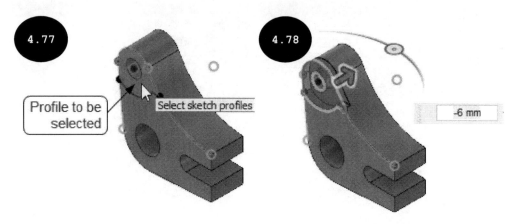

The negative distance value is used for reversing the default direction of extrusion.

12. Ensure that the **Cut** option is selected in the **Operation** drop-down list of the dialog box for creating an extrude cut feature by removing material from the model.

13. Click on the **OK** button in the dialog box. The extrude cut feature is created, see Figure 4.79.

Mirroring a Feature

Now, you need to mirror the previously created extrude cut feature about a mirroring plane.

1. Invoke the **CREATE** drop-down menu in the **SOLID** tab of the **Toolbar** and then click on the **Mirror** tool. The **MIRROR** dialog box appears.

2. Select the **Features** option in the **Pattern Type** drop-down list in the **MIRROR** dialog box for selecting a feature to be mirrored, see Figure 4.80.

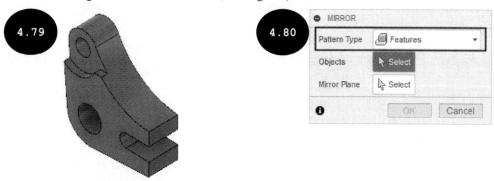

*You can mirror features, faces, bodies, or components about a mirroring plane by selecting the required option in the **Pattern Type** drop-down list of the **MIRROR** dialog box.*

3. Click to select the previously created extrude cut feature in the graphics area or in the **Timeline** available at the lower left corner of the screen, see Figure 4.81.

4. Click on the **Mirror Plane** selection option in the **MIRROR** dialog box for selecting a mirroring plane. The three default planes appear in the graphics area.

5. Click to select the Front plane as the mirroring plane in the graphics area, see Figure 4.82. Alternatively, you can select the Front plane (XZ) in the expanded **Origin** node of the **BROWSER**, see Figure 4.83. A preview of the mirror feature appears in the graphics area.

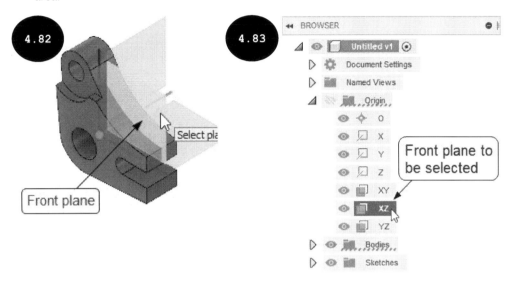

6. Click on the **OK** button in the **MIRROR** dialog box. The mirror feature gets created, see Figure 4.84.

Creating the Second Extrude Cut Feature

1. Click on the **Create Sketch** tool in the **Toolbar** and then select the right planar face of the model as the sketching plane, see Figure 4.85. The right planar face of the model becomes the sketching plane for creating the sketch and it is oriented normal to the viewing direction.

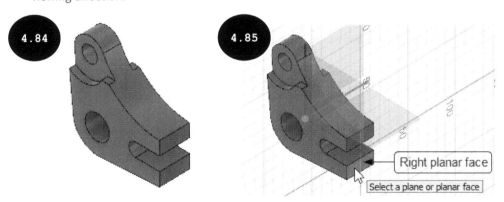

2. Create the sketch of the extrude cut feature, see Figure 4.86.

 In Figure 4.86, a symmetric constraint is applied between the vertical lines of the rectangular sketch and the vertical construction line to make the sketch fully defined. Also, a collinear constraint is applied between the top horizontal line and the edge of the model.

3. After creating the sketch, click on the **SOLID** tab in the **Toolbar** and then click on the **Extrude** tool in the **CREATE** panel or press the E key. The **EXTRUDE** dialog box appears.

4. Change the orientation of the model to isometric by clicking on the Home icon of the ViewCube, if not changed by default.

5. Click to select three closed profiles of the sketch one by one, see Figure 4.87.

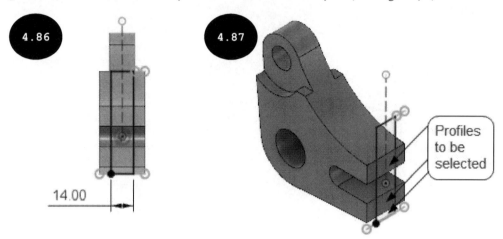

6. Enter -38 in the **Distance** field of the **EXTRUDE** dialog box. The preview of an extrude cut feature appears in the graphics area, see Figure 4.88.

The negative distance value is used for reversing the default direction of extrusion.

7. Ensure that the **Cut** option is selected in the **Operation** drop-down list of the dialog box for creating an extrude cut feature by removing material from the model.

8. Click on the **OK** button in the dialog box. The extrude cut feature is created, see Figure 4.89.

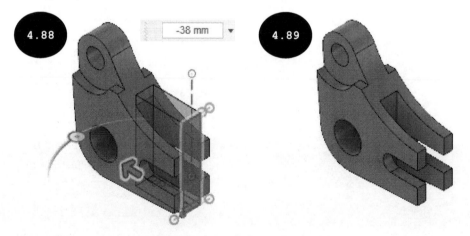

Assigning the Material

Now, you need to assign the Cast Iron material to the model.

1. Right-click on the *name of the design file* in the **BROWSER** and then click on the **Physical**

Material tool in the shortcut menu that appears, see Figure 4.90. The PHYSICAL MATERIAL dialog box appears. Alternatively, to invoke the PHYSICAL MATERIAL dialog box, invoke the MODIFY drop-down menu in the SOLID tab of the Toolbar and then click on the Physical Material tool.

2. Ensure that the Fusion 360 Material Library is selected in the Library drop-down list of the dialog box. The different material categories such as Ceramic, Glass, Metal, Plastic, and Wood available in the material library appear in the dialog box.

3. Click on the Metal material category in the dialog box. The Metal material category gets expanded and all the materials available in this category appear.

4. Scroll down to the list of available materials in the Metal material category and then pause the cursor over the Steel, Mild material, see Figure 4.91.

5. Drag and drop the Steel, Mild material over the model in the graphics area by pressing and holding the left mouse button, see Figure 4.92. The Steel, Mild material is applied to the model. Next, close the PHYSICAL MATERIAL dialog box.

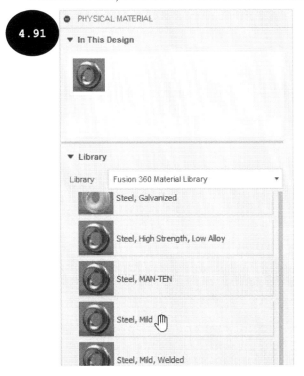

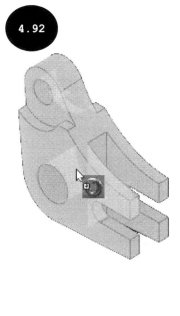

Calculating Mass Properties

Now, you need to calculate the mass properties of the model.

1. Right-click on the *name of the design file* in the **BROWSER** and then click on the **Properties** tool in the shortcut menu that appears, see Figure 4.93. The **PROPERTIES** dialog box appears in the graphics area, which displays the properties of the model including area, mass, volume, bounding box dimensions, center of mass, moment of inertia at center of mass, and moment of inertia at origin, see Figure 4.94.

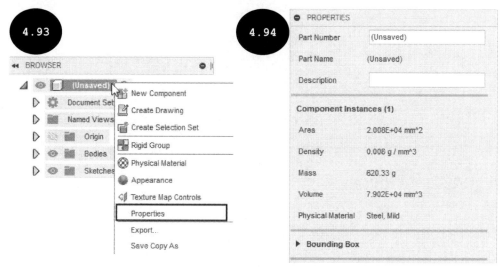

2. The mass of the model is **620.33 grams**.

3. After reviewing the mass properties, exit the **PROPERTIES** dialog box. Figure 4.95 shows the final model after applying the material.

Saving the Model

1. Click on the **Save** tool in the **Application Bar** or press CTRL + S and then enter **Toggle Lever** in the **Name** field of the **Save** dialog box.

2. Make sure the location **Autodesk Fusion 360 Tutorials > Chapter 04** is specified in the **Location** field of the dialog box. To do so, you need to expand the **Save** dialog box by clicking on the down arrow next to the **Location** field of the dialog box.

3. Click on the **Save** button. The model gets saved with the name **Toggle Lever** at the specified location (Autodesk Fusion 360 Tutorials > Chapter 04) in the **Data Panel**.

Tutorial 3: Creating Valve Body

Create the model, as shown in Figure 4.96. After creating the model, assign the Alloy Steel material and calculate the mass properties of the model. All dimensions are in mm.

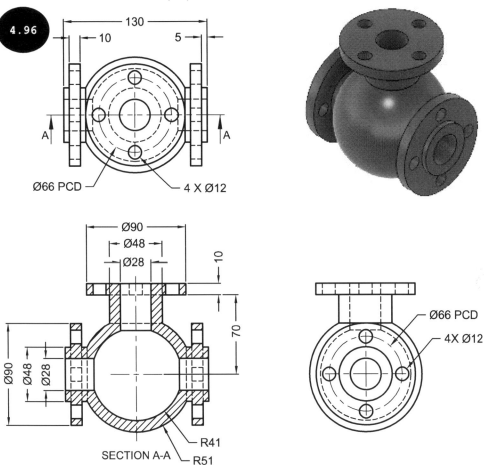

The following sequence summarizes the tutorial outline:

- Starting Fusion 360 and a New Design File
- Creating the Revolve Feature
- Creating the Extrude Feature
- Creating the Second Extrude Feature
- Creating the Extrude Cut Feature
- Creating the Second Extrude Cut Feature
- Creating a Circular Pattern
- Mirroring Features
- Creating the Remaining Features
- Assigning the Material
- Calculating Mass Properties
- Saving the Model

Starting Fusion 360 and a New Design File

1. Start Fusion 360 by double-clicking on the **Autodesk Fusion 360** icon on your desktop.

2. Invoke the **File** drop-down menu in the **Application Bar** and then click on the **New Design** tool, see Figure 4.97. The new design file is started with the default name "**Untitled**".

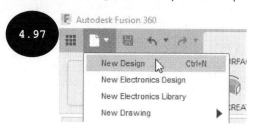

Creating the Revolve Feature

1. Click on the **Create Sketch** tool in the **Toolbar** and then select the Front plane as the sketching plane for creating the sketch of the base feature.

2. Create the sketch of the base feature, see Figure 4.98.

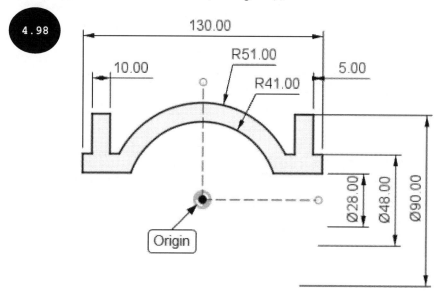

> The sketch of the revolve feature shown in Figure 4.98 is symmetric about the vertical construction line. As a result, you need to apply symmetric constraints to the sketch entities with respect to the vertical construction line. Also, you need to apply equal constraints between the entities of equal length and collinear constraints between the aligned entities of the sketch. You can also create line entities on one side of the vertical construction line and then mirror them to create entities on the other side of the vertical construction line.

3. Click on the **SOLID** tab in the **Toolbar** for displaying the solid modeling tools.

4. Click on the **Revolve** tool in the **CREATE** panel of the **SOLID** tab, see Figure 4.99. The **REVOLVE** dialog box appears. Also, the closed profile of the sketch gets selected automatically and you are prompted to select an axis of revolution, since the **Axis** selection option gets activated in the **REVOLVE** dialog box.

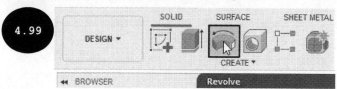

When a single valid profile is available in the graphics area, then it gets selected automatically on invoking the REVOLVE tool.

5. Change the orientation of the sketch to isometric, see Figure 4.100, if not changed by default.

6. Select the horizontal construction line of the sketch as the axis of revolution, see Figure 4.100. The preview of a revolve feature appears in the graphics area, see Figure 4.101.

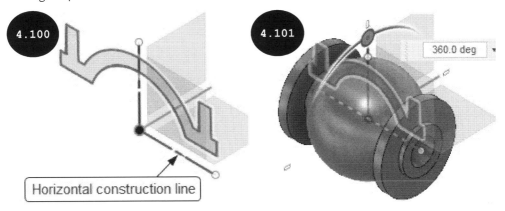

4.100

Horizontal construction line

4.101

360.0 deg

7. Ensure that the **Angle** option is selected in the **Type** drop-down list and the angle of revolution is specified as 360 degrees in the **Angle** field of the dialog box. You can also select the **Full** option in the **Type** drop-down list of the dialog box to revolve the sketch for 360 degrees around the axis of revolution.

8. Click on the **OK** button in the dialog box. The base revolve feature is created, see Figure 4.102.

Creating the Extrude Feature

To create the second feature (extrude) of the model, you first need to create a construction plane at an offset distance of 70 mm from the Top plane.

1. Invoke the **CONSTRUCT** drop-down menu in the **CONSTRUCT** panel of the **SOLID** tab and then click on the **Offset Plane** tool, see Figure 4.103. The **OFFSET PLANE** dialog box appears in the graphics area.

4.102

4.103

CONSTRUCT ▾   INSPECT ▾   INSERT ▾

Offset Plane
Plane at Angle
Tangent Plane
Midplane
Plane Through Two Edges

Offset Plane: The Offset Plane tool is used for creating a construction plane at an offset distance from an existing plane or planar face.

In addition to the three default available construction planes (Front, Top, and Right), you can create a construction plane at an offset distance from an existing plane or planar face, at an angle to an existing plane or planar face, tangent to a cylindrical or conical face, passing through two edges, and so on for a feature of a model by using the respective tool in the CONSTRUCT drop-down menu.

2. Click to select the Top plane as the reference plane for creating an offset construction plane in the graphics area, see Figure 4.104.

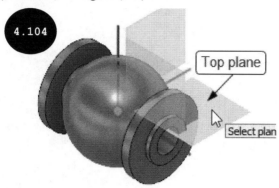

3. Enter **70** in the **Distance** field of the **OFFSET PLANE** dialog box. The preview of an offset plane appears at an offset distance of 70 mm from the Top plane in upward direction, see Figure 4.105.

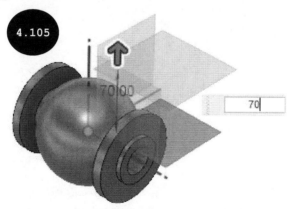

4. Click on the **OK** button in the dialog box. The offset plane is created, see Figure 4.106.

 You can change the default size of the plane by dragging its corner in the graphics area.

Now, you need to create the second feature (extrude) of the model by selecting the newly created plane as the sketching plane.

5. Click on the **Create Sketch** tool in the **Toolbar** and then select the newly created plane as the sketching plane.

6. Create a sketch of the extrude feature (a circle of diameter 48 mm at the origin), see Figure 4.107.

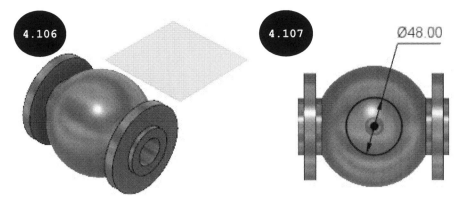

7. Click on the **SOLID** tab in the **Toolbar** for displaying the solid modeling tools.

8. Click on the **Extrude** tool in the **CREATE** panel of the **SOLID** tab or press the **E** key. The **EXTRUDE** dialog box appears and the closed profile of the sketch gets selected automatically.

9. Change the orientation of the model to isometric by clicking on the Home icon in the ViewCube, if not changed automatically.

10. Invoke the **Extent** drop-down list in the **EXTRUDE** dialog box and then select the **To Object** option, see Figure 4.108.

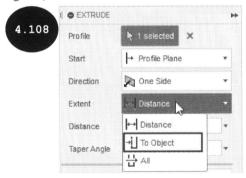

11. Select the outer circular face of the base feature to terminate the extrusion. The preview of an extrude feature appears in the graphics area such that it gets terminated at the intersection with the selected face, see Figure 4.109. Also, the **Solution** and **Chain Faces** areas appear in the dialog box, see Figure 4.110.

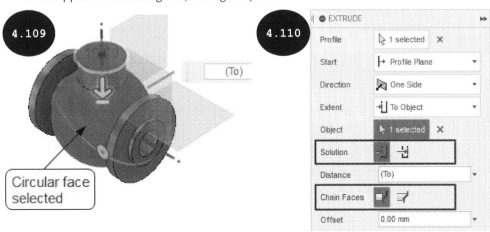

12. Ensure that the **Min Solution** button ⬚ is activated in the **Solution** area of the **EXTRUDE** dialog box to terminate the extrusion at the nearest intersection of the selected face.

13. Ensure that the **Join** option is selected in the **Operation** drop-down list of the dialog box to merge the feature with the existing feature of the model.

14. Click on the **OK** button in the dialog box. The extrude feature is created, see Figure 4.111.

Creating the Second Extrude Feature

1. Click on the **Create Sketch** tool in the **Toolbar** and then select the top planar face of the second feature as the sketching plane, see Figure 4.112.

2. Create the sketch of the third feature (a circle of diameter 90 mm), see Figure 4.113.

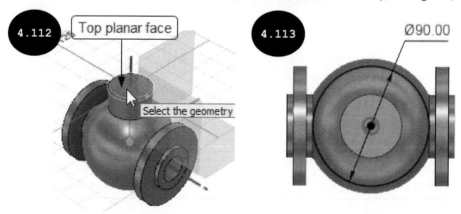

3. Click on the **SOLID** tab in the **Toolbar** for displaying the solid modeling tools.

4. Click on the **Extrude** tool in the **CREATE** panel of the **SOLID** tab or press the E key. The **EXTRUDE** dialog box appears.

5. Select the closed profiles (two profiles) created by the sketch of the third feature, see Figure 4.114.

6. Enter **10** in the **Distance** field of the **EXTRUDE** dialog box. The preview of an extrude feature appears in the graphics area, see Figure 4.115. Ensure that the direction of extrusion is upward. You can reverse the direction of extrusion by entering a negative distance value.

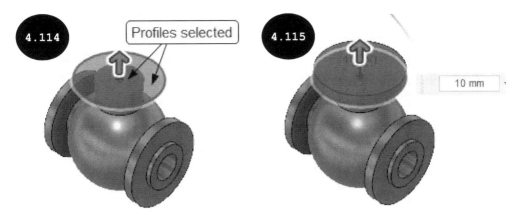

7. Ensure that the **Join** option is selected in the **Operation** drop-down list of the dialog box to merge the feature with the existing features of the model.

8. Click on the **OK** button in the dialog box. The extrude feature (third feature) is created, see Figure 4.116.

Creating the Extrude Cut Feature

1. Click on the **Create Sketch** tool in the **Toolbar** and then select the top planar face of the previously created extrude feature (third feature) as the sketching plane, see Figure 4.117.

2. Create a sketch of the extrude cut feature (a circle of diameter 28 mm), see Figure 4.118.

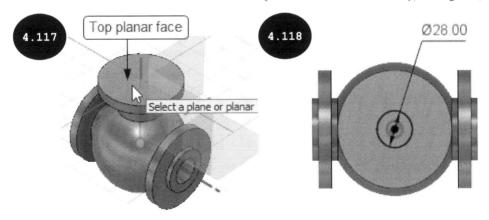

3. Click on the **SOLID** tab in the **Toolbar** for displaying the solid modeling tools.

4. Click on the **Extrude** tool in the **CREATE** panel of the **SOLID** tab or press the **E** key. The **EXTRUDE** dialog box appears.

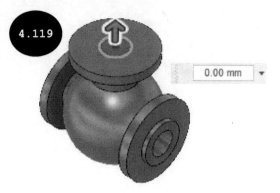

5. Select the closed profile of the sketch, see Figure 4.119.

6. Invoke the **Extent** drop-down list in the **EXTRUDE** dialog box and then select the **To Object** option.

7. Rotate the model such that the inner circular face of the base feature can be viewed, see Figure 4.120.

You can rotate the model by dragging the cursor after pressing and holding the SHIFT + middle mouse button. Alternatively, click on the Orbit tool ⊕ ▾ in the Navigation Bar, which is available in the lower middle section of the screen and then drag the cursor.

8. Click on the inner circular face of the base feature as the face to terminate the creation of the extrude cut feature, see Figure 4.120. A preview of the extrude cut feature appears in the graphics area such that it gets terminated at its nearest intersection with the inner circular face, see Figure 4.121.

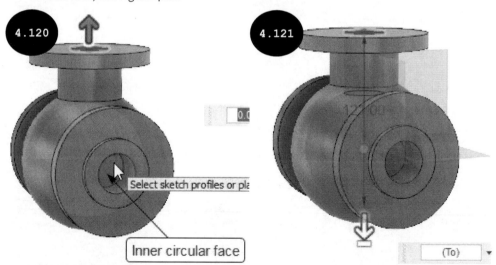

9. Ensure that the **Min Solution** button ⊣ is activated in the **Solution** area of the **EXTRUDE** dialog box to terminate the extrusion at the nearest intersection of the selected face.

10. Ensure that the **Cut** option is selected in the **Operation** drop-down list of the dialog box. Change the orientation of the model back to isometric.

11. Click on the **OK** button in the dialog box. The extrude cut feature is created, see Figure 4.122.

Creating the Second Extrude Cut Feature

1. Click on the **Create Sketch** tool in the **Toolbar** and then select the right planar face of the model as the sketching plane, see Figure 4.123.

2. Create a circle of diameter 12 mm and apply the required dimensions, see Figure 4.124. Note that you need to apply vertical constraint between the origin and the center point of the circle to make it fully defined.

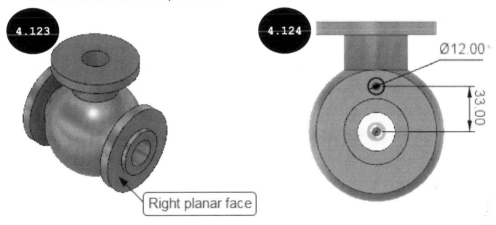

3. Click on the **SOLID** tab in the **Toolbar** and then click on the **Extrude** tool in the **CREATE** panel or press the E key. The **EXTRUDE** dialog box appears.

4. Select the closed profile of the sketch (circle).

5. Ensure that the **Distance** option is selected in the **Extent** drop-down list of the dialog box.

6. Enter **-10** in the in the **Distance** field of the dialog box. The preview of a cut feature appears in the graphics area, see Figure 4.125.

7. Ensure that the **Cut** option is selected in the **Operation** drop-down list of the dialog box.

8. Click on the **OK** button in the dialog box. The extrude cut feature is created, see Figure 4.126.

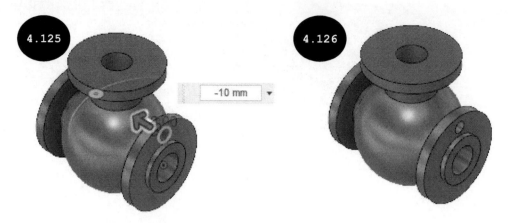

Creating a Circular Pattern

Now, you need to create a circular pattern of the previously created extrude cut feature for creating its remaining instances.

1.   Invoke the **CREATE** drop-down menu in the **SOLID** tab of the **Toolbar** and then click on **Pattern > Circular Pattern**, see Figure 4.127. The **CIRCULAR PATTERN** dialog box appears.

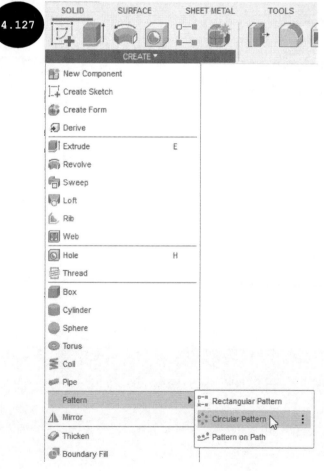

2. Invoke the **Pattern Type** drop-down list in the **CIRCULAR PATTERN** dialog box and then select the **Features** option to select features to be patterned.

3. Select the previously created extrude cut feature in the graphics area or in the **Timeline** as the feature to be patterned.

4. Click on the **Axis** selection option in the **CIRCULAR PATTERN** dialog box and then select the horizontal axis of the model as the pattern axis, see Figure 4.128. The preview of a circular pattern appears with default parameters. Alternatively, you can also select a circular face or circular edge of the model to define the pattern axis.

5. Ensure that the **Full** option is selected in the **Type** drop-down list of the **CIRCULAR PATTERN** dialog box.

6. Enter **4** in the **Quantity** field of the dialog box as the number of pattern instances.

> *The number of pattern instances specified in the **Quantity** field is counted along with the parent or original instance. For example, if 4 is specified in the **Quantity** field, then 4 pattern instances will be created including the parent instance in the respective pattern direction.*

7. Click on the **OK** button in the dialog box. The circular pattern is created, see Figure 4.129.

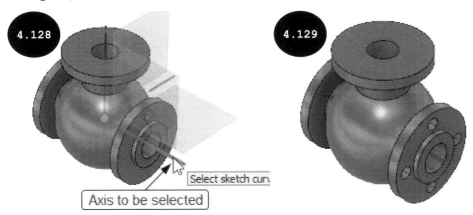

Mirroring Features
Now, you need to mirror the previously created circular pattern and the extrude cut feature.

1. Invoke the **CREATE** drop-down menu in the **Toolbar** and then click on the **Mirror** tool. The **MIRROR** dialog box appears.

2. Select the **Features** option in the **Pattern Type** drop-down list of the **Mirror** dialog box.

3. Select the previously created circular pattern and the extrude cut feature in the **Timeline**, see Figure 4.130.

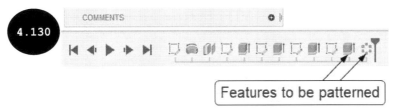

4. Click on the **Mirror Plane** selection option in the **MIRROR** dialog box and then select the Right plane as the mirroring plane, see Figure 4.131.

5. Click on the **OK** button in the dialog box. The mirror feature gets created, see Figure 4.132.

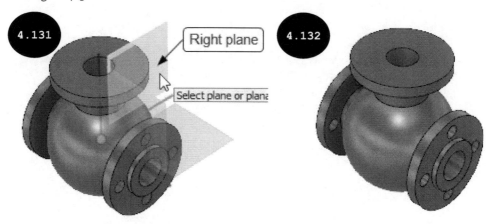

Creating the Remaining Features

1. Create an extrude cut feature of diameter 12 mm on the top planar face of the model, see Figure 4.133. You can refer to Figure 4.96 for dimensions.

2. Create a circular pattern of the previously created cut feature, see Figure 4.134.

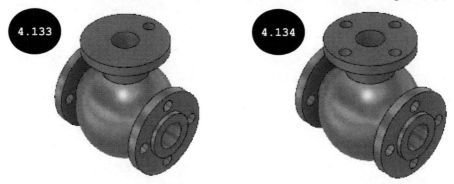

Assigning the Material

1. Right-click on the *name of the design file* in the **BROWSER** and then click on the **Physical Material** tool in the shortcut menu that appears, see Figure 4.135. The **PHYSICAL MATERIAL** dialog box appears.

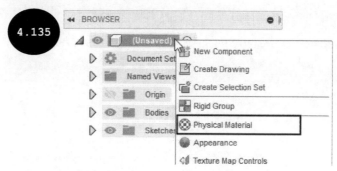

2. Ensure that the **Fusion 360 Material Library** is selected in the **Library** drop-down list.

3. Click on the **Metal** material category in the dialog box. The **Metal** material category gets expanded and all the materials available in this category appear.

4. Scroll down to the list of available materials in the Metal material category and then pause the cursor over the **Steel, Alloy** material, see Figure 4.136.

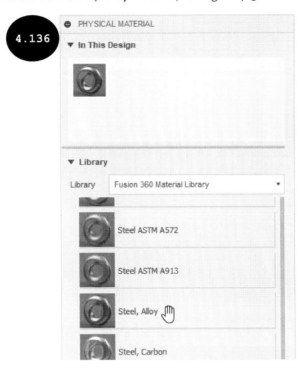

5. Drag and drop the **Steel, Alloy** material over the model in the graphics area by pressing and holding the left mouse button. The **Steel, Alloy** material is applied to the model. Next, close the dialog box.

Calculating Mass Properties

1. Right-click on the *name of the design file* in the **BROWSER** and then click on the **Properties** tool in the shortcut menu that appears, see Figure 4.137. The **PROPERTIES** dialog box appears in the graphics area, which displays the properties of the model including area, mass, volume, bounding box dimensions, center of mass, moment of inertia at center of mass, and moment of inertia at origin, see Figure 4.138.

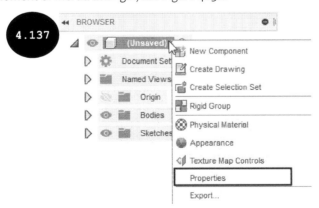

PROPERTIES	
Part Number	Untitled
Part Name	Untitled
Description	
Component Instances (1)	
Area	1.024E+05 mm^2
Density	0.008 g / mm^3
Mass	3503.34 g
Volume	4.532E+05 mm^3
Physical Material	Steel, Alloy
▶ **Bounding Box**	
World X,Y,Z	0.00 mm, 0.00 mm, 0.00 mm
Center of Mass	6.546E-10 mm, 0.00 mm, 11.671 mm

2.   The mass of the model is **3503.34 grams**.

3.   After reviewing the mass properties, exit the **PROPERTIES** dialog box. Figure 4.139 shows the final model after applying the material.

Saving the Model

1.   Click on the **Save** tool in the **Application Bar**. The **Save** dialog box appears.

2.   Enter **Valve Body** in the **Name** field of the dialog box.

3.   Make sure the location **Autodesk Fusion 360 Tutorials > Chapter 04** is specified in the **Location** field of the dialog box to save the file of this tutorial. To specify the location, you need to expand the **Save** dialog box by clicking on the down arrow next to the **Location** field of the dialog box.

4.   Click on the **Save** button in the dialog box. The model gets saved with the name **Valve Body** at the specified location (Autodesk Fusion 360 Tutorials > Chapter 04) in the **Data Panel**.

Exercise 1

Create the model shown in Figure 4.140. After creating the model, assign the Stainless Steel material and calculate the mass properties of the model. All dimensions are in mm.

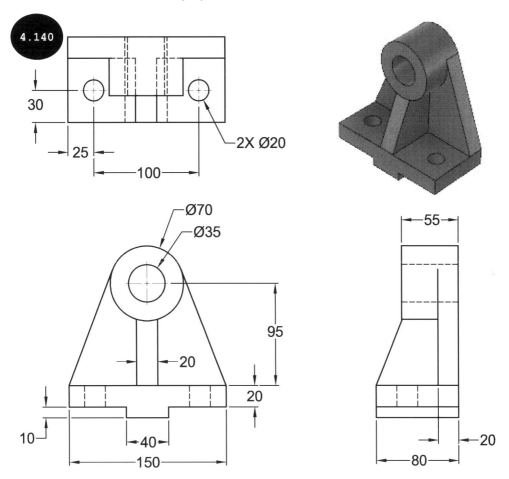

Exercise 2

Create the model shown in Figure 4.141. After creating the model, assign the Aluminium material and calculate the mass properties of the model. All dimensions are in mm.

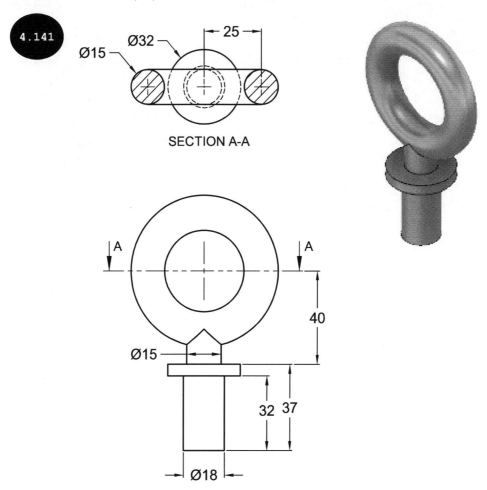

Exercise 3

Create the model shown in Figure 4.142. After creating the model, assign the Aluminium material and calculate the mass properties of the model. All dimensions are in mm.

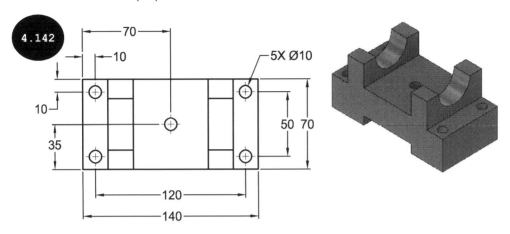

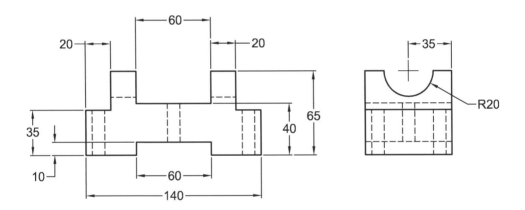

Summary

This chapter discussed the navigate of a 3D model in the graphics area by using various navigation tools, shortcut keys, and ViewCube. It provided a step-by-step explanation for creating multi-feature models by using various modeling tools. The chapter also described methods for creating a rib feature, a chamfer, a circular pattern, and a mirror feature, in addition to creating extrude and revolve features by using their respective tools. Besides, the chapter also explained how to assign a material and calculate the mass properties of a model.

Questions

Answer the following questions:

* The _____ option in the **Extent** drop-down list of the **EXTRUDE** dialog box is used for defining the termination of the extrusion by selecting a face, a plane, a vertex, or a body.

- The _____ option in the **Operation** drop-down list of the dialog box is used for creating an extrude cut feature by removing the material from the model.

- A _____ feature act as a supporting feature and is generally used for increasing the strength of a model.

- The _____ check box in the **Preferences** dialog box is used for projecting edges of the existing features of a model onto the currently active sketching plane as reference, automatically while creating the sketch.

- The _____ option in the **Depth Options** drop-down list of the **RIB** dialog box is used for terminating the rib feature up to its next intersection.

- A _____ is a bevel face that is non perpendicular to its adjacent faces.

- The _____ option in the **Chamfer Type** drop-down list of the **CHAMFER** dialog box is used for creating a chamfer with equal/symmetric distance on both sides of the chamfer edge.

- The _____ tool is used for assigning material to the model.

- The _____ tool is used for invoking the **PROPERTIES** dialog box, which displays the properties of the model including area, mass, volume, bounding box dimensions, center of mass, moment of inertia at center of mass, and moment of inertia at origin.

- The _____ tool is used for projecting the existing edges of the model as sketch entities on to the current sketching plane.

- The _____ tool is used for mirroring features, faces, bodies, or components about a mirroring plane by selecting the required option in the **Pattern Type** drop-down list of the **MIRROR** dialog box.

- The _____ tool is used for creating a construction plane at an offset distance from an existing plane or planar face.

- The _____ tool is used for creating a circular pattern.

- The projection of both the ends of the rib sketch should lie on the geometry of the model. (True/False)

- In Autodesk Fusion 360, the Aluminum material is applied to all active design, by default. (True/False)

Creating Sweep and Loft Features

In this chapter, you will learn the following:

- Introduction to Sweep Features
- Creating a Sweep Feature
- Introduction to Loft Features
- Creating a Loft Feature
- Creating a Loft Cut Feature

Introduction to Sweep Features

A sweep feature is created by adding or removing material by sweeping a profile along a path. Figure 5.1 shows a profile and a path. Figure 5.2 shows the resultant sweep feature created by sweeping the profile along the path. In this figure, the sweep feature is created by adding material. Note that the first feature of a model is essentially created by adding material.

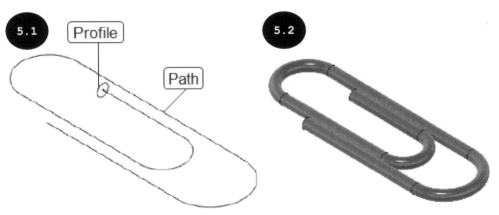

It is evident from the above figures that for creating a sweep feature, you first need to create a profile and a path where the profile follows the path and creates a sweep feature. To create a profile, you need to identify the cross-section of the feature to be created. To create a path, you need to identify a route followed by the profile for creating the feature. In Autodesk Fusion 360, you can create a sweep feature by using the **Sweep** tool available in the **CREATE** drop-down menu of the **SOLID** tab in the **Toolbar**. Note that for creating a sweep feature, you need to ensure the following:

1. The profile must be of a closed sketch. You can also select a face of a model as the profile.
2. The path can be an open or a closed sketch, which is made up of a set of end to end connected sketched entities, a curve, or a set of model edges.
3. The starting point of the path must intersect with the plane of the profile for better results.
4. The profile, the path, and the resultant sweep feature must not self-intersect.

In Autodesk Fusion 360, you can create three types of sweep features: sweep feature with a single path (see Figure 5.3), sweep feature with a path and a guide rail (see Figure 5.4), and sweep feature with a path and a guide surface (see Figure 5.5.).

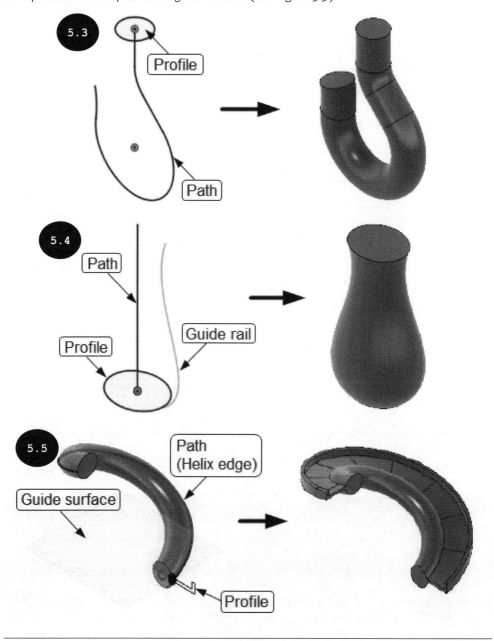

Tutorial 1: Creating a Sweep Feature

Create the model shown in Figure 5.6. The different views and dimensions are given in the same figure. All dimensions are in mm.

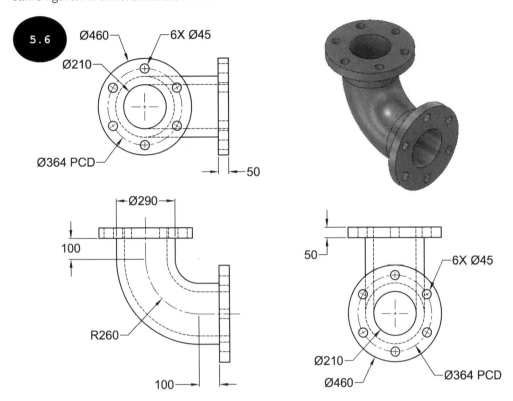

The following sequence summarizes the tutorial outline:

* Starting Fusion 360 and a New Design File
* Creating the Sweep Feature
* Creating the Extrude Feature
* Creating the Extrude Cut Feature
* Creating the Circular Pattern
* Creating Remaining Features
* Saving the Model

Starting Fusion 360 and a New Design File

1. Start Fusion 360 by double-clicking on the **Autodesk Fusion 360** icon on your desktop, if not started already. The startup user interface of Fusion 360 appears.

2. Invoke the **File** drop-down menu in the **Application Bar** and then click on the **New Design** tool, see Figure 5.7. A new design file is started with the default name "Untitled".

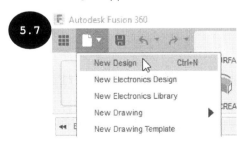

3. Make sure that millimeter (mm) unit is defined as the unit for the currently active design file.

Creating the Sweep Feature

To create a sweep feature, you need to first create a path and a profile.

1.   Click on the **Create Sketch** tool in the **CREATE** panel of the **Toolbar**, see Figure 5.8. The three default planes appear in the graphics area.

2.   Select the Front plane as the sketching plane for creating a path of the sweep feature.

3.   Create a path of the sweep feature by using the sketching tools, see Figure 5.9.

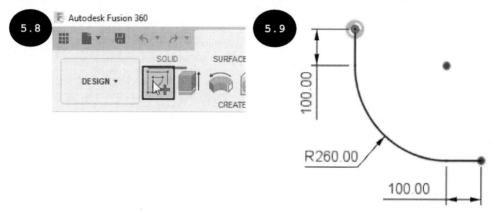

4.   Click on the **FINISH SKETCH** tool in the **SKETCH** contextual tab to finish the creation of sketch.

     After creating the path, you need to create a profile of the sweep feature.

5.   Click on the **Create Sketch** tool in the **Toolbar** and then select the Top plane as the sketching plane to create the profile.

6.   Create the profile (two circles) of the sweep feature, see Figure 5.10.

7.   Click on the **FINISH SKETCH** tool in the **SKETCH** contextual tab to finish the creation of sketch and to exit the Sketching environment.

8.   Change the orientation of the sketch to isometric, see Figure 5.11, if not changed by default.

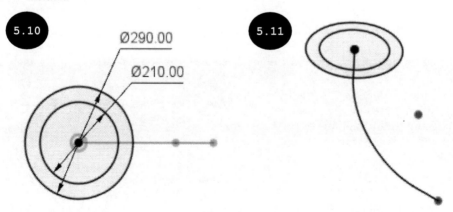

After creating the path and profile, you can create the sweep feature.

9. Invoke the **CREATE** drop-down menu in the **SOLID** tab and then click on the **Sweep** tool, see Figure 5.12. The **SWEEP** dialog box appears, see Figure 5.13.

10. Ensure that the **Single Path** option is selected in the **Type** drop-down list of the **SWEEP** dialog box for creating a sweep feature with a single path.

Type: The **Type** drop-down list of the **SWEEP** dialog box is used for selecting the type of sweep feature to be created. The **Single Path** option is used for creating a sweep feature by sweeping a profile along a path. The **Path + Guide Rail** option is used for creating a sweep feature with a path and a guide rail such that the profile follows the path, while the scale and orientation of the feature is controlled by a guide rail, refer to Figure 5.4. The **Path + Guide Surface** option is used for creating a sweep feature with a path and a guide surface such that the profile follows the path and the orientation of the feature is guided by a guide surface, refer to Figure 5.5.

11. Select the profile of the sweep feature in the graphics area, see Figure 5.14.

12. Click on the **Path** selection option in the **SWEEP** dialog box and then select the path of the sweep feature, see Figure 5.14. A preview of the sweep feature appears in the graphics area, see Figure 5.15. Ensure that the **Chain Selection** check box is selected in the dialog box so that all contiguous entities of the path get selected.

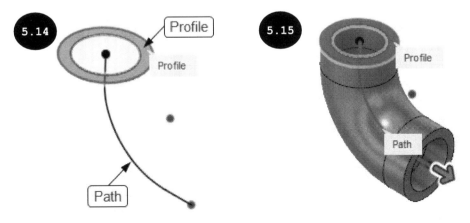

13. Ensure that the distance value 1 is specified in the **Distance** field to sweep the profile along the total length of the path.

14. Ensure that the taper angle and twist angle values are specified as 0 degrees in the respective fields of the dialog box for avoiding tapering and twisting in the resultant sweep feature.

15. Ensure that the **Perpendicular** option is selected in the **Orientation** drop-down list.

*On selecting the **Perpendicular** option in the **Orientation** drop-down list of the SWEEP dialog box, the resultant sweep feature is created by keeping the profile of the feature perpendicular to the path. On selecting the **Parallel** option, the resultant sweep feature is created by keeping the profile of the sweep feature parallel to its sketching plane.*

16. Ensure that the **New Body** option is selected in the **Operation** drop-down list of the dialog box and then click on the **OK** button. The sweep feature is created, see Figure 5.16.

5.16

Creating the Extrude Feature

1. Click on the **Create Sketch** tool in the **Toolbar** and then click on the top planar face of the sweep feature as the sketching plane, see Figure 5.17.

2. Create the sketch (a circle of diameter 460 mm) of the feature, see Figure 5.18.

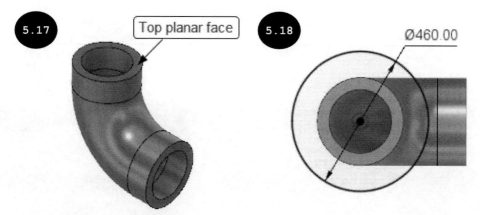

5.17   Top planar face   5.18   Ø460.00

3. Press the **E** key. The **EXTRUDE** dialog box appears.

4. Change the orientation of the model to isometric, if not changed by default.

5. Select the closed profiles (two profiles) for creating the extrude feature, see Figure 5.19.

6. Enter **50** in the **Distance** field. The preview of an extrude feature appears in the graphics area, see Figure 5.20.

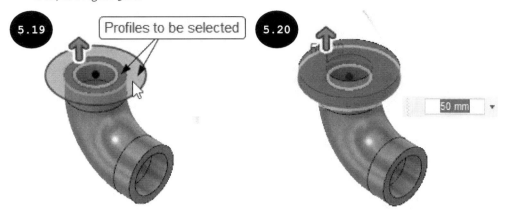

7. Ensure that the **Join** option is selected in the **Operation** drop-down list.

8. Click on the **OK** button in the dialog box. The extrude feature is created, see Figure 5.21.

Creating the Extrude Cut Feature

1. Click on the **Create Sketch** tool in the **Toolbar** and then select the top planar face of the previously created extrude feature as the sketching plane, see Figure 5.22.

2. Create the sketch (a circle of diameter 45 mm) of the feature, see Figure 5.23.

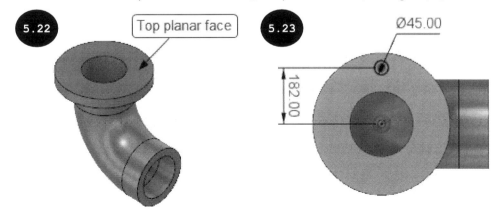

In Figure 5.23, the vertical constraint is applied between the center point of the circle and the origin.

3.   Click on the **SOLID** tab in the **Toolbar** for displaying the solid modeling tools.

4.   Click on the **Extrude** tool in the **CREATE** panel of the **SOLID** tab or press the E key. The **EXTRUDE** dialog box appears.

5.   Select the closed profile of the circle in the graphics area.

6.   Select the **To Object** option in the **Extent** drop-down list of the dialog box.

7.   Rotate the model by dragging the cursor after pressing and holding the SHIFT + middle mouse button such that the back face of the extrude feature can be viewed. Next, select it as the face to terminate the extrude cut feature, see Figure 5.24.

8.   Ensure that the **Cut** option is selected in the **Operation** drop-down list to create the extrude cut feature by removing the material.

9.   Click on the **OK** button in the dialog box. The extrude cut feature is created, see Figure 5.25. Change the orientation of the model to isometric.

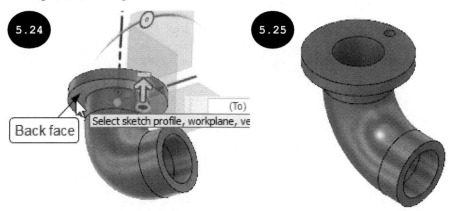

Creating the Circular Pattern

1.   Invoke the **CREATE** drop-down menu in the **SOLID** tab of the **Toolbar** and then click on **Pattern > Circular Pattern**. The **CIRCULAR PATTERN** dialog box appears.

2.   Select the **Features** option in the **Pattern Type** drop-down list in the dialog box.

3.   Select the previously created extrude cut feature in the graphics area or in the **Timeline** as the feature to be patterned.

4.   Click on the **Axis** selection option in the **CIRCULAR PATTERN** dialog box and then select the circular edge of the model to define the pattern axis, see Figure 5.26.

5.   Ensure that the **Full** option is selected in the **Type** drop-down list of the dialog box.

6.   Enter 6 in the **Quantity** field of the dialog box as the number of pattern instances.

7.   Click on the **OK** button. The circular pattern is created, see Figure 5.27.

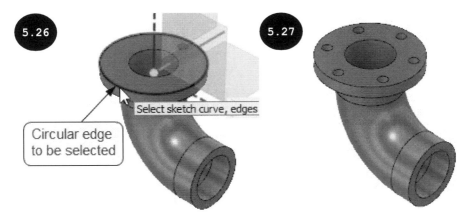

Creating Remaining Features

1. Create a sketch of an extrude feature on the right planar face of the model, see Figure 5.28 and then extrude it to a depth of 50 mm by using the **Extrude** tool, see Figure 5.29.

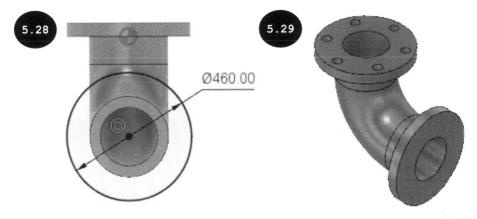

2. Create an extrude cut feature on the right planar face of the model, see Figure 5.30. Note that to create this extrude cut feature, you need to extrude its sketch up to the back planar face of the previously created extrude feature. Refer to Figure 5.6 for the dimensions.

3. Create circular pattern of the previously created extrude cut feature for creating its remaining instances, see Figure 5.31.

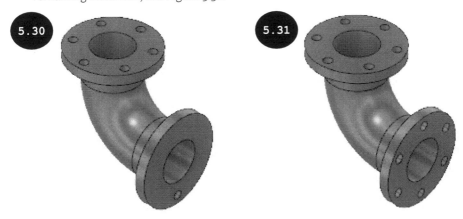

Saving the Model

1. Click on the **Save** tool in the **Application Bar** or press CTRL + S.

2. Enter **Tutorial 1** in the **Name** field of the Save dialog box that appears as the name of the model and then click on the down arrow next to the **Location** field in the dialog box. The expanded **Save** dialog box appears with the **PROJECT** area on its left.

3. Make sure that the **Autodesk Fusion 360 Tutorials** is selected in the **PROJECT** area. All folders created in the selected project appear on the right panel of the dialog box.

4. Create a folder with the name **Chapter 05** inside the **Autodesk Fusion 360 Tutorials** project by using the **New Folder** button of the expanded **Save** dialog box.

5. Double-click on the newly created **Chapter 05** folder and then click on the **Save** button in the dialog box. The model gets saved with the name **Tutorial 1** at the specified location (*Autodesk Fusion 360 Tutorials > Chapter 05*) in the **Data Panel**.

Introduction to Loft Features

A loft feature is created by lofting two or more than two profiles (sections) such that the cross-sectional shape of the loft feature transits from one profile to another. Figure 5.32 shows two dissimilar profiles (sections) created on different planes having an offset distance between each other. Figure 5.33 shows the resultant loft feature.

It is evident from the above figures that for creating a loft feature, you first need to create all the sections that define its shape. In Autodesk Fusion 360, you can create a loft feature by using the **Loft** tool of the **CREATE** drop-down menu in the **SOLID** tab of the **Toolbar**. Note that for creating a loft feature, you need to ensure the following:

1. Two or more than two profiles (similar or dissimilar) must be available in the graphics area before invoking the **Loft** tool.
2. Profiles must be closed. You can select closed profiles of sketches and faces.
3. All profiles must be created as different sketches.
4. The profiles and the resultant lofted feature must not self-intersect.

In Autodesk Fusion 360, you can create three types of loft features: loft feature with profiles (see Figure 5.34), loft feature with profiles and a guide rail (see Figure 5.35), loft feature with profiles and a centerline (see Figure 5.36).

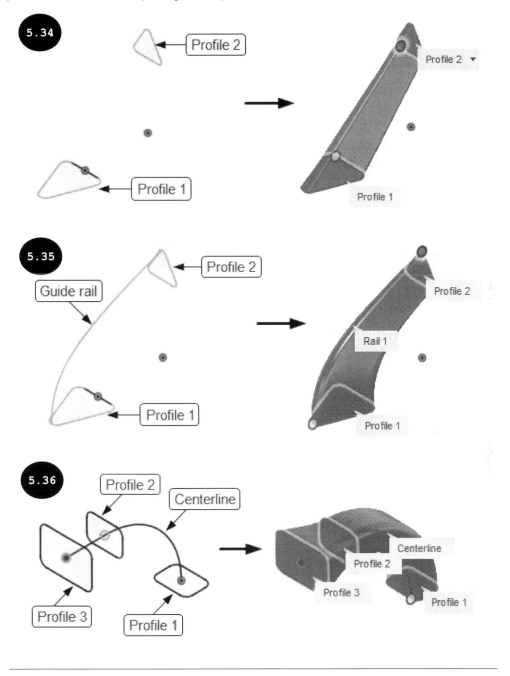

Tutorial 2: Creating a Loft Feature

Create the model shown in Figure 5.37. The different views and dimensions are given in the same figure. All dimensions are in mm.

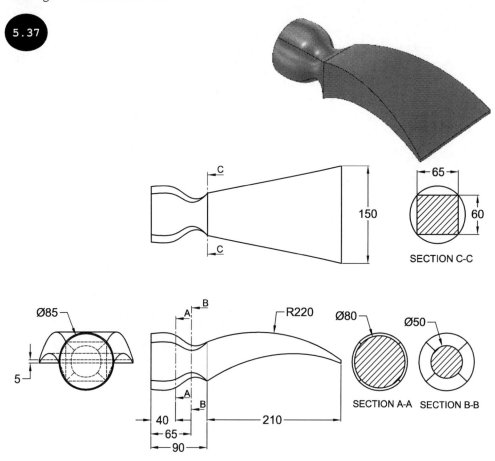

The following sequence summarizes the tutorial outline:

- Starting Fusion 360 and a New Design File
- Creating the Loft Feature
- Creating the Loft Feature with Profiles and a Guide Rail
- Saving the Model

Starting Fusion 360 and a New Design File

1. Start Fusion 360, if not started already and then start a new design file.

2. Ensure that millimeter (mm) unit is defined as the unit for the currently design file.

Creating the Loft Feature

To create the a loft feature of the model, first you need to create all its sections (profiles) on different construction planes.

1. Click on the **Create Sketch** tool in the **Toolbar**, see Figure 5.38 and then select the Right plane as the sketching plane, see Figure 5.39. The Sketching environment gets invoked.

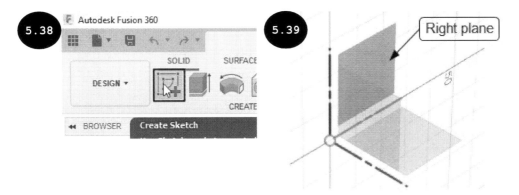

2. Create the first section (profile) of the loft feature, which is a circle of diameter 85 mm, see Figure 5.40. Note that the center point of the circle is at the origin.

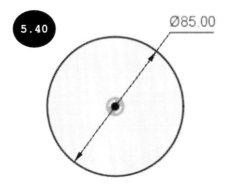

3. Click on the **FINISH SKETCH** tool in the **SKETCH** contextual tab to exit the Sketching environment.

    After creating the first section (profile) of the loft feature, you need to create the second section at an offset distance of 40 mm from the Right plane.

4. Click on the **Offset Plane** tool in the **CONSTRUCT** panel of the **Toolbar** for creating an offset plane, see Figure 5.41. The **OFFSET PLANE** dialog box appears.

5. Click on the Right plane as a reference plane in the graphics area, refer to Figure 5.42. The **Distance** field appears in the **OFFSET PLANE** dialog box and in the graphics area.

6. Enter **40** in the **Distance** filed. The preview of an offset plane appears at an offset distance of 40 mm from the Right plane, see Figure 5.42.

7. Click on the **OK** button in the dialog box. The offset plane is created.

8. Click on the **Create Sketch** tool in the **Toolbar** and then select the newly created construction plane as the sketching plane.

9. Create the second section (a circle of diameter 80 mm) of the loft feature, see Figure 5.43. Next, click on the **FINISH SKETCH** tool in the **SKETCH** contextual tab.

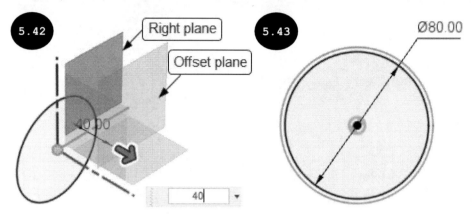

After creating the second section (profile) of the loft feature, you need to create the third section of the feature at an offset distance of 65 mm from the Right plane.

10. Create a construction plane at an offset distance of 65 mm from the Right plane by using the **Offset Plane** tool as discussed earlier, see Figure 5.44.

11. Click on the **Create Sketch** tool in the **Toolbar** and then select the newly created construction plane as the sketching plane.

12. Create the third section (a circle of diameter 50 mm) of the loft feature, see Figure 5.45. Next, click on the **FINISH SKETCH** tool in the **SKETCH** contextual tab.

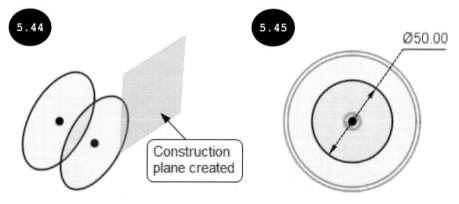

After creating the third section (profile) of the loft feature, you need to create the fourth section at an offset distance of 90 mm from the Right plane.

13. Create a construction plane at an offset distance of 90 mm from the Right plane by using the **Offset Plane** tool, see Figure 5.46.

14. Click on the **Create Sketch** tool in the **Toolbar** and then select the newly created construction plane as the sketching plane.

15. Create the fourth section (a rectangle with dimensions 65 mm X 60 mm) of the loft feature, see Figure 5.47. Next, click on the **FINISH SKETCH** tool in the **SKETCH** contextual tab. All sections of the loft feature get created and appear as shown in Figure 5.48.

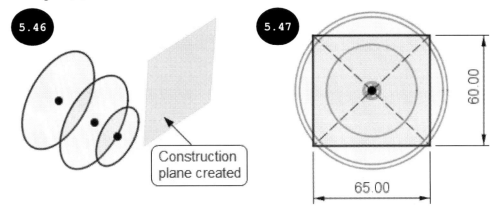

After creating all the sections of the loft feature, you can create the loft feature.

16. Invoke the **CREATE** drop-down menu in the **SOLID** tab and then click on the **Loft** tool, see Figure 5.49. The **LOFT** dialog box appears.

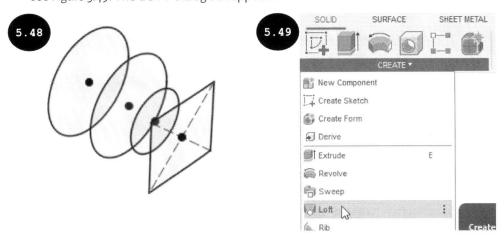

17. Select all the sections (profiles) of the loft feature in the graphics area one by one. The preview of a loft feature appears in the graphics area with connector points, which connect the profiles, see Figure 5.50. Also, the names of the selected profiles appear in the **Profiles** area of the dialog box in the order they are selected, see Figure 5.51.

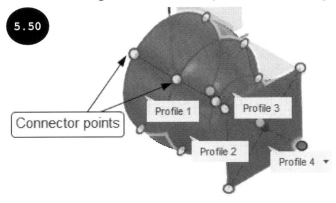

5.51

> If you drag the connector points that appear in the preview of a loft feature, a twist gets
> created in the feature.

18.   Click on the **OK** button in the dialog box. The loft feature is created, see Figure 5.52.

Creating the Loft Feature with Profiles and a Guide Rail

Now, you need to create a loft feature with profiles and a guide rail. A guide rail is used for
guiding the cross-sectional shape of the loft feature. In Autodesk Fusion 360, you can select
multiple guide rails for controlling the shape of the loft feature. Note that the guide rails must
intersect with the profiles of the loft feature.

1.   Create a construction plane at an offset distance of 210 mm from the right planar face of
the base feature by using the **Offset Plane** tool, see Figure 5.53.

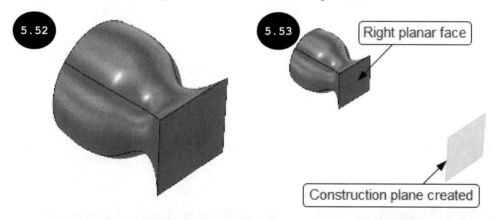

2.   Click on the **Create Sketch** tool in the **Toolbar** and then select the newly created
construction plane as the sketching plane.

3.   Create a section (a rectangle with dimensions 150 mm X 5 mm) of the loft feature,
see Figure 5.54. Note that the center point of the rectangle is at the origin. Next, click
on the **FINISH SKETCH** tool in the **SKETCH** contextual tab to exit the Sketching
environment.

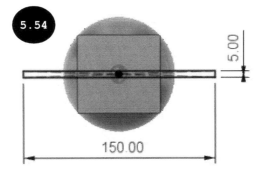

Now, you need to create a guide rail on the Front plane for creating the loft feature.

4. Click on the **Create Sketch** tool in the **Toolbar** and then select the Front plane as the sketching plane.

5. Create the guide rail (an arc of radius 220 mm) of the loft feature, see Figure 5.55. Next, click on the **FINISH SKETCH** tool in the **SKETCH** contextual tab and then change the orientation of the sketch to isometric, if not changed by default.

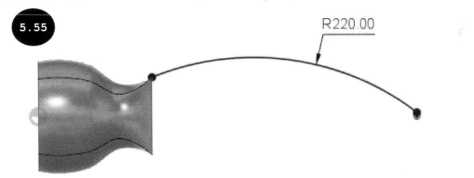

 The endpoints of the guide rail (arc) shown in the Figure 5.55 have coincident constraint with the top entity of the rectangular section of the loft feature and the top edge of the right planar face of the base feature, respectively.

Now, you need to create the loft feature.

6. Invoke the **CREATE** drop-down menu in the **SOLID** tab and then click on the **Loft** tool. The **LOFT** dialog box appears.

7. Select the right planar face of the base feature as the first section of the loft feature and then select the rectangular section (a rectangle with dimensions 150 mm X 5 mm) as the second section of the loft feature in the graphics area. A preview of the loft feature appears in the graphics area, see Figure 5.56.

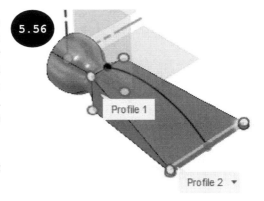

 You can also select a planar face of a model as a profile of the loft feature.

8. Ensure that the **Rails** button is activated in the **Guide Type** area of the dialog box for creating a loft feature with profiles and guide rails, see Figure 5.57.

 *The **Centerline** button available next to the **Rails** button in the **Guide Type** area of the dialog box is used for creating a loft feature with profiles and a centerline. The centerline is used for maintaining a neutral axis of the loft feature and consistent transition between the profiles, refer to Figure 5.36. You can only select one centerline to create a loft feature.*

9. Click on the **Rails Selection** arrow in the dialog box to select the guide rails in the graphics area, see Figure 5.57.

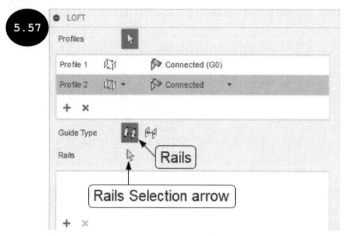

Now, you can select a guide rail to guide the cross-sectional shape of the loft feature.

10. Select the arc of radius 220 mm as the guide rail in the graphics area. A preview of the loft feature appears as shown in Figure 5.58.

11. Ensure that the **Join** option is selected in the **Operation** drop-down list of the dialog box and then click on the **OK** button. The loft feature with profiles and a guide rail is created, see Figure 5.59.

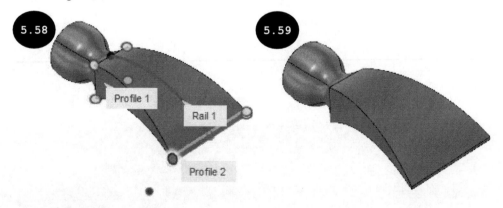

Saving the Model

1. Click on the **Save** tool in the **Application Bar** and then enter **Tutorial 2** in the **Name** field of the **Save** dialog box that appears.

2. Ensure that the location *Autodesk Fusion 360 Tutorials > Chapter 05* is specified in the **Location** field of the dialog box.

3. Click on the **Save** button in the dialog box. The model is saved with the name Tutorial 2 in the specified location (*Autodesk Fusion 360 Tutorials > Chapter 05*).

Tutorial 3: Creating a Loft Cut Feature

Create the model shown in Figure 5.60. The different views and dimensions are given in the same figure. All dimensions are in mm.

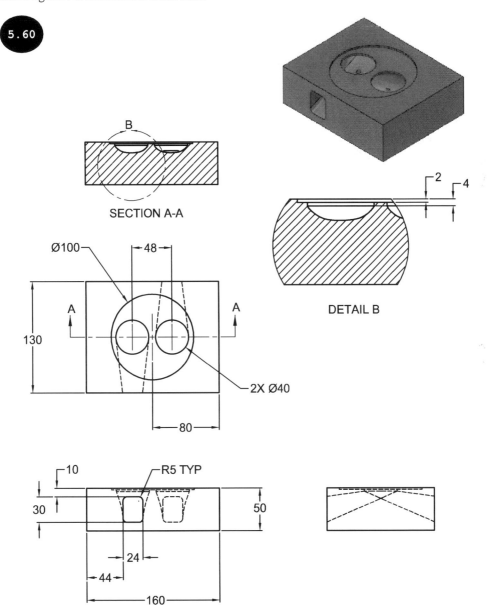

5.60

SECTION A-A

DETAIL B

Ø100

48

2X Ø40

130

80

10

R5 TYP

30

50

24

44

160

The following sequence summarizes the tutorial outline:

- Starting a New Design File and Specifying Units
- Creating the Extrude Feature
- Creating the Extrude Cut Feature
- Creating the Second Extrude Cut Feature
- Creating the Loft Cut Feature
- Creating the Second Loft Cut Feature
- Saving the Model

Starting a New Design File and Specifying Units

1.   Start Fusion 360, if not started already and then start a new design file.

2.   Ensure that millimeter (mm) unit is defined as the unit for the currently active design file.

Creating the Extrude Feature

1.   Click on the **Create Sketch** tool in the **Toolbar** and then select the Top plane as the sketching plane.

2.   Create the sketch of the extrude feature, see Figure 5.61.

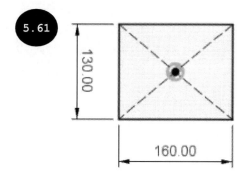

5.61

In Figure 5.61, the rectangle is created by defining its center at the origin, as the model is symmetric about its center.

3.   After creating the sketch, click on the **SOLID** tab in the **Toolbar** for displaying the solid modeling tools, see Figure 5.62.

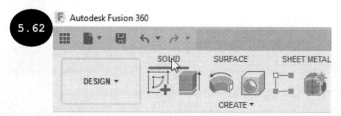

5.62

4.   Click on the **Extrude** tool in the **CREATE** panel of the **SOLID** tab or press the E key. The **EXTRUDE** dialog box appears. Also, the closed profile of the sketch gets selected automatically for extrusion. Next, change the orientation of the sketch to isometric, if not changed by default.

If a single valid profile is available in the graphics area, then it gets selected automatically on invoking the EXTRUDE tool.

5. Enter 50 in the Distance field of the EXTRUDE dialog box as the extrusion distance. The preview of an extrude features appears in the graphics area, see Figure 5.63.

 You can also drag the arrow that appears in the graphics area to set the extrusion distance in the graphics area, dynamically.

6. Click on the OK button in the dialog box. The extrude feature gets created, see Figure 5.64.

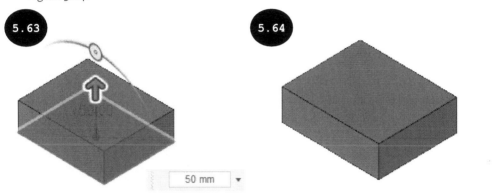

Creating the Extrude Cut Feature

1. Click on the Create Sketch tool in the Toolbar and then select the top planar face of the previously created extrude feature as the sketching plane.

2. Create a circle of diameter 100 mm as the sketch of the extrude cut feature, see Figure 5.65.

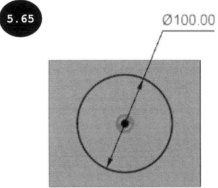

⌀100.00

 In Figure 5.65, the center point of the circle is at the center of the rectangle that is at the origin.

3. After creating the sketch, click on the SOLID tab in the Toolbar for displaying the solid modeling tools.

4. Click on the Extrude tool in the CREATE panel of the SOLID tab or press the E key. The EXTRUDE dialog box appears. Next, change the orientation of the model to isometric.

5.   Click on the closed profile of the sketch, see Figure 5.66. The profile gets selected.

6.   Enter -2 in the **Distance** field of the **EXTRUDE** dialog box as the extrusion distance. The preview of an extrude cut features appears in the graphics area.

7.   Ensure that the **Cut** option is selected in the **Operation** drop-down list of the dialog box for creating an extrude cut feature by removing material from the model.

8.   Click on the **OK** button in the dialog box. The extrude cut feature is created, see Figure 5.67.

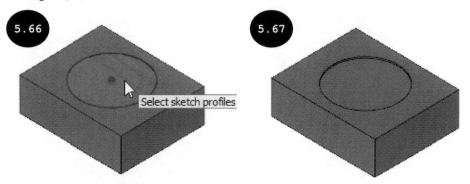

Creating the Second Extrude Cut Feature

1.   Click on the **Create Sketch** tool in the **Toolbar** and then select the top planar face of the previously created extrude cut feature as the sketching plane, see Figure 5.68.

2.   Create two circles as the sketch of the extrude cut feature, see Figure 5.69.

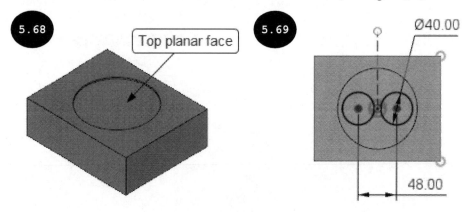

In Figure 5.69, as both the circles are symmetric about the vertical construction line, a symmetric constrain is applied between the center points of the circles and the vertical construction line. Also, an equal constraint is applied on both circles. Moreover, the center points of both the circles are horizontally aligned with the origin.

3.   Press the **E** key. The **EXTRUDE** dialog box appears. Next, change the orientation of the model to isometric, if not changed by default.

4.   Select both the closed profiles of the sketch (circles) one by one in the graphics area and then enter -2 in the **Distance** filed in the **EXTRUDE** dialog box. The preview of an extrude cut feature appears in the graphics area, see Figure 5.70.

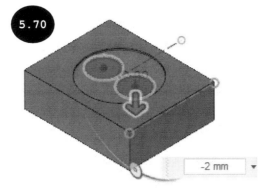

5. Ensure that the **Cut** option is selected in the **Operation** drop-down list of the dialog box for creating an extrude cut feature by removing the material from the model.

6. Click on the **OK** button in the dialog box. The extrude cut feature is created, see Figure 5.71.

Creating the Loft Cut Feature
Now, you need to create the sections of the loft cut feature

1. Click on the **Create Sketch** tool in the **Toolbar** and then select the front planar face of the model as the sketching plane, see Figure 5.72.

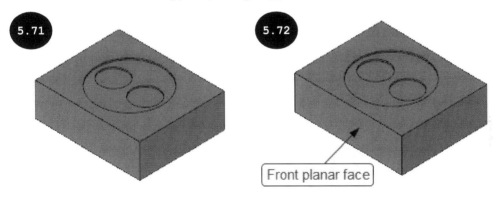

Front planar face

2. Create a section of the loft feature by using the sketching tools, see Figure 5.73.

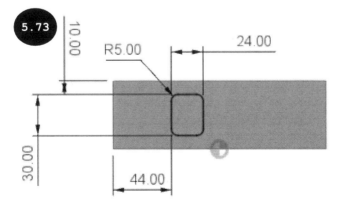

3. Click on the **FINISH SKETCH** tool in the **Toolbar** to exit the Sketching environment. Next, change the orientation of the model to isometric.

Now, you can create the loft feature.

4.   Invoke the **CREATE** drop-down menu in the **SOLID** tab of the **Toolbar** and then click on the **Loft** tool. The **LOFT** dialog box appears.

5.   Select the top left circular face of the model as the first section of the loft feature, see Figure 5.74. Next, select the previously created sketch as the second section of the loft feature. A preview of the loft cut feature appears in the graphics area, see Figure 5.75.

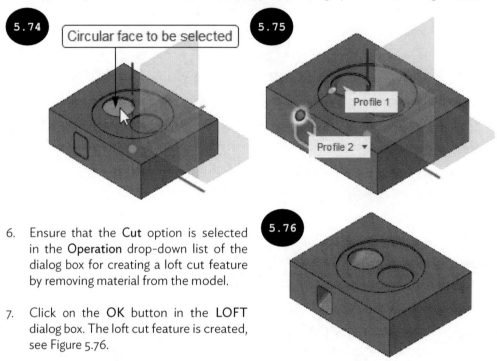

6.   Ensure that the **Cut** option is selected in the **Operation** drop-down list of the dialog box for creating a loft cut feature by removing material from the model.

7.   Click on the **OK** button in the **LOFT** dialog box. The loft cut feature is created, see Figure 5.76.

Creating the Second Loft Cut Feature

1.   Click on the **Create Sketch** tool in the **Toolbar** and then select the front planar face of the model as the sketching plane. Note that you need to rotate the model to select the back planar face of the model by pressing the SHIFT + middle mouse button.

2.   Create a section of the loft feature by using the sketching tools, see Figure 5.77. Next, exit the Sketching environment.

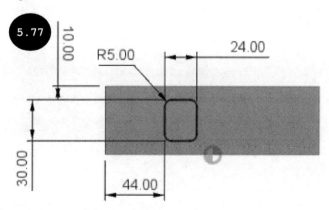

3.   Change the orientation of the model to isometric.

4. Invoke the **CREATE** drop-down menu in the **SOLID** tab of the **Toolbar** and then click on the **Loft** tool. The **LOFT** dialog box appears.

5. Select the top right circular face of the model as the first section of the loft feature, see Figure 5.78. Next, select the previously created sketch as the second section of the loft feature, which is created on the back planar face of the model. A preview of the loft cut feature appears in the graphics area, see Figure 5.79.

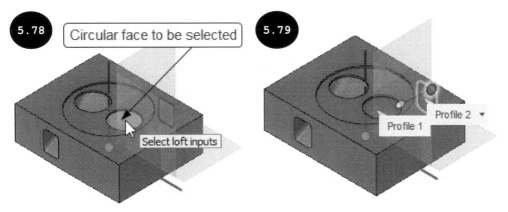

You need to rotate the model by dragging the cursor after pressing and holding the SHIFT + middle mouse button for selecting the back planar face of the model.

6. Ensure that the **Cut** option is selected in the **Operation** drop-down list of the dialog box for creating a loft cut feature by removing material from the model.

7. Click on the **OK** button in the **LOFT** dialog box. The loft cut feature is created, see Figure 5.80.

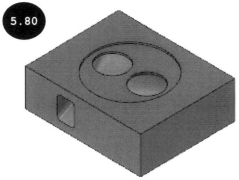

Saving the Model

1. Click on the **Save** tool in the **Application Bar** and then enter **Tutorial 3** in the **Name** field of the **Save** dialog box that appears.

2. Ensure that the location *Autodesk Fusion 360 Tutorials > Chapter 05* is specified in the **Location** field of the dialog box.

3. Click on the **Save** button in the dialog box. The model is saved with the name Tutorial 3 in the specified location (*Autodesk Fusion 360 Tutorials > Chapter 05*).

Exercise 1

Create the model shown in Figure 5.81. The different views and dimensions are given in the same figure. All dimensions are in mm.

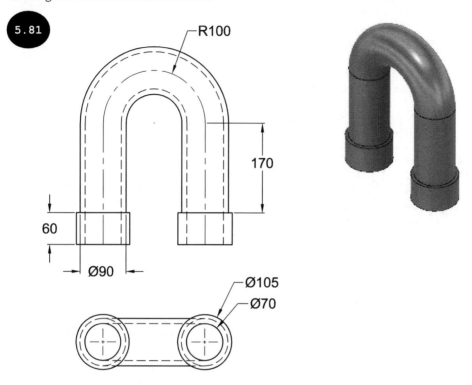

Exercise 2

Create the model shown in Figure 5.82. All dimensions are in mm.

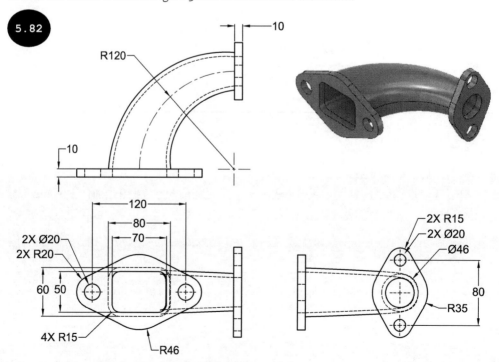

Exercise 3

Create the model shown in Figure 5.83. The different views and dimensions are given in the same figure. All dimensions are in mm.

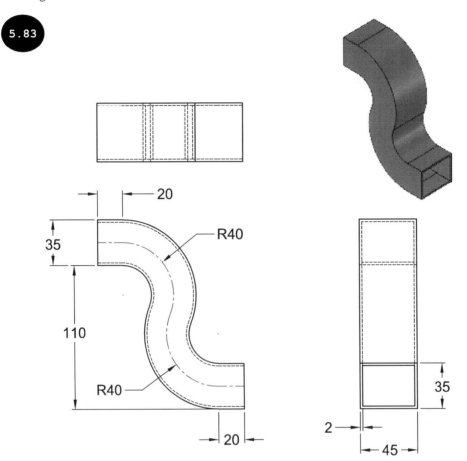

5.83

Summary

This chapter discussed how to create sweep and loft features by using the **Sweep** and **Loft** tools, respectively.

Questions

Answer the following questions:

- A _____ feature is created by sweeping a profile along a path.

- The _____ option is used for creating a sweep feature with a single path.

- On selecting the _____ option in the SWEEP dialog box, the resultant sweep feature is created by keeping the profile of the feature perpendicular to the path.

- A _____ feature is created by lofting two or more than two profiles such that the cross-sectional shape of the feature transits from one profile to another.

- A _____ is used for guiding the cross-sectional shape of a loft feature.

- The _____ option in the **Operation** drop-down list of the **LOFT** dialog box is used for creating a loft cut feature by removing material from the model.

- The _____ button in the **LOFT** dialog box is used for creating a loft feature with profiles and guide rails.

- The _____ button in the **LOFT** dialog box is used for creating a loft feature with profiles and a centerline.

- When the value _____ is specified in the **Distance** field of the **SWEEP** dialog box, the sweep feature is created by sweeping the profile along the total/full length of the path.

- The profile of a sweep feature can be an open or a closed sketch. (True/False)

- The path of a sweep feature can be an open or a closed sketch. (True/False)

- To create a loft feature, two or more than two profiles must be available in the graphics area before invoking the **Loft** tool. (True/False)

- You cannot select multiple guide rails for controlling the shape of the loft feature. (True/False)

CHAPTER

6

Creating Holes, Threads, and Shell Features

In this chapter, you will learn the following:

- Introduction to Holes
- Creating Holes
- Introduction to Threads
- Creating Threads
- Introduction to Shell Features
- Creating a Shell Feature

Introduction to Holes

In Autodesk Fusion 360, you can create Simple, Counterbore, and Countersink hole types by using the **Hole** tool, see Figures 6.1 through 6.3.

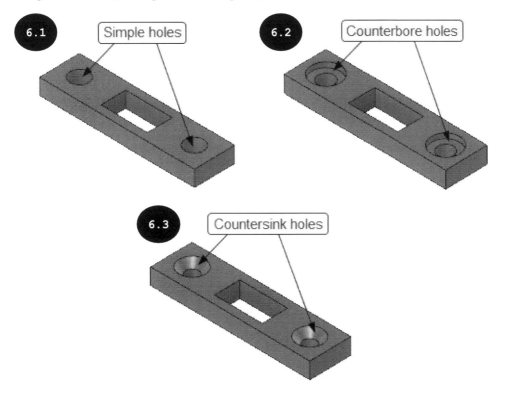

6.1 Simple holes

6.2 Counterbore holes

6.3 Countersink holes

Tutorial 1: Creating Holes

Create a model shown in Figure 6.4. The different views and dimensions are given in the same figure. All dimensions are in mm.

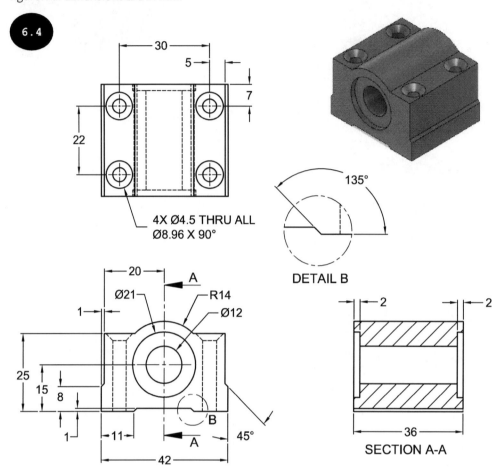

6 . 4

4X Ø4.5 THRU ALL
Ø8.96 X 90°

135°

DETAIL B

SECTION A-A

The following sequence summarizes the tutorial outline:

*   Starting Fusion 360 and a New Design File
*   Creating the Extrude Feature
*   Creating the Extrude Cut Feature
*   Mirroring a Feature
*   Creating a Hole
*   Creating the Rectangular Pattern
*   Saving the Model

Starting Fusion 360 and a New Design File

1.   Start Fusion 360 by double-clicking on the **Autodesk Fusion 360** icon on your desktop, if not started already.

2.   Invoke the **File** drop-down menu in the **Application Bar** and then click on the **New Design** tool, see Figure 6.5. A new design file is started with the default name "**Untitled**".

3.   Make sure that millimeter (mm) unit is defined as the unit of the current design file.

Creating the Extrude Feature

1. Click on the **Create Sketch** tool in the **CREATE** panel of the **Toolbar**, see Figure 6.6. The three default planes appear in the graphics area.

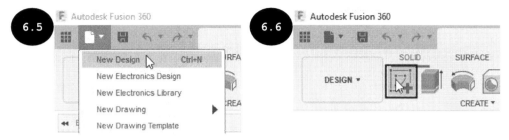

2. Select the Front plane as the sketching plane. The Sketching environment gets invoked.

3. Create a sketch of the extrude feature, see Figure 6.7.

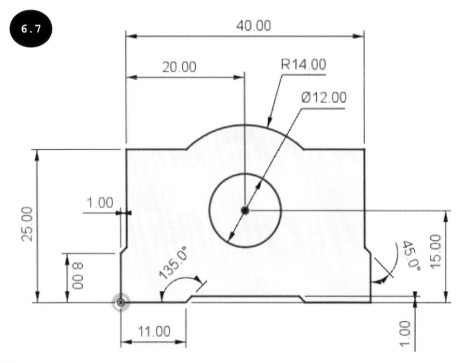

In addition to applying dimensions, you need to apply required constraints to make the sketch fully defined.

4. After creating the sketch, click on the **SOLID** tab in the **Toolbar** for displaying the solid modeling tools, see Figure 6.8.

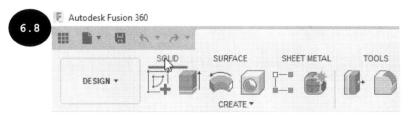

5.   Click on the **Extrude** tool in the **CREATE** panel of the **SOLID** tab or press the E key. The **EXTRUDE** dialog box appears.

6.   Change the orientation of the sketch to isometric by clicking on the Home icon of the ViewCube, if not changed by default.

7.   Click to select the closed profile of the sketch, see Figure 6.9. The profile gets selected.

8.   Enter **36** in the **Distance** field of the **EXTRUDE** dialog box as the extrusion distance. The preview of an extrude feature appears in the graphics area, see Figure 6.10.

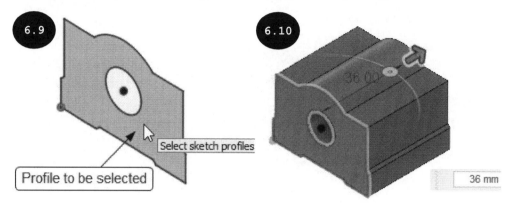

You can also drag the arrow that appears in the graphics area to set the extrusion distance in the graphics area, dynamically.

9.   Select the **Symmetric** option in the **Direction** drop-down list of the dialog box for extruding the sketch profile symmetrically about the sketching plane. The **Half Length** ⊡ and **Whole Length** ⊡ buttons appear below the **Direction** drop-down list in the dialog box.

10. Select the **Whole Length** button ⊡ in the dialog box. The preview of the extrude feature gets modified such that 18 mm material is added on each side of the sketching plane and maintains the total length of the extrusion as 36 mm, see Figure 6.11.

Adding material symmetrically keeps the sketching plane at the middle of the feature, so that it can be used later as a mirroring plane for mirroring a feature about it.

11. Accept the remaining default specified options in the dialog box and then click on the **OK** button. The extrude feature is created, see Figure 6.12.

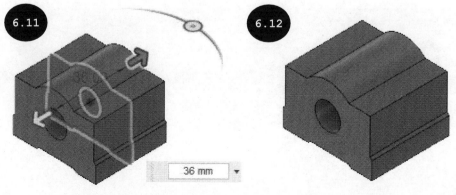

Creating the Extrude Cut Feature

1. Create an extrude cut feature on the front planar face of the model, see Figure 6.13. Refer to Figure 6.4 for dimensions.

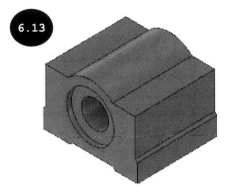

Mirroring a Feature

Now, you need to mirror the previously created extrude cut feature about the Front plane.

1. Invoke the **CREATE** drop-down menu in the **SOLID** tab of the **Toolbar** and then click on the **Mirror** tool. The **MIRROR** dialog box appears, see Figure 6.14.

2. Select the **Features** option in the **Pattern Type** drop-down list of the **MIRROR** dialog box for selecting features to be mirrored.

3. Select the previously created extrude cut feature in the graphics area or in the **Timeline** as the feature to be mirrored.

4. Click on the **Mirror Plane** selection option in the **MIRROR** dialog box for selecting a mirroring plane.

5. Select the Front plane as the mirroring plane in the graphics area, see Figure 6.15. The preview of a mirror feature appears in the graphics area, see Figure 6.16.

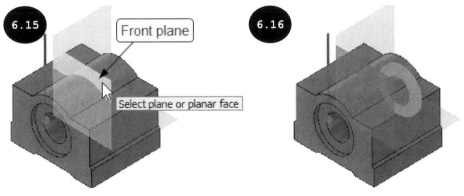

6. Click on the **OK** button in the dialog box. The mirror feature is created, see Figure 6.17. In this figure, the visual style of the model has been changed to "wireframe with hidden edges" visual style for viewing the mirror feature that is created at the back of the model. In this visual style, you can view the hidden edges of the model as dotted lines.

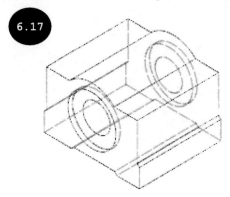

In Autodesk Fusion 360, you can change the visual or display style of a model to shaded, shaded with hidden edges, shaded with visible edges, wireframe, wireframe with hidden edges, or wireframe with visible edges. To do so, click on the Display Settings > Visual Style in the Navigation Bar, see Figure 6.18. A cascading menu appears. In this cascading menu, select the required visual style to be applied for the model.

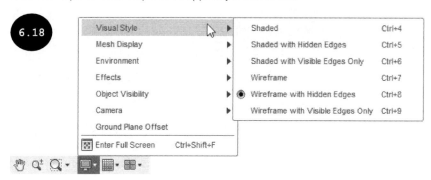

Creating a Hole

Now, you need a hole on the top planar face of the model.

1. Click on the **Hole** tool in the **CREATE** panel of the **Toolbar**, see Figure 6.19. The **HOLE** dialog box appears, Figure 6.20. You can also press the **H** key to invoke the **HOLE** dialog box.

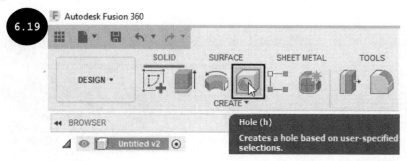

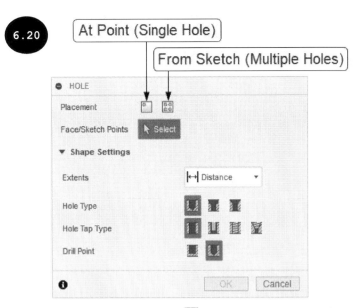

2. Click on the **At Point (Single Hole)** button ⬚ in the **Placement** area of the dialog box for creating a single hole on an existing face of the model.

> 🔘 *The **At Point (Single Hole)** button ⬚ in the **Placement** area of the HOLE dialog box is used for creating a single hole on the existing face of the model, whereas the **From Sketch (Multiple Holes)** button ⬚ is used for creating multiple holes by using the sketch points of a sketch. In the latter case, the holes are created by propagating to each sketch point of the sketch.*

3. Move the cursor over the top planar face of the model in the graphics area. The face gets highlighted and its snap points appear, see Figure 6.21.

4. Click anywhere on the highlighted face of the model or a snap point to define the placement of the hole. The preview of a hole appears on the specified location on the face with default parameters, see Figure 6.22. Also, additional options for creating the hole appear in the **HOLE** dialog box, see Figure 6.23.

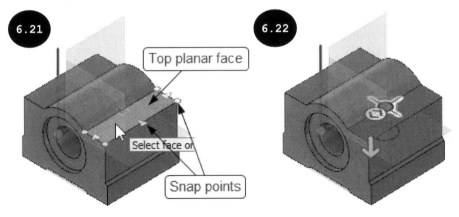

> 🔘 *The availability of additional options in the HOLE dialog box depends up on the type of hole selected in the **Hole Type** area of the dialog box. In Figure 6.23, the **Simple** hole is selected in the **Hole Type** area of the dialog box.*

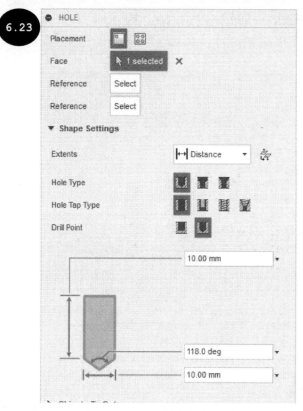

After defining the placement face, you need to define the position of the hole on the selected face of the model.

5. Move the cursor over the top right linear edge of the model, see Figure 6.24 and then click to select it. The **Distance** field appears in the dialog box as well as in the graphics area.

6. Enter **5 mm** in this **Distance** field as the distance between the center of the hole and the selected edge of the model. The position of the hole with respect to the top right edge of the model is defined.

7. Move the cursor over the top front edge of the model, see Figure 6.25 and then click on it when it gets highlighted. Another **Distance** filed appears in the dialog box as well as in the graphics area.

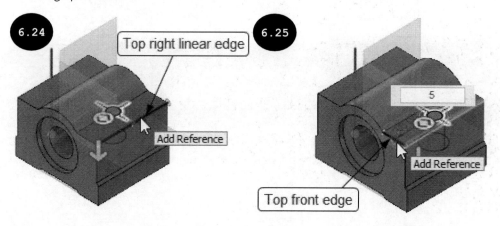

8. Enter **7 mm** in this **Distance** field as the distance between the center of the hole and the selected top front edge of the model. The position of the hole with respective to the selected edges of the model has been defined.

 You can also define the position of the hole by dragging the center point of the hole to the required location on the selected placement face of the model.

After defining the placement face and the position of the hole, you need to select the type of hole to be created.

9. Click to select the **Countersink** button ▮ in the **Hole Type** area of the dialog box as the hole type to be created.

*You can create the required type of hole (Simple, Counterbore, or Countersink) by selecting the respective button in the **Hole Type** area of the dialog box.*

After defining the hole type, you need to define the hole tap type to be created.

10. Click to select the **Simple** button ▮ in the **Hole Tap Type** area of the dialog box as the hole tap type to be created.

*The **Hole Tap Type** area of the dialog box is used for selecting the hole tap type (Simple, Clearance, Tapped or Taper Tapped) to be created.*

11. Click to select the **Flat** button ▮ in the **Drill Point** area of the dialog box for creating the hole with a flat end.

*You can create a hole with either a flat end or an angle end by selecting the respective button (**Flat** ▮ or **Angle** ▮) in the **Drill Point** area of the dialog box.*

12. Select the **All** option in the **Extents** drop-down list in the dialog box for creating the hole throughout the entire model.

13. Specify **8.96** mm as the countersink diameter, **90** degrees as the countersink angle, **4.5** mm as the diameter of the hole in the respective fields of the dialog box, see Figure 6.26.

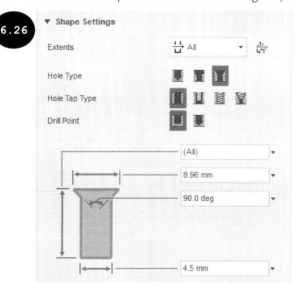
6.26

14. Click on the **OK** button in the **HOLE** dialog box. A countersink hole gets created as per the specified parameters, see Figure 6.27.

6.27

Creating the Rectangular Pattern

Now, you need to create a rectangular pattern of the previously created hole feature for creating its remaining instances.

1. Click on the **Rectangular Pattern** tool in the **CREATE** panel in the **Toolbar**, see Figure 6.28. The **RECTANGULAR PATTERN** dialog box appears, see Figure 6.29. Alternatively, invoke the **CREATE** drop-down menu in the **SOLID** tab and then click on **Pattern > Rectangular Pattern** for invoking the **RECTANGULAR PATTERN** dialog box.

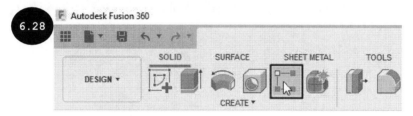

6.28

6.29

2. Select the **Features** option in the **Pattern Type** drop-down list of the RECTANGULAR PATTERN dialog box for selecting a feature to be patterned.

3. Select the previously created countersink hole as the feature to be patterned in the graphics area or in the **Timeline**.

4. Click on the **Directions** selection option in the dialog box for defining the first and second pattern directions for creating a rectangular pattern.

5. Click on the top right linear edge of the model as the first pattern direction, see Figure 6.30. The first pattern direction gets defined. Also, the second pattern direction is defined perpendicular to the first selected direction, automatically.

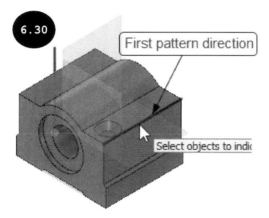

First pattern direction

Select objects to indi

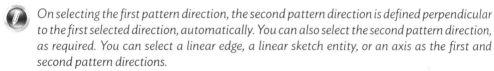

On selecting the first pattern direction, the second pattern direction is defined perpendicular to the first selected direction, automatically. You can also select the second pattern direction, as required. You can select a linear edge, a linear sketch entity, or an axis as the first and second pattern directions.

6. Select the **Spacing** option in the **Distance Type** drop-down list of the dialog box.

*The **Spacing** option of the **Distance Type** drop-down list is used for specifying the spacing between two consecutive pattern instances in the **Distance** field of the dialog box. The **Extent** option is used for specifying the spacing between the first and last pattern instances (total pattern distance) in the **Distance** field of the dialog box.*

7. Enter **2** in the **Quantity** field of the dialog box as the total number of pattern instances to be created in the first pattern direction.

*The number of pattern instances specified in the **Quantity** field is counted along with the parent or original instance. For example, if 2 is specified in the **Quantity** field, then 2 pattern instances will be created including the parent instance in the respective pattern direction.*

8. Enter **22** in the **Distance** field of the dialog box as the distance between two pattern instances in the first pattern direction.

9. Enter **2** in the second **Quantity** field of the dialog box as the total number of pattern instances to be created in second pattern direction.

10. Enter -30 in the second **Distance** field of the dialog box as the distance between two pattern instances in the second pattern direction. The preview of the rectangular pattern appears similar to the one shown in Figure 6.31.

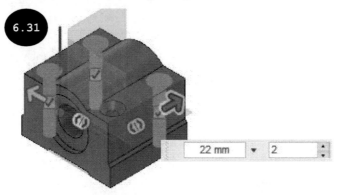

> *The negative distance value is used to reverse the direction of pattern. You can also drag the arrows that appear in the preview of the pattern to increase or decrease the spacing between the pattern instances.*

11. Accept the remaining default options in the dialog box and then click on the **OK** button. The rectangular pattern gets created, see Figure 6.32.

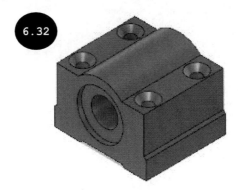

Saving the Model

1. Click on the **Save** tool in the **Application Bar** or press CTRL + S and then enter **Tutorial 1** in the **Name** field of the **Save** dialog box that appears.

2. Click on the down arrow next to the **Location** field in the dialog box. The expanded **Save** dialog box appears with the **PROJECT** area on its left.

3. Make sure that the **Autodesk Fusion 360 Tutorials** project is selected in the **PROJECT** area. All the folders created in the project appear on the right panel of the dialog box.

4. Create a folder with the name **Chapter 06** inside the **Autodesk Fusion 360 Tutorials** project by using the **New Folder** button of the expanded **Save** dialog box.

5. Double-click on the newly created **Chapter 06** folder and then click on the **Save** button. The model gets saved with the name **Tutorial 1** at the specified location (*Autodesk Fusion 360 Tutorials > Chapter 06*) in the **Data Panel**.

Introduction to Threads

You can create internal or external threads on cylindrical faces of a model by using the **Thread** tool, see Figure 6.33. In Autodesk Fusion 360, the threads can be cosmetic threads or modeled threads. A cosmetic thread is not a real thread and is created by applying an appearance of the thread on the selected face, whereas the modeled thread is the real thread and is created by removing material from the selected face of the model. Figure 6.33 shows cosmetic threads and Figure 6.34 shows the modeled thread.

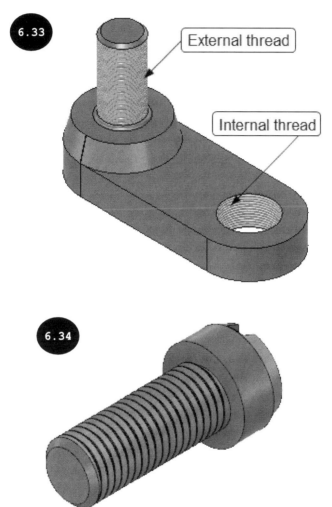

 It is recommended to add cosmetic threads to holes, fasteners, or cylindrical features of a model, as it helps in reducing the complexity of the model and improves the overall performance of the system.

Tutorial 2: Creating Threads

Create a model shown in Figure 6.35. In this model, you need to create modeled threads by removing the material from the model. All dimensions are in mm.

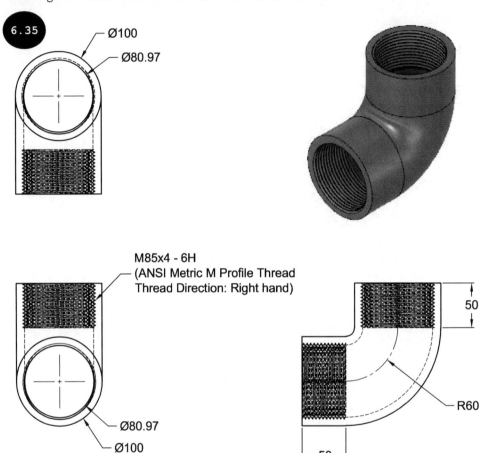

The following sequence summarizes the tutorial outline:

• Starting a New Design File and Specifying Units
• Creating the Sweep Feature
• Creating Threads
• Saving the Model

Starting a New Design File and Specifying Units

1. Launch Autodesk Fusion 360, if not started already.

2. Start a new design file and ensure that the millimeter (mm) unit is defined as the unit of the currently design file.

Creating the Sweep Feature

To create a sweep feature, you need to first create a path and a profile.

1. Click on the **Create Sketch** tool in the **CREATE** panel of the **Toolbar**, see Figure 6.36. The three default planes appear in the graphics area.

2. Select the Right plane as the sketching plane for creating the path of the sweep feature.

3. Create the path of the sweep feature by using the sketching tools, see Figure 6.37.

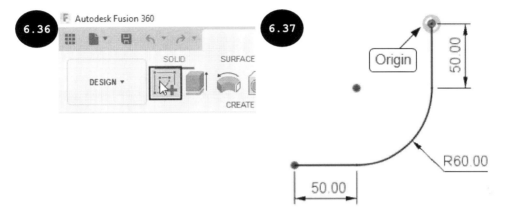

4. Click on the **FINISH SKETCH** tool in the **SKETCH** contextual tab to finish the creation of sketch. Next, change the orientation of the sketch to isometric, if not changed by default.

    After creating the path, you need to create a profile of the sweep feature.

5. Click on the **Create Sketch** tool in the **Toolbar** and then select the Top plane as the sketching plane for creating the profile.

6. Create the profile (two circles) of the sweep feature, see Figure 6.38.

7. Click on the **FINISH SKETCH** tool in the **SKETCH** contextual tab to finish the creation of sketch and to exit the Sketching environment.

8. Change the orientation of the sketch to isometric, see Figure 6.39, if not changed by default.

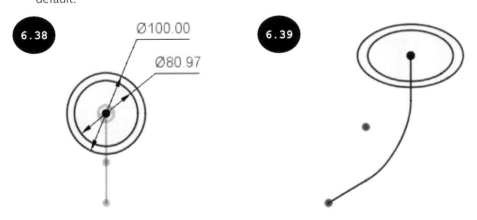

After creating the path and profile, you can create the sweep feature.

9. Invoke the **CREATE** drop-down menu in the **SOLID** tab and then click on the **Sweep** tool, see Figure 6.40. The **SWEEP** dialog box appears, see Figure 6.41.

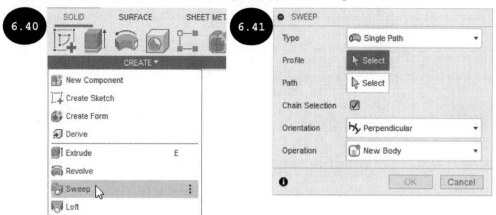

10. Ensure that the **Single Path** option is selected in the **Type** drop-down list of the **SWEEP** dialog box for creating a sweep feature with a single path.

11. Select the profile of the sweep feature in the graphics area, see Figure 6.42.

12. Click on the **Path** selection option in the **SWEEP** dialog box and then select the path of the sweep feature, see Figure 6.42. A preview of the sweep feature appears in the graphics area, see Figure 6.43. Ensure that the **Chain Selection** check box is selected in the dialog box so that all the contiguous entities of the path get selected.

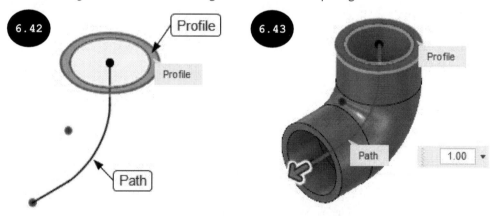

13. Ensure that the distance value 1 is specified in the **Distance** field to sweep the profile along the total length of the path.

14. Ensure that the taper angle and twist angle values are specified as 0 degrees in the respective fields of the dialog box for avoiding any tapering and twisting in the resultant sweep feature.

15. Ensure that the **Perpendicular** option is selected in the **Orientation** drop-down list.

16. Accept the remaining default selected options and then click on the **OK** button in the dialog box. The sweep feature is created, see Figure 6.44.

6.44

Creating Threads

Now, you need to create threads on the model.

1. Invoke the **CREATE** drop-down menu in the **SOLID** tab of the **Toolbar** and then click on the **Thread** tool, see Figure 6.45. The **THREAD** dialog box appears, see Figure 6.46.

6.45   6.46

2. Select the inner circular face of the model for creating an internal thread, see Figure 6.47. A preview of the thread with default specifications appears.

6.47

Circular face selected

You can select internal or external cylindrical/circular faces to create internal or external threads, respectively.

3. Select the **ANSI Metric M Profile** option in the **Thread Type** drop-down list of the dialog box.

4. Select **85.0 mm** as the thread size in the **Size** drop-down list of the dialog box.

5. Select the **M85x4** in the **Designation** drop-down list of the dialog box.

 Where, 85 corresponds to the thread diameter and 4 corresponds to the thread pitch.

6. Select **6H** as the thread class in the **Class** drop-down list of the dialog box.

7. Ensure that the **Right hand** option is selected in the **Direction** drop-down list of the dialog box as the direction of the thread to be created.

8. Select the **Modeled** check box in the **THREAD** dialog box for creating the modeled thread by removing the material from the model. The preview of a thread appears on the selected face of the model as shown in the Figure 6.48.

*If the **Modeled** check box is cleared, a cosmetic thread will be created and if the **Modeled** check box is selected, a modeled thread will be created on the selected face of the model. A modeled thread is an actual thread, created by removing the material from the model, whereas a cosmetic thread is created by only applying an appearance of the thread on the selected face of the model. As discussed earlier, it is recommended to add cosmetic threads, as it helps in reducing the complexity of the model and improves the overall performance of the system. However, as mentioned in the tutorial description, you will create a modeled thread in this tutorial.*

9. Ensure that the **Full Length** check box is selected in the **THREAD** dialog box for creating the thread on the entire length of the selected face of the model.

 *If the **Full Length** check box is cleared, the **Offset** and **Length** fields appear in the dialog box. The **Offset** field is used for creating the thread at an offset distance from the starting point of the selected face. The **Length** field is used for specifying the length of the thread.*

10. Press the CTRL key and then select another inner circular face of the model for creating a thread of similar specifications, see Figure 6.49.

6.48

6.49

Face to be selected

You can select multiple cylindrical/circular faces of a model by pressing the CTRL key for creating threads with the same specifications.

11. Click on the **OK** button in the **THREAD** dialog box. The threads get created. Figure 6.50 shows the final model.

Saving the Model

6.50

1. Click on the **Save** tool in the **Application Bar** and then enter **Tutorial 2** in the **Name** field of the **Save** dialog box that appears.

2. Make sure that the location *Autodesk Fusion 360 Tutorials > Chapter 06* is specified in the **Location** field of the dialog box.

3. Click on the **Save** button in the dialog box. The model is saved with the name Tutorial 2 in the specified location (*Autodesk Fusion 360 Tutorials > Chapter 06*).

Introduction to Shell Features

A shell feature is a thin walled feature, which is created by making a model hollow from inside or by removing the faces of the model, see Figures 6.51 and 6.52. In Figure 6.51, the shell feature is created by making the model hollow, whereas in Figure 6.52, the shell feature is created by removing the top planar face of the model.

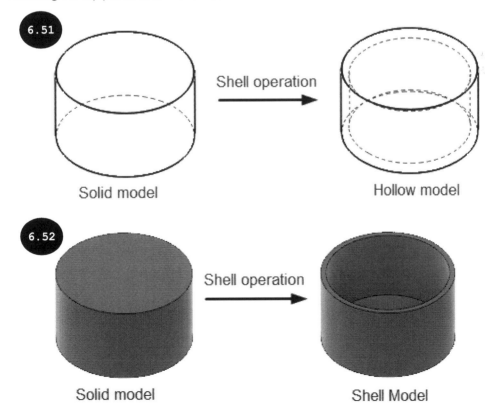

6.51

Shell operation

Solid model   Hollow model

6.52

Shell operation

Solid model   Shell Model

In Figure 6.51, the visual style of the model has been changed to "wireframe with hidden edges" so that the hidden edges of the hollow model can be visualized.

Tutorial 3: Creating a Shell Feature

Create the model shown in Figure 6.53. In this model, you need to create modeled threads by removing the material from the model. All dimensions are in mm.

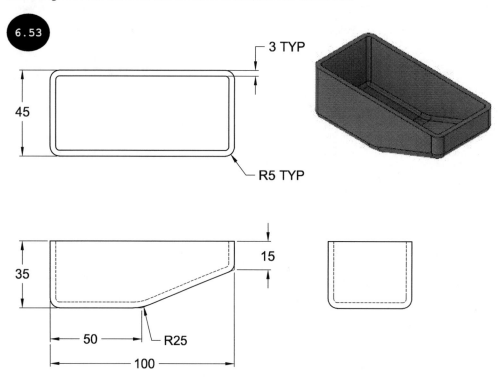

The following sequence summarizes the tutorial outline:

*   Starting a New Design File and Specifying Units
*   Creating the Extrude Feature
*   Creating Fillets
*   Creating the Shell Feature
*   Saving the Model

Starting a New Design File and Specifying Units

1. Launch Autodesk Fusion 360, if not started already.

2. Start a new design file and ensure that millimeter (mm) unit is defined as the unit of the current design file.

Creating the Extrude Feature

1. Click on the **Create Sketch** tool in the **CREATE** panel of the **Toolbar**, see Figure 6.54. The three default planes appear in the graphics area.

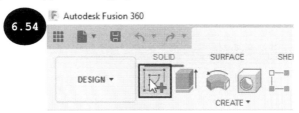

6.54

2. Select the Front plane as the sketching plane and then create the sketch of the extrude feature by using the sketching tools, see Figure 6.55.

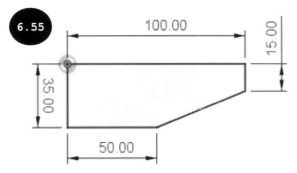

6.55

3. Click on the **SOLID** tab in the **Toolbar** and then click on the **Extrude** tool or press the **E** key. The **EXTRUDE** dialog box appears. Also, the closed profile of the sketch gets selected automatically for extrusion.

4. Change the orientation of the sketch to isometric by clicking on the **Home** icon in the ViewCube.

5. Enter **45** in the **Distance** field of the **EXTRUDE** dialog box as the extrusion distance. The preview of an extrude features appears in the graphics area, see Figure 6.56.

6. Select the **Symmetric** option in the **Direction** drop-down list of the dialog box for extruding the sketch profile symmetrically about the sketching plane.

7. Select the **Whole Length** button in the **Measurement** area of the dialog box. The preview of the extrude feature gets modified such that **22.5 mm** material is added on each side of the sketching plane, maintaining the total length of extrusion as 45 mm, see Figure 6.57.

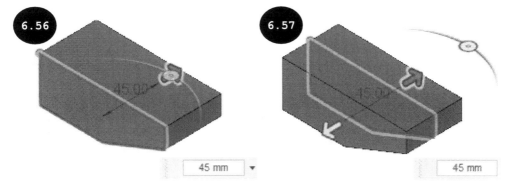

6.56
6.57

8. Accept the remaining default specified options in the dialog box and then click on the OK button. The extrude feature is created, see Figure 6.58.

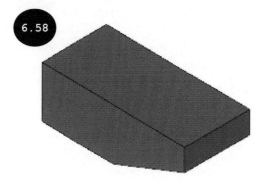

Creating Fillets

Now, you need to create fillets to remove the sharp edges of the model. A fillet is a curved face of a constant or a variable radii and is used for removing sharp edges of a model that may cause injury while handling the model.

1. Click on the **Fillet** tool in the **MODIFY** panel of the **SOLID** tab, see Figure 6.59 or press the **F** key. The **FILLET** dialog box appears, see Figure 6.60.

2. Ensure that the **Fillet** option is selected in the Type drop-down list of the dialog box.

> The **Fillet** option is used for creating a fillet of constant radius, variable radius, or by specifying chord length.

3. Select the **Constant Radius** option in the **Radius Type** drop-down list of the dialog box for creating a constant radius fillet.

By selecting the required option (Constant Radius, Variable Radius, or Chord Length) in the Radius Type drop-down list, you can create constant radius fillets, variable radius fillets, or chord length fillets, respectively.

4. Select the **Constant Radius** option in the **Radius Type** drop-down list of the dialog box for creating a constant radius fillet.

5. Rotate the model such that the bottom edges of the model can be viewed, refer to Figure 6.61.

 You can rotate the model by dragging the cursor after pressing and holding the SHIFT + middle mouse button. Alternatively, click on the Orbit tool ⊕ in the Navigation Bar, which is available in the lower middle section of the screen and then drag the cursor.

6. Select the edge of the model to be filleted, see Figure 6.61. The edge gets selected and an arrow appears along the edge selected. Also, the additional options appear in the dialog box, see Figure 6.62.

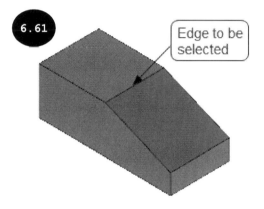

7. Enter **25 mm** in the **Radius** field of the **FILLET** dialog box as the radius of the fillet. The preview of a fillet appears in the graphics area. You can also drag the arrow that appears along the selected edge of the model in the graphics area to set the fillet radius.

You can select multiple edges of a model as a single set by pressing the CTRL key for creating a fillet with same radius.

8. Ensure that the **Tangent (G1)** option is selected in the **Continuity** drop-down list of the dialog box for applying the G1 tangent continuity to the fillet.

*The options in the **Continuity** drop-down list are used for applying the type of continuity: G1 tangent continuity or G2 curvature continuity to the fillet, respectively.*

9. Click on the **Add new selection** button in the **FILLET** dialog box, refer to Figure 6.62 for creating another set of fillets with different radius values.

10. Select two edges of the model to be filleted as another set of fillets, see Figure 6.63. The edges get selected and an arrow appears on the last selected edge of the model.

11. Enter **5 mm** in the **Radius** field of the second set of fillets added in the **FILLET** dialog box. The preview of fillets appears in the graphics area, see Figure 6.64.

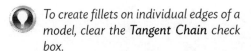

Edges selected

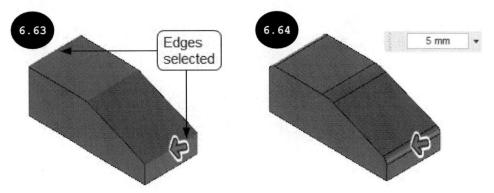

6.64 5 mm

12. Accept the remaining options in the **FILLET** dialog box and then click on the **OK** button. The fillets on the selected edges gets created, see Figure 6.65.

13. Press the **F** key to invoke the **FILLET** dialog box again.

14. Ensure that the **Tangent Chain** check box is selected in the dialog box for including tangentially connected edges of a selected edge for creating a fillet.

*To create fillets on individual edges of a model, clear the **Tangent Chain** check box.*

15. Ensure that the **Constant Radius** option is selected in the **Radius Type** drop-down list for creating a constant radius fillet.

16. Select side edges of the model to be filleted, see Figure 6.66. The edges gets selected.

17. Enter **5 mm** in the **Radius** field of the **FILLET** dialog box as the radius of the fillet. The preview of a fillet appears in the graphics area, see Figure 6.67.

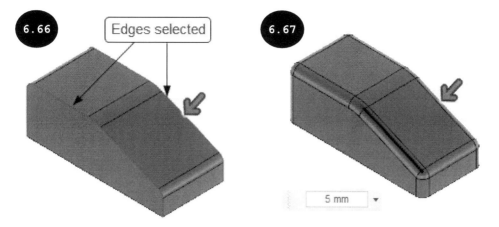

18. Accept the remaining options in the **FILLET** dialog box and then click on the **OK** button. The fillets get created on the selected edges.

19. Click on the **Home** icon in the ViewCube to change the orientation of the model to isometric, see Figure 6.68.

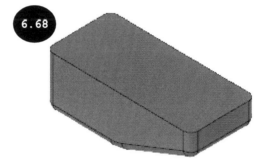

Creating the Shell Feature

Now, you need to create a shell feature of uniform thickness 3 mm and remove the top planar face of the model.

1. Click on the **Shell** tool in the **MODIFY** panel of the **SOLID** tab, see Figure 6.69. The **SHELL** dialog box appears.

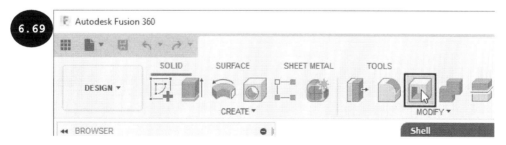

2. Select the top planar face of the model as a face to be removed from the model. The face gets selected, see Figure 6.70. Also, the **Inside Thickness** field appears in the **SHELL** dialog box, see Figure 6.71, since the **Inside** option is selected in the **Direction** drop-down list of the dialog box. The **Inside Thickness** field of the dialog box is used for specifying the wall thickness of the shell feature in the inward direction of the model.

If the *Outside* option is selected in the *Direction* drop-down list, then the *Outside Thickness* field appears for specifying wall thickness of the shell feature outward to the model. If the *Both* option is selected, then the *Inside Thickness* as well as *Outside Thickness* fields appear in the dialog box for specifying wall thickness of the shell feature inward and outward to the model, respectively.

When you invoke the SHELL dialog box, the *Faces/Body* selection option is activated, by default. As a result, you can select faces or a body to create a shell feature of specified wall thickness. You can specify the wall thickness in the *Inside Thickness/Outside Thickness* field of the dialog box. Note that on selecting a body, the closed hollow shell model of specified wall thickness is created. You can select a body in the graphics area or in the *Bodies* node of the *BROWSER*.

3. Ensure that the **Inside** option is selected in the **SHELL** dialog box.

4. Enter **3 mm** in the **Inside Thickness** field of the dialog box as the wall thickness inward to the model. The preview of the model appears in the graphics area, see Figure 6.72.

5. Click on the **OK** button in the **SHELL** dialog box. The shell feature with a uniform wall thickness of 3 mm is created and the selected face of the model gets removed, see Figure 6.73.

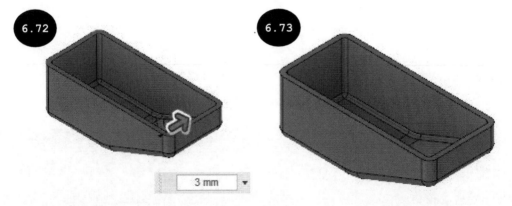

Saving the Model

1. Save the model with the name **Tutorial 3** in the Chapter 06 folder of the Autodesk Fusion 360 Tutorials project by using the **Save** tool.

Exercise 1

Create the model shown in Figure 6.74. In this model, you need to create cosmetic threads. All dimensions are in mm.

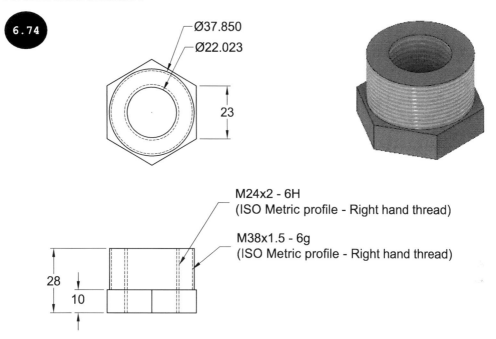

6.74

Ø37.850
Ø22.023
23

M24x2 - 6H
(ISO Metric profile - Right hand thread)

M38x1.5 - 6g
(ISO Metric profile - Right hand thread)

28
10

Exercise 2

Create the model shown in Figure 6.75. All dimensions are in mm.

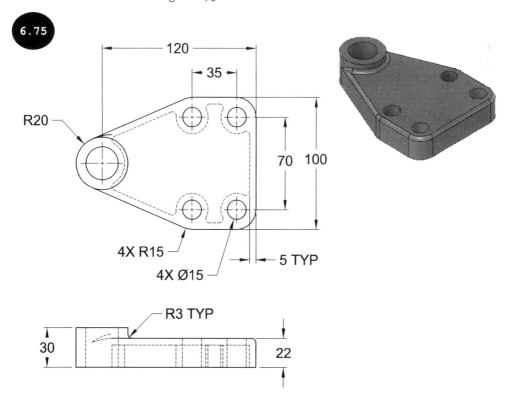

6.75

120
35
R20
70 100
4X R15
5 TYP
4X Ø15

R3 TYP
30
22

Summary

This chapter discussed how to create holes, threads, and shell features. It also described the methods for creating rectangular patterns and fillets.

Questions

Answer the following questions:

- The _____ tool is used for creating Simple, Counterbore, and Countersink hole types.

- Press the _____ key to invoke the **HOLE** dialog box.

- The _____ button in the **HOLE** dialog box is used for creating a single hole on an existing face of the model.

- The **Hole Tap Type** area in the **HOLE** dialog box is used for selecting the _____, _____, _____, or _____ hole tap type to be created.

- The _____ tool is used for creating a rectangular pattern.

- In the _____ pattern, the second pattern direction gets defined perpendicular to the first selected direction, automatically.

- The _____ tool is used for creating cosmetic and modeled threads.

- The _____ thread is the real thread and is created by removing material from the selected face of the model.

- A _____ feature is a thin walled feature, which is created by making a model hollow from inside or by removing the faces of the model.

- The _____ tool is used for creating fillets by removing sharp edges of the model.

- You cannot create a shell feature by removing faces of a model. (True/False)

- You cannot create a hole with an angle end. (True/False)

- A cosmetic thread is created by applying an appearance of the thread on the selected face of the model. (True/False)

- You can select multiple cylindrical/circular faces of a model by pressing the CTRL key for creating threads with same specifications. (True/False)

Creating 3D Sketches and Helical Coils

In this chapter, you will learn the following:

- Introduction to 3D Sketches
- Creating a 3D Sketch
- Introduction to Helical Coils
- Creating a Helical Coil

Introduction to 3D Sketches

In Autodesk Fusion 360, you can create 3D sketches by using the sketching tools such as **Line** and **Spline**. 3D sketches are used as a 3D path and a guide rail for creating features like sweep and loft. Figure 7.1 shows a 3D sketch created by using the **Line** tool and the fillets are created at the corners of the sketch. Figure 7.2 shows a sweep feature created by sweeping a profile along the 3D sketch (path).

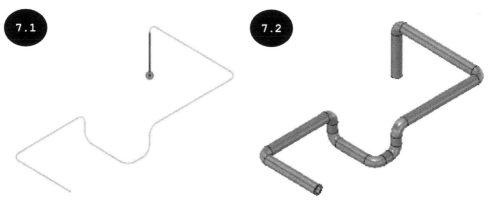

In Autodesk Fusion 360, there is no separate workspace or environment for creating 3D sketches. You can create a 2D sketch as well as a 3D sketch, within the same Sketching environment. To create a 3D sketch in the Sketching environment, you need to select the **3D Sketch** check box in the **SKETCH PALETTE** dialog box that appears in the Sketching environment.

Tutorial 1: Creating a 3D Sketch

Create the model shown in Figure 7.3. The different views and dimensions are given in the same figure. All dimensions are in mm.

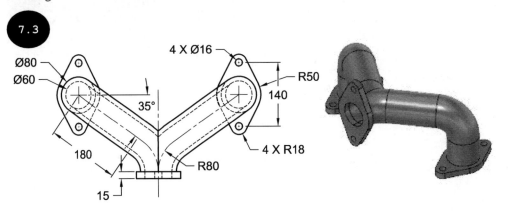

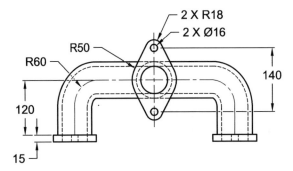

The following sequence summarizes the tutorial outline:

- Starting Fusion 360 and a New Design File
- Creating the 3D Sketch
- Creating the Pipe Feature
- Creating the Mirror Feature
- Combining Bodies
- Creating the Shell Feature
- Creating the Extrude Feature
- Creating the Second Mirror Feature
- Creating the Second Extrude Feature
- Saving the Model

Starting Fusion 360 and a New Design File

1.   Start Fusion 360 by double-clicking on the **Autodesk Fusion 360** icon on your desktop, if not started already. The startup user interface of Fusion 360 appears.

2.   Press the CTRL + N key. A new design file gets started with the default name.

3.   Make sure that millimeter (mm) unit is defined as the unit of the active design file.

Creating the 3D Sketch

Now, you need to create a 3D sketch as the path of the sweep feature.

1. Click on the **Create Sketch** tool in the **Toolbar** and then click on the Top plane as the sketching plane. The Sketching environment gets invoked and the **SKETCH** contextual tab appears in the **Toolbar**.

2. Change the orientation to isometric by clicking on the **Home** icon in the ViewCube.

3. Select the **3D Sketch** check box in the **SKETCH PALETTE** dialog box for creating a 3D sketch, see Figure 7.4.

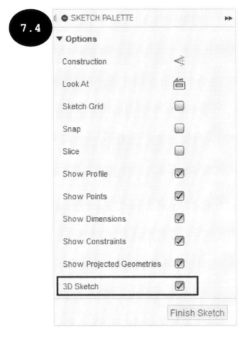

7.4

If the 3D Sketch check box is cleared in the SKETCH PALETTE dialog box, you can create a 2D sketch in the Sketching environment, whereas if this check box is selected, you can create a 3D sketch by using the sketching tools such as Line and Spline.

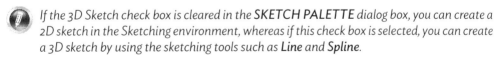

4. Click on the **Line** tool in the **CREATE** panel of the **SKETCH** contextual tab or press the **L** key. The **Line** tool gets activated and the **3D Sketch Manipulator** appears at the origin (0,0) in the graphics area, see Figure 7.5. Also, the Top plane of the **3D Sketch Manipulator** is selected as the sketching plane, by default.

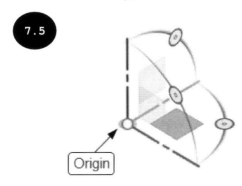

7.5

Origin

You can switch from one sketching plane to another for creating a 3D sketch by clicking on the required plane (Front, Top, or Right) in the 3D Sketch Manipulator.

5.   Move the cursor toward the origin (0,0) and then click to specify the start point of the line when the cursor snaps to it.

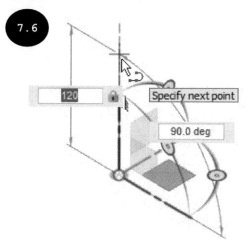

7.6

6.   Move the cursor vertically upward along the axis of the **3D Sketch Manipulator** to a distance. An extension line appears along the axis.

7.   Enter **120** in the Dimension box as the length of the line to be created, see Figure 7.6. The length of the line gets locked to 120 mm.

8.   Click the left mouse button along the extension line that appears. A vertical line of length 120 mm gets created, see Figure 7.7. Also, the origin of the **3D Sketch Manipulator** gets shifted to the last specified point in the graphics area and a rubber band line appears attached to the cursor.

9.   Make sure that the Top plane is selected in the **3D Sketch Manipulator** as the sketching plane.

 You can switch from one sketching plane to another by clicking the required plane in the 3D Sketch Manipulator at any point while creating the sketch.

10.   Move the cursor at an angle to the X axis in the graphics area, see Figure 7.7. Next, enter **180** as the length of the line in the Dimension box that appears in the graphics area. The length of the line gets locked to 180 mm on the current sketching plane, see Figure 7.7.

11.   After specifying the length of the line, press the TAB key for switching to the another Dimension box in the graphics area and then enter **35** degrees as the angle of the line. The length and angle of the line gets locked, see Figure 7.7.

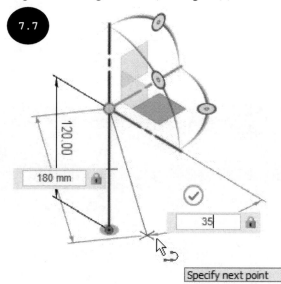

7.7

12. Click to specify the endpoint of the line in the graphics area. A line of length 180 mm at an angle of 35 degrees from the X axis is created. Also, the origin of the **3D Sketch Manipulator** gets shifted to the last specified point and a rubber band line appears attached to the cursor, see Figure 7.8.

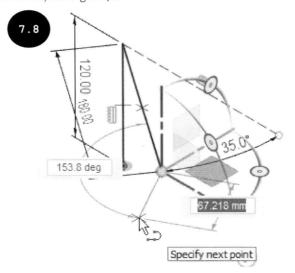

Similarly, you can continue creating line entities of a 3D sketch in different sketching planes.

13. Press the ESC key to exit the **Line** tool.

*Similar to creating a 3D sketch by using the **Line** tool, you can create 3D sketches by using the **Fit Point Spline** and **Control Point Spline** tools. Also, the methods for creating other sketch entities such as rectangle, arc, circle, point, and polygon are same as discussed earlier while creating 2D sketches.*

Now, you need to create a tangent arc.

14. Invoke the **CREATE** drop-down menu and then click on **Arc > Tangent Arc**, see Figure 7.9. The **Tangent Arc** tool gets activated and you are prompted to specify the start point.

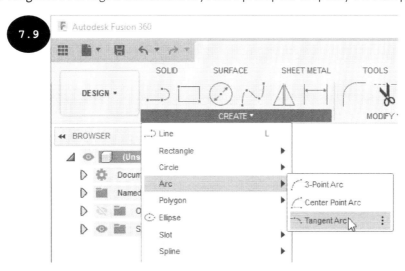

15. Click to specify the start point of the tangent arc at the endpoint of the previously created line, see Figure 7.10. The **3D Sketch Manipulator** appears at the specified start point.

16. Make sure that the Top plane is selected in the **3D Sketch Manipulator** as the sketching plane.

17. Move the cursor to a distance. A preview of an arc, tangent to the line appears.

18. Enter **80** as the radius of the tangent arc in the Dimension box, see Figure 7.11. Next, click anywhere in the graphics area to specify the endpoint of the arc. A tangent arc of radius 80 mm is created, see Figure 7.12. Next, press the ESC key to exit the **Tangent Arc** tool.

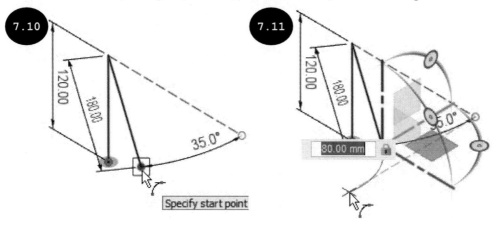

Now, you need to apply a horizontal constraint between the center point and the endpoint of the tangent arc.

19. Change the current orientation of the sketch to the top view by clicking on the TOP face of the ViewCube, see Figure 7.13.

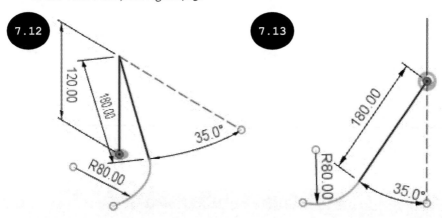

20. Click on the **Horizontal/Vertical** tool in the **CONSTRAINTS** panel of the **SKETCH** contextual tab for applying a horizontal constraint, see Figure 7.14.

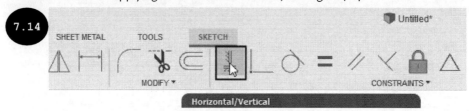

21. Click on the center point of the previously created tangent arc and then its endpoint one by one, see Figure 7.15. The center point and the endpoint of the tangent arc become aligned to each other.

22. Change the orientation of the sketch back to isometric, see Figure 7.16.

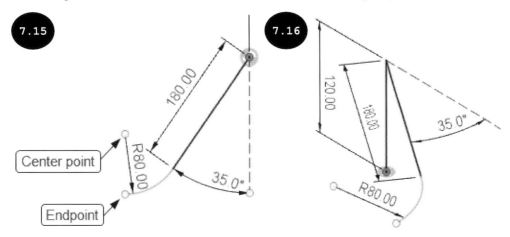

The method of applying constraints and dimensions to a 3D sketch is same as applying constraints and dimensions to a 2D Sketch in the Sketching environment.

Now, you need to add the fillet at the corner of the sketch.

23. Click on the **Fillet** tool in the **MODIFY** panel in the **SKETCH** contextual tab of the **Toolbar**.

24. Click on the vertical line of the sketch as the first entity and then click on the inclined line of length 180 mm as the second entity for creating a fillet. The preview of a fillet appears at the corner of the selected entities, see Figure 7.17.

25. Enter **60** as the radius of the fillet in the **Fillet radius** field that appears in the graphics area, see Figure 7.17.

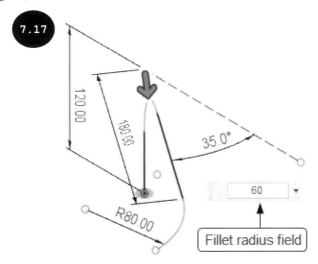

26. Press ENTER to create a fillet of the specified radius value and exit the **Fillet** tool.

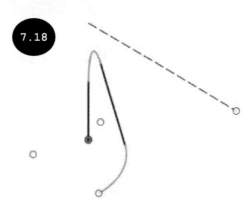

27. After creating the sketch, click on the **FINISH SKETCH** tool in the **SKETCH** contextual tab to finish the creation of the sketch and exit the Sketching environment. The 3D sketch is drawn, see Figure 7.18.

Creating the Pipe Feature

Now, you need to create a pipe feature. In Autodesk Fusion 360, you can create a solid or hollow pipe by using the **Pipe** tool. You can also create a pipe by sweeping a profile along a path by using the **Sweep** tool. In this section, you will create a pipe by using the **Pipe** tool.

1. Invoke the **CREATE** drop-down menu in the **SOLID** tab of the **Toolbar** and then click on the **Pipe** tool, see Figure 7.19. The **PIPE** dialog box appears, see Figure 7.20.

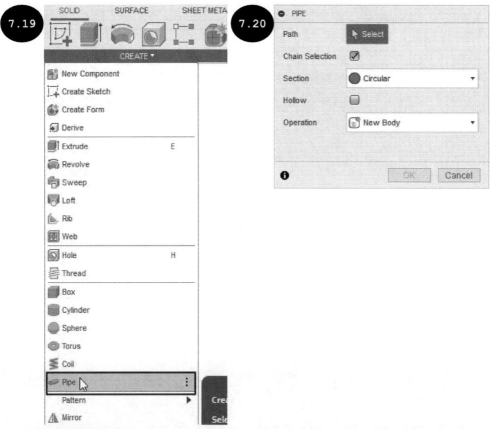

2. Ensure that the **Chain Selection** check box is selected in the dialog box so that all the contiguous entities of the path (3D sketch) get selected.

3. Select the previously created 3D sketch as the path of the pipe in the graphics area. The preview of a pipe with default parameters appears in the graphics area such that the section of the pipe follows the path selected, see Figure 7.21.

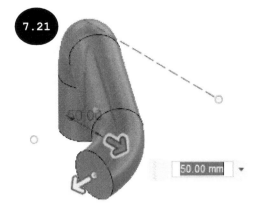

You can select an open or a closed 2D or 3D sketch, or a curve as the path of a pipe. You can also select an edge or a set of model edges as the path of a pipe.

4. Ensure that the distance value **1** is specified in the **Distance** field of the **PIPE** dialog box for creating a pipe of full length along the selected path.

5. Ensure that the **Circular** option is selected in the **Section** drop-down list of the dialog box for creating a pipe of circular section.

*You can create a pipe of circular, square, or triangular section by selecting the respective option in the **Section** drop-down list of the **PIPE** dialog box.*

6. Enter **80 mm** in the **Section Size** field of the dialog box as the diameter of the circular section of the pipe. The preview of a pipe appears similar to the one shown in Figure 7.22.

7. Ensure that the **Hollow** check box is cleared in the **PIPE** dialog box for creating a solid pipe.

*On selecting the **Hollow** check box in the **PIPE** dialog box, a hollow pipe of specified thickness will be created. You can specify the thickness of the hollow pipe in the **Section Thickness** field of the dialog box that appears when the **Hollow** check box is selected.*

8. Click on the **OK** button in the dialog box. A pipe with circular section is created, see Figure 7.23.

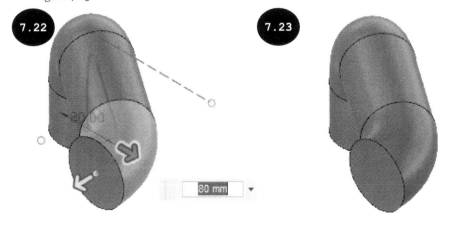

Creating the Mirror Feature

Now, you need to mirror the pipe feature about a construction plane, which passes through the center of the end circular face of the pipe feature and is parallel to the Right plane. To create this construction plane, you need to first create a construction point at the center of the end circular face of the pipe feature.

1. Invoke the **CONSTRUCT** drop-down menu in the **SOLID** tab and then click on the **Point at Center of Circle/Sphere/Torus** tool, see Figure 7.24. The **POINT AT CENTER OF CIRCLE/SPHERE/TORUS** dialog box appears in the graphics area.

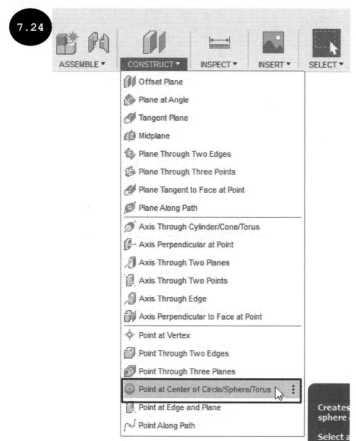

2. Select the circular edge of the pipe, see Figure 7.25. The construction point at the center of the selected circular edge is created, see Figure 7.26.

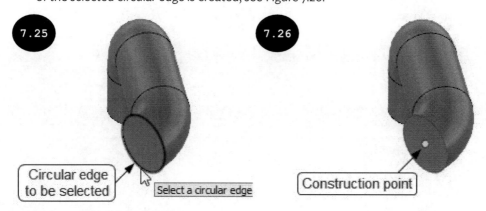

3. Click on the **OK** button in the dialog box.

    After creating the construction point, you can create the construction plane passing through it and parallel to the Right plane.

4. Click on the **Offset Plane** tool in the **CONSTRUCT** panel of the **SOLID** tab, see Figure 7.27. The **OFFSET PLANE** dialog box appears.

5. Select the Right plane as the reference plane and then click on the previously created construction point, see Figure 7.28. The preview of a construction plane passing through the construction point and parallel to the Right plane appears in the graphics area, see Figure 7.28.

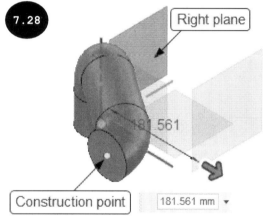

6. Click on the **OK** button in the **OFFSET PLANE** dialog box. The construction plane is created.

    After creating the construction plane, you can mirror the pipe about it.

7. Invoke the **CREATE** drop-down menu in the **SOLID** tab and then click on the **Mirror** tool. The **MIRROR** dialog box appears in the graphics area.

8. Select the **Features** option in the **Pattern Type** drop-down list of the dialog box for selecting a feature to be mirrored.

9. Select the pipe feature in the graphics area or in the **Timeline** as the feature to be mirrored.

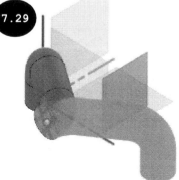

10. Click on the **Mirror Plane** selection option in the **MIRROR** dialog box and then select the newly created construction plane as the mirroring plane in the graphics area. The preview of a mirror feature appears, see Figure 7.29.

11. Click on the **OK** button in the **MIRROR** dialog box. The mirror feature is created as a separate body in the graphics area, see Figure 7.30. Also, the expanded **Bodies** node of the **BROWSER** shows two bodies available in the graphics area.

Now, you need to hide the construction plane in the graphics area.

12. Click on the **Show/Hide** icon in front of the **Construction** node in the **BROWSER** for hiding all the construction geometries in the graphics area, see Figure 7.31.

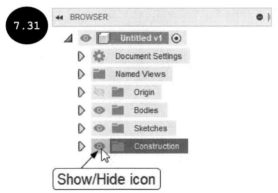

 You can also show or hide the individual construction geometry of the model by expanding the Construction node in the BROWSER and then clicking on the Show/Hide icon of the respective geometry to be shown or hidden.

Combining Bodies

Notice that the newly created mirror feature is created as a new body. As a result, in the **Bodies** node of the **BROWSER**, two separate bodies (**Body1** and **Body2**) are listed. You need to merge these bodies to make a single body.

1. Click on the **Combine** tool in the **MODIFY** panel in the **SOLID** tab, see Figure 7.32. The **COMBINE** dialog box appears.

In Autodesk Fusion 360, you can combine solid bodies by performing boolean operations such as join, cut, or intersect between bodies by using the **Combine** *tool.*

2. Select the base pipe feature as the target body and the mirror feature as the tool body in the graphics area one by one.

3. Ensure that the **Join** option is selected in the **Operation** drop-down list of the dialog box as the boolean operation to be performed on the selected bodies.

4. Ensure that the **New Component** and **Keep Tools** check boxes are cleared in the dialog box.

5. Click on the **OK** button in the dialog box. Both the selected bodies get merged with each other and form a single body.

Creating the Shell Feature

1. Click on the **Shell** tool in the **MODIFY** panel in the **SOLID** tab, see Figure 7.33. The **SHELL** dialog box appears.

2. Click to select three end faces of the model one by one as the faces to be removed, see Figure 7.34. You need to rotate the model for selecting the faces.

3. Ensure that the **Inside** option is selected in the **Direction** drop-down list of the dialog box for adding thickness inside the model.

4. Enter **10** in the **Inside Thickness** field of the **SHELL** dialog box.

5. Click on the **OK** button in the dialog box. The shell feature of specified thickness is created by removing the selected faces of the model, see Figure 7.35.

6. Change the orientation of the model back to isometric by clicking on the **Home** icon in the ViewCube.

Creating the Extrude Feature

1. Click on the **Create Sketch** tool in the **Toolbar** and then select the Top plane as the sketching plane.

2. Ensure that the **3D Sketch** check box is cleared in the **SKETCH PALETTE** dialog box for creating a 2D sketch.

3. Click on the **Look At** tool 🖻 in the **SKETCH PALETTE** dialog box to orient the current sketching plane normal to the viewing direction.

4. Create the sketch of the extrude feature by using the sketching tools, see Figure 7.36.

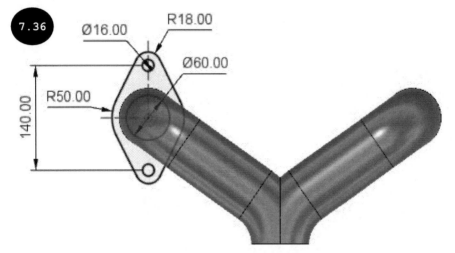

The sketch shown in Figure 7.36 has been fully defined by applying the required dimensions and constraints. You need to apply tangent constraints between each set of connected line and arc entities of the sketch. You also need to apply the symmetric constraint between the center points of the upper and lower arcs of the sketch to the horizontal construction line. Besides, you need to apply equal constraint between the upper and lower arcs and circles of the sketch.

5. Click on the **SOLID** tab in the **Toolbar** for displaying the solid modeling tools.

6. Click on the **Extrude** tool in the **CREATE** panel in the **SOLID** tab or press the E key. The **EXTRUDE** dialog box appears. Next, change the orientation of the model to isometric.

7. Select the closed profile of the sketch in the graphics area, see Figure 7.37.

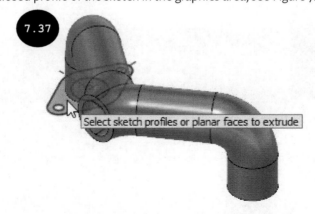

Select sketch profiles or planar faces to extrude

8. Enter -15 in the in the **Distance** field of the dialog box as the extrusion distance. The preview of the extrude feature appears in the downward direction, see Figure 7.38.

The negative value is used for reversing the direction of extrusion to the other side of the sketching plane.

9. Ensure that the **Join** option is selected in the **Operation** drop-down list of the dialog box.

10. Click on the **OK** button in the dialog box. The extrude feature is created, see Figure 7.39.

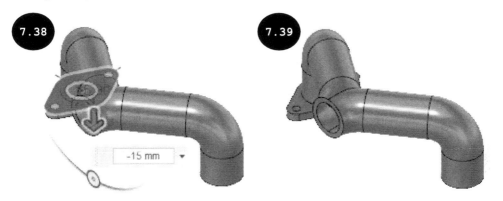

Creating the Second Mirror Feature

1. Invoke the **CREATE** drop-down menu in the **SOLID** tab and then click on the **Mirror** tool. The **MIRROR** dialog box appears in the graphics area.

2. Select the **Features** option in the **Pattern Type** drop-down list of the dialog box.

3. Click on the previously created extrude feature in the graphics area or in the **Timeline** as the feature to be mirrored, see Figure 7.40.

4. Click on the **Mirror Plane** selection option in the dialog box and then select the construction plane (**Plane1**) in the expanded **Construction** node of the **BROWSER** as the mirroring plane, see Figure 7.41. The preview of a mirror feature appears in the graphics area.

5.   Click on the **OK** button in the **MIRROR** dialog box. The mirror feature is created, see Figure 7.42.

Creating the Second Extrude Feature

1.   Click on the **Create Sketch** tool in the **Toolbar** and then select the front planar face of the model as the sketching plane, see Figure 7.43.

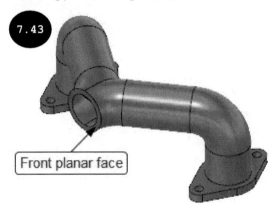

2.   Create a sketch of the extrude feature, see Figure 7.44.

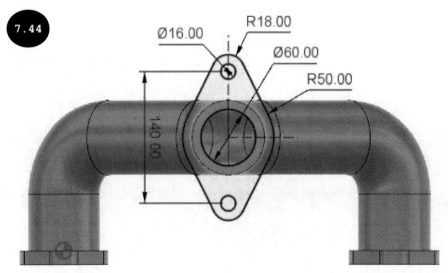

3. Press the **E** key. The **EXTRUDE** dialog box appears in the graphics area. Next, change the orientation of the model to isometric.

4. Select the two closed profiles of the sketch in the graphics area, see Figure 7.45.

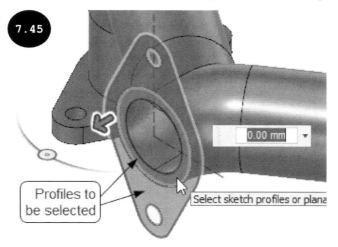

5. Enter **15** in the in the **Distance** field of the dialog box as the extrusion distance. The preview of an extrude feature appears, see Figure 7.46.

6. Ensure that the **Join** option is selected in the **Operation** drop-down list.

7. Click on the **OK** button in the **EXTRUDE** dialog box. The extrude feature is created, see Figure 7.47.

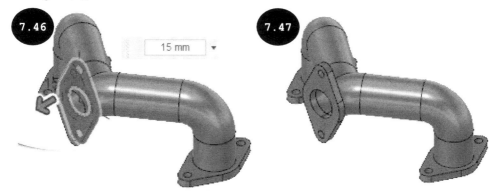

Saving the Model

1. Click on the **Save** tool in the **Application Bar** or press CTRL + S and then enter **Tutorial 1** in the **Name** field of the **Save** dialog box that appears.

2. Click on the down arrow next to the **Location** field in the dialog box.

3. Create a folder with the name **Chapter 07** inside the **Autodesk Fusion 360 Tutorials** project by using the **New Folder** button of the expanded **Save** dialog box.

4. Double-click on the newly created **Chapter 07** folder and then click on the **Save** button. The model gets saved with the name **Tutorial 1** at the specified location (*Autodesk Fusion 360 Tutorials > Chapter 07*) in the **Data Panel**.

Introduction to Helical Coils

In Autodesk Fusion 360, you can create a helical coil with different cross-sectional shapes such as circular, square, triangular (external), or triangular (internal) by using the **Coil** tool. Figure 7.48 shows a helical coil with circular cross-sectional shape. You can also create a spiral coil with different cross-sectional shapes by using the **Coil** tool. Figure 7.49 shows a spiral coil with triangular (external) cross-sectional shape.

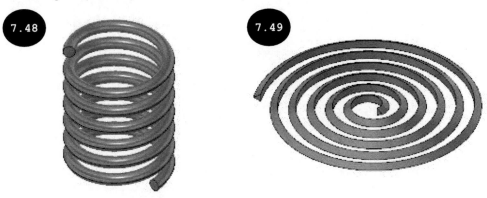

7.48   7.49

Tutorial 2: Creating a Helical Coil

Create the model shown in Figure 7.50. The different views and dimensions are given in the same figure. All dimensions are in mm.

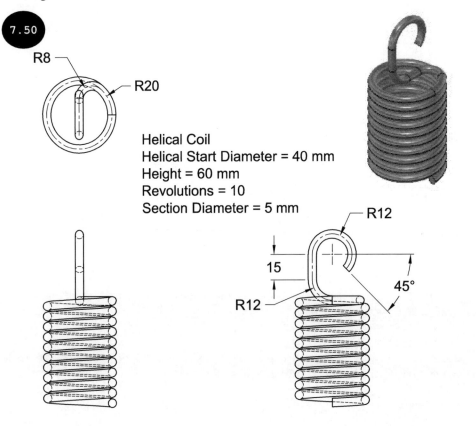

7.50

R8
R20

Helical Coil
Helical Start Diameter = 40 mm
Height = 60 mm
Revolutions = 10
Section Diameter = 5 mm

R12
15
R12
45°

The following sequence summarizes the tutorial outline:

- Starting Fusion 360 and a New Design File
- Creating the Helical Coil
- Creating the Sweep Feature
- Creating the Second Sweep Feature
- Saving the Model

Starting Fusion 360 and a New Design File

1. Start Fusion 360, if not started already.

2. Start a new design file by using the **New Design** tool or by pressing the CTRL + N keys.

3. Ensure that millimeter (mm) unit is defined for the active design file.

Creating the Helical Coil

1. Invoke the **CREATE** drop-down menu in the **SOLID** tab and then click on the **Coil** tool, see Figure 7.51. You are prompted to select a sketching plane.

2. Select the Top plane as the sketching plane. The **Center Diameter Circle** tool gets activated, automatically and you are prompted to specify the center point of the circle.

3. Click to specify the center point of the circle at the origin and then enter **40 mm** in the Dimension box as the diameter of the circle. Next, press ENTER. The preview of a helical coil with default specifications appears in the graphics area, see Figure 7.52. Also, the COIL dialog box appears, refer to Figure 7.53.

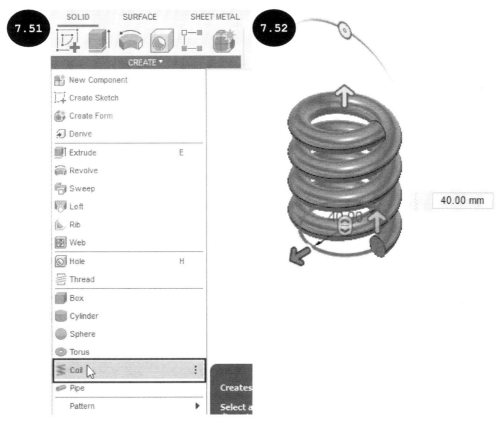

The diameter of the circle drawn defines the start diameter of the helical coil. You can further modify or control the start diameter of the helical coil by entering a new value in the Diameter field of the COIL dialog box.

4.   Select the **Revolution and Height** option in the **Type** drop-down list of the COIL dialog box, see Figure 7.53.

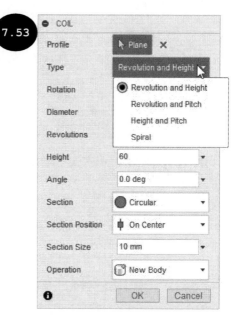

Type: The options in the **Type** drop-down list of the COIL dialog box are used for defining the type of coil (helical or spiral) to be created and the method to be adopted for creating the coil. The **Revolution and Height** option is used for creating a helical coil by defining its number of revolutions and total height in the respective fields of the COIL dialog box. The **Revolution and Pitch** option is used for creating a helical coil by defining its number of revolutions and pitch. The **Height and Pitch** option is used for creating a helical coil by defining its total height and pitch. The **Spiral** option is used for creating a spiral coil by defining its pitch and number of revolutions.

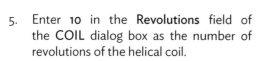

5.   Enter **10** in the **Revolutions** field of the COIL dialog box as the number of revolutions of the helical coil.

6.   Enter **60** in the **Height** field of the dialog box as the total height of the coil.

7.   Ensure that **0** degree is specified in the **Angle** field of the dialog box.

 On specifying a taper angle value in the Angle field of the COIL dialog box, you can create a tapered helical coil. To reverse the taper direction from inward to outward, you need to enter a negative taper angle value in this Angle field.

8.   Ensure that the **Circular** option is selected in the **Section** drop-down list of the dialog box for creating a helical coil of circular cross-sectional shape.

 You can create a helical coil of different cross-sectional shape such as circular, square, triangular (external), or triangular (internal) by selecting the respective option in the Section drop-down list of the COIL dialog box.

9.   Ensure that the **On Center** option is selected in the **Section Position** drop-down list of the dialog box.

 On selecting the On Center option, a helical coil is created by positioning its cross-sectional center on the helical start diameter specified by the circle drawn. On selecting the Inside option, a helical coil is created by positioning its cross-sectional center inside the helical start diameter. On selecting the Outside option, a helical coil is created by positioning its cross-sectional center outside the helical start diameter.

10. Enter **5** in the **Section Size** field of the **COIL** dialog box as the size of the coil section.

11. Ensure that the **New Body** option is selected in the **Operation** drop-down list in the dialog box.

12. Click on the **OK** button in the **COIL** dialog box. A helical coil of required specifications is created, see Figure 7.54.

7.54

Creating the Sweep Feature

To create the path of the sweep feature, you need to create a construction plane at an offset distance of 60 mm from the Top plane.

1. Create a construction plane at an offset distance of 60 mm from the Top plane by using the **Offset Plane** tool, see Figure 7.55.

   After creating the construction plane, you can create the path of the sweep feature.

2. Click on the **Create Sketch** tool in **Toolbar** and then select the newly created construction plane as the sketching plane.

3. Create a sketch of the path by using the sketching tools, see Figure 7.56.

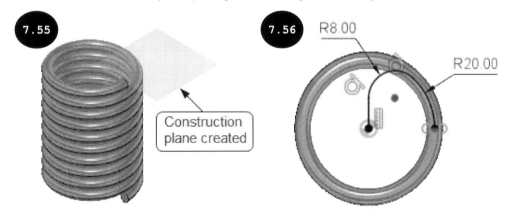

7.55

Construction plane created

7.56 R8.00 R20.00

4. Click on the **SOLID** tab in the **Toolbar** for displaying the solid modeling tools.

5. Invoke the **CREATE** drop-down menu in the **SOLID** tab and then click on the **Sweep** tool. The **SWEEP** dialog box appears. Next, change the orientation of the model to isometric.

6. Ensure that the **Single Path** option is selected in the **Type** drop-down list in the dialog box.

7. Rotate the model and then select the top planar face of the helical coil as the profile of the sweep feature, see Figure 7.57.

8. Click on the **Path** selection option in the **SWEEP** dialog box and then select the path of the sweep feature, see Figure 7.57. The preview of a sweep feature appears in the graphics area.

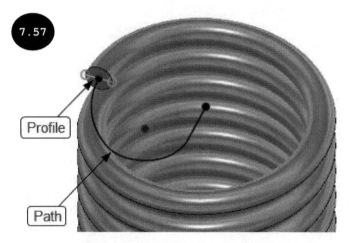

7.57

Profile

Path

9. Ensure that the distance value **1** is specified in the **Distance** field of the dialog box for sweeping the profile along the full length of the path.

10. Ensure that the **Join** option is selected in the **Operation** drop-down list of the dialog box for merging the sweep feature with the helical coil.

11. Click on the **OK** button in the dialog box. The sweep feature is created. Next, change the orientation of the model to isometric. Figure 7.58 shows the model after creating the sweep feature.

Creating the Second Sweep Feature

1. Click on the **Create Sketch** tool in **Toolbar** and then select the Right plane as the sketching plane for creating the path of the sweep feature, see Figure 7.59.

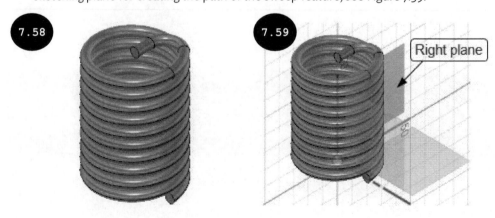

7.58

7.59

Right plane

2. Create the path of the sweep feature by using the sketching tools, see Figure 7.60.

3. Click on the **SOLID** tab in the **Toolbar** for displaying the solid modeling tools.

4. Invoke the **CREATE** drop-down menu in the **SOLID** tab and then click on the **Sweep** tool. The **SWEEP** dialog box appears. Next, change the orientation of the model to isometric.

5. Ensure that the **Single Path** option is selected in the **Type** drop-down list of the dialog box.

6. Click to select the top planar face of the previously created feature as the profile of the sweep feature, see Figure 7.61.

7. Click on the **Path** selection option in the dialog box and then select the path of the sweep feature, see Figure 7.61. The preview of a sweep feature appears in the graphics area, see Figure 7.62.

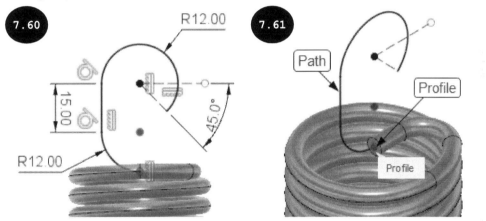

8. Ensure that the distance value 1 is specified in the **Distance** field of the dialog box for sweeping the profile along the full length of the path.

9. Ensure that the **Join** option is selected in the **Operation** drop-down list of the dialog box.

10. Click on the **OK** button in the dialog box. The sweep feature is created, see Figure 7.63.

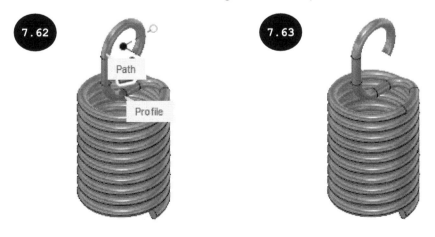

Saving the Model

1.   Click on the **Save** tool in the **Application Bar** and then enter **Tutorial 2** in the **Name** field of the **Save** dialog box that appears.

2.   Make sure that the location *Autodesk Fusion 360 Tutorials > Chapter 07* is specified in the **Location** field of the dialog box.

3.   Click on the **Save** button in the dialog box. The model is saved with the name Tutorial 2 in the specified location (*Autodesk Fusion 360 Tutorials > Chapter 07*).

Exercise 1

Create a model shown in Figure 7.64. The different views and dimensions are given in the same figure. All dimensions are in mm.

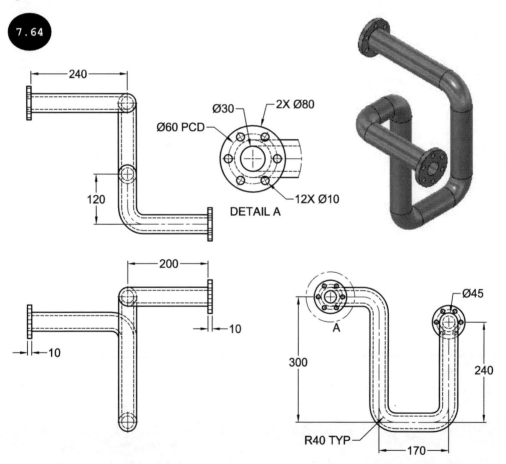

7.64

Exercise 2

Create the model shown in Figure 7.65. All dimensions are in mm.

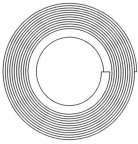

Helical Coil
Helical Start Diameter = 60 mm
Revolutions = 12
Pitch = 5 mm
Taper Angle = 12 degrees
Section Diameter = 4 mm

Summary

This chapter discussed how to create 3D sketches in the Sketching environment by using the sketching tools. Methods for creating helical and spiral coils of different cross-sections have been explained in addition to methods for creating a solid or a hollow pipe and combining multiple solid bodies into a single body by performing boolean operations such as join, cut, or intersect.

Questions

Answer the following questions:

- On selecting the _____ check box in the **SKETCH PALETTE** dialog box, you can create a 3D sketch by using the sketching tools.

- The _____ tool is used for creating a solid or hollow pipe.

- You can create a pipe of _____, _____, or _____ section.

- The _____ tool is used for combining solid bodies by performing boolean operations such as join, cut, or intersect.

- You can create a helical coil with different cross-sectional shapes by using the _____ tool.

- The _____ tool is used for creating a helical or a spiral coil.

- The _____ option in the COIL dialog box is used for creating a helical coil by defining its total height and pitch.

- You can create a tapered helical coil by specifying a taper angle value in the _____ field of the COIL dialog box.

- In Autodesk Fusion 360, you can create a 2D sketch and a 3D sketch, within the same Sketching environment. (True/False)

- You can switch from one sketching plane to another by clicking the required plane in the 3D Sketch Manipulator at any point while creating a 3D sketch. (True/False)

- You can only select a 2D sketch as the path of a pipe. (True/False)

- The method of applying constraints and dimensions to a 3D sketch is same as applying constraints and dimensions to a 2D Sketch in the Sketching environment. (True/False)

Creating Assemblies - I

In this chapter, you will learn the following:

- Introduction to Bottom-up Assembly
- Working with Joints
- Creating the Single Cylinder Engine Assembly
- Creating the Blow Off Cock Assembly
- Creating the Manual Press Assembly

In earlier chapters, you have learned about the basic and advanced techniques of creating real world mechanical components. In this chapter, you will learn about different techniques of creating mechanical assemblies. An assembly is made up of two or more than two components assembled together by applying joints. Figure 8.1 shows an assembly, in which multiple components are assembled together by applying the required joints.

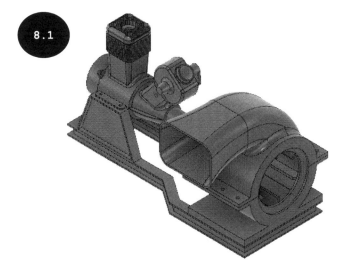

8.1

In Autodesk Fusion 360, you can create an assembly by using two approaches: Bottom-up assembly approach and Top-down assembly approach. You can also use a combination of both these approaches for creating an assembly. The method for creating an assembly by using the Top-down assembly approach is discussed in the next chapter. In this chapter, you will learn about creating assemblies by using the Bottom-up assembly approach.

 In Autodesk Fusion 360, there is no separate workspace or environment for creating assemblies. You can create a component as well as an assembly, within a design file of the DESIGN workspace.

Introduction to Bottom-up Assembly

The Bottom-up Assembly Approach is the most widely used approach for assembling components. In this approach, first all the components of an assembly are created one by one as a separate design file and saved in a common location. Later, all the components are inserted one by one in a design file and then assembled by applying the required joints. Before you start creating assemblies by using the bottom-up assembly approach, it is important to first understand about various types of joints.

 Autodesk Fusion 360 has bidirectional association capabilities. As a result, if any change or modification is made in a component, the same change reflects in the component used in the assembly as well as in the drawing and other workspaces of Fusion 360, automatically on updating the respective file.

Working with Joints

Joints are used for fixing the required degrees of freedom and defining the relationship between the components of an assembly. For example, the function of a shaft in an assembly is to rotate about its axis therefore, you need to apply a joint such that the rotational degree of freedom of the shaft remains free to rotate. You can apply various types of joints such as rigid, revolute, slider, cylindrical, pin-slot, ball, and planar between the components of an assembly for defining the relationship by using the **Joint** and **As-built Joint** tools. You will learn about applying joints using the **As-built Joint** tool in the next chapter, while creating an assembly using the Top-down assembly approach. In this chapter, you will learn about applying joints using the **Joint** tool. Different types of joints are discussed below:

 Every component has six degrees of freedom: three translational and three rotational. This means that a free component within a 3D space can move along the X, Y, and Z axes as well as rotate about the X, Y, and Z axes. You need to apply joints to fix the required degrees of freedom and define the relationship between the components.

Rigid Joint

The rigid joint is used for locking or fixing the components together by removing all degrees of freedom and does not allow any relative motion between the components, see Figure 8.2. The rigid joint is mainly applied between the components that are welded or bolted together with no allowable motion between them.

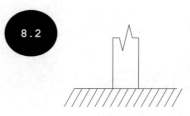

Rigid Joint
(No translational and no rotational movements)

Revolute Joint

The revolute joint allows a component to rotate about an axis by removing all its degrees of freedom except one rotational degree of freedom, see Figure 8.3. This joint type is used for rotating the component around an axis.

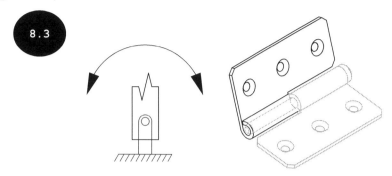

Revolute Joint
(Only one rotational movement is allowed)

Slider Joint

The slider joint is used for translating or sliding a component along a single axis by removing all its degrees of freedom except one translational degree of freedom, see Figure 8.4.

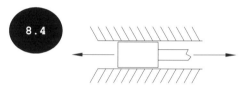

Slider Joint
(Only one translational movement is allowed)

Cylindrical Joint

The cylindrical joint is used for translating as well as rotating a component along the same axis by removing all its degrees of freedom except one translational and one rotational, see Figure 8.5. It is mainly used for forming a screw mechanism between the components.

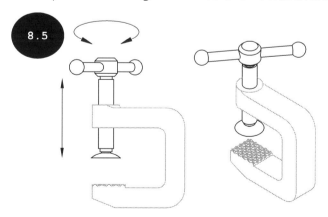

Cylindrical Joint
(One translational and one rotational movement is allowed along the same axis)

Pin-slot Joint

The pin-slot joint is used for translating a component along an axis and rotating about a different axis by removing all its degrees of freedom except one translational and one rotational, see Figure 8.6. It is mainly used for forming a pin-slot mechanism between the components such that the pin translates along the slot and rotates about its axis.

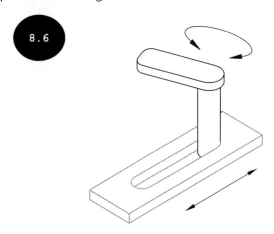

Pin-slot Joint
(One translational movement along an axis and one rotational movement about another axis is allowed)

Planar Joint

The planar joint is used for translating the component along two axes in addition to rotating about a single axis, see Figure 8.7. In this joint, you can restrain the component to a planar face of another component such that its movement in the direction normal to the planar face gets restricted and allows movement within the plane of the face. It also allows a rotational movement along an axis normal to the planar face. For example, an object can move on the planar face of a table top as well as rotate about an axis normal to the planar face.

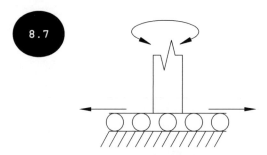

Planar Joint
(Translational movement freely within the plane of face and rotational movement about an axis are allowed)

Ball Joint

The ball joint is used for rotating a component about all its three rotational axes, see Figure 8.8. In this joint, all translational degrees of freedom of the component get restricted and the component can rotate about its three axes.

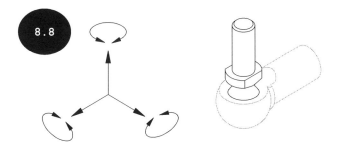

Ball Joint
(All three rotational movements are allowed)

Tutorial 1: Creating the Single Cylinder Engine Assembly

Create the assembly shown in Figure 8.9 by applying all the required joints and then animate it. The exploded view of the assembly is shown in Figure 8.10 for your reference only. Different views and dimensions of individual components of the assembly are shown in Figures 8.11 through 8.15. You can also download all components of the assembly by logging on to the SDCAD Academy website (www.sdcadacademy.com). All dimensions are in mm.

PARTS LIST				
ITEM	QTY	PART NUMBER	DESCRIPTION	MATERIAL
1	1	CRANK CASE		STEEL
2	1	CRANK SHAFT		STEEL
3	1	CONNECTING ROD		STEEL
4	1	PISTON		STEEL
5	1	PISTON PIN		STEEL

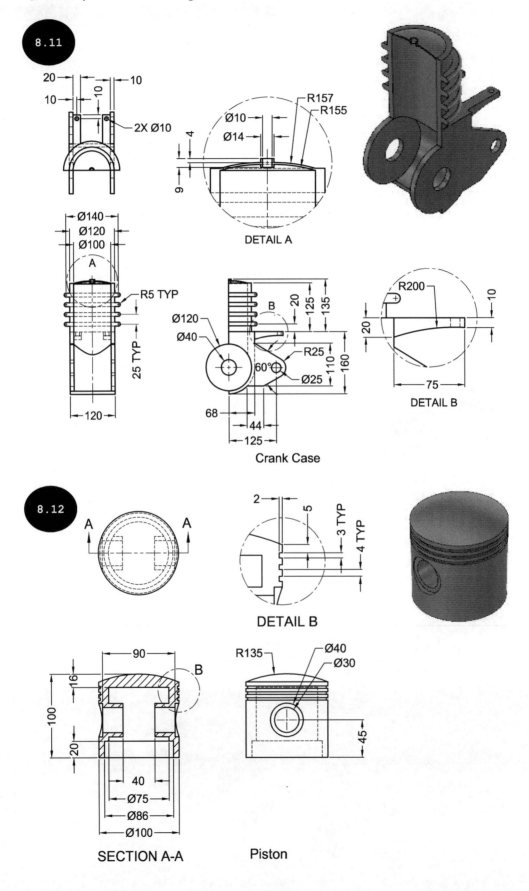

8.11

DETAIL A

Crank Case

DETAIL B

8.12

DETAIL B

SECTION A-A   Piston

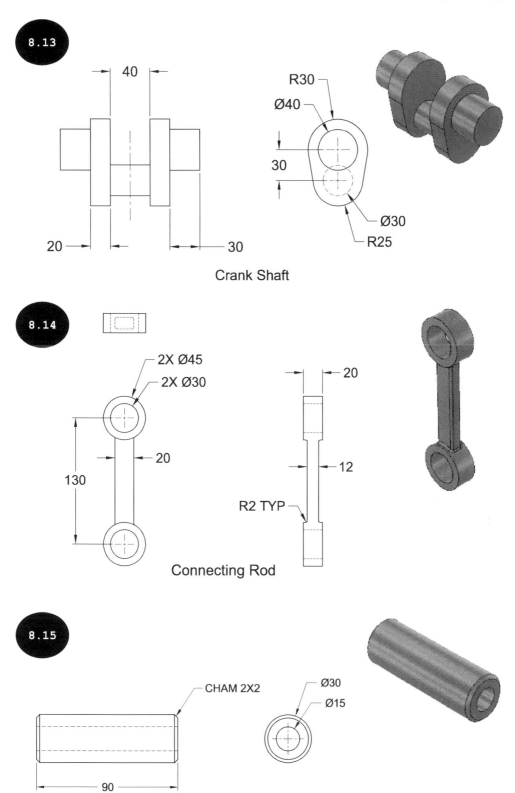

8.13

40

R30

Ø40

30

20

30

Ø30

R25

Crank Shaft

8.14

2X Ø45

2X Ø30

20

20

130

12

R2 TYP

Connecting Rod

8.15

CHAM 2X2

Ø30

Ø15

90

Piston Pin

The following sequence summarizes the tutorial outline:

- Starting Fusion 360 and Creating all Components
- Inserting the First Component into a Design File
- Grounding/Fixing the First Component
- Inserting the Second Component of the Assembly
- Applying the Revolute Joint
- Inserting and Assembling the Third Component
- Inserting and Assembling the Fourth Component
- Inserting and Assembling the Fifth Component
- Applying the Slider Joint
- Hiding the Joint Symbols in the Graphics Area
- Animating the Assembly
- Saving the Model

Starting Fusion 360 and Creating all Components

1. Start Fusion 360 by double-clicking on the Autodesk Fusion 360 icon on your desktop.

2. Create all the components of the assembly one by one in a separate design file. Refer to Figures 8.11 through 8.15 for dimensions of each component. After creating all the components, save them at a common location *Autodesk Fusion 360 Tutorials > Chapter 8 > Tutorial 1* in the **Data Panel**. You need to create these folders in the **Data Panel**.

 You can also download all the components of the assembly by visiting our website www.sdcadacademy.com.

Inserting the First Component into a Design File

1. Start a new design file by invoking the **File** drop-down menu in the **Application Bar** and then clicking on the **New Design** tool, see Figure 8.16.

 As discussed earlier, in Autodesk Fusion 360, there is no separate workspace or environment for creating assemblies. You can create a component as well as an assembly, within a design file of the DESIGN workspace.

2. Ensure that the **DESIGN** workspace is selected in the **Workspace** drop-down menu of the **Toolbar** as the workspace for the active design file, refer to Figure 8.17.

    Before you insert components of the assembly, you need to save the design file.

3. Click on the **Save** tool on the **Application Bar**, see Figure 8.17. The **Save** dialog box appears.

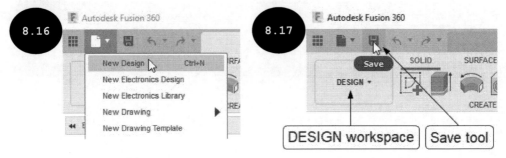

4. Enter **Single Cylinder Engine** in the **Name** field of the **Save** dialog box as the name of the design file.

5. Ensure that the location **Autodesk Fusion 360 Tutorials > Chapter 8 > Tutorial 1** is specified in the **Location** field of the dialog box for saving the design file.

> *It is recommended to save the design file with a unique name of the assembly, in the same location where all the components of the assembly are saved.*

6. Click on the **Save** button in the dialog box. The design file is saved with the name **Single Cylinder Engine** at the specified location (*Autodesk Fusion 360 Tutorials > Chapter 8 > Tutorial 1*) in the **Data Panel**.

Now, you can insert the first component of the assembly into the currently active design file (Single Cylinder Engine).

7. Display the **Data Panel** by clicking on the **Show Data Panel** tool in the **Application Bar**, see Figure 8.18.

8. Browse to the location where all the components of the assembly have been saved (**Autodesk Fusion 360 Tutorials > Chapter 8 > Tutorial 1**) in the **Data Panel**. A thumbnail view of all the components of the assembly appears in the **Data Panel**, see Figure 8.19.

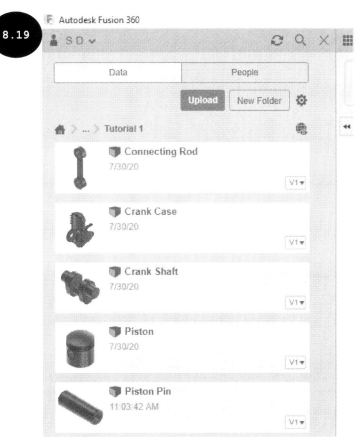

Now, you can insert the first component of the assembly into the active design file.

 Before inserting a component into a design file, the component icon appears in front of the name of the design file in the BROWSER, see Figure 8.20. This means that the currently active design file represents a component file. However, as soon as you insert a component into the currently active design file, the component icon changes to the assembly icon in the BROWSER, which represents the design file as an assembly file.

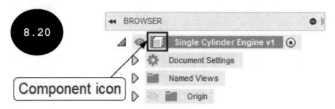

9. Right-click on the **Crank Case** component in the **Data Panel** and then click on the **Insert into Current Design** tool in the shortcut menu that appears, see Figure 8.21. The **Crank Case** component gets inserted into the design file with the display of translational and manipulator handles attached to it, see Figure 8.22. Also, the **MOVE/COPY** dialog box appears in the graphics area.

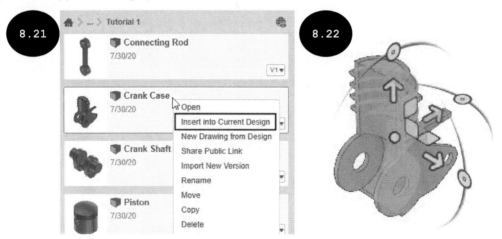

 The component icon in front of the name of the design file gets changed to the assembly icon in the BROWSER and the inserted component (Crank Case) is added into it with a link icon, see Figure 8.23. The link icon indicates that the component is inserted as an external file.

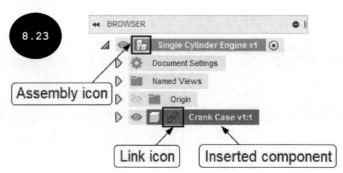

You can drag the translational and manipulator handles that appear attached to the inserted components in the graphics area to define their position and orientation, as required in the graphics area. By default, the component is placed at the origin of the design file.

10. Accept the default position of the component in the graphics area and then click on the OK button in the **MOVE/COPY** dialog box. The **Crank Case** component gets inserted into the design file, see Figure 8.24. Next, close the **Data Panel** by clicking on the cross mark at its top right corner.

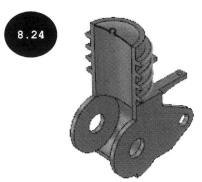
8.24

 *You can also insert a component into the active design file by dragging and dropping it from the **Data Panel** to the design file.*

Grounding/Fixing the First Component

Now, you need to ground the first component of the assembly, in order to fix all its degrees of freedom.

 In Autodesk Fusion 360, the component you insert into the design file is a floating component whose all degrees of freedom are free. A floating component is free to move or rotate in any direction in the graphics area. It is recommended to ground or fix the first component of the assembly, before you insert the second component into the design file. A grounded or fixed component does not allow any translational or rotational movement.

1. Right-click on the name of the component (**Crank Case**) in the BROWSER and then click on the **Ground** option in the shortcut menu that appears, see Figure 8.25. The **Crank Case** component becomes the grounded component and all its degrees of freedom get fixed such that its cannot move or rotate in any direction. Also, a push-pin symbol 📌 appears on its component icon in the BROWSER representing it as a grounded component.

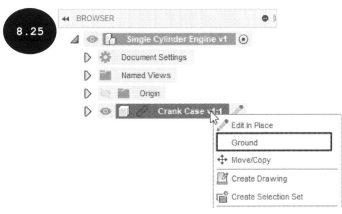
8.25

You can also change a grounded component to a floating component, whose all degrees of freedom are free. To do so, right-click on the grounded component in the BROWSER and then click on the Unground option in the shortcut menu that appears.

Inserting the Second Component of the Assembly

After the first component becomes a grounded component, you need to insert the second component of the assembly into the design file.

1. Display the **Data Panel** by clicking on the **Show Data Panel** tool ▦ in the **Application Bar.**

2. Right-click on the **Crank Shaft** component in the **Data Panel** and then click on the **Insert into Current Design** tool in the shortcut menu that appears, see Figure 8.26. The **Crank Shaft** component gets inserted into the design file with the display of translational and manipulator handles attached to it. Also, the **MOVE/COPY** dialog box appears in the graphics area.

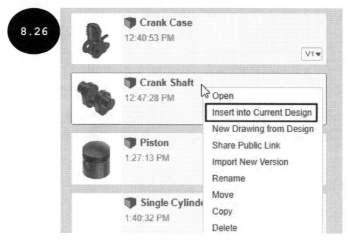

Now, you need to change the position the **Crank Shaft** component in the graphics area.

3. Change the position of the second component (**Crank Shaft**) in the graphics area by dragging its translational and manipulator handles such that it does not intersect with the first component, see Figure 8.27.

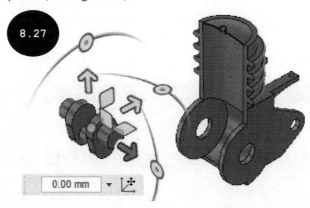

4. Click on the **OK** button in the **MOVE/COPY** dialog box. The **Crank Shaft** component gets inserted and placed in the specified position in the design file. Next, close the **Data Panel** by clicking on the cross mark at its top right corner.

After inserting the second component, you need to assemble it with the first component by applying the required joint.

Applying the Revolute Joint

Now, you need to apply the revolute joint between the second and the first components of the assembly, so that the second component can only rotate about an axis.

1. Click on the **Joint** tool in the **ASSEMBLE** panel of the **SOLID** tab, see Figure 8.28. Alternatively, press the **J** key. The **JOINT** dialog box appears, see Figure 8.29. Also, the first component (grounded component) becomes transparent in the graphics area and you are prompted to define the position of the joint origin on the second component (moveable component).

 To apply a joint between two components, you need to specify the position of the joint origin on each component one by one.

2. Ensure that the **Simple** button ⊙ is selected in the **Component 1** rollout of the **Position** tab in the **JOINT** dialog box for defining the joint origin on a face, an edge, or a point of the component.

    Component 1: The options of the **Component 1** rollout in the **Position** tab of the dialog box are used for defining the joint origin on the moveable component. By default, the **Simple** button ⊙ is selected in the **Mode** area of this rollout. As a result, you can define the joint origin on a face, an edge, or a point of the component. On selecting the **Between Two Faces** button, you can define the joint origin on a plane at the center of two selected faces of the component. On selecting the **Two Edge Intersection** button, you can define the joint origin at the intersection of two edges of the component.

3. Move the cursor over the right circular edge of the second component (**Crank Shaft**), see Figure 8.30. The edge gets highlighted and the joint origin snaps to the snap point that appears at the center of the circular edge.

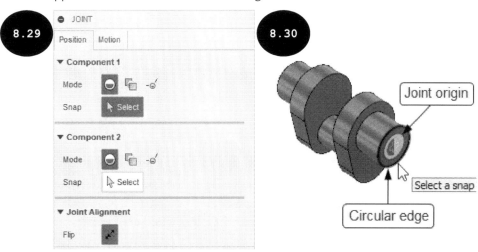

4. Click the left mouse button when the joint origin snaps to the center of the right circular edge of the **Crank Shaft** component, refer to Figure 8.30. The position of the joint origin is defined at the center of the circular edge. Also, the **Crank Shaft** component becomes transparent in the graphics area and you are prompted to define the position of the joint origin on the first component (**Crank Case**).

5. Ensure that the **Simple** button ⊚ is selected in the **Mode** area of the **Component 2** rollout in the dialog box for defining the joint origin on a face, an edge, or a point.

6. Move the cursor over the right circular edge of the first component (**Crank Case**), see Figure 8.31. The edge gets highlighted and the joint origin snaps to the center of the edge.

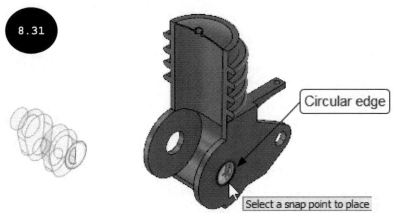

7. Click the left mouse button when the joint origin snaps to the center of the edge, refer to Figure 8.31. The position of the joint origin is defined and the second component (**Crank Shaft**) moves toward the first component such that the defined joint origins of both the components get coincident to each other in the graphics area, see Figure 8.32. Also, the component animates in the graphics area based on the default joint type selected in the **Motion** tab of the dialog box.

8. Enter -10 in the **Offset Z** field of the **Joint Alignment** rollout in the dialog box as an offset distance between the joint origins of the connected components, refer to Figure 8.33.

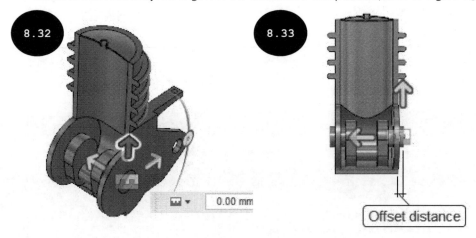

In Figure 8.33, the view orientation of the assembly has changed to Front view for better understanding of the offset distance between the joint origins of the components.

Now, you need to define the joint to be applied between the components.

9. Click on the **Motion** tab in the **JOINT** dialog box for defining a joint between the components, see Figure 8.34.

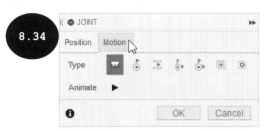

 The options in the Position tab of the JOINT dialog box are used for defining the components to be joined and their alignment, whereas the options in the **Motion** *tab are used for defining the type of joint to be applied between the components.*

10. Click on the **Revolute** button in the **Type** area of the dialog box as the joint to be applied between the components. The **Crank Shaft** component starts rotating for a while about an axis which is selected in the **Rotate** drop-down list of the dialog box.

11. Ensure that the **Z Axis** option is selected in the **Rotate** drop-down list of the dialog box as the axis of revolution.

The **Preview joint motion** *button in the* **Animate** *area in the* **Motion** *tab of the dialog box is used for animating the allowable motion between the components after applying the joint. It helps to identify the free degrees of freedom of the component based on the joint applied.*

12. Click on the **OK** button in the **JOINT** dialog box. The revolute joint is applied such that all degrees of freedom of the second component become fixed except one rotational degree of freedom. As a result, the second component (**Crank Shaft**) can rotate about its axis. Figure 8.35 shows the assembly after applying the revolute joint between the **Crank Shaft** and **Crank Case** components of the assembly.

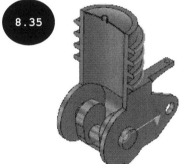

 By default, the visibility of applied joints is turned on. As a result, the symbols of applied joints appear in the graphics area. To turn on or off the visibility of applied joints in the graphics area, click on the **Display Settings > Object Visibility** *in the* **Navigation Bar,** *see Figure 8.36. Next, select or clear the* **Joints** *check box in the cascading menu that appears, respectively.*

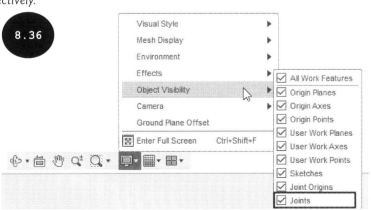

Inserting and Assembling the Third Component

Now, you need to insert and assemble the **Connecting Rod** component of the assembly.

1. Display the **Data Panel** by clicking on the **Show Data Panel** tool ⊞ in the **Application Bar.**

2. Right-click on the **Connecting Rod** component in the **Data Panel** and then click on the **Insert into Current Design** tool in the shortcut menu that appears, see Figure 8.37. The **Connecting Rod** component gets inserted into the design file with the display of translational and manipulator handles attached to it. Also, the **MOVE/COPY** dialog box appears in the graphics area.

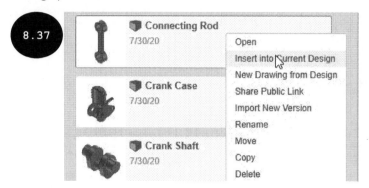

3. Change the position of the third component (**Connecting Rod**) in the graphics area by dragging its translational and manipulator handles such that it does not intersect with the existing components of the assembly.

4. Click on the **OK** button in the **MOVE/COPY** dialog box. The **Connecting Rod** component gets inserted and placed in the specified position in the design file, see Figure 8.38. Next, close the **Data Panel** by clicking on the cross mark at its top right corner.

Now, you need to assemble the third component (**Connecting Rod**).

5. Click on the **Joint** tool in the **ASSEMBLE** panel of the **SOLID** tab, see Figure 8.39. Alternatively, press the **J** key. The **JOINT** dialog box appears.

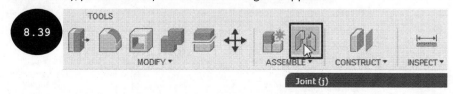

*If the **Fusion360** message window appears, which informs you that some components have been moved from their previous position, then click on the **Capture Position** button to capture the current position of the components, see Figure 8.40. If you click on the **Continue** button in this message window, then the components will revert back to their previous position.*

6. Ensure that the **Simple** button ⊝ is selected in the **Component 1** rollout of the **Position** tab in the **JOINT** dialog box for defining the joint origin on a face, an edge, or a point of the component.

7. Move the cursor over the bottom inner circular face of the **Connecting Rod** component, see Figure 8.41. The face gets highlighted and its three snap points appear.

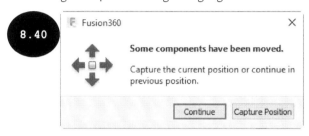

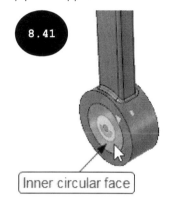

 A triangular snap point indicates a midpoint, a circular snap point indicates a corner, and a square snap point indicates a center.

8. Press and hold the CTRL key to lock the highlighted face (inner circular face) so that you can easily select the middle snap point of the face to define the position of the joint origin.

 You can lock a face or an edge of the component to select its required snap point easily by pressing the CTRL key.

9. Move the cursor over the middle snap point of the highlighted face and then click the left mouse button when the joint origin snaps to it, see Figure 8.42. The position of the joint origin on the third component is defined. Next, release the CTRL key.

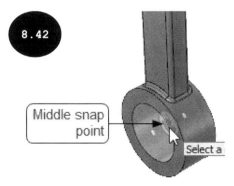

10. Ensure that the **Simple** button ⊝ is selected in the **Component 2** rollout in the dialog box for defining the joint origin on a face, an edge, or a point of another component.

11. Move the cursor over the middle circular face of the second component (**Crank Shaft**), see Figure 8.43. The face gets highlighted and its snap points appear.

12. Press the CTRL key and then click the left mouse button when the joint origin snaps to the middle snap point of the highlighted face of the second component (**Crank Shaft**), see Figure 8.43. The position of the joint origin is defined and the third component moves toward the second component such that the defined joint origins of both the components get coincident to each other in the graphics area, see Figure 8.44. Also, the component animates in the graphics area based on the default joint type selected in the **Motion** tab of the dialog box.

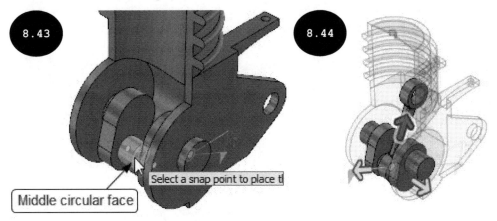

Now, you need to define the joint to be applied between the components.

13. Click on the **Motion** tab in the **JOINT** dialog box and then click on the **Revolute** button in the **Type** area of the dialog box as the joint to be applied between the components, see Figure 8.45.

14. Ensure that the **Z Axis** option is selected in the **Rotate** drop-down list of the dialog box as the axis of revolution.

15. Click on the **OK** button in the **JOINT** dialog box. The revolute joint is applied such that all degrees of freedom of the third component (**Connecting Rod**) become fixed except one rotational degree of freedom. As a result, the **Connecting Rod** component can rotate about its axis. Figure 8.46 shows the assembly after assembling the **Connecting Rod** component.

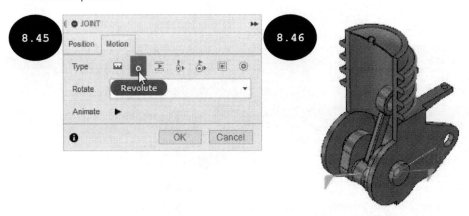

Inserting and Assembling the Fourth Component

Now, you need to insert and assemble the **Piston Pin** component of the assembly.

1. Display the **Data Panel** by clicking on the **Show Data Panel** tool ▦ in the **Application Bar.**

2. Right-click on the **Piston Pin** component in the **Data Panel** and then click on the **Insert into Current Design** tool in the shortcut menu that appears. The **Piston Pin** component gets inserted into the design file with the display of translational and manipulator handles attached.

3. Change the position of the **Piston Pin** component in the graphics area by dragging its translational and manipulator handles such that it does not intersect with the existing components of the assembly.

4. Click on the **OK** button in the **MOVE/COPY** dialog box. The **Piston Pin** component gets inserted and placed in the specified position in the design file, see Figure 8.47. Next, close the **Data Panel** by clicking on the cross mark at its top right corner.

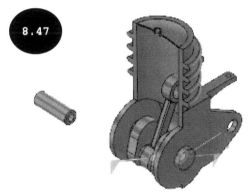

Now, you need to assemble the fourth component (**Piston Pin**).

5. Press the **J** key. The **JOINT** dialog box appears.

 *If the **Fusion360** message window appears, which informs you that some components have been moved from their previous position, then click on the **Capture Position** button to capture the current position of the components. If you click on the **Continue** button in this message window, then the components will revert back to their previous position.*

6. Ensure that the **Simple** button ◎ is selected in the **Component 1** rollout of the **Position** tab in the **JOINT** dialog box for defining the joint origin on a face, an edge, or a point of the component.

7. Move the cursor over the circular face of the **Piston Pin** component, see Figure 8.48. The face gets highlighted and its snap points appear.

8. Click the left mouse button when the joint origin snaps to the middle snap point of the highlighted face, see Figure 8.48. The position of the joint origin is defined on the **Piston Pin** component.

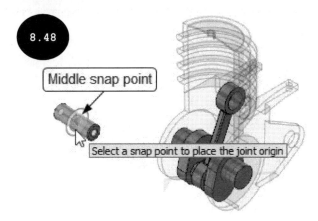

8.48

Middle snap point

Select a snap point to place the joint origin

Now, you need to define the joint origin on another component (**Connecting Rod**).

9. Move the cursor over the top inner circular face of the **Connecting Rod** component, refer to Figure 8.49. The face gets highlighted and its three snap points appear.

10. Press the CTRL key to lock the highlighted face and then click when the joint origin snaps to the middle snap point of the highlighted face, see Figure 8.49. The position of the joint origin is defined and the **Piston Pin** component moves toward the **Connecting Rod** component such that the defined joint origins of both the components get coincident to each other in the graphics area, see Figure 8.50.

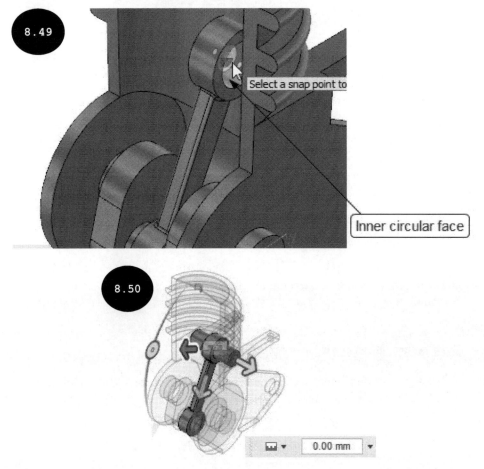

8.49

Select a snap point to

Inner circular face

8.50

0.00 mm

Now, you need to define the joint to be applied between the components.

11. Click on the **Motion** tab in the **JOINT** dialog box and then click on the **Revolute** button in the **Type** area of the dialog box as the joint to be applied between the components, see Figure 8.51.

12. Click on the **OK** button in the **JOINT** dialog box. The revolute joint is applied such that all degrees of freedom of the **Piston Pin** component become fixed except one rotational degree of freedom. Figure 8.52 shows the assembly after assembling the **Piston Pin** component.

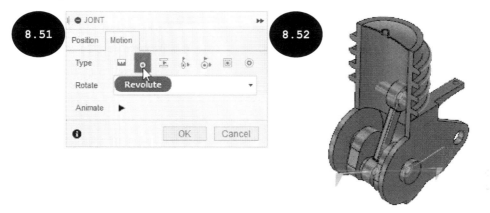

Inserting and Assembling the Fifth Component

Now, you need to insert the **Piston** component of the assembly.

1. Display the **Data Panel** and then right-click on the **Piston** component. Next, click on the **Insert into Current Design** tool in the shortcut menu that appears. The **Piston** component gets inserted into the design file with the display of translational and manipulator handles attached.

2. Change the position of the **Piston** component in the graphics area by dragging its translational and manipulator handles such that it does not intersect with the existing components of the assembly and appears similar to the one shown in Figure 8.53.

3. Drag the **Piston Pin** component to change its position similar to the one shown in Figure 8.54 such that it does not intersect with the **Crank Case** component of the assembly.

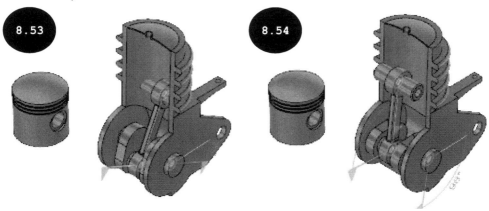

You can translate or rotate a component along or about its free degrees of freedom.

Now, you need to assemble the fifth component (**Piston**).

4.   Click on the **Joint** tool in the **ASSEMBLE** panel of the **SOLID** tab or press the J key. The **Fusion360** message window appears.

 The Fusion 360 message window appears, if some components of the assembly have moved from their position. The Capture Position button is used to capture the current position of the components, whereas the Continue button is used to revert the components back to their previous position.

5.   Click on the **Capture Position** button in the **Fusion360** message window. The **JOINT** dialog box appears.

6.   Move the cursor over the inner circular edge of the **Piston** component, see Figure 8.55. The edge gets highlighted and the joint origin snaps to the center of the edge.

7.   Click the left mouse button when the joint origin snaps to the center of the circular edge, see Figure 8.55. The position of the joint origin is defined on the **Piston** component and you are prompted to define the position of the joint origin on the other component.

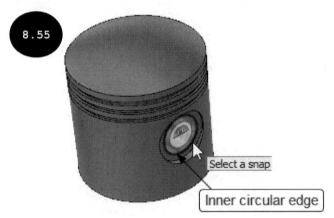

8.   Move the cursor over the right circular edge of the **Piston Pin** component, see Figure 8.56. The edge gets highlighted and the joint origin snaps to the center of the edge.

9.   Click the left mouse button when the joint origin snaps to the center of the circular edge, see Figure 8.56. The defined joint origins of both the components get coincident to each other in the graphics area, see Figure 8.57.

10. Click on the **Motion** tab in the **JOINT** dialog box and then click on the **Revolute** button in the **Type** area of the dialog box as the joint to be applied between the components.

11. Click on the **OK** button in the **JOINT** dialog box. The revolute joint is applied such that all degrees of freedom of the **Piston** component become fixed except one rotational degree of freedom. Figure 8.58 shows the assembly after assembling the **Piston** component.

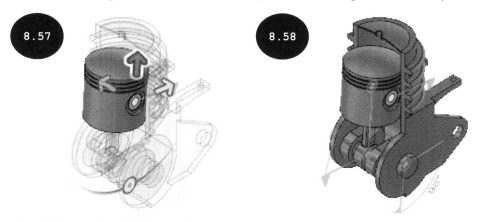

Applying the Slider Joint

Now, you need to apply the slider joint between the **Piston** and the **Crank Case** components of the assembly, so that **Piston** can translate or slide along an axis of the **Crank Case**.

1. Click on the **Joint** tool in the **ASSEMBLE** panel of the **SOLID** tab, see Figure 8.59. Alternatively, press the J key. The **JOINT** dialog box appears.

2. Move the cursor over the lower circular edge of the **Piston** component and then click when the joint origin snaps to its center point, see Figure 8.60. The joint origin is defined on the **Piston** component.

3. Move the cursor over the inner cylindrical face of the **Crank Case** component and then click when the joint origin snaps to its top snap point, see Figure 8.61. The joint origins are defined and the component animates for a while in the graphics area based on the joint type selected in the **Motion** tab of the dialog box.

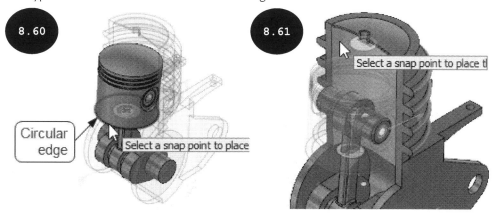

4. Click on the **Motion** tab in the **JOINT** dialog box and then click on the **Slider** button in the **Type** area of the dialog box as the joint to be applied between the components. The **Piston** component starts translating or sliding for a while along an axis of the **Crank Case** component.

5. Ensure that the **Z Axis** option is selected in the **Slide** drop-down list of the dialog box as the sliding axis for the **Piston** component.

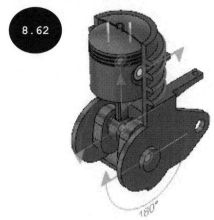

6. Click on the **OK** button in the **JOINT** dialog box. The slider joint is applied such that all degrees of freedom of the **Piston** component become fixed except one translational degree of freedom. Figure 8.62 shows the final assembly after assembling all its components.

Hiding the Joint Symbols in the Graphics Area

By default, the visibility of applied joints is turned on. As a result, the symbols of applied joints appear in the graphics area.

1. Click on the **Display Settings > Object Visibility** in the **Navigation Bar**, see Figure 8.63. A cascading menu appears.

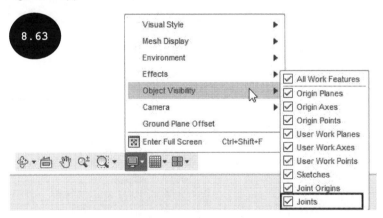

2. Clear the **Joints** check box in the cascading menu. The joint symbols of the applied joints get hidden in the graphics area, see Figure 8.64.

Animating the Assembly

Now, you can animate the assembly to review its working conditions and the behavior of its individual components with respect to each other.

1. Expand the **Joints** node in the **BROWSER** by clicking on the arrow in front of it, see Figure 8.65. A list of all the applied joints appear under the **Joints** node.

2. Right-click on the first revolute joint applied between the **Crank Shaft** and the **Crank Case** components in the expanded **Joints** node as the joint for animating the assembly, see Figure 8.66. A shortcut menu appears.

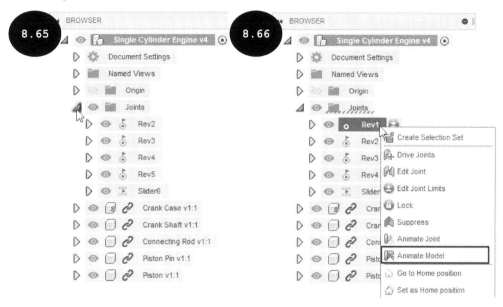

*The **Animate Joint** option in the shortcut menu is used for animating only the selected joint of the assembly and its respective component.*

3. Click on the **Animate Model** option in the shortcut menu. The assembly starts animating in the graphics area such that the **Crank Shaft** rotates about its axis, simultaneously the **Piston** slides up and down, which is connected to the **Crank Shaft** through the **Connecting Rod**.

4. After reviewing the working conditions and the behavior of individual components of the assembly, press the ESC key to stop the animation.

Saving the Model

1. Click on the **Save** tool in the **Application Bar**. The **Add Version Description** window appears as the design is already saved, see Figure 8.67. In this window, you can enter a description for the new version of the assembly, if needed.

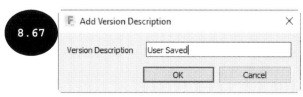

In Autodesk Fusion 360, every time you save a design file, a new version of the file gets saved without overriding its existing versions.

2.   Click on the **OK** button in the window. A new updated version of the assembly file is saved at the specified location (**Autodesk Fusion 360 Tutorials** > **Chapter 8** > **Tutorial 1**).

Tutorial 2: Creating the Blow Off Cock Assembly

Create an assembly shown in Figure 8.68 by applying all the required joints. The section view of the assembly is shown in Figure 8.69 for your reference only. Different views and dimensions of individual components of the assembly are shown in Figures 8.70 through 8.74. You can also download all components of the assembly by logging on to the SDCAD Academy website (www.sdcadacademy.com). All dimensions are in mm.

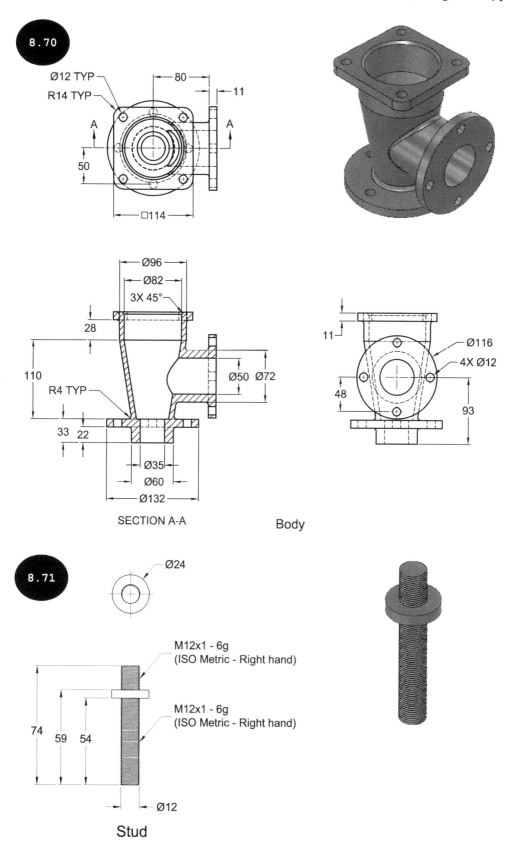

8.70

Ø12 TYP
R14 TYP
80
11
A
A
50
□114

Ø96
Ø82
3X 45°
28
110
R4 TYP
33 22
Ø35
Ø60
Ø132
Ø50 Ø72

SECTION A-A

11
Ø116
4X Ø12
48
93

Body

8.71

Ø24

M12x1 - 6g
(ISO Metric - Right hand)

M12x1 - 6g
(ISO Metric - Right hand)

74 59 54

Ø12

Stud

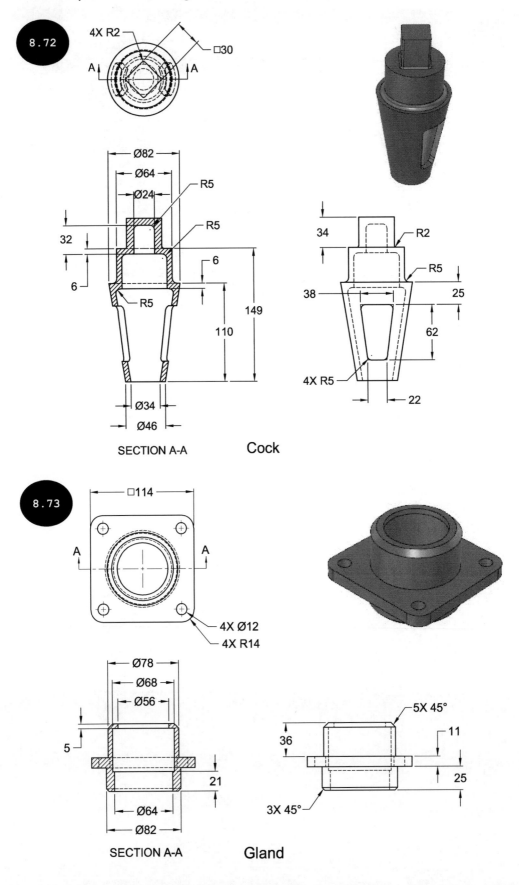

8.72

4X R2

□30

A   A

Ø82

Ø64

Ø24

R5

R5

32

R5

6

6

R5

6

149

110

Ø34

Ø46

SECTION A-A   Cock

34

R2

R5

38

25

62

4X R5

22

8.73

□114

A   A

4X Ø12

4X R14

Ø78

Ø68

Ø56

5

21

Ø64

Ø82

SECTION A-A   Gland

5X 45°

36

11

25

3X 45°

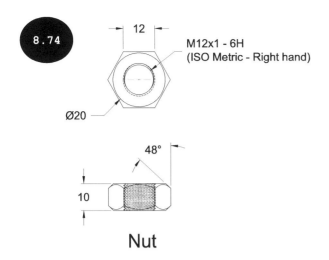

Nut

The following sequence summarizes the tutorial outline:

- Starting Fusion 360 and Creating all Components
- Inserting the First Component into a Design File
- Grounding/Fixing the First Component
- Creating the Section View of an Assembly
- Inserting the Second Component of the Assembly
- Applying the Revolute Joint
- Turning Off the Section View
- Inserting the Third Component
- Applying the Rigid Joint
- Inserting and Assembling the Fourth Component
- Inserting and Assembling the Fifth Component
- Inserting and Assembling the Remaining Components
- Saving the Model

Starting Fusion 360 and Creating all Components

1. Start Fusion 360 by double-clicking on the Autodesk Fusion 360 icon on your desktop.

2. Create all the components of the assembly one by one in a separate design file. Refer to Figures 8.70 through 8.74 for dimensions of each component. After creating all the components, save them at a common location *Autodesk Fusion 360 Tutorials > Chapter 8 > Tutorial 2* in the **Data Panel**. You need to create these folders in the **Data Panel**.

 You can also download all the components of the assembly by visiting our website www.sdcadacademy.com.

Inserting the First Component into a Design File

1.   Start a new design file by invoking the **File** drop-down menu in the **Application Bar** and then clicking on the **New Design** tool, see Figure 8.75.

2.   Ensure that the **DESIGN** workspace is selected in the **Workspace** drop-down menu of the **Toolbar** as the workspace for the active design file, refer to Figure 8.76.

Before you insert components of the assembly, you need to save the design file.

3.   Click on the **Save** tool on the **Application Bar**, see Figure 8.76. The **Save** dialog box appears.

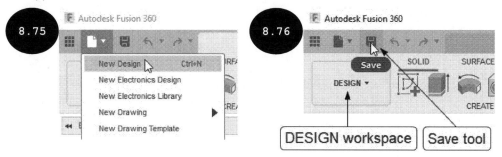

4.   Enter **Blow Off Cock** in the **Name** field of the **Save** dialog box as the name of the design file.

5.   Ensure that the location **Autodesk Fusion 360 Tutorials > Chapter 8 > Tutorial 2** is specified in the **Location** field of the dialog box for saving the design file.

It is recommended to save the design file with a unique name of the assembly, in the same location where all the components of the assembly are saved.

6.   Click on the **Save** button in the dialog box. The design file is saved with the name **Blow Off Cock** at the specified location (*Autodesk Fusion 360 Tutorials > Chapter 8 > Tutorial 2*) in the **Data Panel**.

Now, you can insert the first component of the assembly into the currently active design file (**Blow Off Cock**).

7.   Display the **Data Panel** by clicking on the **Show Data Panel** tool in the **Application Bar**, see Figure 8.77.

8.   Browse to the location where all the components of the assembly have been saved (**Autodesk Fusion 360 Tutorials > Chapter 8 > Tutorial 2**) in the **Data Panel**. A thumbnail view of all the components of the assembly appears in the **Data Panel**, see Figure 8.78.

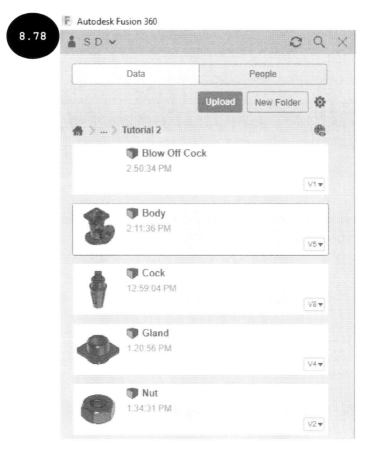

Now, you can insert the first component of the assembly into the active design file.

9. Right-click on the **Body** component in the **Data Panel** and then click on the **Insert into Current Design** tool in the shortcut menu that appears, see Figure 8.79. The **Body** component gets inserted into the design file with the display of translational and manipulator handles attached to it, see Figure 8.80. Also, the **MOVE/COPY** dialog box appears in the graphics area.

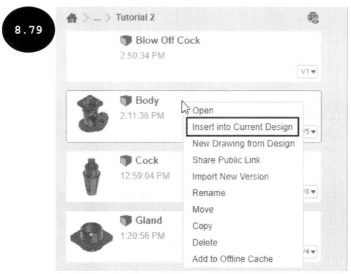

10. Accept the default position of the component in the graphics area and then click on the OK button in the MOVE/COPY dialog box. The **Body** component gets inserted into the design file, see Figure 8.81. Next, close the **Data Panel** by clicking on the cross mark at its top right corner.

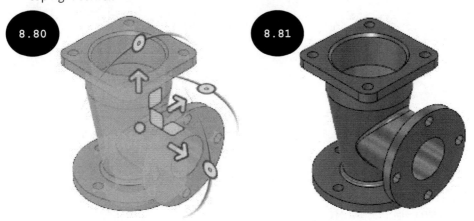

The component icon in front of the name of the design file gets changed to the assembly icon in the BROWSER, which represents the current design file as an assembly file.

You can also insert a component into the active design file by dragging and dropping it from the Data Panel to the design file.

Grounding/Fixing the First Component

Now, you need to ground the first component of the assembly.

1. Right-click on the name of the component (**Body**) in the **BROWSER** and then click on the **Ground** option in the shortcut menu that appears, see Figure 8.82. The **Body** component becomes the grounded component and all its degrees of freedom get fixed such that its cannot move or rotate in any direction. Also, a push-pin symbol 📌 appears on its component icon in the **BROWSER** representing it as a grounded component.

Creating the Section View of an Assembly

Now, you need to create a section view of an assembly for displaying its internal details.

1. Invoke the **INSPECT** drop-down menu in the **SOLID** tab of the **Toolbar** and then click on

the **Section Analysis** tool, see Figure 8.83. The **SECTION ANALYSIS** dialog box appears. Also, three default planes appear in the graphics area.

2. Click on the Front plane as the cutting plane for creating the section view of the model. A preview of the section view appears such that the geometry of the model in front of the selected plane gets hidden, see Figure 8.84. Also, additional options for manipulating the section plane appear in the **SECTION ANALYSIS** dialog box.

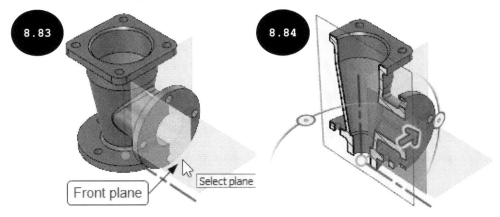

*By default, the 0 mm value is entered in the **Y Distance** field in the **SECTION ANALYSIS** dialog box. As a result, the section view is created by cutting the model exactly at the selected plane. You can specify an offset distance in the **Y Distance** file for creating a section view at an offset distance from the selected plane. You can also drag the arrow that appears in the graphics area to define the offset distance for creating the section view. Additionally, you can define an angle value in the **X Angle** and **Z Angle** fields for creating the section view at an angle to the respective axes.*

3. Click on the **OK** button in the **SECTION ANALYSIS** dialog box. The section view is created, see Figure 8.85. Also, the **Analysis** node gets added in the **BROWSER** with the display of **Section1** under it, see Figure 8.86.

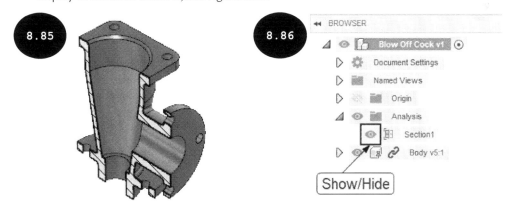

Creating a section view does not change or modify the geometry of the model. It is only used for viewing the internal features or components of a design.

*You can turn on or off the display of section view in the graphics area by clicking on the **Show/Hide** icon in front of the **Section1** option under the expanded **Analysis** node in the BROWSER. You can create multiple section views on a model.*

Inserting the Second Component of the Assembly

1. Display the **Data Panel** by clicking on the **Show Data Panel** tool ▦ in the **Application Bar**.

2. Right-click on the **Cock** component in the **Data Panel** and then click on the **Insert into Current Design** tool in the shortcut menu that appears, see Figure 8.87. The **Cock** component gets inserted into the design file with the display of translational and manipulator handles attached to it. Also, the **MOVE/COPY** dialog box appears in the graphics area.

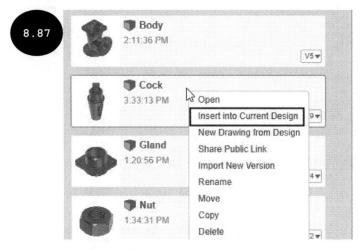

3. Define the position of the second component (**Cock**) by dragging its translational handle, back side of the section plane in the graphics area so that it does not get sectioned, see Figure 8.88.

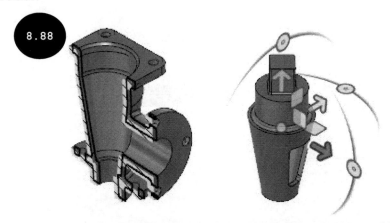

🔘 *If you specify the placement of the component on the front side of the assembly section plane then the placed component will also be sectioned by the section plane and it will not be visible or partial visible in the graphics area.*

4. Click on the **OK** button in the **MOVE/COPY** dialog box. The **Cock** component gets inserted and placed in the specified position in the design file. Next, close the **Data Panel** by clicking on the cross mark at its top right corner.

Applying the Revolute Joint

Now, you need to apply the revolute joint between the second and the first components of the assembly, so that the second component can only rotate about an axis.

1. Click on the **Joint** tool in the **ASSEMBLE** panel of the **SOLID** tab, see Figure 8.89. Alternatively, press the **J** key. The **JOINT** dialog box appears. Also, the first component (grounded component) becomes transparent in the graphics area and you are prompted to define the position of the joint origin on the second component (moveable component).

2. Ensure that the **Simple** button ⊙ is selected in the **Component 1** rollout of the **Position** tab in the **JOINT** dialog box for defining the joint origin on a face, an edge, or a point of the component.

3. Move the cursor over the bottom circular edge of the second component (**Cock**), see Figure 8.90. The edge gets highlighted and the joint origin snaps to the snap point that appears at the center of the circular edge.

4. Click the left mouse button when the joint origin snaps to the center of the bottom circular edge of the **Cock** component, see Figure 8.90. The position of the joint origin is defined at the center of the circular edge. Also, the **Cock** component becomes transparent in the graphics area and you are prompted to define the position of the joint origin on the first component (**Body**).

5. Ensure that the **Simple** button ⊙ is selected in the **Mode** area of the **Component 2** rollout in the dialog box for defining the joint origin on a face, an edge, or a point.

6. Move the cursor over the inner circular edge of the first component (**Body**), see Figure 8.91. The edge gets highlighted and the joint origin snaps to its center.

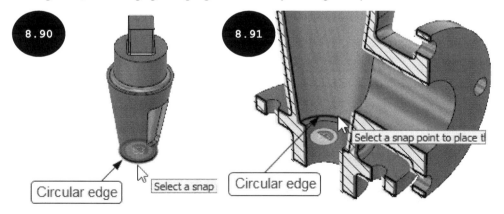

7. Click the left mouse button when the joint origin snaps to its center, refer to Figure 8.91. The position of the joint origin is defined and the second component (**Cock**) moves toward the first component such that the defined joint origins of both the components

get coincident to each other in the graphics area, see Figure 8.92. Also, the component animates in the graphics area based on the default joint type selected in the **Motion** tab of the dialog box.

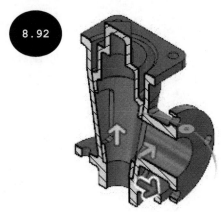

8. Click on the **Motion** tab in the **JOINT** dialog box and then click on the **Revolute** button as the joint to be applied between the components, see Figure 8.93.

9. Click on the **OK** button in the **JOINT** dialog box. The revolute joint is applied such that all degrees of freedom of the second component become fixed except one rotational degree of freedom. As a result, the second component (**Cock**) can rotate about its axis. Figure 8.94 shows the assembly after assembling the **Cock** component.

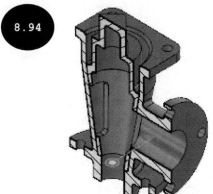

*You can also edit an already applied joint of an assembly. To do so, expand the **Joints** node in the **BROWSER** and then right-click on the joint to be edited. Next, click on the **Edit Joint** tool in the shortcut menu that appears. The **EDIT JOINT** dialog box appears. In this dialog box, you can define new positions for the joint origins of the components, edit the alignment, change the joint type, and so on.*

Turning Off the Section View

1. Expand the **Analysis** node in the BROWSER and then click on the **Show/Hide** icon in front of the **Section1** option, see Figure 8.95. The display of the section view gets turned off in the graphics area and the full assembly appears as shown in Figure 8.96.

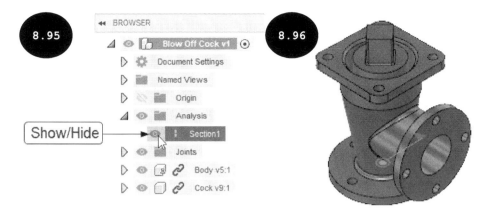

Show/Hide

Inserting the Third Component

1. Display the **Data Panel** by clicking on the **Show Data Panel** tool ▦ in the **Application Bar**.

2. Drag and drop the **Gland** component from the **Data Panel** to any point in the graphics area. The **Gland** component gets inserted into the design file with the display of translational and manipulator handles attached to it. Also, the **MOVE/COPY** dialog box appears in the graphics area.

3. Change the position of the third component (**Gland**) in the graphics area by dragging its translational and manipulator handles such that it does not intersect with the existing components of the assembly.

4. Click on the **OK** button in the **MOVE/COPY** dialog box. The **Gland** component gets inserted and placed in the specified position in the design file, see Figure 8.97. Next, close the **Data Panel** by clicking on the cross mark at its top right corner.

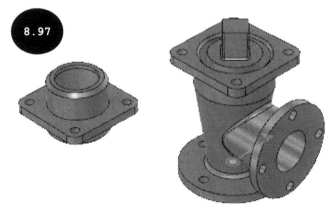

Applying the Rigid Joint

Now, you need to apply the rigid joint.

1. Press the **J** key. The **JOINT** dialog box appears.

2. Rotate the third component (**Gland**) in the graphics area such that you can view its bottom circular edge, see Figure 8.98.

3. Move the cursor over the outer circular edge of the third component (**Gland**), see Figure 8.98. The edge gets highlighted and the joint origin snaps to its center.

4. Click the left mouse button when the joint origin snaps to the center of the outer circular edge of the **Gland** component, see Figure 8.98. The position of the joint origin is defined at the center of the circular edge. Also, the **Gland** component becomes transparent in the graphics area and you are prompted to define the position of the joint origin on another component.

5. Change the orientation of the assembly to isometric by clicking on the **Home** icon in the ViewCube.

6. Move the cursor over the top inner circular edge of the first component (**Body**), see Figure 8.99. The edge gets highlighted and the joint origin snaps to its center.

7. Click the left mouse button when the joint origin snaps to the center of the top inner circular edge of the **Body** component, see Figure 8.99. The defined joint origins of both the components get coincident to each other in the graphics area, see Figure 8.100.

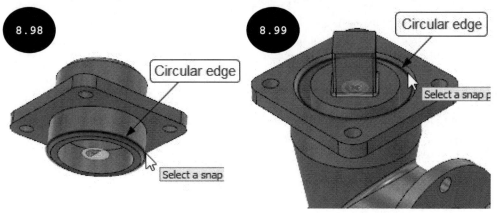

8. Click on the **Motion** tab in the **JOINT** dialog box and then click on the **Rigid** button as the joint to be applied between the components, see Figure 8.101.

9. Click on the **OK** button in the **JOINT** dialog box. The rigid joint is applied such that all degrees of freedom of the **Gland** component become fixed and it cannot move or rotate in any direction. Figure 8.102 shows the assembly after assembling the **Gland** component.

Inserting and Assembling the Fourth Component

Now, you need to insert and assemble the **Stud** component of the assembly.

1. Display the **Data Panel** and then insert the **Stud** component into the design file by dragging and dropping it from the **Data Panel** to any point in the graphics area. The **Stud** component gets inserted into the design file with the display of translational and manipulator handles attached to it.

2. Change the position of the **Stud** component in the graphics area by dragging its translational and manipulator handles such that it does not intersect with the existing components of the assembly.

3. Click on the **OK** button in the **MOVE/COPY** dialog box. The **Stud** component gets inserted and placed in the specified position in the design file, see Figure 8.103. Next, close the **Data Panel** by clicking on the cross mark at its top right corner.

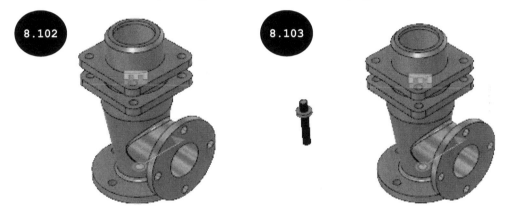

Now, you need to assemble the fourth component (**Stud**).

4. Click on the **Joint** tool in the **ASSEMBLE** panel of the **SOLID** tab or press the J key. The **JOINT** dialog box appears.

5. Rotate the assembly such that you can view the bottom face of the **Stud** component, refer to Figure 8.104.

6. Move the cursor over the bottom circular edge of the **Stud** component in the graphics area, see Figure 8.104.

7. Click the left mouse button when the joint origin snaps to the center of the circular edge, see Figure 8.104. The position of the joint origin is defined on the **Stud** component and you are prompted to define the position of the joint origin on the other component.

8. Change the orientation of the assembly back to isometric.

9. Move the cursor over the top circular edge of a hole of the **Gland** component, see Figure 8.105 and then click the left mouse button when the joint origin snaps to its center. The defined joint origins of both the components get coincident to each other in the graphics area, see Figure 8.106.

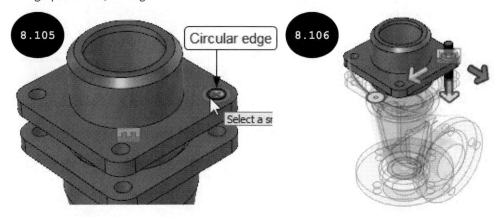

10. Click on the **Motion** tab in the **JOINT** dialog box and then ensure that the **Rigid** button is activated in the dialog box.

11. Click on the **OK** button in the **JOINT** dialog box. The rigid joint is applied between the components. Figure 8.107 shows the assembly after assembling the **Stud** component.

 In Figure 8.107, the visibility of applied joints is turned off. To turn off the visibility of applied joints, click on the Display Settings > Object Visibility in the Navigation Bar and then clear the Joints check box in the cascading menu that appears.

Inserting and Assembling the Fifth Component
Now, you need to insert and assemble the **Nut** component of the assembly.

1. Display the **Data Panel** and then insert the **Nut** component into the design file by dragging and dropping it from the **Data Panel** to anywhere in the graphics area. The **Nut** component gets inserted into the design file with the display of translational and manipulator handles attached to it.

2. Change the position of the **Nut** component in the graphics area by dragging its translational and manipulator handles such that it does not intersect with the existing components of the assembly.

3. Click on the **OK** button in the **MOVE/COPY** dialog box. The **Nut** component gets inserted and placed in the specified position in the design file, see Figure 8.108. Next, close the **Data Panel** by clicking on the cross mark at its top right corner.

   Now, you need to assemble the fifth component (**Nut**).

4. Click on the **Joint** tool in the **ASSEMBLE** panel of the **SOLID** tab or press the J key. The **JOINT** dialog box appears.

5. Move the cursor over the top planar face of the **Nut** component. The face gets highlighted and all its snap points appear, see Figure 8.109.

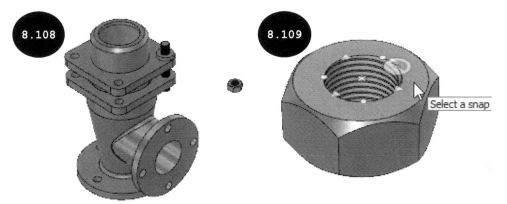

6. Press and hold the CTRL key to lock the highlighted face and then move the cursor over the center snap point of the highlighted face, see Figure 8.110.

   You can lock a face or an edge of the component to select its required snap point easily by pressing the CTRL key.

7. Click the left mouse button when the joint origin snaps to the center of the highlighted face, see Figure 8.110. The position of the joint origin on the fifth component is defined. Next, release the CTRL key.

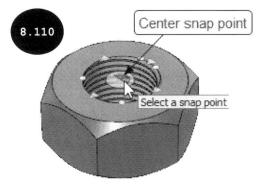

8. Rotate the assembly and then move the cursor over the bottom planar face of the **Body** component, see Figure 8.111. The face gets highlighted and all its snap points appear.

9. Press and hold the CTRL key to lock the highlighted face and then move the cursor over the center snap point of the hole circular edge.

10. Click the left mouse button when the joint origin snaps to the center of the hole circular edge of the highlighted face, see Figure 8.111. The defined joint origins of both the components get coincident to each other in the graphics area, refer to Figure 8.112.

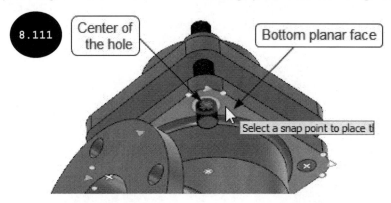

11. Click on the **Motion** tab in the **JOINT** dialog box and then ensure that the **Rigid** button is activated in the dialog box.

12. Click on the **OK** button in the **JOINT** dialog box. The rigid joint is applied between the components, see Figure 8.112. Next, change the orientation of the assembly to isometric, see Figure 8.113.

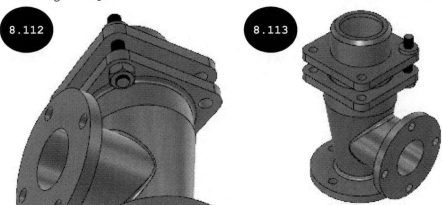

Inserting and Assembling the Remaining Components

1. Insert and assemble the remaining instances of the **Stud** and **Nut** components of the assembly one by one in a manner similar to discussed earlier. Figure 8.114 shows the final assembly after assembling all the instances of the **Stud** and **Nut** components. Figure 8.115 shows the section view of the final assembly.

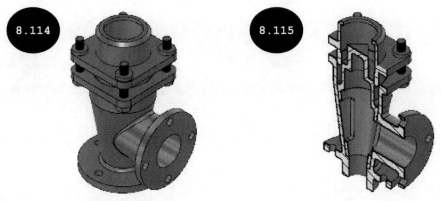

*You can also create rectangular pattern of **Stud** and **Nut** components for creating their remaining instances by using the **Rectangular Pattern** tool.*

Saving the Model

1. Click on the **Save** tool in the **Application Bar**. The **Add Version Description** window appears as the design is already saved. In this window, you can enter a description for the new version of the assembly, if needed.

2. Click on the **OK** button in the window. A new updated version of the assembly file is saved at the specified location (**Autodesk Fusion 360 Tutorials > Chapter 8 > Tutorial 2**).

Tutorial 3: Creating the Manual Press Assembly

Create the Manual Press assembly shown in Figure 8.116 by applying all the required joints. Different views and dimensions of individual components of the assembly are shown in Figures 8.117 through 8.125. You can also download all components of the assembly by logging on to the SDCAD Academy website (www.sdcadacademy.com). All dimensions are in mm.

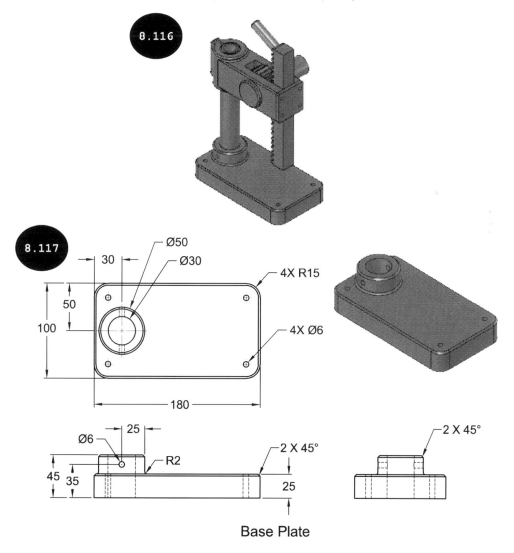

Base Plate

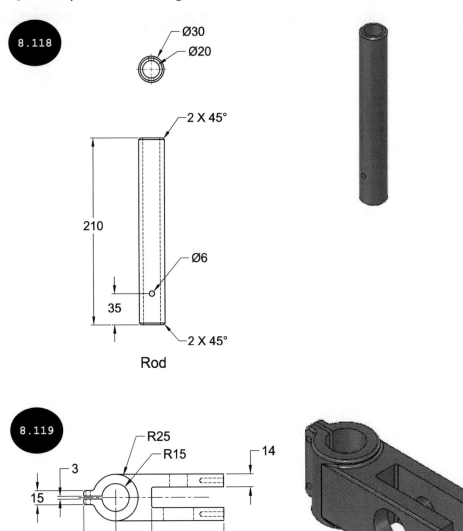

Rod

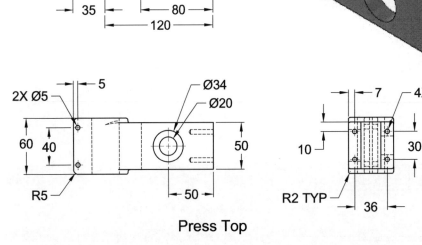

Press Top

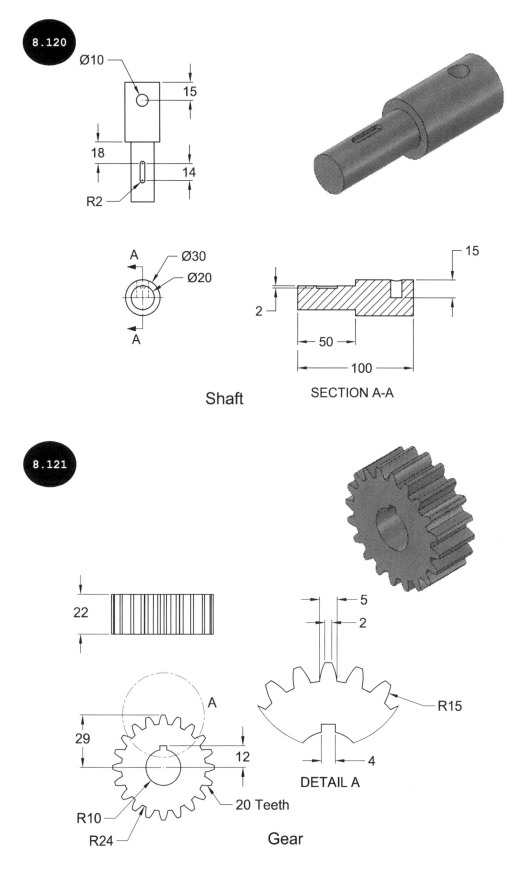

8.120

Ø10

15

18

14

R2

A

Ø30

Ø20

A

Shaft

15

2

50

100

SECTION A-A

8.121

22

A

29

12

5

2

R15

4

DETAIL A

R10

R24

20 Teeth

Gear

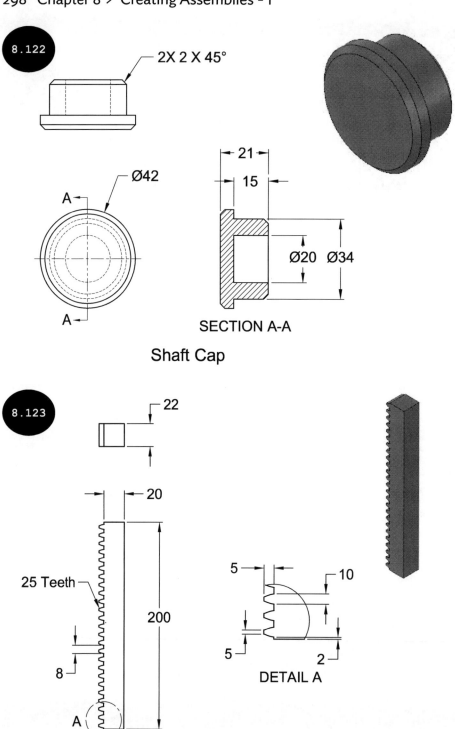

8.122

2X 2 X 45°

Ø42

A

21

15

Ø20   Ø34

SECTION A-A

Shaft Cap

8.123

22

20

25 Teeth

200

8

A

5

5

10

2

DETAIL A

Rack

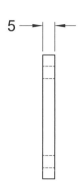

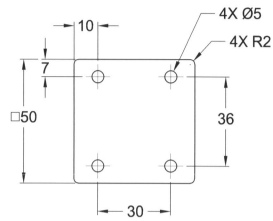

5

4X Ø5

4X R2

10

7

□50

36

30

Cover Plate

Ø16

2 X 45°

75

90

Ø10

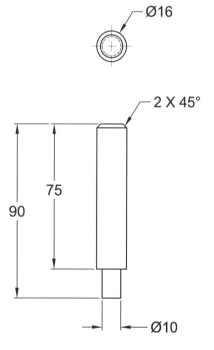

Handle

The following sequence summarizes the tutorial outline:

- Starting Fusion 360 and Creating all Components
- Inserting the First Component into a Design File
- Grounding/Fixing the First Component
- Inserting the Second Component of the Assembly
- Applying the Rigid Joint
- Inserting and Assembling the Third Component
- Inserting and Assembling the Fourth Component
- Inserting and Assembling the Fifth Component
- Inserting and Assembling the Sixth Component
- Inserting the Seventh Component
- Applying the Slider Joint
- Defining the Joint Limits
- Inserting and Assembling the Remaining Components
- Defining Relative Motion between Two Joints
- Saving the Model

Starting Fusion 360 and Creating all Components

1. Start Fusion 360 by double-clicking on the Autodesk Fusion 360 icon on your desktop.

2. Create all the components of the assembly one by one in a separate design file. Refer to Figures 8.117 through 8.125 for dimensions of each component. After creating all the components, save them at a common location *Autodesk Fusion 360 Tutorials > Chapter 8 > Tutorial 3* in the **Data Panel**. You need to create the **Tutorial 3** folder inside the **Chapter 8** folder of the **Autodesk Fusion 360 Tutorials** project in the **Data Panel**.

   You can also download all the components of the assembly by visiting our website www.sdcadacademy.com.

Inserting the First Component into a Design File

1. Start a new design file pressing the CTRL + N key.

2. Save the design file with the name **Manual Press** by using the **Save** tool at the **Autodesk Fusion 360 Tutorials > Chapter 8 > Tutorial 3** location in the **Data Panel**.

   It is recommended to save the design file with a unique name of the assembly, in the same location where all the components of the assembly are saved.

Now, you can insert the first component of the assembly into the currently active design file (**Manual Press**).

3. Display the **Data Panel** by clicking on the **Show Data Panel** tool in the **Application Bar**, see Figure 8.126.

4. Browse to the location where all the components of the assembly have saved (**Autodesk Fusion 360 Tutorials > Chapter 8 > Tutorial 3**) in the **Data Panel**. A thumbnail view of all the components of the assembly appears in the **Data Panel**, refer to Figure 8.127.

5. Right-click on the **Base Plate** component in the **Data Panel** and then click on the **Insert into Current Design** tool in the shortcut menu that appears, see Figure 8.127. The **Base Plate** component gets inserted into the design file with the display of translational and manipulator handles attached to it. Also, the **MOVE/COPY** dialog box appears in the graphics area.

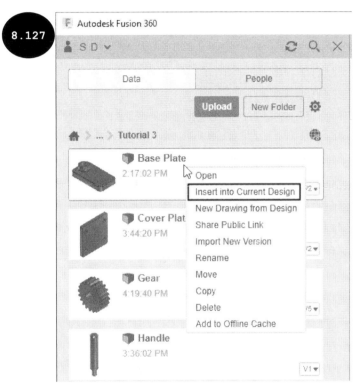

6. Accept the default position of the component in the graphics area and then click on the **OK** button in the **MOVE/COPY** dialog box. The **Base Plate** component gets inserted into the design file, see Figure 8.128. Next, close the **Data Panel** by clicking on the cross mark at its top right corner.

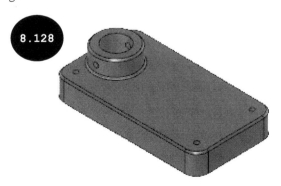

Grounding/Fixing the First Component

1. Right-click on the name of the component (**Base Plate**) in the BROWSER and then click on the **Ground** option in the shortcut menu that appears, see Figure 8.129. The **Base Plate** component becomes the grounded component and all its degrees of freedom get fixed such that its cannot move or rotate in any direction. Also, a push-pin symbol ![] appears on its component icon in the BROWSER representing it as a grounded component.

8.129

Inserting the Second Component of the Assembly

1. Display the **Data Panel** by clicking on the **Show Data Panel** tool ![] in the **Application Bar**.

2. Right-click on the **Rod** component in the **Data Panel** and then click on the **Insert into Current Design** tool in the shortcut menu that appears. The **Rod** component gets inserted into the design file with the display of translational and manipulator handles attached to it.

3. Define the position of the second component (**Rod**) by dragging its translational handle such that it does not intersect with the first component of the assembly, refer to Figure 8.130.

4. Click on the **OK** button in the **MOVE/COPY** dialog box. The **Rod** component gets inserted and placed in the specified position in the design file, see Figure 8.130. Next, close the **Data Panel** by clicking on the cross mark at its top right corner.

8.130

Applying the Rigid Joint

1. Click on the **Joint** tool in the **ASSEMBLE** panel of the **SOLID** tab, see Figure 8.131. Alternatively, press the J key. The **JOINT** dialog box appears. Also, the first component (grounded component) becomes transparent in the graphics area and you are prompted to define the position of the joint origin on the second component (moveable component).

2. Ensure that the **Simple** button ⊙ is selected in the **Component 1** rollout of the **Position** tab in the **JOINT** dialog box for defining the joint origin on a face, an edge, or a point of the component.

3. Move the cursor over the bottom hole face of the second component (**Rod**), see Figure 8.132. The face gets highlighted and its snap points appear.

4. Click the left mouse button when the joint origin snaps to its front snap point, see Figure 8.132. The position of the joint origin is defined on the **Rod** component and it becomes transparent in the graphics area. Also, you are prompted to define the position of the joint origin on the first component (**Base Plate**).

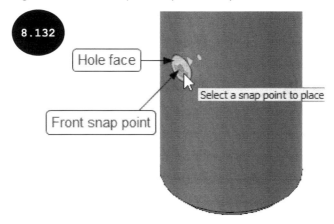

5. Move the cursor over the hole face of the first component (**Base Plate**), see Figure 8.133. The face gets highlighted and its three snap points (front, middle, and back) appear.

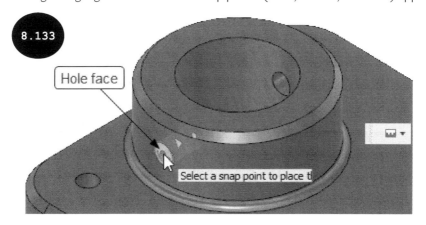

6. Press and hold the CTRL key to lock the highlighted face and then move the cursor over its back snap point, see Figure 8.134.

7. Click the left mouse button when the joint origin snaps to the back snap point of the highlighted face, see Figure 8.134. The position of the joint origin is defined and the second component (**Rod**) moves toward the first component such that the defined joint origins of both the components get coincident to each other in the graphics area, see Figure 8.135. Also, the component animates in the graphics area based on the default joint type selected in the **Motion** tab of the dialog box. Release the CTRL key.

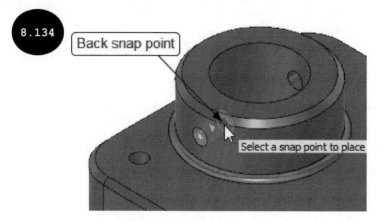

8. Click on the **Motion** tab in the **JOINT** dialog box and then click on the **Rigid** button as the joint to be applied between the components, see Figure 8.136.

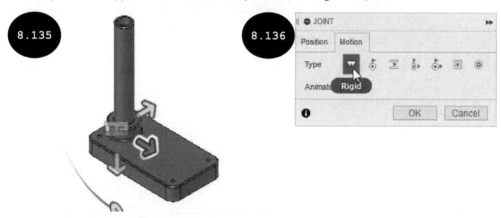

9. Click on the **OK** button in the **JOINT** dialog box. The rigid joint is applied such that all degrees of freedom of the **Rod** component become fixed and it cannot move or rotate in any direction. Figure 8.137 shows the assembly after assembling the **Rod** component.

*In Figure 8.137, the visibility of applied joints is turned off. To turn off the visibility of applied joints, click on the **Display Settings** > **Object Visibility** in the **Navigation Bar** and then clear the **Joints** check box in the cascading menu that appears.*

Inserting and Assembling the Third Component

1. Display the **Data Panel** by clicking on the **Show Data Panel** tool ⊞ in the **Application Bar.**

2. Drag and drop the **Press Top** component from the **Data Panel** to any point in the graphics area. The **Press Top** component gets inserted into the design file.

3. Change the position of the third component (**Press Top**) in the graphics area by dragging its translational and manipulator handles that appear such that it does not intersect with the existing components of the assembly.

4. Click on the **OK** button in the **MOVE/COPY** dialog box. The **Press Top** component gets inserted and placed in the specified position in the design file, see Figure 8.138. Next, close the **Data Panel** by clicking on the cross mark at its top right corner.

Now, you need to assemble the **Press Top** component.

5. Press the **J** key. The **JOINT** dialog box appears.

6. Move the cursor over the top circular face of the third component (**Press Top**) and then click when the joint origin snaps to its center snap point, see Figure 8.139. The position of the joint origin is defined on the **Press Top** component and it becomes transparent in the graphics area. Also, you are prompted to define the position of the joint origin on another component.

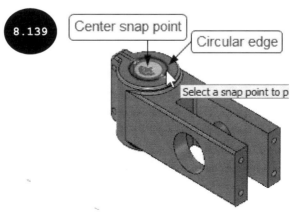

7. Move the cursor over the top circular edge of the second component (**Rod**) and then click when the joint origin snaps to its center, see Figure 8.140. The defined joint origins of both the components get coincident to each other in the graphics area, refer to Figure 8.141.

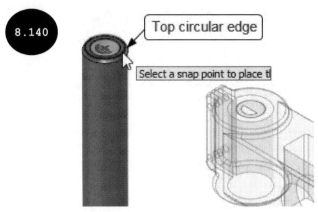

8. Click on the **Motion** tab in the **JOINT** dialog box and then ensure that the **Rigid** button is activated as the joint to be applied between the components.

9. Click on the **OK** button in the **JOINT** dialog box. The rigid joint is applied such that all degrees of freedom of the **Press Top** component become fixed. Figure 8.141 shows the assembly after assembling the **Press Top** component.

Inserting and Assembling the Fourth Component

1. Display the **Data Panel** by clicking on the **Show Data Panel** tool ▦ in the **Application Bar.**

2. Drag and drop the **Shaft** component from the **Data Panel** to anywhere in the graphics area. The **Shaft** component gets inserted into the design file.

3. Change the position of the fourth component (**Shaft**) in the graphics area by dragging its translational and manipulator handles that appear such that it does not intersect with the existing components of the assembly.

4. Click on the **OK** button in the **MOVE/COPY** dialog box. The **Shaft** component gets inserted and placed in the specified position in the design file, see Figure 8.142. Next, close the **Data Panel** by clicking on the cross mark at its top right corner.

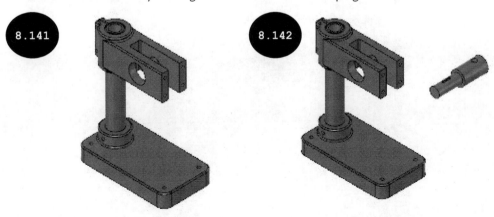

Now, you need to assemble the **Shaft** component.

5. Press the **J** key. The **JOINT** dialog box appears.

6. Move the cursor over the circular edge of the fourth component (**Shaft**) and then click when the joint origin snaps to its center, see Figure 8.143. The position of the joint origin is defined on the **Shaft** component and it becomes transparent in the graphics area. Also, you are prompted to define the position of the joint origin on another component.

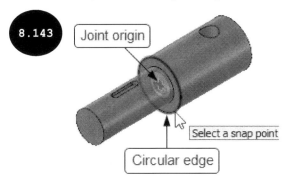

7. Rotate the model and then move the cursor over the circular edge of the back face of the third component (**Press Top**) and then click when the joint origin snaps to its center snap point, see Figure 8.144. The defined joint origins of both the components get coincident to each other in the graphics area, see Figure 8.145.

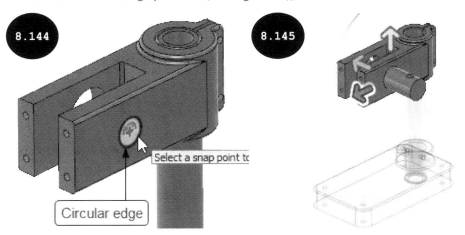

8. Change the orientation of the assembly to isometric.

9. Click on the **Motion** tab in the **JOINT** dialog box and then click on the **Revolute** button as the joint to be applied between the components, see Figure 8.146.

10. Click on the **OK** button in the **JOINT** dialog box. The revolute joint is applied such that all degrees of freedom of the fourth component (**Shaft**) become fixed except one rotational degree of freedom. Figure 8.147 shows the assembly after assembling the **Shaft** component.

Inserting and Assembling the Fifth Component

1. Display the **Data Panel** and then insert the **Gear** component by dragging and dropping it at any point in the design file.

2. Change the position of the **Gear** component by dragging its translational and manipulator handles that appear in the graphics area such that it does not intersect with the existing components of the assembly.

3. Click on the **OK** button in the **MOVE/COPY** dialog box. The **Gear** component gets inserted and placed in the specified position in the design file, see Figure 8.148. Next, close the **Data Panel** by clicking on the cross mark at its top right corner.

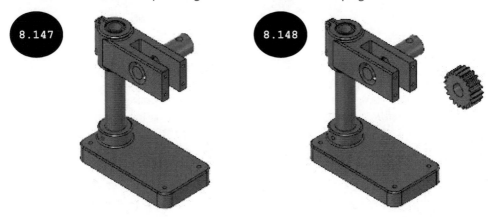

Now, you need to assemble the **Gear** component with the **Shaft** component.

4. Hide the **Press Top** component (third component) of the assembly by clicking on the Show/Hide icon available in front of its name in the **BROWSER**, see Figure 8.149. It helps in easily assembling the **Gear** component with the **Shaft** component.

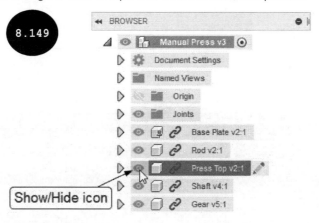

5. After hiding the **Press Top** component, press the J key. The **JOINT** dialog box appears.

6. Move the cursor over the inner circular face of the **Gear** component, see Figure 8.150. The circular face gets highlighted and its snap points (front, middle, and back) appear.

7. Press and hold the CTRL key to lock the highlighted face and then move the cursor over its middle snap point, see Figure 8.151.

8. Click the left mouse button when the joint origin snaps to the middle snap point of the highlighted face, see Figure 8.151. The position of the joint origin is defined and you are prompted to define the position of the joint origin on another component. Next, release the CTRL key.

9. Move the cursor over the outer circular face of the **Shaft** component and then click when the joint origin snaps to its middle snap point, see Figure 8.152. The defined joint origins of both the components get coincident to each other in the graphics area, see Figure 8.153.

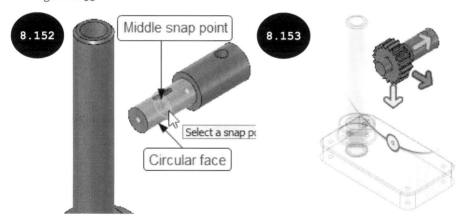

10. Click on the **Motion** tab in the **JOINT** dialog box and then click on the **Rigid** button as the joint to be applied between the components.

11. Click on the **OK** button in the **JOINT** dialog box. The rigid joint is applied such that all degrees of freedom of the **Gear** component become fixed with respect to the **Shaft** of the assembly.

    Now, you can turn on the display of **Press Top** component in the graphics area.

12. Click on the **Show/Hide** icon in front of the **Press Top** component in the BROWSER to turn on its display in the graphics area. Figure 8.154 shows the assembly after assembling the **Gear** component and turning on the display of the **Press Top** component.

8.154

Inserting and Assembling the Sixth Component

1. Display the **Data Panel** and then insert the **Shaft Cap** component by dragging and dropping it at any point in the design file.

2. Change the position of the **Shaft Cap** component by dragging its translational and manipulator handles that appear in the graphics area such that it does not intersect with the existing components of the assembly.

3. Click on the **OK** button in the **MOVE/COPY** dialog box. The **Shaft Cap** component gets inserted and placed in the specified position in the design file, see Figure 8.155. Next, close the **Data Panel** by clicking on the cross mark at its top right corner.

   Now, you need to assemble the **Shaft Cap** component.

4. Press the J key. The **JOINT** dialog box appears.

5. Rotate the assembly and then move the cursor over the circular edge of the **Shaft Cap** component, see Figure 8.156. Next, click when the joint origin snaps to its center. The position of the joint origin is defined and you are prompted to define the position of the joint origin on the another component.

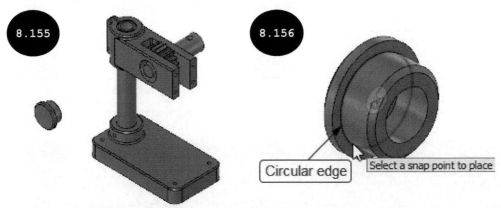

8.155

8.156

Circular edge | Select a snap point to place

6. Change the orientation of the assembly back to isometric.

7. Move the cursor over the circular edge of the front face of the **Press Top** component, see Figure 8.157. Next, click when the joint origin snaps to its center. The defined joint origins of both the components get coincident to each other, see Figure 8.158.

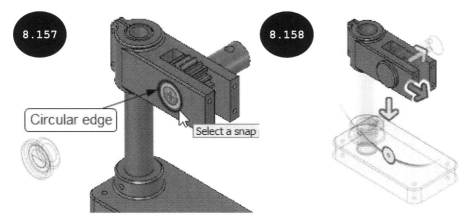

8.   Click on the **Motion** tab in the **JOINT** dialog box and then ensure that the **Rigid** button is activated as the joint to be applied between the components.

9.   Click on the **OK** button in the **JOINT** dialog box. The rigid joint is applied such that all degrees of freedom of the **Shaft Cap** component become fixed.

Inserting the Seventh Component

1.   Display the **Data Panel** and then insert the **Rack** component by dragging and dropping it at any point in the design file.

2.   Change the position of the **Rack** component by dragging its translational and manipulator handles that appear in the graphics area such that it does not intersect with the existing components of the assembly.

3.   Click on the **OK** button in the **MOVE/COPY** dialog box. The **Rack** component gets inserted and placed in the specified position in the design file, see Figure 8.159. Next, close the **Data Panel**.

Applying the Slider Joint

1.   Press the **J** key to invoke the **JOINT** dialog box.

2.   Move the cursor over the vertical edge of the **Rack** component and then click when the joint origin snaps to its middle snap point, see Figure 8.160. The position of the joint origin is defined and you are prompted to define the position of the joint origin on another component.

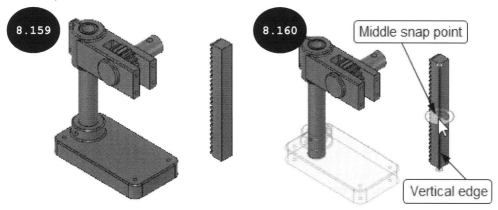

3. Move the cursor over the front vertical edge of the **Press Top** component and then click when the joint origin snaps to its middle snap point, see Figure 8.161. The defined joint origins of both the components get coincident to each other, see Figure 8.162.

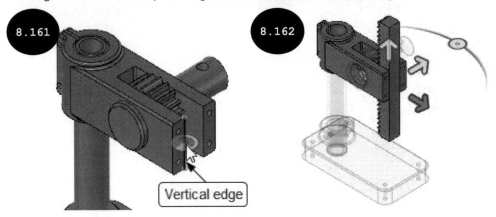

Vertical edge

4. Click on the **Motion** tab in the **JOINT** dialog box and then click on the **Slider** button as the joint to be applied between the components.

5. Click on the **OK** button in the **JOINT** dialog box. The slider joint is applied such that all degrees of freedom of the **Rack** component become fixed except one translational degree of freedom. Figure 8.163 shows the assembly after assembling the **Rack** component.

Defining the Joint Limits

Now, you need to define the maximum and minimum joint limits for the previously applied slider joint such that it can slide or translate within the specified limits only.

 In Autodesk Fusion 360, when you apply a joint, the component is free to rotate or translate, without any limitation along its free degrees of freedom. Consider the case of the slider joint, where the component can translate freely, without any limitation along the specified direction, see Figure 8.163. You can avoid this by defining the maximum and minimum limits for the joint to control its movement along/about its free degrees of freedom.

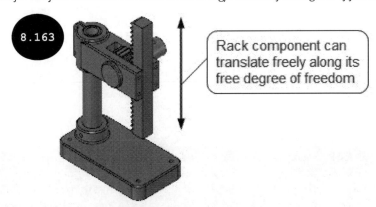

Rack component can translate freely along its free degree of freedom

1. Expand the **Joints** node in the **BROWSER** by clicking on the arrow in front if it, refer to Figure 8.164. A list of all the applied joints appears.

2. Move the cursor over the **Slider** joint in the expanded **Joints** node. The **Edit Joint Limits** icon 😀 appears next to the name of the joint, see Figure 8.164.

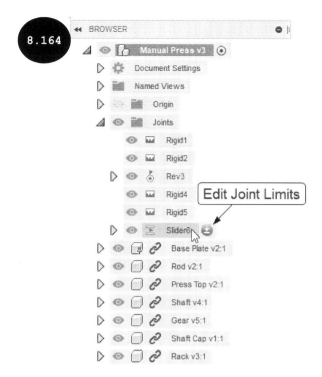

3. Click on this **Edit Joint Limits** icon, refer to Figure 8.164. The **EDIT JOINT LIMITS** dialog box appears, see Figure 8.165.

*You can also right-click on the joint in the expanded **Joints** node of the **BROWSER** or in the Timeline and then click on the **Edit Joint Limits** option in the shortcut menu that appears to invoke the **EDIT JOINT LIMITS** dialog box.*

4. Ensure that the **Slide** option is selected in the **Motion** drop-down list of the dialog box.

*The slider joint has only one slide motion. As a result, only the **Slide** option is available in the Motion drop-down list for defining its limits. However, in case of cylindrical joint, the **Rotate** and **Slide** options are available in the **Motion** drop-down list of the **EDIT JOINT LIMITS** dialog box. This is because, the cylindrical joint has two motions: rotational and translational. You can define the limits for the available motions of the joint by selecting them in the Motion drop-down list.*

5. Select the **Minimum** check box in the **EDIT JOINT LIMITS** dialog box. Next, enter -55 in the field that appears below the **Minimum** check box in the dialog box as the minimum limit for the slider joint.

6. Select the **Maximum** check box in the **EDIT JOINT LIMITS** dialog box. Next, enter **60** in the field that appears below the **Maximum** check box in the dialog box as the maximum limit for the slider joint, see Figure 8.166.

The minimum and maximum limits are measured between the locations of the joint origins defined on the components.

You can define the rest position of the component anywhere between the minimum and maximum limits by selecting the **Rest** check box in the dialog box. The rest position of the component is the position where the component will come into rest after the motion.

7. Click on the **OK** button in the **EDIT JOINT LIMITS** dialog box. The minimum and maximum joint limits for the slider joint is defined. Now, the **Rack** component can translate or slide within the specified minimum and maximum joint limits.

Inserting and Assembling the Remaining Components

1. Insert the **Cover Plate** component in the design file and then assemble it by applying the rigid joint with the **Press Top** component, see Figure 8.167.

2. Insert the **Handle** component into the design file and then assemble it by applying the rigid joint with the **Shaft** component, see Figure 8.168.

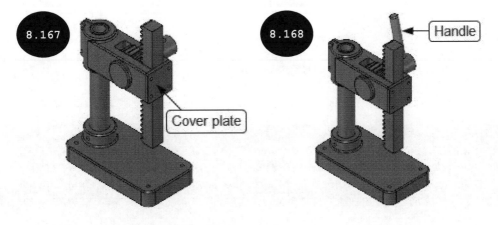

Defining Relative Motion between Two Joints

Now, you need to define the relative motion between the revolute joint of the **Shaft** component and the slider joint of the **Rack** component such that the rotational motion of the **Shaft** component translates to the translational motion of the **Rack** component and vice-versa.

 In Autodesk Fusion 360, you can define relative motion between two joints by using the ***Motion Link*** *tool. For example, you can define the relative motion between the slider and revolute joints such that the rotational motion of one component translates to the translational motion of another component and vice-versa.*

1. Invoke the **ASSEMBLY** drop-down menu in the **Toolbar** and then click on the **Motion Link** tool, see Figure 8.169. The **MOTION LINK** dialog box appears.

2. Expand the **Joints** node in the **BROWSER** and then select the revolute joint (**Rev3**) applied to the **Shaft** and the slider joint (**Slider6**) applied to the **Rack** component of the assembly one by one, refer to Figure 8.170. On selecting the joints, the **MOTION LINK** dialog box gets modified with additional options, which are used for controlling the relative motion between the selected joints, see Figure 8.171.

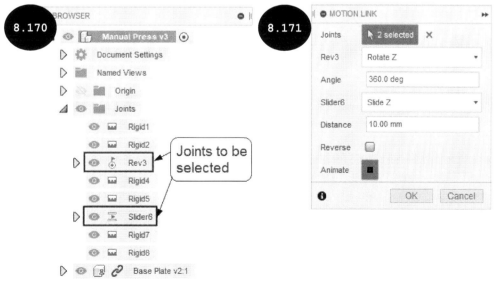

The relative motion between the selected joints animates in the graphics area as per the default values specified in the respective fields of the MOTION LINK dialog box.

Now, you need to define the distance travelled by **Rack** component with respect to the angle of revolution of the **Shaft** component in the **Distance** and **Angle** fields of the **MOTION LINK** dialog box, respectively.

3.   Ensure that **360 degrees** is specified in the **Angle** field of the dialog box as the angle of revolution of the **Shaft** component.

4.   Enter **160** in the **Distance** field of the dialog box as the distance travelled by the **Rack** component per 360 degrees of revolution of the **Shaft** component.

5.   You can reverse the direction of motion by selecting the **Reverse** check box in the dialog box, if needed.

You can play or stop the animation of the relative motion between the selected joints in the graphics area by using the Play/Stop button in the Animate area of the dialog box, respectively.

6.   Click on the **OK** button in the dialog box. The relative motion between the selected joints is defined and you can review it by dragging the respective components in the graphics area, refer to Figure 8.172. This figure shows the section view and the isometric view of the final assembly.

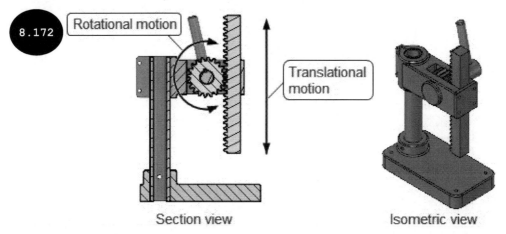

8.172

Section view   Isometric view

Saving the Model

1.   Click on the **Save** tool in the **Application Bar**. The **Add Version Description** window appears as the design is already saved. In this window, you can enter a description for the new version of the assembly, if needed.

2.   Click on the **OK** button in the window. A new updated version of the assembly file is saved at the specified location (**Autodesk Fusion 360 Tutorials > Chapter 8 > Tutorial 3**).

Exercise 1

Create the assembly, as shown in Figure 8.173 by applying the required joints. The exploded view of the assembly is shown in Figure 8.174 for your reference only. Different views and dimensions of individual components of the assembly are shown in Figures 8.175 through 8.182. You can also download all components of the assembly by logging on to the SDCAD Academy website (www.sdcadacademy.com).

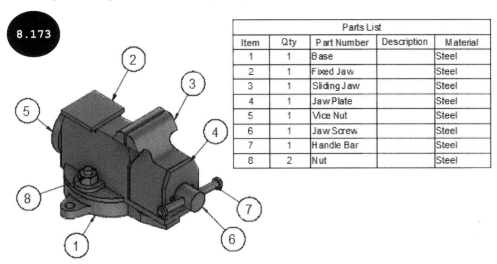

Parts List				
Item	Qty	Part Number	Description	Material
1	1	Base		Steel
2	1	Fixed Jaw		Steel
3	1	Sliding Jaw		Steel
4	1	Jaw Plate		Steel
5	1	Vice Nut		Steel
6	1	Jaw Screw		Steel
7	1	Handle Bar		Steel
8	2	Nut		Steel

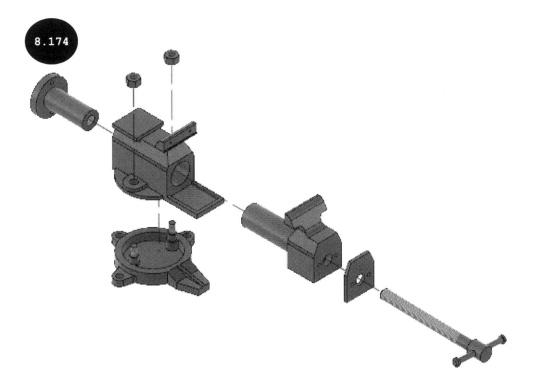

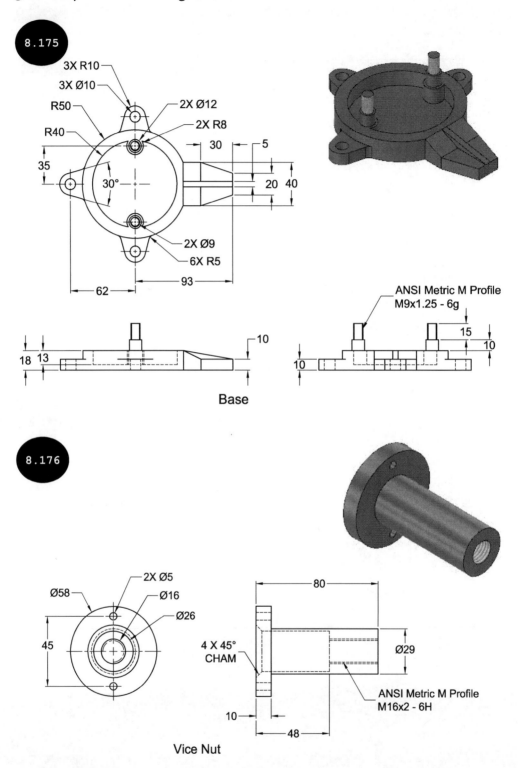

8.175

3X R10
3X Ø10
R50
R40
35
30°
62
2X Ø12
2X R8
30
5
20   40
93
2X Ø9
6X R5

ANSI Metric M Profile
M9x1.25 - 6g
15
10
10
18 13
10

Base

8.176

2X Ø5
Ø58
Ø16
Ø26
45
4 X 45°
CHAM
80
Ø29
ANSI Metric M Profile
M16x2 - 6H
10
48

Vice Nut

8.177

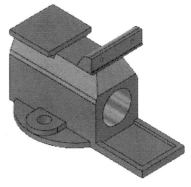

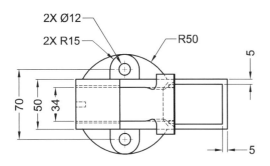

2X Ø12
2X R15
R50
70
50
34
5
5

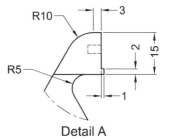

R10
R5
3
2
15
1

Detail A

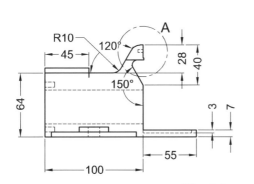

R10
120°
150°
45
28
40
3
7
64
55
100
A

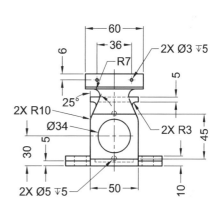

60
36
2X Ø3 ▽5
R7
6
25°
5
2X R10
Ø34
2X R3
45
30
5
2X Ø5 ▽5
50
10

Fixed Jaw

8.178

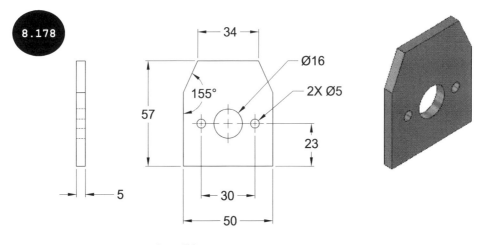

34
Ø16
2X Ø5
155°
57
23
5
30
50

Jaw Plate

8.179

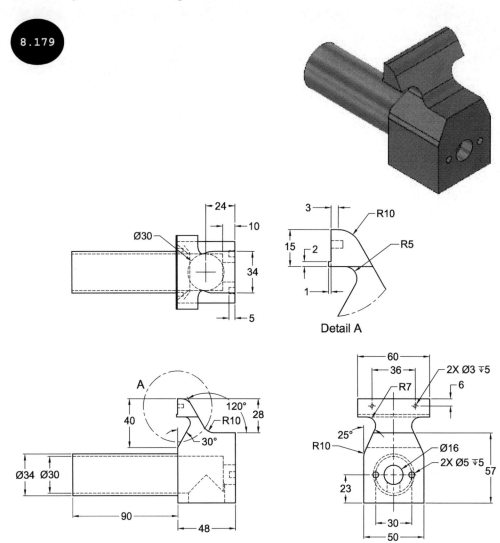

Detail A

Sliding Jaw

8.180

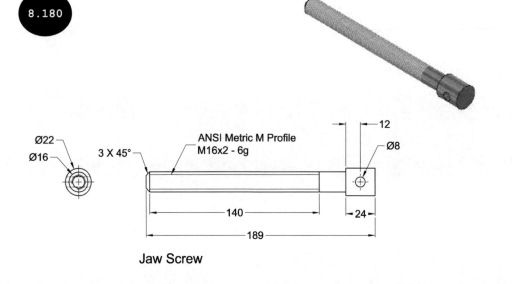

ANSI Metric M Profile
M16x2 - 6g

3 X 45°

Ø22
Ø16
Ø8

12
140
24
189

Jaw Screw

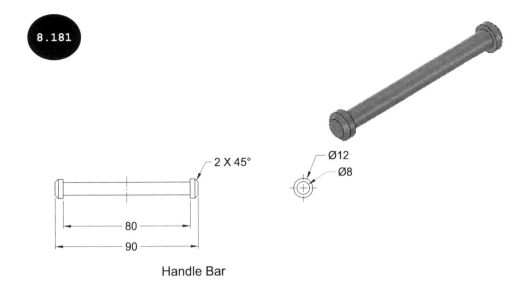

8.181

2 X 45°

Ø12
Ø8

80
90

Handle Bar

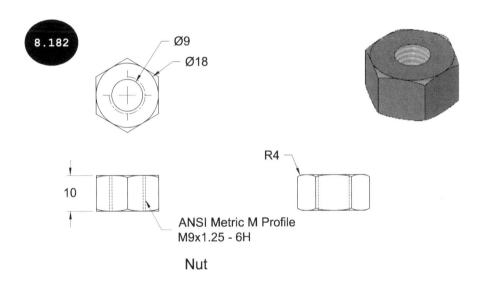

8.182

Ø9
Ø18

R4

10

ANSI Metric M Profile
M9x1.25 - 6H

Nut

Summary

This chapter discussed how to create assemblies by using the bottom-up assembly approach. It explained the application of rigid, revolute, slider, cylindrical, pin-slot, planar, and ball joints to assemble components of an assembly and define relative motion with respect to each other. The chapter also discussed how to insert components into a design file, ground the first component, apply various types of joints, define joint limits, animate a joint, animate a model, and define relative motion between two joints.

Questions

Answer the following questions:

- In Autodesk Fusion 360, you can create assemblies by using the _____ and _____ approaches.

- Autodesk Fusion 360 has _____ capabilities. As a result, if any change is made in a component, the same change reflects in the component used in the assembly as well as in the drawing and other workspaces of Autodesk Fusion 360, automatically on updating the respective file.

- The _____ dialog box appears every time on inserting a component into a design file and allows you to define the position and orientation of the component in the design file.

- A free component of an assembly has _____ degrees of freedom.

- The _____ joint allows the component to rotate about an axis by removing all degrees of freedom except one rotational degree of freedom.

- The _____ joint allows the component to translate along a single axis by removing all degrees of freedom except one translational degree of freedom.

- The _____ joint allows the component to translate along an axis as well as rotate about a different axis.

- The _____ tool is used for animating the model or assembly to review its working conditions and the behavior of its individual components with respect to each other.

- You can move the individual components of an assembly along its degrees of freedom. (True/False)

- You can define minimum and maximum limits for a joint. (True/False)

- In Autodesk Fusion 360, you cannot define relative motion between two joints. (True/False)

- In Autodesk Fusion 360, you can edit an already applied joint. (True/False)

Creating Assemblies - II

In this chapter, you will learn the following:

- Introduction to Top-down Assembly
- Creating Components within a Design File
- Creating the V Block Assembly

In the previous chapter, you have learned about creating assemblies by using the Bottom-up Assembly Approach. You have also learned about various types of joints, their application to assemble components with respect to each other, animating a model, and so on. In this chapter, you will learn about creating assemblies by using the Top-down Assembly Approach.

Introduction to Top-down Assembly

In the Top-down Assembly approach, all the components of an assembly are created within a single design file. It helps in taking reference from the existing components of the assembly. By using this approach, you can create a concept-based design, where new components of an assembly can be created by taking reference from the existing components.

Creating Components within a Design File

In Autodesk Fusion 360, you can create components of an assembly within a single design file by using one of the following methods:

Creating a New Empty Component

The method for creating a new empty component within a design file is discussed below:

1. Invoke the **ASSEMBLE** drop-down menu in the **SOLID** tab and then click on the **New Component** tool, see Figure 9.1. The **NEW COMPONENT** dialog box appears, see Figure 9.2.

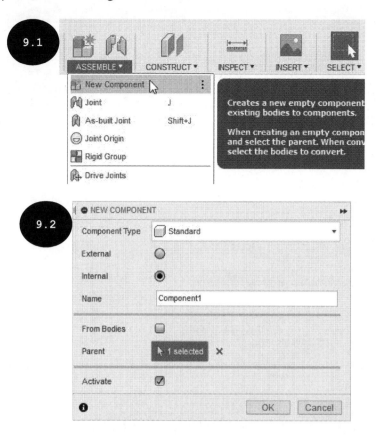

You can also invoke the **NEW COMPONENT** dialog box by right-clicking on the name of the component (parent component) in the **BROWSER** and then click on the **New Component** tool in the shortcut menu that appears, see Figure 9.3.

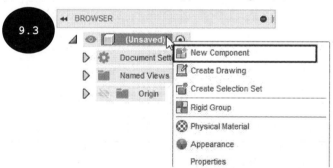

2. Ensure that the **Standard** option is selected in the **Component Type** drop-down list of the **NEW COMPONENT** dialog box for creating an empty standard solid component.

3. Select the **Internal** radio button in the **NEW COMPONENT** dialog box for creating an empty component within the current design file as an internal component. Note that an internal component is saved internally within the current design file.

*You can also create an empty component within the current design file as an external component by selecting the **External** radio button in the **NEW COMPONENT** dialog box. An external component is saved externally in a separate design file. On selecting the **External** radio button, the **Location** selection field appears in the dialog box. By clicking on this selection field, you can define the location for saving the new component, externally.*

4. Enter a unique name for the new component in the **Name** field of the dialog box.

5. Ensure that the **From Bodies** check box is cleared in the dialog box.

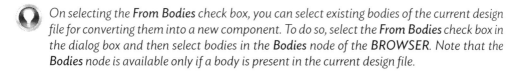 *On selecting the **From Bodies** check box, you can select existing bodies of the current design file for converting them into a new component. To do so, select the **From Bodies** check box in the dialog box and then select bodies in the **Bodies** node of the BROWSER. Note that the **Bodies** node is available only if a body is present in the current design file.*

6. Accept the default selection of the parent for the new component in the **Parent** selection field in the dialog box.

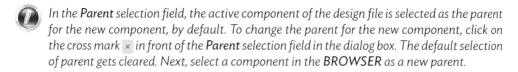 *In the **Parent** selection field, the active component of the design file is selected as the parent for the new component, by default. To change the parent for the new component, click on the cross mark ☒ in front of the **Parent** selection field in the dialog box. The default selection of parent gets cleared. Next, select a component in the BROWSER as a new parent.*

7. Ensure that the **Activate** check box is selected in the dialog box for making the new component as an active component of the design file.

8. Click on the **OK** button in the dialog box. A new empty component gets created and its name appears in the **BROWSER**, see Figure 9.4. Also, it becomes an active component of the design file.

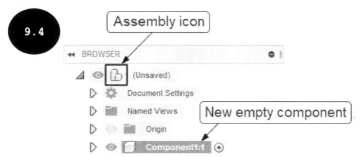

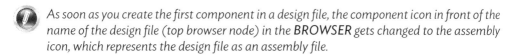 *As soon as you create the first component in a design file, the component icon in front of the name of the design file (top browser node) in the BROWSER gets changed to the assembly icon, which represents the design file as an assembly file.*

9. Similarly, you can create multiple empty components within a design file one by one.

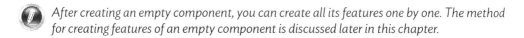 *After creating an empty component, you can create all its features one by one. The method for creating features of an empty component is discussed later in this chapter.*

Creating a New Component from Existing Bodies

The method for creating a new component from existing bodies of a design file is discussed below:

1. Expand the **Bodies** node in the **BROWSER** of a design file, refer to Figure 9.5.

2. Select a body in the expanded **Bodies** node to be converted into a new component and then right-click to display a shortcut menu, see Figure 9.5.

3. Click on the **Create Components from Bodies** option in the shortcut menu, see Figure 9.5. The selected body of the design file gets converted into a new component.

You can also select multiple bodies of a design file together by pressing the CTRL key in the expanded **Bodies** node for converting them into new individual components. Moreover, to convert all the bodies of a design file into individual components at a time, right-click on the **Bodies** node in the **BROWSER** and then click on the **Create Components from Bodies** option in the shortcut menu that appears. All the bodies of the design file get converted into individual new components.

Creating a Component During an Active Tool

In Autodesk Fusion 360, you can also create a component during an active tool such as **Extrude**, **Revolve**, or **Sweep** in a design file and the method for the same is discussed below:

1. While creating a solid feature such as extrude, revolve, or sweep by using the respective solid modeling tool in a design file, select the **New Component** option in the **Operation** drop-down list of the respective dialog box that appears, see Figure 9.6. This figure shows the **Operation** drop-down list of the **EXTRUDE** dialog box. Next, click on the **OK** button in the dialog box. A new component gets created in the design file.

*After creating an empty component, you can create its feature. To do so, you need to first ensure that it is an active component. To make a component active, move the cursor over its name in the BROWSER. The **Activate Component** radio button appears, see Figure 9.7. Next, click to select this radio button. The component gets activated and allows you to create its features.*

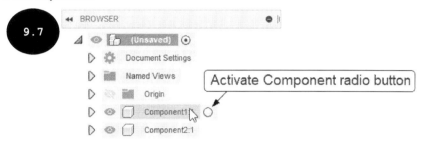

Tutorial 1 - Creating the V-Block Assembly

Create an assembly as shown in Figure 9.8 by using the Top-down Assembly approach. Different views and dimensions of the each component are shown in Figures 9.9 through 9.11. After creating the assembly, you need to apply joints. All dimensions are in mm.

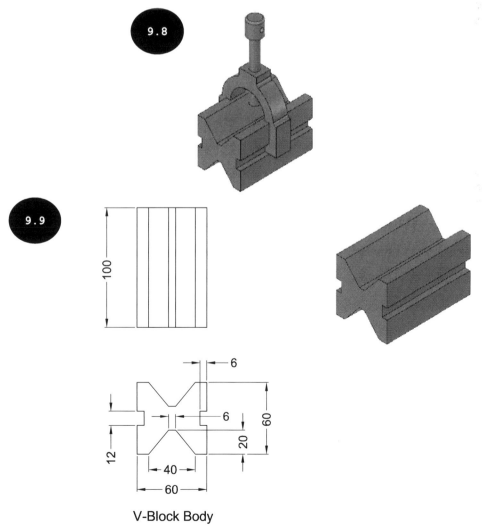

V-Block Body

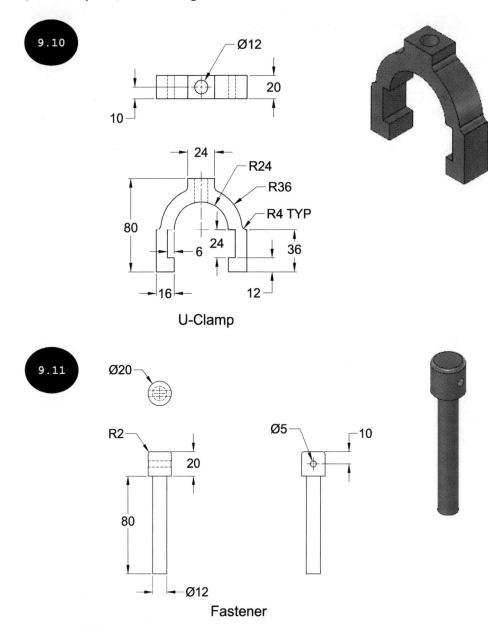

U-Clamp

Fastener

The following sequence summarizes the tutorial outline:

- Starting Fusion 360 and a New Design File
- Creating the First Component within a Design File
- Creating the Second Component within the Design File
- Creating the Third Component
- Activating the Parent Assembly
- Applying As-built Joint
- Saving the Assembly File

Starting Fusion 360 and a New Design File

1. Start Fusion 360 by double-clicking on the **Autodesk Fusion 360** icon on your desktop, if not started already. The startup user interface of Autodesk Fusion 360 appears.

2. Invoke the **File** drop-down menu in the **Application Bar** and then click on the **New Design** tool, see Figure 9.12. A new design file is started with the default name "**Untitled**".

   Now, you can create components of the assembly within the design file one by one.

Creating the First Component within a Design File

1. Invoke the **ASSEMBLE** drop-down menu in the **SOLID** tab of the **Toolbar** and then click on the **New Component** tool, see Figure 9.13. The **NEW COMPONENT** dialog box appears, see Figure 9.14.

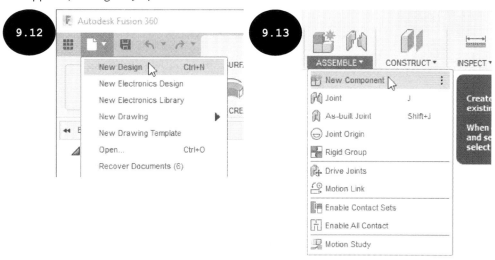

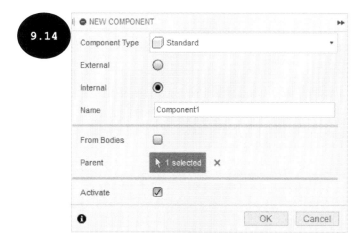

2. Ensure that the Standard option is selected in the Component Type drop-down list of the **NEW COMPONENT** dialog box for creating a standard component.

3. Ensure that the **Internal** radio button is selected for creating an empty component within the current design file as an internal component.

4.   Enter **V-Block Body** in the **Name** field of the dialog box as the name of the new component.

5.   Ensure that the **Activate** check box is selected in the dialog box for making the new component as an active component of the design file.

6.   Click on the **OK** button in the **NEW COMPONENT** dialog box. A new empty component is added in the **BROWSER**, see Figure 9.15 and the component icon of the top browser node changes to an assembly icon. Also, the **Activate Component** radio button that appears next to the name of the newly added component in the **BROWSER** is selected, by default. This indicates that the newly added component is an active component and you can add its features.

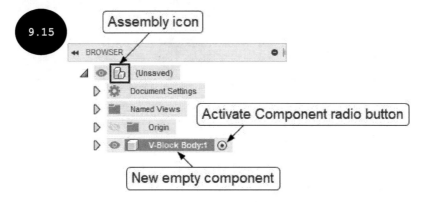

Now, you can add features to the newly created empty component.

7.   Click on the **Create Sketch** tool in the **Toolbar**, see Figure 9.16. Next, select the Front plane as the sketching plane to create the sketch of the first feature. The sketching plane becomes normal to the viewing direction and the **SKETCH** contextual tab appears in the **Toolbar**. Also, the **SKETCH PALETTE** dialog box appears in the graphics area.

8.   Ensure that the **3D Sketch** check box is cleared in the **SKETCH PALETTE** dialog box for creating a 2D sketch.

9.   Draw the sketch of the first feature of the component, see Figure 9.17.

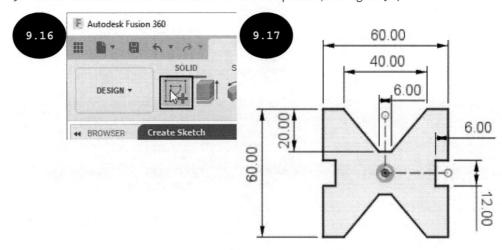

10. After creating the sketch, click on the **SOLID** tab in the **Toolbar** and then click on the **Extrude** tool or press the **E** key. The **EXTRUDE** dialog box appears in the graphics area. Also, the closed sketch profile gets selected, automatically.

 If a single valid profile is available in the graphics area, then it gets selected automatically on invoking the EXTRUDE dialog box.

11. Change the orientation of the sketch to isometric.

12. Select the **Symmetric** option in the **Direction** drop-down list of the **EXTRUDE** dialog box and then enter **50 mm** in the **Distance** field of the dialog box. Ensure that the **Half Length** button ⚏ is activated in the **Measurement** area of the dialog box for creating an extrude feature of total extrusion depth 100 mm.

13. Click on the **OK** button in the dialog box. The extrude feature of the component gets created, see Figure 9.18.

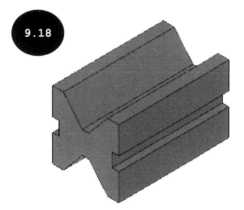

9.18

 The method for creating features of a component is same as discussed while creating multi-featured models in earlier chapters.

Creating the Second Component within the Design File

After creating the first component, you need to create the second component of the assembly.

1. Right-click on the top browser node in the **BROWSER**, see Figure 9.19. Next, click on the **New Component** tool in the shortcut menu that appears. The **NEW COMPONENT** dialog box appears. Alternatively, invoke the Assembly drop-down menu and then click on the **New Component** tool for invoking the **NEW COMPONENT** dialog box.

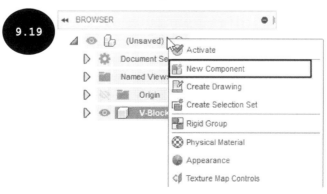

9.19

2. Enter **U-Clamp** in the **Name** field of the dialog box as the name of the second component.

 *In the **Parent** selection field of the dialog box, the active component of the design file is selected as the parent for the new component, by default. As a result, the first component (**V-Block Body**) is selected as the parent for the second component, which you need to change to the top browser node.*

3. Click on the cross mark ⊠ in front of the **Parent** selection field in the dialog box for clearing the default selection of parent.

4. Click on the top browser node in the **BROWSER** as the parent for the second component, see Figure 9.20.

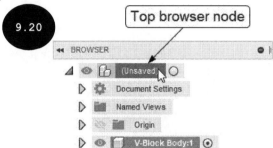

5. Ensure that the **Activate** check box is selected in the dialog box for making the new component as an active component of the design file.

6. Click on the **OK** button in the **NEW COMPONENT** dialog box. A new empty component (**U-Clamp**) is added as a child of the selected parent (top browser node) in the **BROWSER** and becomes an active component by default, see Figure 9.21. Also, the first component becomes transparent in the graphics area so that you can easily create the second component (**U-Clamp**) by taking reference from the first component.

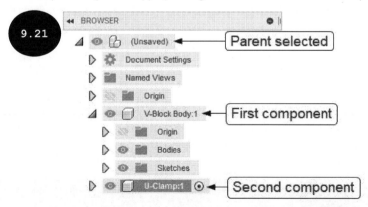

Now, you can add features to the newly created empty component (**U-Clamp**).

 To add features in a component, you need to ensure that the component is active.

7. Click on the **Create Sketch** tool in the **Solid** tab of the **Toolbar** and then select the Front plane as the sketching plane to create the sketch of the first feature of the second component. The sketching plane becomes normal to the viewing direction and the **SKETCH** contextual tab appears in the **Toolbar**.

8. Draw the sketch of the first feature of the second component, see Figure 9.22.

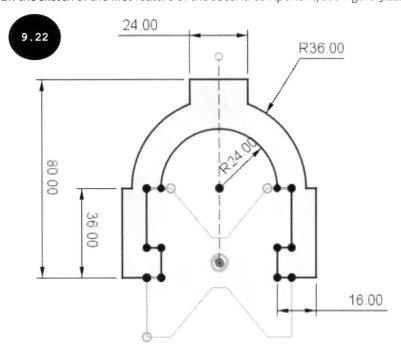

In Figure 9.22, the sketch is created by taking references from the edges/vertices of the existing component. You can also project the respective edges of the first component onto the sketching plane by using the **Project** tool for creating some of the sketch entities.

9. After creating the sketch, click on the **SOLID** tab in the **Toolbar** and then click on the **Extrude** tool or press the **E** key. The **EXTRUDE** dialog box appears in the graphics area. Also, the closed sketch profile gets selected, automatically.

10. Change the orientation of the model to isometric, see Figure 9.23.

11. Select the **Symmetric** option in the **Direction** drop-down list of the **EXTRUDE** dialog box and then enter **10 mm** in the **Distance** field of the dialog box. Ensure that the **Half Length** button 🖵 is activated in the **Measurement** area of the dialog box for creating an extrude feature of total extrusion depth 20 mm. The preview of the extrude features appears in the graphics area similar to the one shown in Figure 9.24.

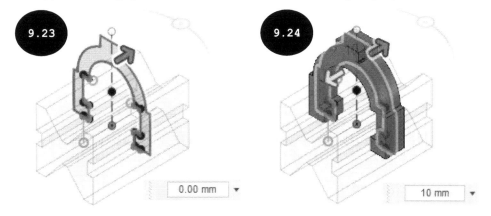

12. Ensure that the **New Body** option is selected in the **Operation** drop-down list of the dialog box.

13. Click on the **OK** button in the dialog box. The first feature of the second component is created, see Figure 9.25.

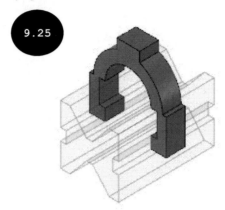

9.25

Now, you need to create the second feature of the component. The second feature of the component is a cut feature.

14. Click on the **Create Sketch** tool in the **Solid** tab of the **Toolbar** and then select the top planar face of the previously created feature of the second component as the sketching plane, see Figure 9.26.

15. Create a circle of diameter 12 mm as the sketch of the second feature, see Figure 9.27.

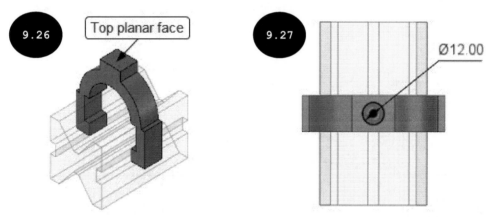

9.26   Top planar face

9.27   Ø12.00

16. Press the E key to invoke the **EXTRUDE** dialog box. Next, change the orientation of the model to isometric.

17. Select the sketch profile in the graphics area.

18. Select the **To Object** option in the **Extent** drop-down list of the dialog box and then select the bottom semi-circular face of the first feature as the object to terminate the extrude cut feature, see Figure 9.28. The preview of the cut feature appears in the graphics area up to the selected face, see Figure 9.29, since the **Cut** option gets selected automatically in the **Operation** drop-down list of the dialog box.

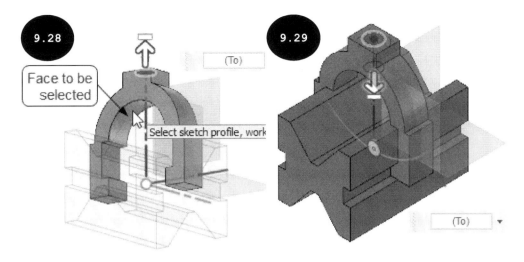

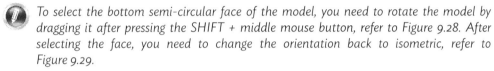

> *To select the bottom semi-circular face of the model, you need to rotate the model by dragging it after pressing the SHIFT + middle mouse button, refer to Figure 9.28. After selecting the face, you need to change the orientation back to isometric, refer to Figure 9.29.*

19. Click on the **OK** button in the dialog box. The second feature (extrude cut feature) of the **U-Clamp** component is created, see Figure 9.30.

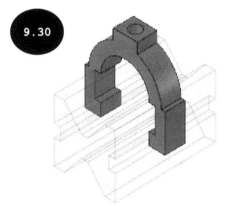

Now, you need to create the third feature of the second component. The third feature of the component is a fillet feature.

20. Click on the **Fillet** tool in the **MODIFY** panel of the **Toolbar** or press the **F** key. The **FILLET** dialog box appears.

21. Select the 4 edges of the second component (**U-Clamp**) to be filleted, see Figure 9.31.

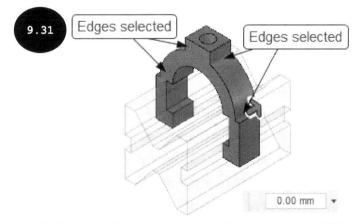

22. Enter 4 in the **Radius** field of the dialog box and then click on the **OK** button. The third feature (fillet) of the **U-Clamp** component is created, see Figure 9.32. Also, it remains active in the graphics area.

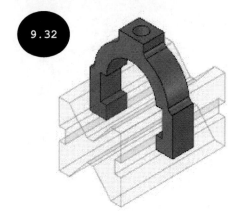

9.32

Creating the Third Component

Now, you need to create the third component of the assembly.

1. Invoke the **ASSEMBLE** drop-down menu in the **SOLID** tab of the **Toolbar** and then click on the **New Component** tool, see Figure 9.33. The **NEW COMPONENT** dialog box appears.

2. Enter **Fastener** in the **Name** field of the dialog box as the name of the third component.

3. Click on the cross mark [x] in front of the **Parent** selection field in the dialog box for clearing the default selection of parent.

    By default, the second component (U-Clamp) is selected as the parent for the third component, since it is the active component of the assembly.

4. Click on the top browser node in the **BROWSER** as the parent for the third component, see Figure 9.34.

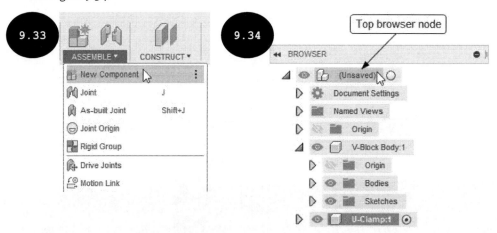

9.33

9.34

Top browser node

5. Ensure that the **Activate** check box is selected in the dialog box for making the new component as an active component of the design file.

6. Click on the **OK** button in the **NEW COMPONENT** dialog box. A new empty component (**Fastener**) is added as a child of the selected parent (top browser node) in the **BROWSER** and becomes an active component by default, see Figure 9.35. Also, the other components become transparent in the graphics area.

Now, you can add features to the newly created empty component (**Fastener**).

7. Click on the **Create Sketch** tool in the **Toolbar** and then select the top planar face of the second component as the sketching plane, see Figure 9.36.

8. Create a circle of diameter 12 mm as the sketch of the first feature, see Figure 9.37.

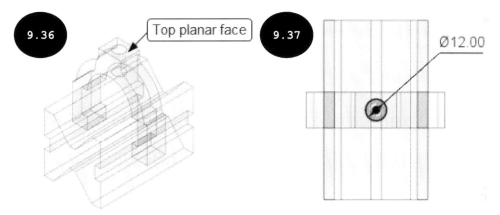

*Instead of creating a circle of diameter 12 mm, you can also project the top circular edge of the second component by using the **Project** tool.*

9. After creating the sketch, extrude it to a total distance of 80 mm, symmetrically on both sides of the sketching plane by using the **Extrude** tool, see Figure 9.38. Note that the total extrusion distance is 80 mm (40 mm on each side of the sketching plane). The first feature of the third component (**Fastener**) gets created.

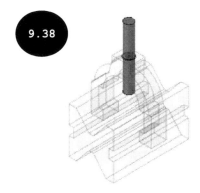

Now, you need to create the second feature of the **Fastener** component.

10. Click on the **Create Sketch** tool in the **Toolbar** and then select the top planar face of the previously created feature of the third component (**Fastener**) as the sketching plane.

11. Create a circle of diameter 20 mm as the sketch of the second feature, see Figure 9.39.

12. After creating the sketch, extrude it to a distance of 20 mm in the upward direction by using the **Extrude** tool, see Figure 9.40. Ensure that the **Join** option is selected in the **Operation** drop-down list of the **EXTRUDE** dialog box.

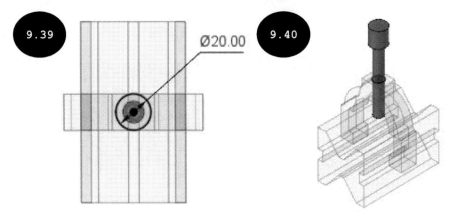

Now, you need to create the third feature of the **Fastener** component.

13. Click on the **Create Sketch** tool in the **Toolbar** and then select the Right plane as the sketching plane.

14. Create a circle of diameter 5 mm as the sketch of the third feature, see Figure 9.41.

15. Invoke the **EXTRUDE** dialog box and then select the sketch profile.

16. Select the **Symmetric** option in the **Direction** drop-down list and the **All** option in the **Extent** drop-down list of the dialog box for creating an extrude cut feature, through all the model on both sides of the sketching plane. The preview of the cut feature appears, since the **Cut** option gets selected automatically in the **Operation** drop-down list of the dialog box.

17. Click on the **OK** button. The extrude cut feature gets created, see Figure 9.42.

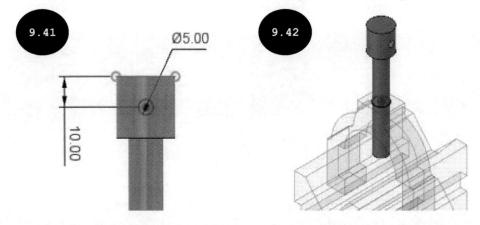

Now, you need to create the fourth feature of the third component (**Fastener**). The fourth feature is a fillet.

18. Create a fillet of radius 2 mm on the top circular edge of the third component (**Fastener**) by using the **Fillet** tool, see Figure 9.43.

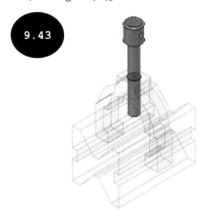

9.43

Activating the Parent Assembly

Now, you need to activate the parent assembly (top browser node).

1. Move the cursor over the parent assembly (top browser node) in the **BROWSER**. The **Activate Component** radio button appears, see Figure 9.44.

9.44

Activate Component radio button

2. Click to select the **Activate Component** radio button. The parent assembly (top browser node) becomes activated and all its child components appear in default visual style, see Figure 9.45. Click anywhere in the graphics area to exit the current selection set.

9.45

Applying As-built Joint

Now, you need to apply joints to define the relative motion between the components. As all the components of the assembly are in correct position, you can apply joints by using the **As-built Joint** tool. However, before you apply joints between the components, you need to fix or ground the first component.

 *The **As-built Joint** tool is used for applying joints such as rigid, revolute, slider, cylindrical, pin-slot, ball, and planar to define the relative motion between the components in their current position as they are built. It is mainly used when the components of an assembly are created in-context to each other by using the Top-down assembly approach and are already positioned properly with respect to each other.*

1. Right-click on the **V-Block Body** component in the **BROWSER** and then click on the **Ground** option in the shortcut menu that appears, see Figure 9.46. The first component becomes the fixed component and cannot move or rotate in any direction.

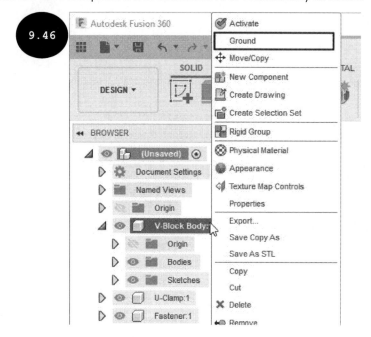

Now, you can apply joints between the components.

2. Invoke the **ASSEMBLE** drop-down menu in the **SOLID** tab and then click on the **As-built Joint** tool, see Figure 9.47. The **AS-BUILT JOINT** dialog box appears, see Figure 9.48. Alternatively, press the SHIFT + J keys to invoke the **AS-BUILT JOINT** dialog box.

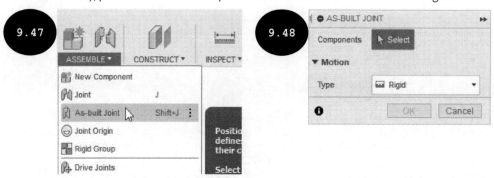

3. Select the **U-Clamp** component (moveable component) and then the **V-Block Body** component (fixed component) in the graphics area one by one to apply a joint. The components get selected and the moveable component animates for a while in the graphics area based on the default joint type selected in the **Type** drop-down list of the dialog box.

4. Select the **Slider** option in the **Type** drop-down list of the dialog box as the joint to be applied between the selected components. The **Position** selection field appears in the dialog box and you are prompted to specify the position of the joint origin.

5. Move the cursor over a linear edge of the first component (**V-Block Body**) to define the position of the joint origin and the direction of translation, see Figure 9.49. The edge gets highlighted and its snap points appear.

6. Press the CTRL key to lock the highlighted edge and then click to specify the position of the joint origin when the cursor snaps to the middle snap point of the highlighted edge. The **U-Clamp** component (moveable component) starts sliding along the joint origin defined. Next, release the CTRL key.

7. Click on the **OK** button in the dialog box. The slider joint is applied between the selected components.

   Now, you need to apply a cylindrical joint between the **Fastener** and **U-Clamp** components of the assembly.

8. Press the SHIFT + J keys to invoke the **AS-BUILT JOINT** dialog box and then select the **Fastener** and **U-Clamp** components in the graphics area one by one.

9. Select the **Cylindrical** option in the **Type** drop-down list of the dialog box. The **Position** selection field appears in the dialog box and you are prompted to specify the position of the joint origin.

10. Move the cursor over the cylindrical face of the **Fastener** component, see Figure 9.50. The face gets highlighted and its snap points appear.

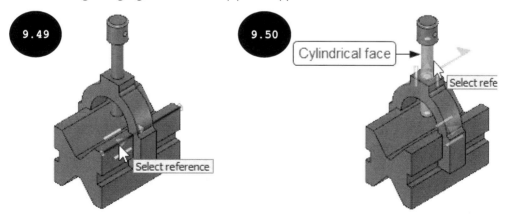

11. Press the CTRL key to lock the highlighted face and then click to specify the position of the joint origin, when the cursor snaps to its middle snap point. The **Fastener** component starts sliding as well as rotating about the joint origin defined. Next, release the CTRL key.

12. Click on the **OK** button in the dialog box. The cylindrical joint is applied between the selected components. Figure 9.51 shows the final assembly after applying the joints.

In Figure 9.51, the visibility of the applied joints symbols is turned off in the graphics area. To do so, click on the **Display Settings > Object Visibility** in the **Navigation Bar**, see Figure 9.52. Next, clear the **Joints** check box in the cascading menu that appears.

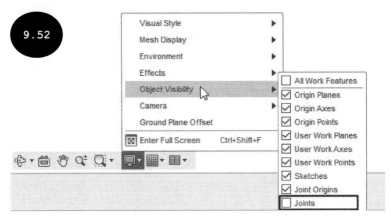

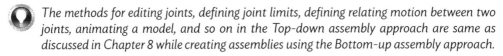

The methods for editing joints, defining joint limits, defining relating motion between two joints, animating a model, and so on in the Top-down assembly approach are same as discussed in Chapter 8 while creating assemblies using the Bottom-up assembly approach.

Saving the Assembly File

1. Click on the **Save** tool in the **Application Bar**. The **Save** dialog box appears.

2. Enter **V-Block Assembly** in the **Name** field of the dialog box.

3. Ensure that the location *Autodesk Fusion 360 Tutorials > Chapter 9 > Tutorial 1* is specified in the **Location** field of the dialog box to save the file of this tutorial. Note that you need to create these folders in the **Data Panel**.

4. Click on the **Save** button in the dialog box. The assembly is saved with the name **V-Block Assembly** in the specified location.

Exercise 1

Create an assembly, as shown in Figure 9.53 by using the Top-down approach. Different views and dimensions of the individual components of the assembly are shown in Figures 9.54 through 9.59. After creating the assembly, you need to apply the joints by using the **As-built Joint** tool. All dimensions are in mm.

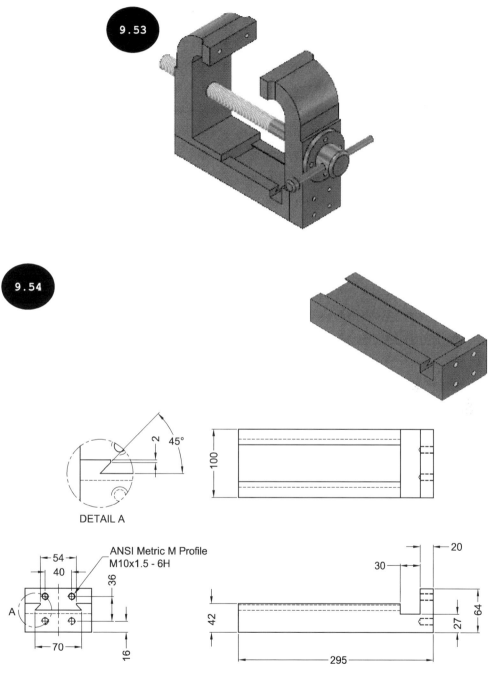

9.53

9.54

DETAIL A

ANSI Metric M Profile
M10x1.5 - 6H

54
40
36
70
16
A

2
45°
100

30
20
42
295
27
64

Base

9.55

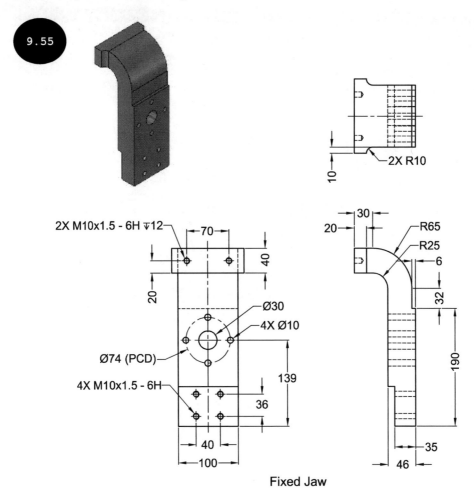

2X M10x1.5 - 6H ▽12

70

40

20

Ø30

4X Ø10

Ø74 (PCD)

4X M10x1.5 - 6H

139

36

40

100

10

2X R10

30

20

R65

R25

6

32

190

35

46

Fixed Jaw

9.56

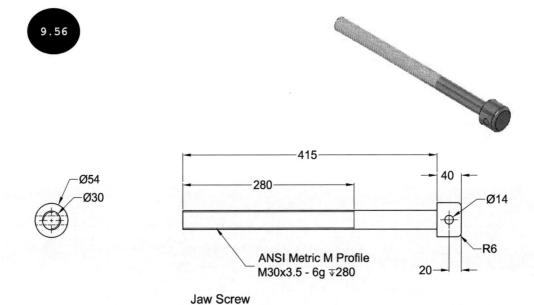

415

280

40

Ø14

Ø54

Ø30

ANSI Metric M Profile
M30x3.5 - 6g ▽280

R6

20

Jaw Screw

9.57

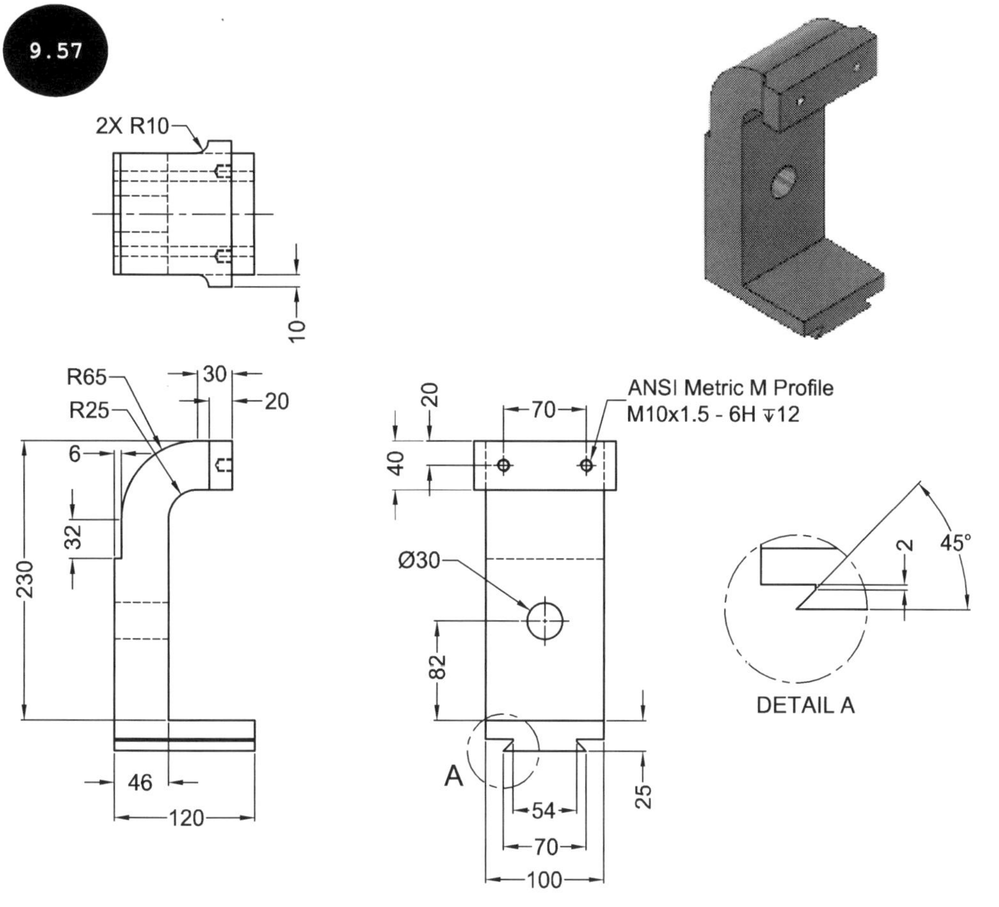
2X R10
10
R65
R25
30
20
6
32
230
46
120
20
70
ANSI Metric M Profile
M10x1.5 - 6H ↧12
40
Ø30
82
A
54
70
100
25
2
45°
DETAIL A

Moveable Jaw

9.58

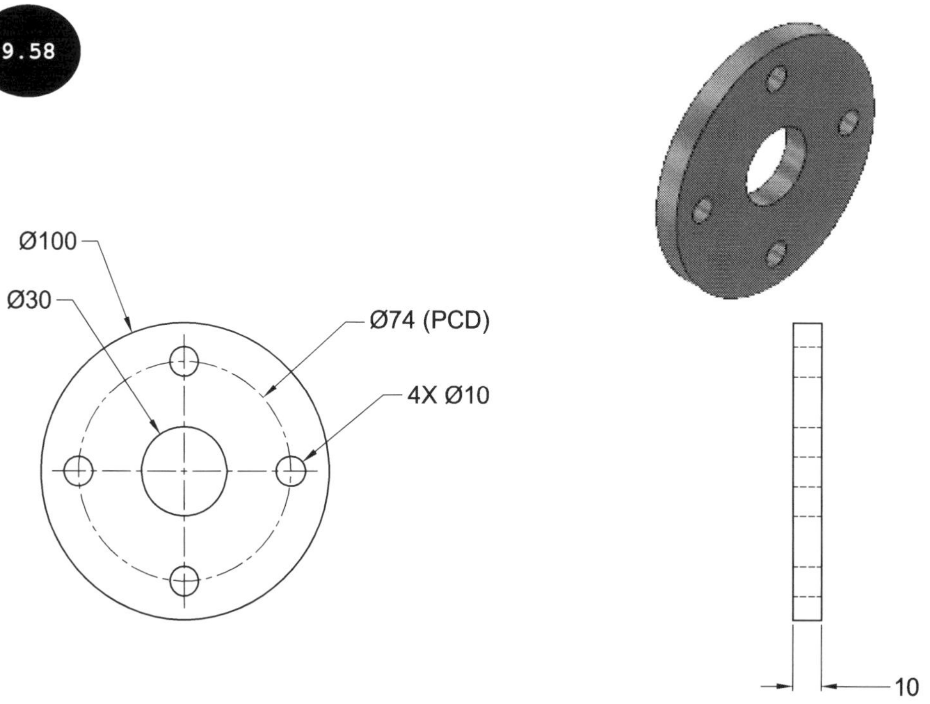
Ø100
Ø30
Ø74 (PCD)
4X Ø10
10

Washer

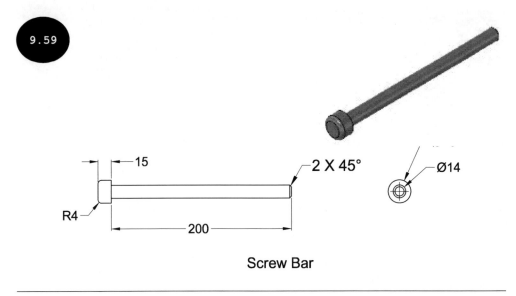

Screw Bar

Summary

This chapter discussed how to create assemblies by using the Top-down assembly approach. Various methods of creating all components of an assembly within a design file have been explained in addition to the method for applying as-built joints between the components of the assembly by using the **As-built Joint** tool.

Questions

Answer the following questions:

- In the _____ approach, all components of an assembly are created within a single design file.

- The _____ dialog box is used for creating an empty component or converting the existing bodies into a component.

- The _____ tool is used for applying joints to define the relative motion between the components in their current position as they are built.

- On selecting the _____ radio button in the **NEW COMPONENT** dialog box, an empty component is created within the current design file as an internal component.

- By default, the active component of the design file is selected as the parent for the new component. (True/False)

- In Autodesk Fusion 360, to add features in a component, you need to ensure that the component is active. (True/False)

- In Autodesk Fusion 360, you cannot edit components of the assembly created by using the Top-down assembly approach. (True/False)

CHAPTER

10

Creating Animation and Exploded Views

In this chapter, you will learn the following:

- Invoking the ANIMATION Workspace
- Capturing Views on the Timeline
- Capturing Actions on the Timeline
- Customizing Views and Actions
- Deleting Views and Actions of a Storyboard
- Creating a New Storyboard
- Toggling On or Off Capturing Views
- Playing and Publishing Animation
- Creating Exploded View of the Blow Off Cock Assembly

In Autodesk Fusion 360, you can animate a design to represent how the components of an assembly are assembled, operated, or repaired. Also, it serves as a great marketing tool to present your product or explain its functioning clearly. In Autodesk Fusion 360, you can create an animation of a design in the ANIMATION workspace. The method for invoking the ANIMATION workspace and creating the animation of a design is discussed next.

Invoking the ANIMATION Workspace

After creating an assembly in the DESIGN workspace, you need to switch to the ANIMATION workspace for creating its animation. To do so, invoke the **Workspace** drop-down menu in a design file, see Figure 10.1 and then click on **ANIMATION**. The startup user interface of the ANIMATION workspace appears, see Figure 10.2.

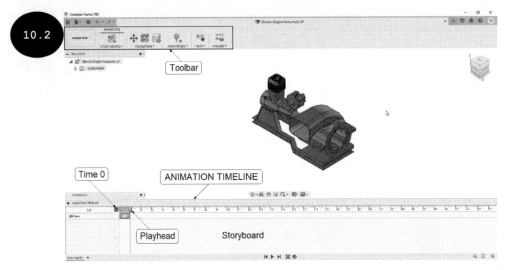

In Autodesk Fusion 360, to create an animation of a design, you need to capture views and actions along the **Timeline** in a storyboard, see Figure 10.3. Note that all navigating operations such as zoom in, zoom out, and orbit, performed at a given point in time on the design or assembly are captured on the **Timeline** as views, whereas, all the transforming operations such as move and rotate, performed at a given point in time on individual components of an assembly are captured on the **Timeline** as actions. The method for capturing views and actions on the **Timeline** of a storyboard are discussed next.

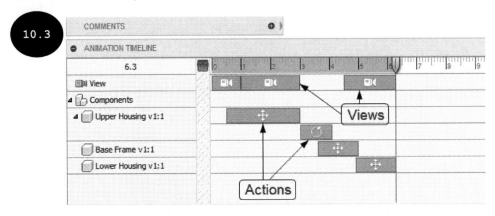

Capturing Views on the Timeline

To capture a view such as zoom or orbit, you need to first define the position of the **Playhead** on the **Timeline** at a positive point in time, see Figure 10.4. In this figure, the **Playhead** is placed on the **Timeline** at time 2 seconds. Note that, if the position of the **Playhead** is defined on the **Timeline** at **Time 0** ■ (red mark), then the view will not be captured on performing any navigating operation on the design or assembly, see Figure 10.5. You can also turn on or off the recording or capturing of views by clicking on the **View** tool in the **Toolbar**, respectively.

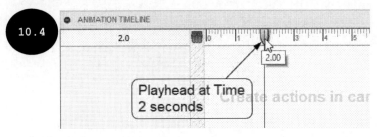

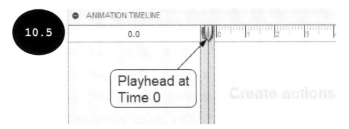

Playhead at Time 0

After defining the **Playhead** position at a positive point in time, perform a navigating operation on the design or assembly by using the mouse buttons or the navigating tools. The navigating operation performed is captured as a view on the **Timeline** at a defined point in time, see Figure 10.6. Now, you can play the animation to review the captured view by clicking on the **Play** button in the lower middle part of the storyboard, see Figure 10.6. You can similarly capture multiple views on the **Timeline** at different points in time.

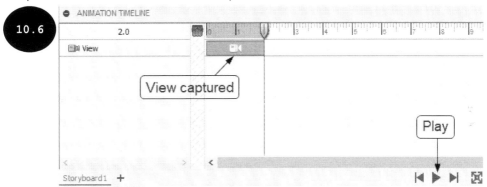

View captured

Play

After capturing a view, if you further perform any navigating operation without changing the Playhead position on the Timeline, then the existing view gets overridden by the newly performed navigating operation.

Capturing Actions on the Timeline

In Autodesk Fusion 360, you can capture actions at a given point in time on the **Timeline** by performing operations such as move and rotate on individual components of an assembly. You can also capture actions by creating exploded views of an assembly, turning on or off the visibility of the components, and creating callouts with annotations. The methods for capturing actions are discussed next.

Transforming Components (Move or Rotate)

As discussed, any transforming operation such as move or rotate performed at a given point in time on a component of an assembly is captured as an action. You can perform a transforming operation by using the **Transform Components** tool. To do so, first define the position of the **Playhead** on the **Timeline** at a positive point in time, see Figure 10.7. In this figure, the **Playhead** is positioned on the **Timeline** at time 4 seconds.

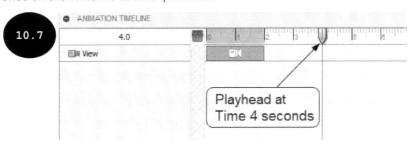

Playhead at Time 4 seconds

*If the position of the **Playhead** is defined on the **Timeline** at Time 0 (red mark), then the action will not be captured.*

After defining the **Playhead** position at a positive point in time, click on the **Transform Components** tool in the **Toolbar**, see Figure 10.8 or press the M key. The **TRANSFORM COMPONENTS** dialog box appears, see Figure 10.9. Next, select a component to be transformed in the graphics area. You can also select multiple components by pressing the CTRL key. The **TRANSFORM COMPONENTS** dialog box gets modified, see Figure 10.10. Also, the translational and manipulator handles appear on the selected component in the graphics area, see Figure 10.11. Now, you can transform (move and rotate) the selected component by dragging the translational and manipulator handles or by entering the distance and angle values in the respective fields of the dialog box.

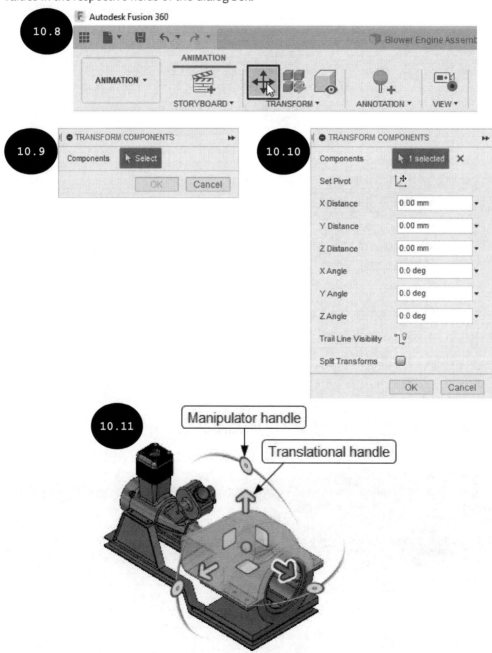

The **Trail Line Visibility** button of the **TRANSFORM COMPONENTS** dialog box is used for toggling the visibility of the trail line in the graphics area. The trail line defines the path and the direction in which the component is assembled, see Figure 10.12. By default, the **Split Transforms** check box is cleared in the dialog box. As a result, a straight trail line appears in the graphics area, see Figure 10.12. On selecting the **Split Transforms** check box, the trail line gets split into horizontal and vertical lines in the graphics area depending upon the transforming operation performed, see Figure 10.13.

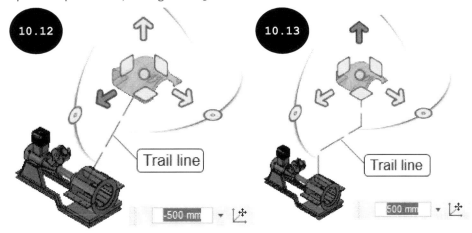

After transforming a component, click on the **OK** button in the **TRANSFORM COMPONENTS** dialog box. The transforming operation performed on the component is captured as an action on the **Timeline** at the defined point in time, see Figure 10.14. In Autodesk Fusion 360, after creating an action, you can customize it by editing its start and end times. You will learn about customizing an action later in this chapter.

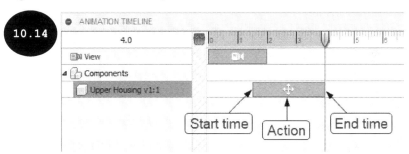

If you move as well as rotate the component by dragging the translational and manipulator handles or by entering the distance and angle values in the respective fields of the TRANSFORM COMPONENTS dialog box, then both the move and rotate actions will be captured separately on the Timeline, see Figure 10.15.

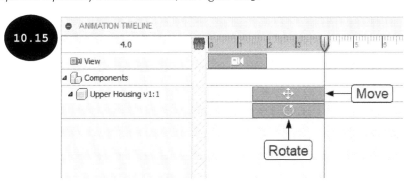

You can similarly capture multiple actions on the **Timeline** at different points in time by performing transforming operations on other components of the assembly one by one. After capturing the actions on the **Timeline** of a storyboard, you can play the animation by clicking on the **Play** button in the lower middle part of the storyboard.

Creating an Exploded View of an Assembly

In Autodesk Fusion 360, you can also capture actions on the **Timeline** by creating an exploded view of an assembly. An exploded view of an assembly helps in easily identifying the position of each component in the assembly. You can create exploded views by using the **Auto Explode: One Level**, **Auto Explode: All Levels**, or **Manual Explode** tools available in the **TRANSFORM** drop-down menu of the **Toolbar**, see Figure 10.16. The different tools for exploding an assembly are discussed next.

Auto Explode: One Level Tool

The **Auto Explode: One Level** tool is used for exploding only the first level children components of the assembly, automatically. This means that, if the assembly consists of sub-assemblies, then the components of sub-assemblies will not be exploded. To do so, expand the **Components** node in the **BROWSER** and then click to select the assembly, see Figure 10.17. All the components of the assembly get selected and highlighted in the graphics area. Next, invoke the **TRANSFORM** drop-down menu in the **Toolbar**, refer to Figure 10.16 and then click on the **Auto Explode: One Level** tool. The process of exploding the first level children components of the selected assembly gets started and once it is completed, the preview of the exploded view of the assembly and the **Auto Explode** toolbar appear in the graphics area, see Figure 10.18. Also, the actions of the exploded view of individual components of the assembly are captured on the **Timeline**, and the Green and Red sliders appear, see Figure 10.19.

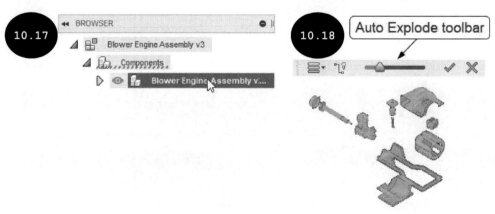

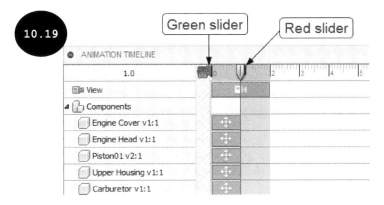

The Green slider defines the start time and the Red slider (appearing at the background of the **Playhead**) defines the end time of the exploded view on the **Timeline**. You can change the start and end times of the exploded view by dragging them along the **Timeline**, as required.

The **Auto Explode** toolbar that appears in the graphics area is used for controlling the type, trail line visibility, and explosion scale of the exploded view, see Figure 10.20. By default, the **One-Step Explosion** option is selected as the type of explosion in the **Type** drop-down list, see Figure 10.21. As a result, all components of the assembly get exploded at the same time. To explode each component of the assembly in a sequential order, select the **Sequential Explosion** option in the **Type** drop-down list of the **Auto Explode** toolbar. Note that, depending upon the option selected in the **Type** drop-down list, the actions of the exploded view are captured accordingly on the **Timeline**. Figure 10.22 shows the actions captured on the **Timeline** when the **One-Step Explosion** option is selected and Figure 10.23 shows the actions captured on the **Timeline** when the **Sequential Explosion** option is selected.

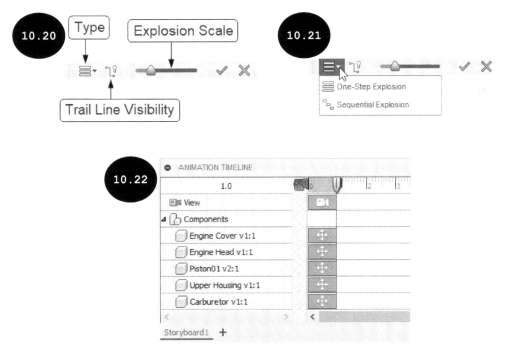

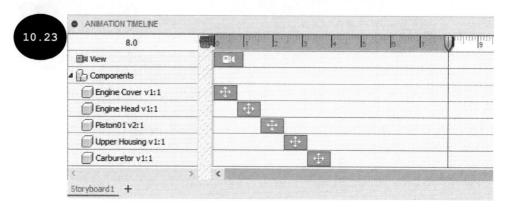

After defining the required options for the exploded view, click on the **OK** button (green tick-mark) in the **Auto Explode** toolbar. The exploded view is created and the actions of each exploded component of the assembly are captured on the **Timeline**. Now, you can animate the exploded view by clicking on the **Play** button of the Storyboard.

Auto Explode: All Levels Tool

The **Auto Explode: All Levels** tool is used for exploding all levels of the assembly, automatically. This means that, if the assembly consists of sub-assemblies, then the components of sub-assemblies will also be exploded. The method for exploding all levels of the assembly by using the **Auto Explode: All Levels** tool is same as discussed earlier.

Manual Explode Tool

The **Manual Explode** tool is used for exploding the components of the assembly, manually. To do so, invoke the **TRANSFORM** drop-down menu in the **Toolbar** and then click on the **Manual Explode** tool or press the **E** key. The **Auto Explode** toolbar appears in the graphics area. Also, the Green and Red sliders appear on the **Timeline**, see Figure 10.24. Next, select a component to be exploded in the graphics area, manually. A Triad with different axes appears along with the selected component in the graphics area, see Figure 10.25.

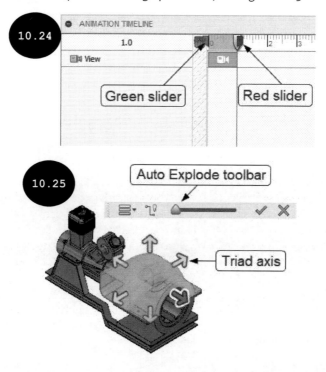

Select an axis of the Triad as the direction of explosion for the selected component in the graphics area. You can also select a set of components by pressing the CTRL key and define their direction of explosion. After selecting the components and defining the direction of explosion, specify the type of explosion (**One-Step Explosion** or **Sequential Explosion**), trail lines visibility, and explosion scale in the **Auto Explode** toolbar, as discussed earlier. A preview of the exploded view of the selected components appears in the graphics area. Also, the exploded actions are captured on the **Timeline**. Now, specify the start and end times for the exploded actions by dragging the Red and Green sliders that appear in the **Timeline**. Next, click on the **OK** button (green tick-mark) in the **Auto Explode** toolbar. The exploded view is created and the exploded actions are captured on the **Timeline**. You can similarly explode other components of the assembly, manually. After creating the exploded view, you can animate it by clicking on the **Play** button of the storyboard.

Toggling on or off the Visibility of Components

In Autodesk Fusion 360, you can capture actions on the **Timeline** by turning on or off the visibility of components at a given point in time on the **Timeline**. To do so, first define the position of the **Playhead** on the **Timeline** at a positive point in time, where the visibility of the component is to be turned off. Next, select the component in the graphics area. After selecting the component, click on the **Show/Hide** tool in the **TRANSFORM** panel of the **Toolbar**, see Figure 10.26. The visibility of the selected component gets turned off in the graphics area. Also, a visibility action is captured and added below the name of the selected component on the **Timeline**, see Figure 10.27.

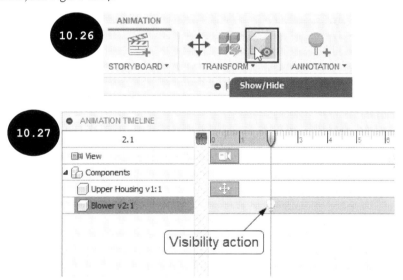

Visibility action

Now, when you play the animation, you will notice that the visibility of the selected component gets turned off instantly at the specified point in time. This is because, the **Instant** option is defined for the visibility action, by default. You can define the start and end times for the visibility action so that the component gets faded slowly. To do so, right-click on the light bulb icon of the visibility action in the **Timeline** and then click on the **Edit Start/End** option in the shortcut menu that appears, see Figure 10.28. The **Start/End** toolbar appears with the **Start** field only, see Figure 10.29. Click on the arrow next to the **Instant** option in the **Toolbar** and then select the **Duration** option. Both **Start** and **End** fields appear in the **Toolbar**, see Figure 10.30. Now, you can specify the start and end times of the action in the respective fields of the **Toolbar** and then click on the **OK** button. After defining the start and end times, when you play the animation, you will notice that the component starts fading from its start time and gets hidden at its end time on the **Timeline**.

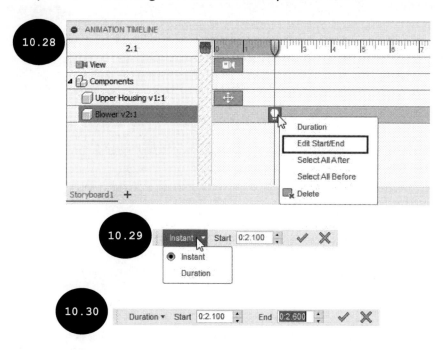

Creating a Callout with Annotation

In Autodesk Fusion 360, you can also capture an action on the **Timeline** by tagging a callout with text or annotation on a component. To do so, first define the position of the **Playhead** on the **Timeline** and then click on the **Create Callout** tool in the **ANNOTATION** panel of the **Toolbar**, see Figure 10.31. A callout gets attached to the cursor. Next, click on the component to tag the callout. A Text window appears, see Figure 10.32. Enter the information to be tagged with the selected component in the Text window and then click on the green tick-mark that appears above it. The callout is tagged to the selected component. Also, the callout action is captured at the specified point in time on the **Timeline**. Now, when you hover the cursor over the callout, the text appears in the graphics area.

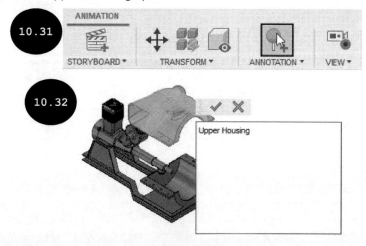

Customizing Views and Actions

After capturing views and actions on the **Timeline**, you can customize them by editing their start and end times. To edit the start time of an action, move the cursor over its start time (left end) on the **Timeline** until the cursor changes to a double arrow, see Figure 10.33. Next, drag the cursor to set the new start time for the action on the **Timeline**. You can similarly edit the end time of the action, as required. On editing the start and end times of an action, you can control the total duration of the action on the **Timeline**. You can also edit the duration of an action as discussed earlier.

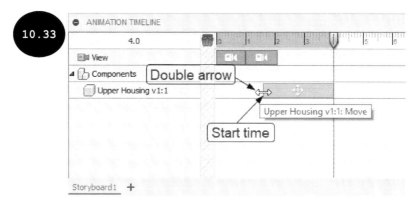

In addition to editing the start and end times of an action to control its duration, you can move the action to a different point in time on the **Timeline**. To do so, move the cursor over the action on the **Timeline**. The cursor changes to the move cursor, see Figure 10.34. Next, drag and drop the action to a new location on the **Timeline** to define its new position.

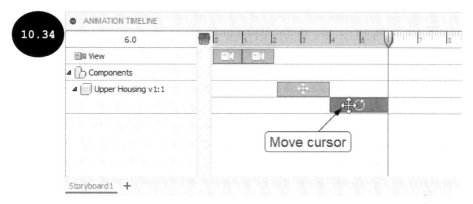

After creating required actions and views for a storyboard, you can play the animation by clicking on the **Play** button available at the lower middle part of the storyboard.

Deleting Views and Actions of a Storyboard

You can also delete views and actions of a storyboard that are no longer required. To do so, right-click on a view or an action to be deleted on the **Timeline** of a storyboard and then click on the **Delete** option in the shortcut menu that appears, see Figure 10.35. The selected view or action gets deleted from the **Timeline** of the storyboard.

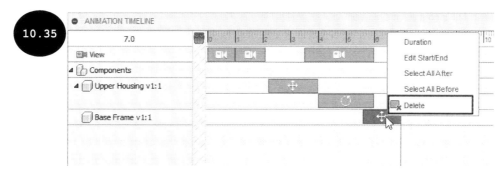

Creating a New Storyboard

In Autodesk Fusion 360, on invoking the **ANIMATION** workspace, an empty storyboard is created with a default name (**Storyboard1**) automatically, at the bottom of the screen. In addition to the default storyboard created, you can create a new storyboard and add the required views and actions. To do so, click on the **New Storyboard** tool in the **STORYBOARD** panel of the **Toolbar**, see Figure 10.36. The **NEW STORYBOARD** dialog box appears, see Figure 10.37. On selecting the **Clean** option in the **Storyboard Type** drop-down list of the dialog box, a new empty storyboard is created with no action and the transformation of the components is the same as they are brought from the **DESIGN** workspace. On selecting the **Start from end of previous** option, a new empty storyboard is created with no action and the transformation of the components is the same as they are at the end of the previous storyboard.

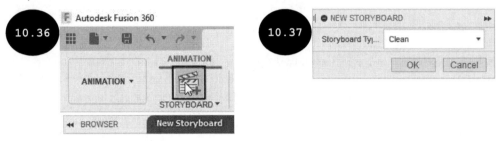

After selecting the required option in the **Storyboard Type** drop-down list of the **NEW STORYBOARD** dialog box, click on the **OK** button. A new empty storyboard is created with a default name and becomes the active storyboard, see Figure 10.38. Now, you can add different views and actions for the newly created storyboard, as discussed earlier. Alternatively, you can create a new storyboard by clicking on the Plus sign next to the existing storyboard tab, see Figure 10.38.

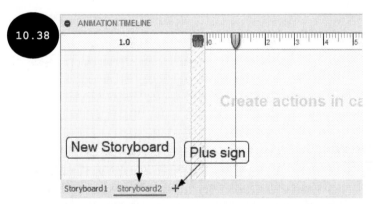

 *When you publish the animation of a storyboard, the name of the storyboard appears on the web as its title. As a result, it is recommended to rename the storyboard, as required. To do so, right-click on the storyboard tab at the lower left corner of the screen and then click on the **Rename** option in the shortcut menu that appears, see Figure 10.39. Now, you can enter a new name for the storyboard. You will learn about publishing the animation of a storyboard later in this chapter.*

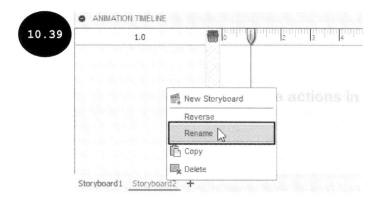

Toggling On or Off Capturing Views

When the **Playhead** is positioned at a positive point in time on the **Timeline**, the views get captured or recorded automatically on performing the navigating operations such as zoom or pan. However, to setup a scene in preparation of animation, you may need to turn off the capturing of views. To do so, click on the **View** tool in the **Toolbar**, see Figure 10.40 or press CTRL + R. The automatic capturing of navigating operations as views gets turned on or off, respectively. Note that it is a toggle button.

Playing and Publishing Animation

After capturing all views and actions on the **Timeline** of a storyboard, you can play the animation as well as publish it to a video file format. To play the animation, click on the **Play** button at the lower middle part of the storyboard, see Figure 10.41.

To publish the animation as a video file format, click on the **Publish Video** tool in the PUBLISH panel of the **Toolbar**, see Figure 10.42 or press the P key. The **Video Options** dialog box appears, see Figure 10.43. In the **Video Scope** drop-down list of the dialog box, specify whether to publish the animation of all storyboards or only the currently active storyboard by selecting the **All Storyboards** or the **Current Storyboard** option, respectively. In the **Video Resolution** area of the dialog box, specify the resolution/size of the video file to be published. The **Current Document Window Size** option in this area is used for publishing the video using the pixel size and resolution of the current environment. Next, click on the **OK** button in the dialog box. The **Save As** dialog box appears. In this dialog box, enter the name of the video file and specify the location to save the video in a local drive of your computer. Next, click on the **Save** button. The video file (*.avi*) is saved in the specified location.

Tutorial 1 - Creating Exploded View of the Blow Off Cock Assembly

Open the Blow Off Cock assembly created in Tutorial 2 of Chapter 8, see Figure 10.44 and then create its exploded view in the **ANIMATION** workspace, see Figure 10.45.

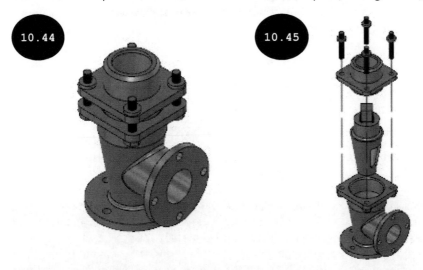

The following sequence summarizes the tutorial outline:

- Opening Tutorial 2 of Chapter 8
- Invoking the ANIMATION Workspace
- Creating the Exploded View
- Renaming the Storyboard

- Playing the Animation
- Publishing and Saving the Animation
- Saving the Model

Opening Tutorial 2 of Chapter 8

1. Start Autodesk Fusion 360.

2. Display the **Data Panel** by clicking on the **Show Data Panel** tool in the **Application Bar** and then browse to **Autodesk Fusion 360 Tutorials > Chapter 8 > Tutorial 2** location.

3. Double-click on the **Blow Off Cock** assembly file in the **Data Panel**. The **Blow Off Cock** assembly gets opened in Autodesk Fusion 360. Next, close the **Data Panel** by clicking on the cross mark at its top right corner.

Invoking the ANIMATION Workspace

1. Invoke the **Workspace** drop-down menu and then click on **ANIMATION**, see Figure 10.46. The startup user interface of the **ANIMATION** workspace appears, see Figure 10.47.

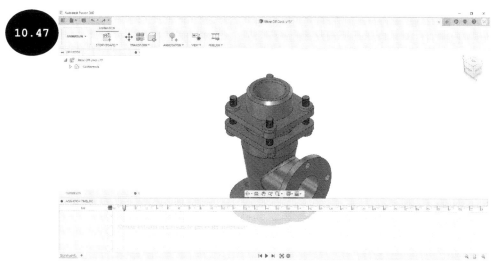

Creating the Exploded View

1. Define the **Playhead** position to time 2 seconds on the **Timeline** to capture the view by dragging it, see Figure 10.48.

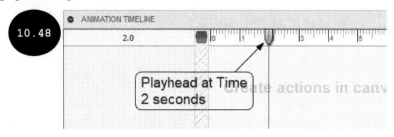

2. Navigate the assembly such that it fits within the screen. The view is captured at time 2 seconds on the **Timeline**, see Figure 10.49.

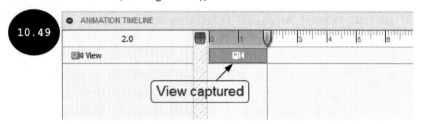

Now, you need to transform all instances of the **Stud** components.

3. Define the **Playhead** position to time 4 seconds on the **Timeline** by dragging it.

4. Click on the **Transform Components** tool in the **TRANSFORM** panel of the **Toolbar**, see Figure 10.50 or press the **M** key. The **TRANSFORM COMPONENTS** dialog box appears in the graphics area.

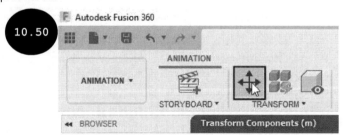

5. Select the **Stud** components (all four instances) by pressing the CTRL key, see Figure 10.51. The translational and manipulator handles appear on the last selected instance in the graphics area.

6. Drag the vertical translational handle upward in the graphics area up to a distance of 400 mm, see Figure 10.52. You can also enter **400 mm** distance value in the **Z Distance** field of the **TRANSFORM COMPONENTS** dialog box.

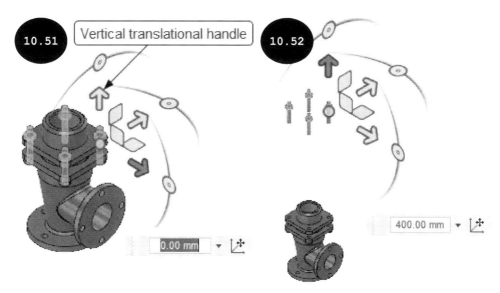

Vertical translational handle

10.51

10.52

400.00 mm

0.00 mm

While dragging the vertical translational handle upward to a distance 400 mm, you may need to zoom out the model by scrolling the middle mouse button such that it can fit inside the screen and the same zooming operations get captured on the Timeline as views.

7. Click on the **Trail Line Visibility** button to activate it in the dialog box. The visibility of the trail lines gets turned on in the graphics area.

8. Click on the **OK** button in the **TRANSFORM COMPONENTS** dialog box. The transforming operation performed on the **Stud** components gets captured as actions on the **Timeline**, see Figure 10.53.

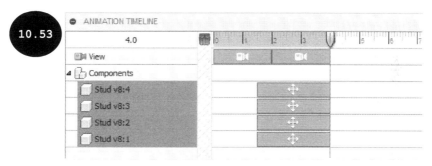

Now, you need to transform the **Gland** component.

9. Define the **Playhead** position to time 6 seconds on the **Timeline** by dragging it.

10. Click on the **Transform Components** tool in the **TRANSFORM** panel of the **Toolbar** or press the M key. The **TRANSFORM COMPONENTS** dialog box appears.

11. Select the **Gland** component of the assembly in the graphics area. The translational and manipulator handles appear, see Figure 10.54.

12. Enter **300 mm** in the **Z Distance** field of the **TRANSFORM COMPONENTS** dialog box. The **Gland** component gets transformed to 300 mm along the z-axis direction, see Figure 10.55.

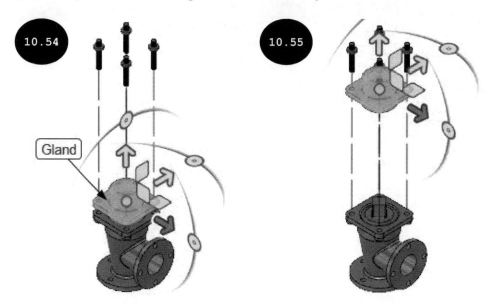

13. Click on the **OK** button in the dialog box. The transforming operation performed on the Gland component gets captured as an action on the **Timeline**.

Now, you need to transform the **Cock** component.

14. Define the **Playhead** position to time 7 seconds on the **Timeline** by dragging it.

15. Click on the **Transform Components** tool in the **TRANSFORM** panel of the **Toolbar** or press the **M** key. The **TRANSFORM COMPONENTS** dialog box appears.

16. Select the **Cock** component of the assembly in the graphics area. The translational and manipulator handles appear, see Figure 10.56.

17. Enter **200 mm** in the **Z Distance** field of the **TRANSFORM COMPONENTS** dialog box. The **Cock** component gets transformed to 200 mm along the z-axis direction, see Figure 10.57.

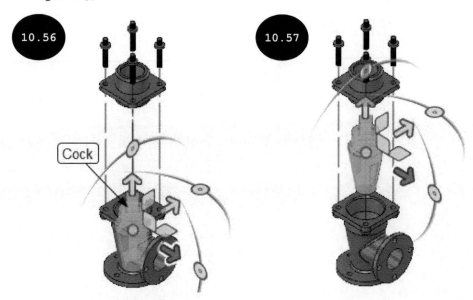

18. Click on the **OK** button in the dialog box. The transforming operation performed on the **Cock** component gets captured as an action on the **Timeline**, see Figure 10.58.

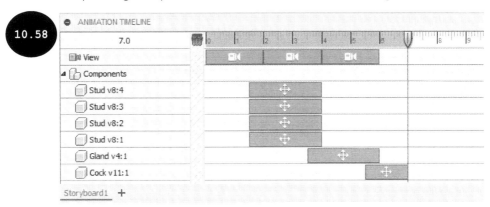

10.58

19. Click anywhere in the graphics area to exit the current selection set. Figure 10.59 shows the final assembly after exploding all its components.

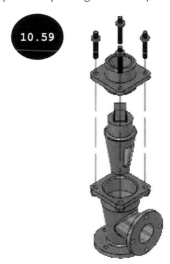

10.59

Renaming the Storyboard

1. Right-click on the **Storyboard** tab at the lower left corner of the screen. The shortcut menu appears, see Figure 10.60.

10.60

2.   Click on the **Rename** option in the shortcut menu. An edit field appears.

3.   Enter **Exploded View Animation** in the edit field as the name of the storyboard and then press ENTER. The name of the storyboard gets changed.

Playing the Animation

1.   Click on the **Play** button at the lower middle part of the storyboard. The animation of the exploded view starts in the graphics area.

Publishing and Saving the Animation

1.   Click on the **Publish Video** tool in the PUBLISH panel of the **Toolbar**. The **Video Options** dialog box appears, see Figure 10.61.

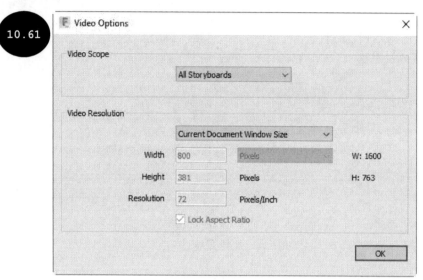

2.   Select the **Current Storyboard** option in the **Video Scope** drop-down list of the dialog box.

3.   Accept the remaining options of the dialog box and then click on the **OK** button. The **Save As** dialog box appears.

4.   Enter **Blow Off Cock Exploded View** in the **Name** field of the dialog box as the name of the video file.

5.   Select the **Save to my computer** check box in the dialog box for saving the video file in the local drive of your system.

6.   Click on the **Browse** button ⋯ available on the right of the **Save to my computer** field. The **Save to my computer** dialog box appears.

7.   Browse to the location where you want to save the video file in the local drive of your computer.

8.   Click on the **Save** button in the dialog box. The **Publish Video** window appears, which displays the process of publishing the video and once the process is completed, the video file is saved with the specified name in the *.avi* file format.

Saving the Model

1. Click on the **Save** tool in the **Application Bar**. The **Add Version Description** window appears as the design is already saved. In this window, you can enter a description for the new version of the assembly, if needed.

2. Click on the **OK** button in the window. A new updated version of the assembly file is saved at the location (**Autodesk Fusion 360 Tutorials > Chapter 8 > Tutorial 2**).

Exercise 1

Open the assembly created in Exercise 1 of Chapter 8, see Figure 10.62 and then create its exploded view manually by exploding its components one by one in the **ANIMATION** workspace, see Figure 10.63. After creating the exploded view, save the animated video in the .avi file format in a local drive of your computer.

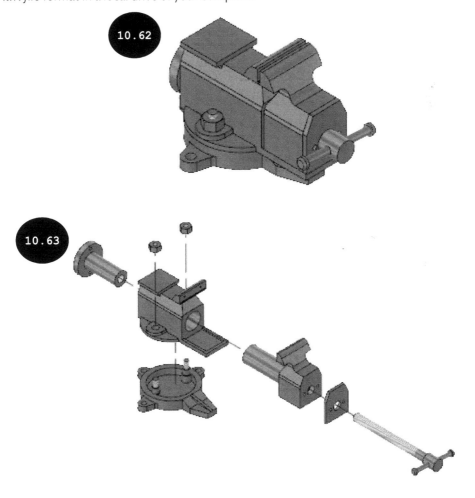

Summary

This chapter discussed how to create an animation of an assembly in the **ANIMATION** Workspace. To animate an assembly, you need to capture various views and actions on the **Timeline** of a storyboard, the method for which has been described. Various methods for creating exploded views of the assembly (manually or automatically), turning on or off the visibility of the components, and creating callouts have also been discussed in addition to methods for customizing and deleting views and actions on the **Timeline**, creating new storyboards, turning on or off the recording of the views, and publishing animation as .avi file format.

Questions

Answer the following questions:

- In Autodesk Fusion 360, you can create the animation of a design in the _____ workspace.

- If the position of the **Playhead** is defined at _____ on the **Timeline**, then the views and actions will not be captured.

- In Autodesk Fusion 360, any transforming operation such as move or rotate performed at a point in time on a component of an assembly is captured as an _____.

- The _____ button of the **TRANSFORM COMPONENTS** dialog box is used for toggling the visibility of the trail line on or off in the graphics area.

- The _____ tool is used for exploding the first level children components of the assembly, automatically.

- The _____ tool is used for exploding all levels of the assembly including the sub-assemblies components, automatically.

- The _____ tool is used for turning on or off the visibility of components at a point in time on the **Timeline**.

- The _____ tool is used for adding a callout with text or annotation on a component.

- The _____ tool is used for creating a new empty storyboard.

- The _____ tool is used for publishing the animation as a video file format.

- In Autodesk Fusion 360, after capturing views and actions on the **Timeline**, you can customize them by editing their start and end times. (True/False)

- You cannot delete views and actions of a storyboard. (True/False)

- When you publish the animation of a storyboard, the name of the storyboard appears on the web as its title. (True/False)

Creating 2D Drawings

In this chapter, you will learn the following:

- Introduction to 2D Drawings
- Creating Drawing Views of the Valve Body Component
- Creating Drawing Views of the Blow Off Cock Assembly

Introduction to 2D Drawings

A 2D drawing is not just a drawing, but also a language used by engineers for communication of ideas and information about engineered products. By using 2D drawings, a designer can clearly and fully communicate information about components to be manufactured to the engineers on the shop floor. Underscoring the importance of 2D drawings, the role of designers becomes very important in generating accurate drawings for production. Inaccurate or missing information about a component in drawings can lead to faulty production. Keeping this in mind, Autodesk Fusion 360 provides you with a separate workspace (DRAWING) that allows you to generate error-free 2D drawings.

In the **DRAWING** workspace of Fusion 360, you can create drawings of a design (component or assembly) created in the **DESIGN** workspace as well as the exploded views of the assembly created in the **ANIMATION** workspace.

Tutorial 1 - Creating Drawing Views of the Valve Body Component

Open the model created in Tutorial 3 of Chapter 4 and then create different drawing views: front, top, side, isometric, section, and detail, as shown in Figure 11.1 in the B (17in x 11in) sheet size. After creating the drawing views, apply dimensions.

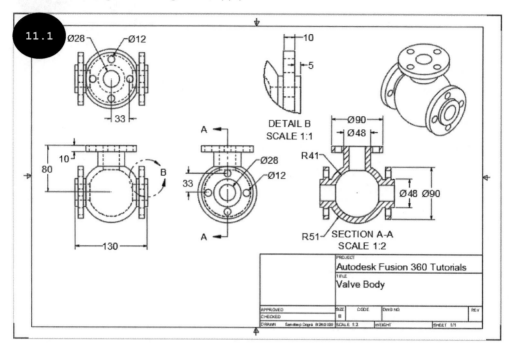

Figure 11.1

The following sequence summarizes the tutorial outline:

- Opening the Tutorial 3 of Chapter 4
- Defining the Angle of Projection
- Invoking the DRAWING Workspace and Creating Base View
- Creating Projected Views
- Creating the Section View
- Creating the Detail View
- Applying Dimensions
- Editing Dimensions
- Saving the Model

Opening the Tutorial 3 of Chapter 4

1. Launch Autodesk Fusion 360 and then open the **Valve Body** model created in Tutorial 3 of Chapter 4, see Figure 11.2.

    Now, you need to save the model in Chapter 11 folder of the project.

2. Click on **File > Save As** in the **Application Bar**. The **Save As** dialog box appears.

3. Save the **Valve Body** model in **Autodesk Fusion 360 Tutorials > Chapter 11 > Tutorial 1** location. Note that you need to create these folders inside the "**Autodesk Fusion 360 Tutorials**" project folder in the **Data Panel**. Next, close the **Data Panel**.

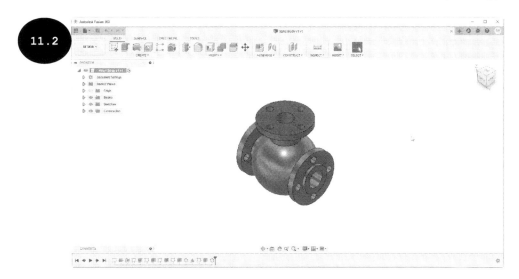

Defining the Angle of Projection

Before invoking the DRAWING workspace, you can define the angle of projection and drawing properties for creating the drawing views of the model.

Engineering drawings follow two types of angles of projection: first angle of projection and third angle of projection. In the first angle of projection, the object is assumed to be kept in the first quadrant and the viewer views the object from the direction as shown in Figure 11.3. As the object has been kept in the first quadrant, its projections of views are on the respective planes as shown in Figure 11.3. Now on unfolding the planes of projections, the front view appears on the upper side and the top view appears on the bottom side. Also, the right side view appears on the left and the left side view appears on the right side of the front view, refer to Figure 11.4. Similarly, in the third angle of projection, the object is assumed to be kept in the third quadrant, refer to Figure 11.3. In this case, the projection of the front view appears on the bottom and the projection of the top view appears on the top side in the drawing. Also, the right side view appears on the right and the left side view appears on the left of the front view, refer to Figure 11.5.

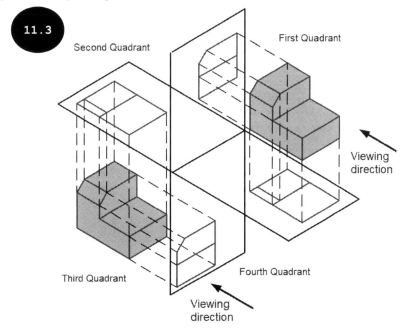

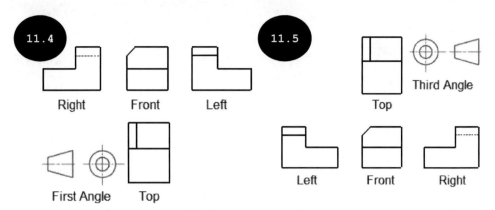

1. Click on your name in the upper right corner of Autodesk Fusion 360. The **User Account** drop-down menu appears, see Figure 11.6.

2. Click on the **Preferences** tool in the drop-down menu. The **Preferences** dialog box appears.

3. Click on the **Drawing** option under the **General** node in the left panel of the **Preferences** dialog box, see Figure 11.7.

*By default, the **Inherit From Design** option is selected in the **Standard** and **Annotation** Units drop-down lists of the dialog box. As a result, each new drawing uses the standard and units specified for the design.*

4. Select the **ASME** drawing standard in the **Standard** drop-down list on the right panel of the dialog box, see Figure 11.7. The **Third Angle** option gets selected in the **Projection Angle** drop-down list of the dialog box, automatically, since for the ASME standard, the third angle of projection is used for generating the drawing views, by default.

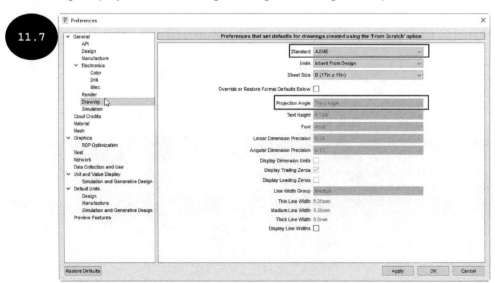

*By default, when you create a drawing as per the ISO standard, the first angle of projection is used for generating the drawing views, whereas when creating a drawing as per the ASME standard, the third angle of projection is used. However, you can customize the default angle of projection for a drawing standard. To do so, select the **Override or Restore Format Defaults Below** check box in the **Preferences** dialog box. All the default properties of the selected drawing standard become editable in the dialog box. Next, select the projection angle, as required in the **Projection Angle** drop-down list of the dialog box. Besides, you can also edit the default drawing preferences or properties such as text height, font, linear dimension precision, angular dimension precision, units, and so on in their respective fields of the dialog box.*

5. Click on the **Apply** button and then the **OK** button in the **Preferences** dialog box.

 *The changes made in the projection angle or drawing properties for a standard in the **Preferences** dialog box will be applied only to new drawings and does not reflect on the current drawing or any of the existing drawings. Therefore, it is recommended to make these changes before invoking the DRAWING workspace.*

Invoking the DRAWING Workspace and Creating Base View

Now, you need to invoke the **DRAWING** workspace for creating different drawing views of the model.

1. Invoke the **Workspace** drop-down menu and then click on **DRAWING > From Design**, see Figure 11.8. The **CREATE DRAWING** dialog box appears, see Figure 11.9.

 *You can also invoke the **CREATE DRAWING** dialog box by clicking on **File > New Drawing > From Design** in the **Application Menu**, see Figure 11.10 or right-clicking on the name of the design (**Valve Body**) in the **BROWSER** and then clicking on the **Create Drawing** option in the shortcut menu that appears, see Figure 11.11.*

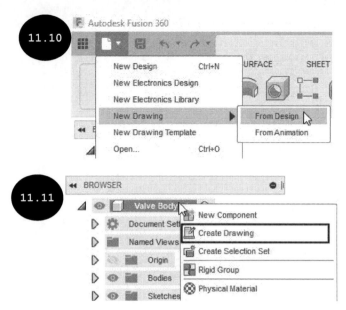

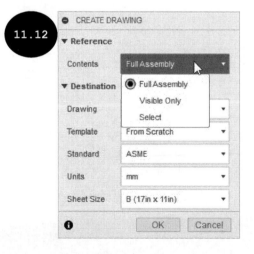

*Autodesk Fusion 360 allows you to invoke the **DRAWING** workspace from a design or an animation file by selecting the respective option: **From Design** or **From Animation**, refer to Figures 11.8 and 11.10. The **From Design** option is used for creating drawing views from the design file (component or assembly), whereas the **From Animation** option is used for creating the exploded view of the assembly on the drawing sheet that is created in the **ANIMATION** workspace.*

2. Ensure that the **Full Assembly** option is selected in the **Contents** drop-down list of the **CREATE DRAWING** dialog box.

Contents: The Contents drop-down list of the dialog box contains three options: **Full Assembly**, **Visible Only**, and **Select**, see Figure 11.12. On selecting the **Full Assembly** option, all the components of the assembly gets selected automatically for creating the drawing. Even if the visibility of some of the components of the assembly is turned off or hidden in the graphics area, still they will also be included in the selection set for creating the drawing. On selecting the **Visible Only** option, only the visible components of the assembly gets selected for creating the drawing. On selecting the **Select** option, the **Components** selection option appears in the dialog box, which is used for selecting components of the assembly for creating the drawing.

3. Ensure that the **Create New** option is selected in the **Drawing** drop-down list of the dialog box for creating a new drawing.

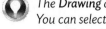 *The **Drawing** drop-down list also displays a list of existing drawings created for the design. You can select an existing drawing in this drop-down list. On doing so, you can add a new sheet of drawing or create drawing views in a sheet of the existing drawing.*

4. Ensure that the **From Scratch** option is selected in the **Template** drop-down list of the dialog box for creating a new drawing from scratch in the default drawing template.

   Template: The **Template** drop-down list appears in the dialog box when the **Create New** option is selected in the **Drawing** drop-down list. The **From Scratch** option is used for creating a new drawing from scratch in the default drawing template. You can also select an existing template to create the new drawing. To do so, select the **Browse** option in the **Template** drop-down list. The **Select Template** dialog box appears. In this dialog box, browse to the location where the drawing template is saved and then select it. Next, click on the **Select** button in the dialog box.

5. Select the **ASME** standard in the **Standard** drop-down list of the dialog box.

    The Standard drop-down list is enabled in the dialog box only on creating a new drawing and is used for selecting a drawing standard such as ASME or ISO for creating the drawing.

6. Ensure that **mm** unit is selected in the **Units** drop-down list of the dialog box.

7. Select the **B (17in x 11in)** sheet size in the **Sheet Size** drop-down list of the dialog box.

8. After selecting the required options in the **CREATE DRAWING** dialog box, click on the **OK** button. The **DRAWING** workspace is invoked and a drawing sheet with the specified standard and size appears, see Figure 11.13. Also, the **DRAWING VIEW** dialog box appears on the right side of the drawing sheet and a preview of the default base view appears attached to the cursor, see Figure 11.13.

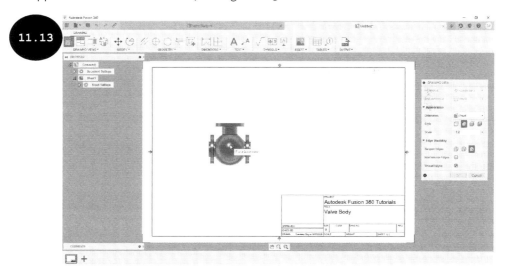

11.13

 In Autodesk Fusion 360, every time on invoking the DRAWING workspace, the DRAWING VIEW dialog box appears, since the Base View tool gets activated in the Toolbar, automatically on invoking the DRAWING workspace. The options in the DRAWING VIEW dialog box are used for specifying the parameters such as orientation, style, and scale for the base view to be created.

Now, you need to create the base view by defining its parameters and placement location on the drawing sheet.

The base view is an independent view of a design. It is also known as the first or the parent view for generating the orthogonal and isometric projected views of the design.

9. Select the **Front** option in the **Orientation** drop-down list of the **DRAWING VIEW** dialog box for creating the front view of the model as the base view, see Figure 11.14.

10. Ensure that the **Visible and Hidden Edges** button 🗗 is activated in the **Style** area of the dialog box, see Figure 11.14.

    Style: The Style area of the dialog box is used for specifying a visual style for the base view to be created. You can select the **Visible Edges**, **Visible and Hidden Edges**, **Shaded**, or **Shaded with Hidden Edges** button in this area to define the visual style.

11. Select **1:2** in the **Scale** drop-down list of the dialog box as the scale factor of the base view, see Figure 11.14.

12. Ensure that the **Off** button 🗗 is activated in the **Tangent Edges** area of the dialog box to turn off the display of tangent edges on the base view, see Figure 11.14.

    Tangent Edges: The Tangent Edges area of the dialog box is used for controlling the display of the tangent edges of the model in the base view. Tangent edges are a smooth transition between the faces and the rounded edges (filleted edges). The **Full Length** button 🗗 is used for displaying full length tangent edges of the model in the base view. The **Shortened** button 🗗 is used for displaying shortened tangent edges in the base view. The **Off** button 🗗 is used for turning off the display of tangent edges in the base view.

13. Ensure that the **Interference Edges** check box is cleared in the dialog box.

 The Interference Edges check box is used for turning on or off the display of interference edges of the model in the base view. Interference edges are edges which occur when the faces of two components intersect each other.

14. Ensure that the **Thread Edges** check box is selected in the dialog box.

 On selecting the Thread Edges check box in the dialog box, the thread edges are represented as dash lines in the drawing view, whereas on clearing this check box, the thread edges representation gets turned off in the drawing view.

    Now, you need to define the placement point of the base view on the drawing sheet.

15. Click to specify the position of the base view in the lower left corner of the drawing sheet, see Figure 11.15. The Front view is placed in the specified location and the **DRAWING VIEW** dialog box is still displayed.

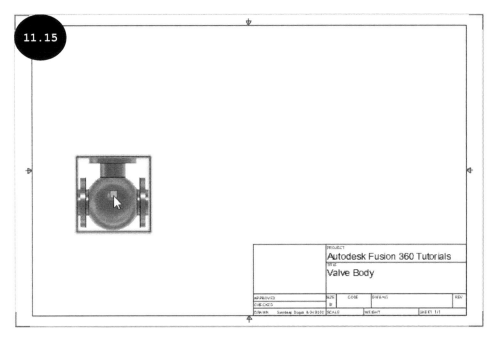

You can control the parameters such as orientation, style, and scale for the base view before and after defining its placement point in the drawing sheet in the DRAWING VIEW dialog box.

16. After defining all the required parameters for the base view in the **DRAWING VIEW** dialog box, click on the **OK** button. The Front view of the model is placed in the specified location as per the parameters specified in the dialog box, see Figure 11.16.

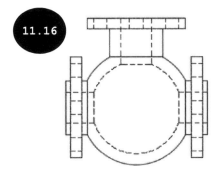

As discussed earlier, every time on invoking the DRAWING workspace, the DRAWING VIEW dialog box appears automatically for creating the base view of the model. Besides, you can also invoke the DRAWING VIEW dialog box for creating the base view by clicking on the Base View tool in the DRAWING VIEWS panel of the Toolbar, see Figure 11.17.

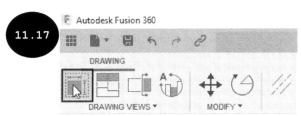

Creating Projected Views

Now, you need to create the projected views of the Base view.

 Projected views are orthogonal and isometric views of an object, which are created by viewing the object from different projection sides such as top, front, side, and at an angle of 45 degrees, refer to Figures 11.18 and 11.19. Note that the creation of orthogonal projected views depends upon the angle of projection defined for the drawing sheet.

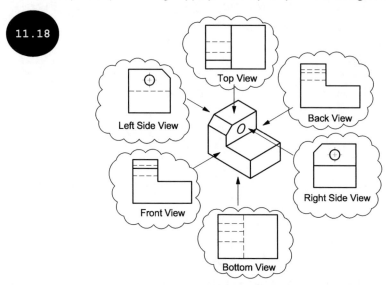

Projected Views

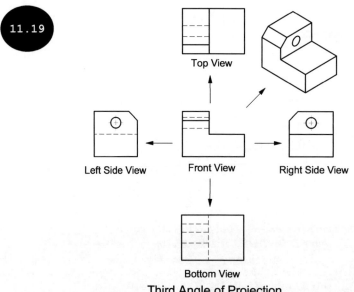

Third Angle of Projection

1. Click on the **Projected View** tool in the **DRAWING VIEWS** panel in the **Toolbar**, see Figure 11.20 or press the **P** key. You are prompted to select a parent view.

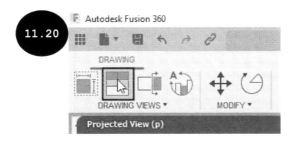

2. Select the Front view as the parent view for creating the projected views. A projected view is attached to the cursor.

3. Move the cursor vertically upward. The projected view (Top view) appears attached to the cursor, see Figure 11.21.

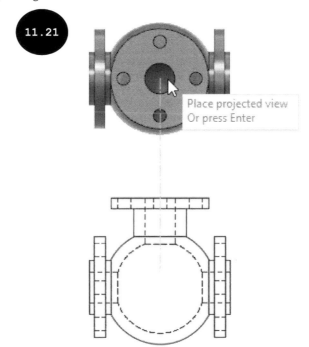

4. Click on the drawing sheet to specify the position of the Top view, refer to Figure 11.22.

5. Move the cursor horizontally towards right. The projected view (Right view) of the model appears attached to the cursor.

6. Click on the drawing sheet to specify the position of the Right view, refer to Figure 11.22.

7. Move the cursor at an angle to the Front view (Base view). The isometric view of the model appears attached to the cursor. Next, click to specify its position on the upper right corner of the drawing sheet, see Figure 11.22.

The creation of projected views; orthogonal or isometric; depends upon the movement of the cursor. When the cursor is moved at a right angle (horizontally or vertically) to the base view, an orthogonal view gets created, whereas when it is moved at an angle of 45 degrees to the base view, an isometric view gets created.

8.   After creating all the projected views, press ENTER to exit the tool. The projected views are created.

     Now, you need to change the visible style of the isometric projected view. By default, the properties of the parent view (Front view) are propagated to the projected views.

9.   Double-click on the isometric projected view. The **DRAWING VIEW** dialog box appears. In this dialog box, the **From Parent** button is activated in the **Style** area, by default. As a result, properties of the parent view are propagated to its projected view.

> *You can change the properties of any existing drawing view by double-clicking on it and then defining its new properties in the respective dialog box that appears.*

10. Click on the **Visible Edges** button in the dialog box to change the visible style of the isometric projected view.

11. Click on the **Close** button to exit the dialog box. Figure 11.22 shows the drawing sheet after creating all the projected views.

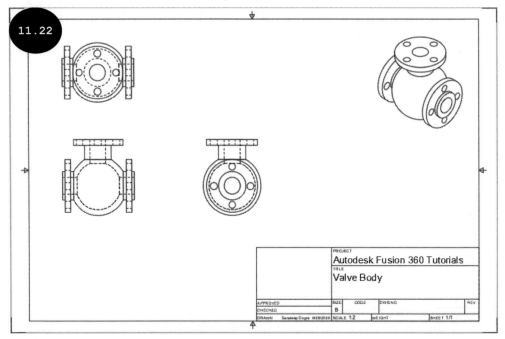

11.22

	PROJECT	
	Autodesk Fusion 360 Tutorials	
	TITLE	
	Valve Body	

APPROVED		SIZE	CODE	DWG NO		REV
CHECKED		B				
DRAWN	Sandeep Dogra 8/28/2020	SCALE 1:2		WEIGHT	SHEET 1/1	

> *You can change the position of an existing drawing view by dragging and dropping it to a new position on the drawing sheet.*

Creating the Section View

Now, you need to create the section view by selecting the Right view as the parent view.

> *A section view is created by cutting an object by using an imaginary cutting plane or a section line and then viewing the object from a direction normal to the section line. It is used for illustrating internal features of an object. It also reduces the number of hidden-detail lines, facilitates the dimensioning of internal features, shows cross-sections, and so on.*

1. Click on the **Section View** tool in the DRAWING VIEWS panel in the **Toolbar**, see Figure 11.23. You are prompted to select the parent view.

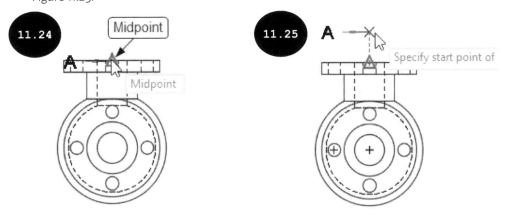

2. Select the Right view as the parent view for creating the section view. The **DRAWING VIEW** dialog box appears and you are prompted to specify the start point of the section line.

3. Move the cursor to the midpoint of the upper horizontal edge of the Right view, see Figure 11.24 and then move the cursor vertically upward. A tracking line appears, see Figure 11.25.

4. Follow the tracking line and then click to specify the start point of the section line at a small distance outside the top edge, refer to Figure 11.26.

5. Move the cursor vertically downward and then click to specify the endpoint of the section line anywhere outside the bottom of the Right view, refer to Figure 11.26.

You can create a section line by specifying multiple points one after the other.

6. Press ENTER to end the creation of section lines. A preview of the section view appears attached to the cursor, see Figure 11.26. Also, you are prompted to specify its placement in the drawing sheet.

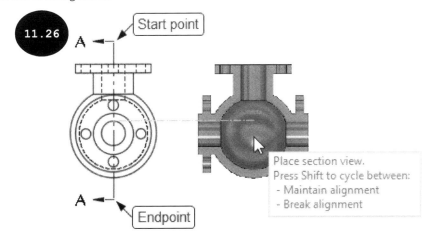

By default, the section view maintains a horizontal or vertical alignment to the section line, see Figure 11.26. To break the alignment, press the SHIFT key. You can again press the SHIFT key to restore the horizontal or vertical alignment of the section view.

7. Move the cursor horizontally toward right and then click to specify the position of the section view on the drawing sheet, refer to Figure 11.27. After defining the placement for the section view, you can define the appearance, scale, and visibility of tangent edges in the section view by using the **DRAWING VIEW** dialog box. The options in this dialog box are same as discussed earlier, except the **Section Depth** and **Objects To Cut** rollouts, which is discussed next.

Section Depth: By default, the **Full** option is selected in the **Depth** drop-down list of the **Section Depth** rollout in the dialog box. As a result, the section view is created such that all geometries of the object beyond the section line are visible in the resultant section view. On selecting the **Slice** option, the sliced section view is created such that only the geometries that cut through the section line are visible. On selecting the **Distance** option, the **Distance** field gets enabled below the drop-down list. In this field, you can specify a distance of viewing in the object beyond the section line.

Objects To Cut: The Objects To Cut rollout in the **DRAWING VIEW** dialog box displays a list of bodies included in the section cut. If you are creating the section view of a component, then it displays only one body. On the other hand, if you are creating the section view of an assembly, then it displays a list of all bodies included in the section cut. As a result, you can clear the check boxes that appear in front of the bodies like fasteners, for excluding them from the section cut.

8. Accept the default option in the **DRAWING VIEW** dialog box and then click on the **OK** button in the dialog box. The section view is created, see Figure 11.27.

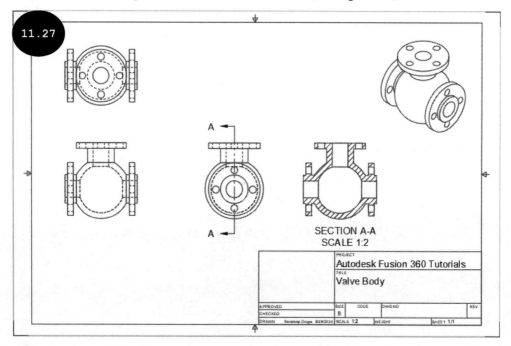

SECTION A-A
SCALE 1:2

PROJECT
Autodesk Fusion 360 Tutorials
TITLE
Valve Body

The text of the section view overlaps with the title block. You need to place this text below the section view such that it should not overlap with the title block. You can move the text

by selecting it and then dragging its grip point. Also, if there is insufficient space between the title block and the section view for placing the text in between then you can move the Front view to a small distance upward by dragging it. On moving the Front view upward, the Right view and the Section view also get moved, accordingly.

Creating the Detail View

Now, you need to create the detail view of a portion of the Front view.

 A detail view is used for showing a portion of an existing drawing view in an enlarged scale. You can define the portion of an existing drawing view to be enlarged by drawing a circular boundary.

1. Click on the **Detail View** tool in the **DRAWING VIEWS** panel in the **Toolbar**, see Figure 11.28. You are prompted to select the parent view.

2. Select the Front view as the parent view for creating the detail view. The **DRAWING VIEW** dialog box appears and you are prompted to specify the center point of the detail boundary.

3. Move the cursor over the upper right most vertex of the Front view and then click to specify the center point of the detail boundary when the cursor snaps to it, see Figure 11.29. You are prompted to specify the size of the detail boundary.

4. Move the cursor to a small distance and then click to define the size of the boundary anywhere in the drawing sheet, refer to Figure 11.30. The preview of the detail view of the portion that lies inside the boundary appears attached to the cursor.

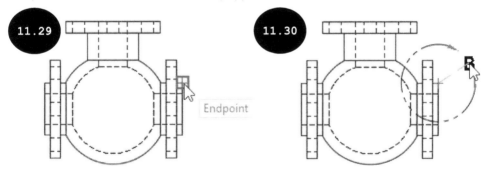

5. Click to specify the position of the detail view on the drawing sheet, refer to Figure 11.31.

6. Ensure that the **1:1** is specified as the scale factor of the detail view in the **DRAWING VIEW** dialog box. You can also specify other properties of the detail view in the dialog box. The options in the **DRAWING VIEW** dialog box are discussed earlier.

7. Accept the default option in the **DRAWING VIEW** dialog box and then click on the **OK** button. A detail view is created in the specified position, see Figure 11.31. Note that, if the text of the detail view intersects with any existing drawing view, then you need to change its position such that it should not intersect with any drawing view.

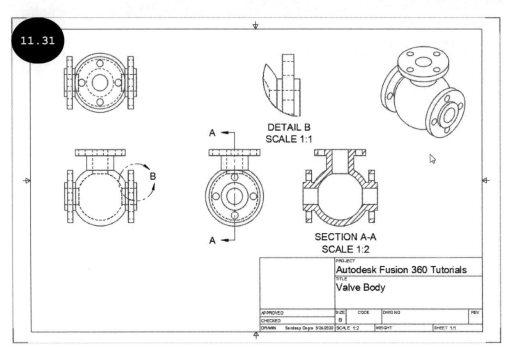

11.31

DETAIL B
SCALE 1:1

SECTION A-A
SCALE 1:2

PROJECT					
Autodesk Fusion 360 Tutorials					
TITLE					
Valve Body					
APPROVED		SIZE	CODE	DWG NO	REV
CHECKED		B			
DRAWN	Sandeep Dogra 8/26/2020	SCALE 1:2	WEIGHT		SHEET 1/1

On editing the boundary of a detail view, the detail view gets updated, dynamically. To edit the boundary of a detail view, click on it, the grips of the boundary appear, see Figure 11.32. You can edit the boundary by using these grips. For example, to change the location of the boundary, click on its center grip and then specify its new position on the drawing view by clicking the left mouse button. Similarly, to increase or decrease the size of the boundary, click on a grip appearing along the boundary and then click to specify its new position.

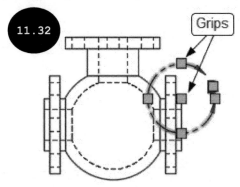

11.32

Grips

Applying Dimensions

Now, you need to apply the required dimensions to the drawing views.

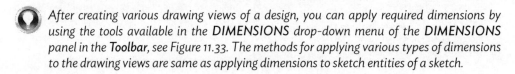

After creating various drawing views of a design, you can apply required dimensions by using the tools available in the DIMENSIONS drop-down menu of the DIMENSIONS panel in the Toolbar, see Figure 11.33. The methods for applying various types of dimensions to the drawing views are same as applying dimensions to sketch entities of a sketch.

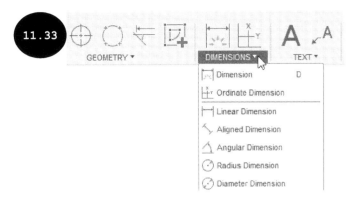

1. Click on the **Dimension** tool in the **DIMENSIONS** panel in the **Toolbar** or press the D key. You are prompted to select an edge or specify points to apply dimensions.

*The dimension applied by using the **Dimension** tool depends upon the type of entity selected. For example, if you select a circular edge, the diameter dimension is applied and if you select a linear edge, the linear dimension is applied.*

2. Click on the upper right most vertex of the Section view, see Figure 11.34. You are prompted to specify the second point to apply dimension.

3. Click on the lower right most vertex of the Section view, see Figure 11.34. The linear dimension between the selected vertices is attached to the cursor. Next, click on the right side of the Section view to define the position of the dimension. The linear dimension is applied between the selected vertices, see Figure 11.34.

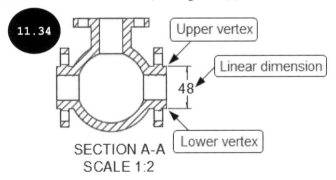

*In Figure 11.34, the text height of the dimension has increased. To change the text height of the dimension in the current drawing sheet, expand the **Document Settings** node in the **BROWSER** by clicking on the arrow in front of it. Next, move the cursor over the **Text Height** option in the expanded **Document Settings** node and then click on the **Change Text Height** button that appears, see Figure 11.35. The **DOCUMENT SETTINGS** dialog box appears, see Figure 11.36. In this dialog box, you can edit the current document settings such as text font, dimension unit, text height, and so on. Select the required text height (0.24 in) in the **Text Height** drop-down list of the dialog box as the new height of the text and then click on the **OK** button. The text height of the dimensions get changed, as specified.*

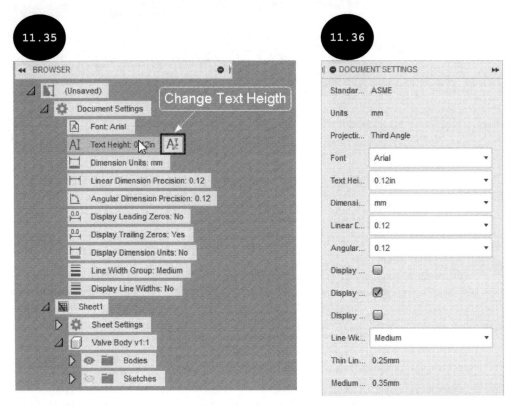

4. Apply the remaining dimensions on the drawing views by using the **Dimension** tool, see Figure 11.37.

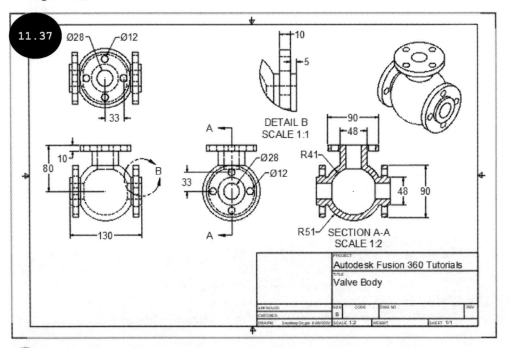

After applying a dimension, you may need to change its position to avoid any intersection or overlapping with other dimensions. To do so, select a dimension and then click on its grip point that appears on the dimension text. Next, specify the new position for the dimension in the drawing sheet.

Editing Dimensions

Now, you need to edit the linear dimensions applied on the Section view to insert the diameter symbol.

1. Double-click on the linear dimension 90 mm that is applied on the Section view. The **DIMENSION** dialog box appears. Also, the dimension value appears as "<value>" in an edit field on the drawing sheet.

2. Place the cursor in front of the dimension value (outside the bracket) in the edit field and then invoke the **Insert Symbol** flyout in the **DIMENSION** dialog box, see Figure 11.38.

3. Select the **Diameter** symbol in the **Insert Symbol** flyout and then click on the **Close** button to exit the dialog box. The diameter symbol is inserted in front of the dimension value, see Figure 11.39.

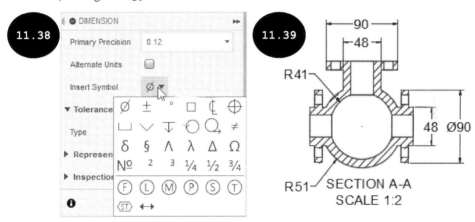

You can also override the original dimension value by entering a new dimension value in the edit field that appears.

4. Similarly, insert the diameter symbol to another linear dimensions of the Section view, see Figure 11.40.

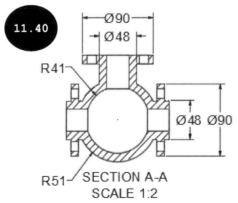

5. Arrange the position of the dimensions to maintain proper spacing between each other, if needed. Figure 11.41 shows the final drawing after creating all the drawing views and applying dimensions.

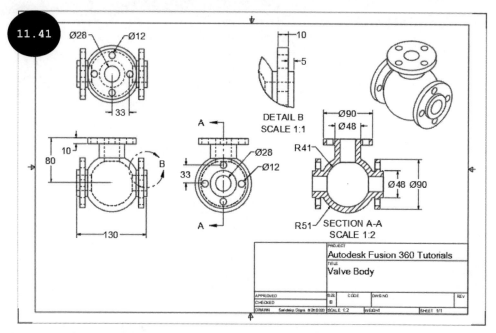

Saving the Model

1.   Click on the **Save** tool in the Application Bar and then ensure that the location to save the file is specified as *Autodesk Fusion 360 Tutorials > Chapter 11 > Tutorial 1*. Next, click on the **Save** button in the dialog box. The drawing file is saved in the specified location.

Tutorial 2 - Creating Drawing Views of the Blow Off Cock Assembly

Open the Blow Off Cock assembly created in Tutorial 2 of Chapter 8 and then create the different drawing views: Top, Section, and Right in the C (22in x 17in) sheet size, see Figure 11.42. Also, create an exploded view of the assembly and add the Parts list with balloons.

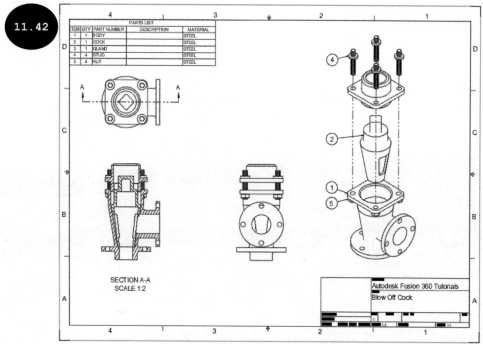

The following sequence summarizes the tutorial outline:

- Opening the Tutorial 2 of Chapter 8
- Invoking the DRAWING Workspace and Creating Base View
- Creating the Section View
- Creating the Projected View
- Creating the Exploded View
- Creating the Bill of Material (BOM) and Adding Balloons
- Exporting the Parts List as a CSV File
- Exporting the Drawing as a PDF File
- Saving the Model

Opening the Tutorial 2 of Chapter 8

1. Launch Autodesk Fusion 360 and then open the **Blow Off Cock** assembly created in Tutorial 2 of Chapter 8, see Figure 11.43.

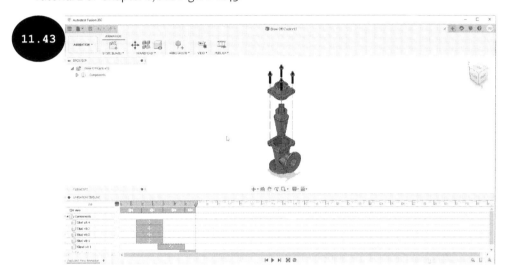

 *The exploded view of the **Blow Off Cock** assembly can be opened in the **ANIMATION** workspace, see Figure 11.43, since in Tutorial 1 of Chapter 10, the exploded view of the assembly is created in the ANIMATION workspace.*

Now, you need to save the model in Chapter 11 folder of the project.

2. Click on **File > Save As** in the **Application Bar**. The **Save As** dialog box appears.

3. Expand the **Save As** dialog box and then specify **Autodesk Fusion 360 Tutorials > Chapter 11 > Tutorial 2** as the location for saving the assembly. Note that you need to create **Tutorial 2** folder inside the "**Chapter 11**" folder of the project in the **Data Panel**. Next, close the **Data Panel**.

 *You cannot save an assembly file of a project to a folder of another project in the **Data Panel**.*

Invoking the DRAWING Workspace and Creating Base View

Now, you need to invoke the **DRAWING** workspace and create the Top view as the base view of the assembly.

1. Invoke the **Workspace** drop-down menu and then click on **DRAWING** > **From Design**, see Figure 11.44. The **CREATE DRAWING** dialog box appears, see Figure 11.45.

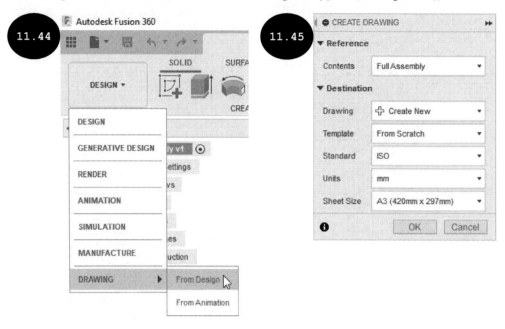

2. Ensure that the **Full Assembly** option is selected in the **Contents** drop-down list of the dialog box for including all the components of the assembly in the drawing view.

3. Select the **ASME** standard in the **Standard** drop-down list of the dialog box.

4. Ensure that **mm** unit is selected in the **Units** drop-down list of the dialog box.

5. Select the **C (22in x 17in)** sheet size in the **Sheet Size** drop-down list of the dialog box.

6. After selecting the required options in the **CREATE DRAWING** dialog box, click on the **OK** button. The **DRAWING** workspace is invoked and a drawing sheet with the specified standard and size appears, see Figure 11.46. Also, the **DRAWING VIEW** dialog box appears on the right side of the drawing sheet and a preview of the default base view appears attached to the cursor, see Figure 11.46.

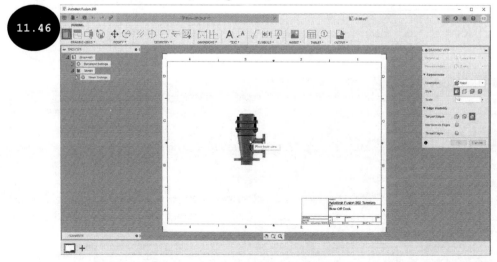

Now, you need to create the base view by defining its parameters and placement location on the drawing sheet.

7. Select the **Top** option in the **Orientation** drop-down list of the **DRAWING VIEW** dialog box for creating the Top view of the model as the base view.

8. Ensure that the **Visible Edges** button is activated in the **Style** area of the dialog box.

9. Select **1:2** in the **Scale** drop-down list of the dialog box as the scale of the base view.

10. Ensure that the **Off** button is activated in the **Tangent Edges** area of the dialog box to turn off the display of tangent edges on the base view.

    After defining the required parameters for the base view, you need to define its placement on the drawing sheet.

11. Click to specify the position of the base view in the top left corner of the drawing sheet, see Figure 11.47. The Top view is placed in the specified location and the **DRAWING VIEW** dialog box is still displayed.

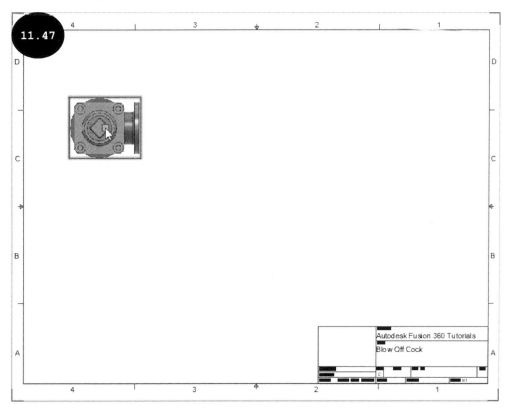

*You can control the parameters such as orientation, style, and scale for the base view before and after defining its placement on the drawing sheet by using the **DRAWING VIEW** dialog box.*

12. After defining all the required parameters for the base view in the **DRAWING VIEW** dialog box, click on the **OK** button. The Top view of the model is placed in the specified location as per the parameters specified in the dialog box, see Figure 11.48.

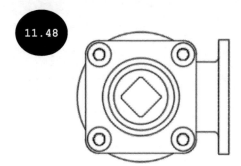

Creating the Section View

Now, you need to create the section view by selecting the Top view as the parent view.

1. Click on the **Section View** tool in the **DRAWING VIEWS** panel in the **Toolbar**, see Figure 11.49. You are prompted to select the parent view.

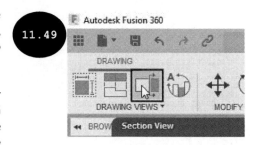

2. Select the Top view as the parent view for creating the section view. The **DRAWING VIEW** dialog box appears and you are prompted to specify the start point of the section line.

3. Move the cursor to the center of the Top view, see Figure 11.50 and then move it horizontally to the left. A tracking line appears, see Figure 11.51.

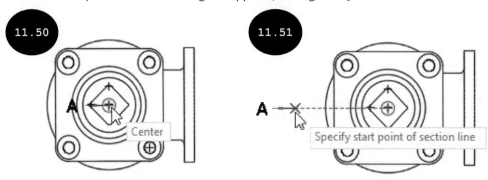

4. Follow the tracking line and then click to specify the start point of the section line at a small distance outside the Top view, refer to Figure 11.52. You are prompted to specify the endpoint of the section line.

5. Move the cursor horizontally toward the right and then click to specify the endpoint of the section line anywhere outside the Top view on its right, refer to Figure 11.52.

6. Right-click on the drawing sheet and then click on the **Continue** option in the Marking Menu that appears to end the creation of the section line. A preview of the section view appears attached to the cursor, see Figure 11.52. Also, you are prompted to specify its placement in the drawing sheet.

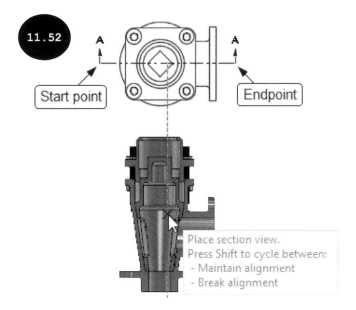

7. Move the cursor vertically downward and then click to specify the position of the section view on the drawing sheet, refer to Figure 11.53.

After defining the placement for the section view, you can define its appearance, scale, and visibility of tangent edges by using the **DRAWING VIEW** dialog box.

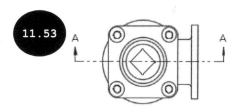

8. Ensure that the **Full** option is selected in the **Depth** drop-down list of the **DRAWING VIEW** dialog box for displaying all the geometries of the object that are beyond the section line.

 *The **Objects To Cut** rollout in the DRAWING VIEW dialog box displays a list of all the components of the assembly that are included in the section cut. Also, the check box in front of each component is selected for including them in the section cut. You can clear the check boxes of the components to be excluded from the section cut.*

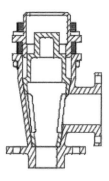

SECTION A-A
SCALE 1:2

9. Accept the remaining default options in the **DRAWING VIEW** dialog box and then click on the **OK** button in the dialog box. The section view is created, see Figure 11.53.

Creating the Projected View

Now, you need to create the projected view of the Section view.

1. Click on the **Projected View** tool in the **DRAWING VIEWS** panel in the **Toolbar**, see Figure 11.54 or press the **P** key. You are prompted to select a parent view.

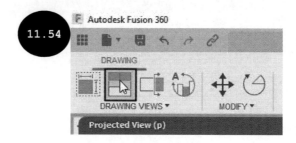

2. Select the Section view as the parent view for creating the projected view. A projected view is attached to the cursor.

3. Move the cursor horizontally toward right. The projected view (Side view) appears attached to the cursor, see Figure 11.55.

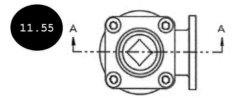

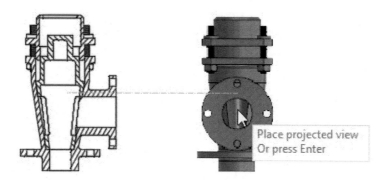

Place projected view
Or press Enter

SECTION A-A
SCALE 1:2

4. Click on the drawing sheet to specify the position of the Side view, see Figure 11.56.

5. After creating all the projected views, press ENTER or right-click on the drawing sheet and then click on the **OK** button in the Marking Menu that appears. The projected view (Side view) gets created, see Figure 11.56.

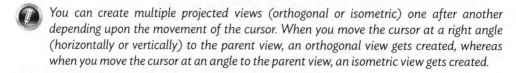

You can create multiple projected views (orthogonal or isometric) one after another depending upon the movement of the cursor. When you move the cursor at a right angle (horizontally or vertically) to the parent view, an orthogonal view gets created, whereas when you move the cursor at an angle to the parent view, an isometric view gets created.

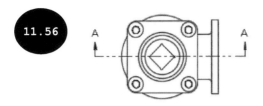

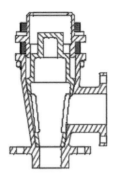

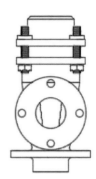

SECTION A-A
SCALE 1:2

Creating the Exploded View

Now, you need to create the exploded view of the assembly.

1. Click on the **Base View** tool in the **DRAWING VIEWS** panel in the **Toolbar**, see Figure 11.57. The **DRAWING VIEW** dialog box appears.

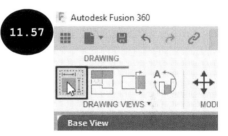

2. Ensure that the **Create New** option is selected in the **Reference** drop-down list of the dialog box.

*The **Create New** option in the **Reference** drop-down list of the dialog box is used for adding a new base view reference in the **BROWSER** for the base view to be created. Figure 11.58 shows a base view reference of the drawing sheet. The **Reference** drop-down list also displays a list of existing base view references created in the current drawing. You can select any of the existing base view references in this drop-down list as a reference for the base view to be created. Note that the **Reference** drop-down list is not enabled, when the **DRAWING VIEW** dialog box is invoked automatically on invoking the **DRAWING** workspace.*

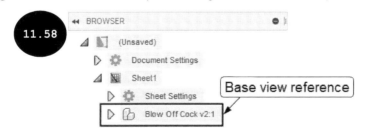

3. Invoke the **Representation** drop-down list in the **DRAWING VIEW** dialog box and then select the **Exploded View Animation** option (name of the storyboard representing the

exploded view) as the representation of the base view to be created, see Figure 11.59. A preview of the exploded view appears attached the cursor.

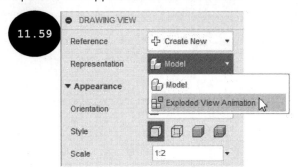

The **Representation** drop-down list in the dialog box displays a list of storyboards created for the current design in the **ANIMATION** workspace. By default, the **Model** option is selected in this drop-down list when the **DRAWING** workspace is invoked from a design. So, the base view is represented as a model. You can select a storyboard in this drop-down list to create an exploded view of the design as the base view. Note that the Representation drop-down list is not enabled, when the **DRAWING VIEW** dialog box is invoked automatically on invoking the **DRAWING** workspace from a design.

Now, you need to define the placement for the exploded view on the drawing sheet.

4.   Click to specify the placement for the exploded view above the title block on the drawing sheet, refer to Figure 11.60.

5.   Accept the remaining selected options in the **DRAWING VIEW** dialog box and then click on the **OK** button. The exploded view of the assembly gets created at the specified location on the drawing sheet, see Figure 11.60.

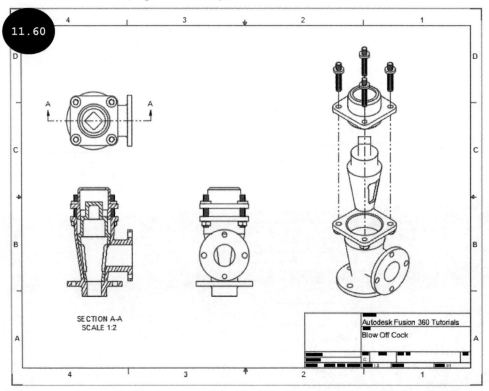

Creating the Bill of Material (BOM) and Adding Balloons

Now, you need to create the Bill of Material (BOM)/Parts list of the assembly and add balloons to each of its components.

 After creating all the required drawing views of an assembly, you need to create the Bill of Material/Parts list. The Bill of Material (BOM)/Parts list contains all the required information such as the number of parts used in an assembly, part number, quantity of each part, material, and so on. Since the Bill of Material (BOM) contains all the information, it serves as a primary source of communication between the manufacturer and the vendors as well as the suppliers.

1. Click on the **Table** tool in the **TABLES** panel of the **Toolbar**, see Figure 11.61. The **TABLE** dialog box appears, see Figure 11.62. Also, you are prompted to select a drawing view for creating the Parts list (BOM) and adding the balloons.

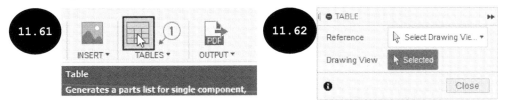

 *If the current drawing sheet has only one base view reference created or available, then on invoking the **Table** tool, a drawing view for creating the Parts list (BOM) and adding balloons gets automatically selected and the preview of a table appears attached to the cursor.*

2. Click on the exploded view of the assembly on the sheet as the view for creating the Parts list (BOM). The preview of a table appears attached to the cursor.

3. Move the cursor toward the top left corner of the drawing sheet and then click to define the position of the Parts list (BOM) when the cursor snaps to it, see Figure 11.63. The BOM/Parts list is placed in the specified position on the drawing sheet and the balloons are added to each component of the assembly in the selected drawing view, see Figure 11.64.

 Before specifying the position of the Parts list, you can flip it to other side of the cursor by pressing the SHIFT key, if needed.

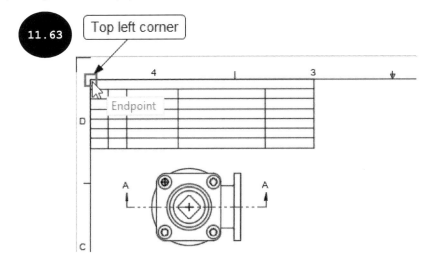

11.64

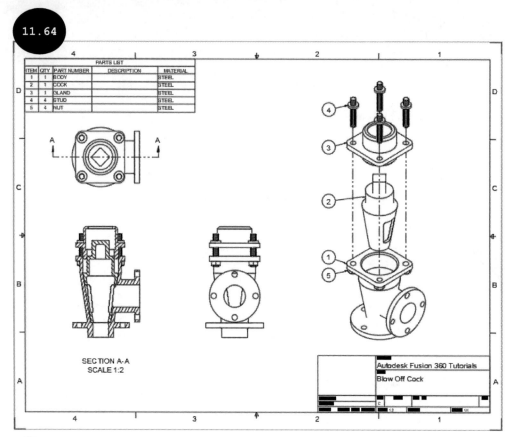

The following table is the Parts List from the drawing:

ITEM	QTY	PART NUMBER	DESCRIPTION	MATERIAL
1	1	BODY		STEEL
2	1	COCK		STEEL
3	1	GLAND		STEEL
4	4	STUD		STEEL
5	4	NUT		STEEL

SECTION A-A
SCALE 1:2

Autodesk Fusion 360 Tutorials
Blow Off Cock

 If the Parts list (BOM) overlaps with the Top view of the drawing sheet, then you need to change the position of the Top view, a bit downward. To change the position of a view, click on it on the drawing sheet and then drag it to a new position by using its grip that appears.

Also, as the balloons gets added automatically to each component of the assembly on inserting the parts list, you may need to change their locations to arrange them properly on the drawing sheet. To do so, select the balloon and then move it to a new location in the drawing sheet by using its grip.

 In Autodesk Fusion 360, you can also customize the BOM/Parts list by adding or removing item columns, as required in the BOM. To do so, double-click on the Parts list in the drawing sheet. The **PARTS LIST** dialog box appears. In this dialog box, you can select the check boxes of the columns to be added in the Parts list and clear the check boxes of the columns to be removed or not included in the Parts list. Next, close the dialog box.

Exporting the Parts List as a CSV File

After creating the Parts list (BOM) of an assembly, you can export or output it as a CSV file.

1.   Invoke the OUTPUT drop-down menu in the **Toolbar** and then click on the **Output** CSV tool, see Figure 11.65. The **Output Table** dialog box appears.

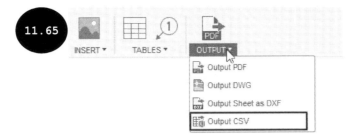

2. Enter the name of the CSV file in the **File name** field in the dialog box. Next, browse to the required location in a local drive of your system for saving the file.

3. Click on the **Save** button. The CSV file of the Parts list is saved in the specified location.

Exporting the Drawing as a PDF File

After creating the drawing, you can export or output it as a PDF file.

1. Click on the **Output PDF** tool in the **Toolbar**, see Figure 11.66. The **OUTPUT PDF** dialog box appears, see Figure 11.67.

2. Select the **Current Sheet** option in the **Sheets** drop-down list of the dialog box for including only the current drawing sheet in the output PDF file.

    Sheets: The **All Sheets** option in the **Sheets** drop-down list is used for including all the drawing sheets in the output PDF file. The **Current Sheet** option is used for including only the current drawing sheet in the output PDF file. The **Range** option is used for specifying a range of sheets to be included in the PDF file. The **Selected Sheets** option is used for including only the selected drawing sheets in the output PDF file. You can select multiple sheets in the bottom left corner by pressing the CTRL key.

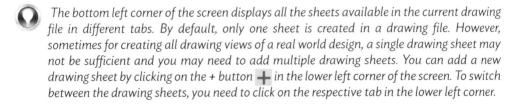

The bottom left corner of the screen displays all the sheets available in the current drawing file in different tabs. By default, only one sheet is created in a drawing file. However, sometimes for creating all drawing views of a real world design, a single drawing sheet may not be sufficient and you may need to add multiple drawing sheets. You can add a new drawing sheet by clicking on the + button ➕ in the lower left corner of the screen. To switch between the drawing sheets, you need to click on the respective tab in the lower left corner.

3. Select the **Open PDF** file check box in the dialog box to automatically open the PDF file when the output file is generated.

4. Select the **Lineweights** check box in the dialog box for generating the PDF file with thicker drawing outlines. To generate the PDF file with thinner drawing outline, you can clear this check box,

5. After selecting the required options in the dialog box, click on the **OK** button. The **Output PDF** dialog box appears. In this dialog box, specify the name of the PDF file in the **File name** field and then browse to the required location for saving the file.

6. Click on the **Save** button. The PDF file is saved in the specified location.

 You can also export or output the current drawing as DWG and DXF files by using the **Output DWG** *and* **Output Sheet as DXF** *tools available in the* **OUTPUT** *drop-down menu of the* **Toolbar,** *respectively.*

Saving the Model

1. Click on the **Save** tool in the Application Bar and then ensure that the location to save the file is specified as *Autodesk Fusion 360 Tutorials > Chapter 11 > Tutorial 2* in the **Location** field of the **Save** dialog box that appears.

2. Click on the **Save** button in the dialog box. The drawing file is saved in the specified location with default specified name "Blow Off Cock Drawing ".

Exercise 1

Open the model created in Tutorial 1 of Chapter 5 and then create different drawing views as shown in Figure 11.68 in the B (17in x 11in) sheet size.

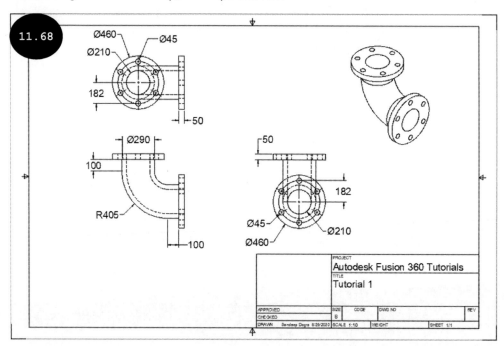

*HINT: You can add center marks for identifying the center of the rounded or circular edges in the drawing view. To do so, click on the **Center Mark** tool in the **GEOMETRY** panel of the **Toolbar** and then click on a circular edge of the drawing view. The center mark gets added at the center of the selected circular edge. You can select multiple circular or rounded edges one after the other for adding the center marks.*

*Moreover, you can add center mark pattern geometry for identifying the center and PCD (Pitch Circle Diameter) of the pattern feature in the drawing views. To do so, click on the **Center Mark Pattern** tool in the **GEOMETRY** panel in the **Toolbar**. The **CENTER MARK PATTERN** dialog box appears. Next, click on a circular or rounded edge of a pattern instance. Center marks are created on all the pattern instances along with the addition of the PCD, since the **Auto-complete** check box is selected in the dialog box, by default. If you clear this check box, then a center mark is created at the center of the selected circular edge only. You can create multiple circular edges of the other patter instances as well. You can also add center mark to represent the center of the PCD by selecting the **Center Mark** check box in the dialog box. Next, click on the **OK** button. The center mark pattern gets added on the drawing view.*

Summary

The chapter discussed how to create 2D drawings of components and assemblies. It also explained the concept and definition of angle of projections, and the method to edit the annotations and sheet settings. The chapter also describes methods for creating exploded views of an assembly, applying and editing dimensions, creating the Bill of Material (BOM)/Parts list, adding balloons, exporting the Parts list (BOM) as a CSV file, and exporting the current drawing as a PDF, DWG, or DXF file.

Questions

Answer the following questions:

- In _____ workspace, you can generate 2D drawings of a design.

- Autodesk Fusion 360 allows you to invoke the DRAWING workspace from a design or an animation file by selecting the respective option: _____ and _____.

- On selecting the _____ option in the **CREATE DRAWING** dialog box, you can select individual components of the assembly for creating the drawing.

- Engineering drawings follow the _____ and the _____ angles of projections.

- Projected views are _____ and _____ views of an object, which are created by viewing the object from its different projection sides.

- A _____ view is created by cutting an object by using an imaginary cutting plane or a section line and then viewing the object from the direction normal to the section line.

- On creating the section view of an assembly, a list of all bodies included in the section cut appears in the _____ rollout of the **DRAWING VIEW** dialog box.

402 Chapter 11 > Creating 2D Drawings

- The _____ contains all the required information of an assembly such as part number, quantity, material, and so on.

- In Autodesk Fusion 360, after creating a drawing view, you can edit its properties such as orientation, style, scale, and visibility of tangent edges. (True/False)

- In Fusion 360, after applying a dimension, you can edit it to override its dimension value, insert symbol, specify tolerances, and so on. (True/False)

INDEX

Index

Symbols

Made in the USA
Monee, IL
09 December 2020